American Perceptions of Immigrant and Invasive Species

American Perceptions of Immigrant and Invasive Species

Strangers on the Land

Peter Coates

UNIVERSITY OF CALIFORNIA PRESS
Berkeley   Los Angeles   London

University of California Press, one of the most distinguished
university presses in the United States, enriches lives around
the world by advancing scholarship in the humanities, social
sciences, and natural sciences. Its activities are supported by
the UC Press Foundation and by philanthropic contributions
from individuals and institutions. For more information, visit
www.ucpress.edu.

University of California Press
Berkeley and Los Angeles, California

University of California Press, Ltd.
London, England

Library of Congress Cataloging-in-Publication Data

Coates, Peter A., 1957–.
    American perceptions of immigrant and invasive species : strangers
on the land / Peter A. Coates.
        p.   cm.
    Includes bibliographical references and index.
    ISBN-13: 978-0-520-24930-1 (cloth : alk. paper)
    ISBN-10: 0-520-24930-5 (cloth : alk. paper)
    1. Introduced organisms—United States—History.   I. Title.

QH353.C62   2007
333.95'230973—dc22   2006025834

Manufactured in the United States of America
15   14   13   12   11   10   09   08   07   06
10   9   8   7   6   5   4   3   2   1
This book is printed on New Leaf EcoBook 60, containing 60%
post-consumer waste, processed chlorine free; 30% de-inked recycled
fiber, elemental chlorine free; and 10% FSC-certified virgin fiber,
totally chlorine free. EcoBook 60 is acid-free and meets the minimum
requirements of ANSI/ASTM D5634-01 (*Permanence of Paper*).

I dedicate this book to the memory of my father, Robert Allan Coates.

CONTENTS

ACKNOWLEDGMENTS

For their contributions in a wide variety of forms (sometimes simply for good conversation), I thank Johnny Ajluni, William Beinart, Bill Cronon, Chris Dunford, Tom Dunlap, Marcus Hall, Elizabeth Arnold Hull, Nancy Jackson, Joe Jisser, Peter Kaufman, Rob Lambert, David Lowenthal, Rich Minnich, Cheryl Oakes, Alix Reiskind, Chris Smout, Rene Sugasawarra, Julidta Tarver, Donald Worster, and, for their hospitality, all the relatives in San Jose. At the University of California Press, I wish to thank Chuck Crumly, Danette Davis, Mary Severance, and, for his terrific copyediting, John Thomas. I have also received welcome feedback from those who attended various seminars and sessions at which I've presented material from this book over the past few years: the University of Keele's American Studies Department; the Johnson Scholars visiting speakers' program at the University of North Carolina, Chapel Hill; the European Society for Environmental History's conferences at Prague and Florence; and the British Academy in London. I also thank Dave Boyd and California State Parks for granting access to files on the Angel Island eucalyptus removal project. Flora Davis, Frank Goodall, David Haase, Nancy Lubamersky, Jean Severinghaus, Dorothy Trezevant, and Bill West (on behalf of his parents, John and Anne West) graciously consented to the publication of material from letters they wrote to the California Department of Parks and Recreation. The National Arbor Day Foundation kindly granted permission to use of one of their posters as an illustration. Some parts of chapter 2 first appeared in my article "Eastenders Go West: English Sparrows, Immigrants, and the Nature of Fear," *Journal of American Studies* 39, 3 (2005): 431–62, copyright Cambridge University Press, reproduced with permission. Research leave funded by the Arts and Humanities Research Board (now the Arts and Humanities Research Council) and matched by the University of Bristol's Department of Historical Studies provided a sabbatical year in 2000/1 that was crucial to the project's launch. The Research Fund of the University of Bristol's Arts Faculty helped finance a couple of research trips to the United States and various journeys to libraries closer to home in Oxford and Cambridge. Not least, I owe an enormous debt to Graziella Mazza for tolerating the not infrequent occasions on which I disappeared into the study in the evenings and on weekends (and when I appeared distracted over the breakfast table). Yet I dedicate this book to the memory of my father, Allan, who died just as the idea for it was taking root. We never had a chance to talk about the nationality of animals and plants, but one of his greatest pleasures was strolling down to the National Trust reserve in the pinewoods at Formby Point on the Lancashire coast where I grew up to see the red squirrels frolic in an environment without the presence of their larger North American immigrant cousin, the gray squirrel.

Peter Coates, Bristol, U.K., April 19, 2006

Chapter 1

Strangers and Natives

KNOWING NATURE THROUGH NATIONALITY

"The United States is having a problem with aliens," announced the National Safety Council's Environmental Health Center as the twentieth century drew to a close. "Not illegal immigrants or space invaders," elaborated the Center—a division of a parent organization more commonly associated with efforts to enforce seat belt laws, combat drunk driving, and promote the careful use of fire extinguishers—"but plants and animals that reach the shores and stay." A California journalist had adopted the same approach the previous year, opening his article about immigrants with the remark that "the strangers come from far and wide." "Then they make themselves so much at home, helping themselves to food and water while producing offspring," he went on to explain, with the result that "the original occupants are forced to move." Then, once more, comes the unexpected twist: "These strangers are plants, not people."[1]

A host of similar pronouncements that play on words and subvert familiar notions indicate that discussions of undesirable immigrants in the United States are now just as likely to include flora and fauna as they are to involve the more conventional human variety. Organisms from elsewhere cause concern because they can be invasive species—which President Clinton's executive order of 1999 on the subject defined as "an alien species whose introduction does or is likely to cause economic or environmental harm or harm to human health."[2] Invasive aliens have affected individual native species through competition, predation, hybridization, and disease.[3] Arriving in ever-increasing numbers, they may also initiate fundamental transformations in ecosystems, changing them almost beyond recognition.[4] Thirty years ago, a biologist claimed that an international medley of overseas species had left Florida "biologically traumatized." Thanks to this multinational assault, a "south Floridian could conceivably watch a walking Siamese catfish crawl out of a canal choked with the Asian weed hydrilla, while Columbian iguanas scampered through Australian pines beneath a squadron of Amazonian parakeets."[5]

In the trans-Mississippi West, fire-adapted cheatgrass from Eurasia encroaches on scrublands hitherto dominated by sagebrush. As a result, fire incidence has increased from once every 60–110 years to once every 3–5 years—a punishing rate that native flora cannot withstand. Expanding standard conceptions of natural disaster, Interior Secretary Babbitt announced in 1998 that the "invasion of noxious weeds has created a level of destruction to America's environment and economy that is matched only by the damage caused by floods, earthquakes, wildfire, hurricanes and mudslides."[6] In fact, many scientists increasingly believe that invasive "biological immigrants" are second only to habitat loss as the major cause of the depletion, endangerment, and extinction of indigenous species.[7] Even George W. Bush is doing his bit to rein them in. One of the president's favorite activities at his 1,600-acre ranch in Crawford, Texas, is clearing the "plague" of tamarisk, a tree from North Africa (also known as salt cedar) that desiccates the soil and elbows out native trees; meanwhile, the First Lady is planting buffalo grass—part of a wider plan to restore the ranch to its native splendor. And, as part of efforts to promote his environmentalist credentials during a pre-election trip to Florida in April 2004, the president took up an enormous pair of pruning shears and hacked away at earleaf acacia, a fast-growing evergreen from Australia that displaces native vegetation. Introduced as an urban shade tree in the early 1900s, the acacia is widely dispersed via its seeds by a variety of birds (prominent among them another foreign species, the European starling).

In some instances, nonnative plants and animals have become the primary threat to native biodiversity.[8] The National Park Service ranks these "habitat snatchers" ahead of air pollution, off-road vehicles, excessive visitor pressure, and oil drilling on adjacent lands as threats to the integrity of certain parklands. After more conventional pressures on them are relieved, native species can rebound. The recovery of heavily denuded eastern deciduous forests since 1900 is one of the great success stories of spontaneous ecological restoration. Yet some ecologists would argue that the impact of a European insect such as the balsam woolly adelgid (which probably arrived with imported conifers) is far less reversible than agents of change such as logging or even acid rain. These tiny, sap-sucking, aphid-like insects are killing off massive quantities of old growth Fraser fir unique to southern Appalachia's woodlands. A "growing army" of invasive exotics is "overrunning" the country, jeopardizing the nation's "biological heritage," warn Don Schmitz and Daniel Simberloff.[9] Highlighting a neglected facet of homeland security—biosecurity—some conservation biologists advocate a zero tolerance entry policy for nonhuman biota combined with a "shoot first, ask questions later" approach to any species that slips through the net.

Is American anxiety over what some see as a crisis of ecological identity essentially a recent phenomenon? In this book I seek to provide a longer and deeper perspective on this highly topical current environmental preoccupation by examining some earlier manifestations of unease over fauna and flora from other countries. Though the burgeoning nontechnical literature on invasive species sometimes alludes to examples from the past, contextualizing the problem historically is not the purpose of recent calls to arms that mix popular science with investigative reporting.[10] Edward Tenner's *Why Things Bite Back: Technology and the Revenge of Unintended Consequences*, a wide-ranging study of the unexpected fallout from a broad spectrum of human activities, provides the most scholarly treatment to date from a historical perspective, with chapters on nonnative plants, insects, and other animals. Otherwise, there is a strong sense in much of the current literature that today's level of concern over invasive nonnative species is unprecedented.[11]

The desire to throw current American attitudes to nonnative species into sharper relief by examining past perspectives on some earlier arrivals provides the general impetus for this study. A historical study that embraces the past century and a half indicates that claims for the novelty of the problem in recent times are often exaggerated. More particularly, though, this historical approach aims to heighten our appreciation of how ideas of nationality have influenced our understandings of the nonhuman world of nature. Recent historical study of American interactions with the natural world has emphasized how work and recreation shaped these relationships. (We also have a far keener awareness of how the variables of race, class, and gender molded the dialogue between people and the rest of nature.) We know less, though, about how notions of nationality structured understandings. "Knowing nature through labor" and "knowing nature through leisure" have become common phrases in the environmental historian's lexicon. "Knowing nature through nationality" has a less familiar ring.[12]

How certain landforms, places, and creatures were appropriated in the late nineteenth and early twentieth centuries to help create a sense of national identity and became central ingredients of a naturalized form of patrimony is, of course, a classic area of American environmental history—and of growing interest to those studying expressions of cultural nationalism in other white "settler" colonies such as Australia, New Zealand, and South Africa. Yet we know far less about an essential counterpoint to this valorization of native nature. As Americans were establishing national parks and embracing the redwood and the buffalo, they were distancing themselves from certain biotic forms not American in origin. These symbiotic processes of identification and rejection created a nature of inclusion and a nature of exclusion by distinguishing between native species and those that fell beyond the pale.

American Perceptions of Immigrant and Invasive Species breaks fresh ground by situating the history of immigrant flora and fauna and their relations with native species within the wider history of human immigration. Just as historians of immigration have neglected the parallel and sometimes intersecting tales of immigrant flora and fauna, commentators on exotic plants and animals—apart from a few passing references and superficial analogies—have largely overlooked the wider framework provided by the history of human immigration. By bringing the perspective of the environmental historian to bear, and asking when attitudes to plants and animals tell us about people and when attitudes to people tell us about plants and animals, this study supplies a larger, more natural context for human history and embeds the saga of human relations with the rest of nature more firmly within the broader social and cultural environment.

In terms of the quantity and intensity of responses to exotic species since the mid-nineteenth century—favorable and unfavorable—two periods stand out: the late nineteenth and early twentieth centuries and the era since 1945. These are the periods when the volume of arrivals was the heaviest; between 1790 and the 1840s, numbers were trivial.[13] During the second half of the nineteenth century, intercontinental transplantation of species was all the rage, a passion shared by private individuals, acclimatization societies (whose ranks included the native-born and immigrant alike), and officials in the Department of Agriculture. Enthusiasm waned toward century's end as the unanticipated drawbacks of certain promising introductions—notably the English (house) sparrow—became increasingly apparent. Restrictive measures ensued and acclimatization societies and their promotional activities became discredited and defunct. Moreover, a fresh value was stamped on the native nature that became synonymous with what Thomas Dunlap calls "national nature," and which nonnative species were seen to menace.[14]

As import bans and quarantines took effect and the desire to recreate old, recognizable biotic worlds dissipated, the introduction of terrestrial invertebrates, fishes, and mollusks slowed down for a while, as, to a lesser extent, did the influx of plants, plant pathogens, and insects (later, the six categories of entrant employed in a seminal congressional report [1993] on nonindigenous problem species).[15] Deliberate imports eased off. Yet inadvertent arrivals soon replaced them as intercontinental contacts multiplied with burgeoning trade, tourism, and travel in ever bigger and quicker vessels facilitated by the shift from sail to steam; between 1970 and 1996, the world's merchant shipping trade virtually doubled. The arrival of commercial air transportation reinforced these trends.

The shrinking of physical distance, not least, enhanced the odds of survival for globe-trotting organisms. In all six categories, therefore, the total numbers of entering species during the twentieth century were greater than they had been in the nineteenth. In fact, the figures were the highest since the spate of planned and accidental exchanges during the epoch of European exploration and expansion between 1492 and the mid-1600s.[16] The rate accelerated markedly after World War II with the exponential growth of global trade—not least in horticultural and aquarium products—and shows no signs of abating as we enter a new millennium dominated by the ethos of unfettered international trade.

Looking at these two eras of faunal and floral immigration, I am particularly interested in the connections between the representation and reception of foreign species of flora and fauna and attitudes to human immigrants. And my overriding purpose within this remit is to clarify the nature of the relationship between criticism of invasive nonnative species on the one hand and of human immigration on the other. The two periods I have identified as the most important for plant and animal arrivals over the past two centuries happen to coincide (more or less) with the high watermarks of human immigration to the United States—not that this overlap has anything directly to do with national immigration policy; open doors for people does not automatically mean open doors for floral and faunal immigrants, more of which have entered in packing crates, shipping containers, and ballast water than in suitcases or stuck to the soles of shoes. After the introduction of restrictive quotas in the early 1920s, the number of arrivals was relatively low for four decades. But they rose again after 1965, when the national origins system that had worked against immigrants from outside northwest Europe was eliminated. As with the tenor of responses to nonhuman immigrants, the pitch of public debate over immigration's merits rose and fell in line with these statistical fluctuations. And just like the disputes over their nonhuman counterparts, this more familiar controversy over human arrivals has been squarely framed in terms of immigrant promise and desirability and immigrant menace and undesirability.

My investigations of promise and menace with reference to floral and faunal immigrants in American history are informed by some big and basic questions. How do we weigh up what is good and bad in nature? Clean and dirty? Healthy and unhealthy? Beautiful and ugly? How do we determine what is natural (and native) in nature? How do we measure improvements and losses in nature? At the forefront, though, are several more specific questions. Why are some overseas species embraced while others struggle for acceptance, no matter how firmly established they become? Are the problems associated with nonnatives primarily of a material order—ecological and economic, in other words? Or are social and cultural factors—especially notions of nationality—uppermost in identifying troublesome species? And, insofar as considerations of national identity are operative in the characterization of dangerous intruders, how does this nature of fear intersect with a wider culture of fear engendered by human immigrants?[17] In short, what do American attitudes to nonnative flora and fauna tell us about American attitudes to immigrant people at various points during the past century and a half?

Although I focus on the period between the 1890s and the 1920s and on the final three decades of the twentieth century, this study is not organized around these periods. Though by no means indifferent to chronological considerations, it is divided into three biotic categories: wild animals, agricultural plants (including associated insects), and trees. In his seminal works on international species transfer, *The Columbian Exchange: Biological and Cultural Consequences of 1492* and *Ecological Imperialism: The Biological Expansion of Europe, 900–1900*, Alfred Crosby examined livestock transplantation in some depth.[18] Yet the pigs, goats, sheep, and cattle in his books left little room for wild animals or much smaller creatures such as birds and insects. Crosby also discussed the colonizing role of crops (and plants known as weeds). But he covered a period mostly prior to American independence and generally dwelt on the initial centuries of European expansion when what are now staple American food crops and livestock were readily incorporated into the biotic polity. The story of agricultural plants brought to the United States since the Civil War is more obscure. Historians studying biotic interchange have also neglected trees, whether their period has been nineteenth century, twentieth century, or early modern.

By prioritizing the nonhuman protagonists, by allowing some telling animal and plant stories to drive the narrative forward, I maximize coverage of the nonhuman actors environmental history seeks to restore to the heart of the human experience. To preserve the physical integrity of my selected animals and plants, I disperse my coverage of the broader social and scientific landscape. Context and background are important. Yet content and foreground are more important.

My coverage of wild animals pivots on one of the problematic "wild foreigners" named in the National Safety Council's aforementioned news alert: the "English" sparrow.[19] British ecologist Charles Elton, in his pioneering study of the global "ecological explosions" triggered by invasive species, alluded to the sparrow only once. And this feathered foreigner made a very tardy cameo appearance in Crosby's books as a leitmotif of North America's Europeanized natural world. Yet the sparrow exemplifies the acclimatizer's desire to manipulate existing environments through transplantation, thereby creating an "authored ecosystem."[20] The bird's American tale illustrates dramatically how an ecosystem author's initial belief in immigrant promise can be challenged and eventually replaced by a more widespread perception of immigrant menace—and how rapidly this reversal can occur.

The bird's introduction illustrates most of the forces behind late nineteenth- and early twentieth-century plant and animal transplantation. But one motive in particular stands out. Underlying the English sparrow's introduction, one fervent opponent believed, was the "pestilent superstition which has done so much harm in the United States—that anything European must of necessity be better than anything native."[21] The English sparrow controversy in the late nineteenth- and early twentieth-century United States shows to particularly good effect how animate forms of nature can become embroiled in the cultural politics of nationalism.

Though it originated beyond its borders, a "problem species" like the English sparrow is indisputably naturalized in the United States. So is another European transplant that looms large on the American skyscape and features within this wildlife chapter in a subsidiary capacity: the starling. Naturalization in its scientific sense refers to an organism's capacity to form free-living populations by reproducing spontaneously and in self-replacing fashion beyond human care and cultivation. This means, in other words, that it has begun to make it on its own and to hold its own amidst the existing residents, or, to use a suggestive phrase, to behave "like a native."[22] A naturalized organism is thus one that has rooted itself firmly in new soil. Whether this success has earned these organisms the right to be considered *of* a new country as well as *in* it is another matter entirely. Concepts of national citizenship based on the contrasting principles of *jus soli* and *jus sanguinis* are highly relevant to these deliberations over the citizenship of birds and plants. According to *jus soli* (Latin for "right of territory"; literally "right of soil"), place of birth determines citizenship. On the basis of *jus sanguinis* ("right of blood" or descent), citizenship is determined by the citizenship of the parents, regardless of place of birth. Some would argue that nineteenth-century transplants like the English sparrow, European starling, European carp, and (Chinese) ring-necked pheasant—regardless of their impact on indigenous species, the economic toll they extract, or the pleasure they give—have produced sufficient American-born generations to merit their animal citizenship. (South Dakotans have gone further in extending formal recognition. They adopted the ring-necked pheasant as their state bird in 1943.) But as the story of the English sparrow illustrates (as does chapter 4's major case study), there is no unambiguous point at which a naturalized (nondomestic) species becomes eligible for faunal or floral citizenship or honorary native status. A plant or animal may have been in a new place or country for decades without the emergence of a consensus that it is also of that place or country.

Next, in chapter 3 I look at the introduction of crop, forage, and horticultural plants since the 1860s. This topic reveals how the notions of immigrant promise and immigrant menace were often closely tied, as certain parties identified the insects that sometimes accompanied these otherwise eminently desirable and uncontroversial imports as major threats to agricultural production. Though only 54 percent of the nonindigenous species investigated for a landmark congressional report in 1993 were insects, these were responsible for 96 percent of total economic costs.[23] And between the 1860s and 1920s, these "pests" provoked some of the most potent articulations of anxiety and hostility toward "alien" creatures.

In this connection, Mark Fiege's notion of "mobile nature" can be profitably adopted. Fiege's discussion was limited to weeds in Montana in the 1930s (and only incidentally concerned with their nationality). His term is equally relevant, however, to insects and a larger geographical and historical canvas.[24] All introduced organisms are self-evidently mobile. But "mobile nature" means more than just transplanted nature or "authored" nature, terms that convey the impression of humans with a clear plan who are firmly in control of their introductions. What happens when orderly introductions are accompanied by unanticipated and unruly fellow travelers who go their own ways and create disorder? And what do we call these self-willed, transgressive biota? "Mobile nature" works well for the United States as a whole.

There is no botanical distinction between trees and other plants. And a few trees sprout up here and there as part of my coverage of agricultural species in chapter 3. But in chapter 4 I shift focus decisively to trees and shrubs (no hard and fast distinction here, either) and transfer the discussion of immigrants of all types to another part of the United States. If chapter 2 can be pinned down to a specific geographical locale, it is New York City, where house sparrows and starlings and the people who debated their eligibility as biotic citizens were particularly thick on the ground (or in the air). The chapter on seeds, bulbs, and bugs can also be situated on the East Coast: in and around Washington, D.C., in the offices, laboratories, and fields stations of the federal government's botanists and entomologists. Chapter 4 also begins on the eastern seaboard, with a tree famous for defying the odds and thriving in Brooklyn. But attention soon switches to the West Coast, where it stays for the remainder of the chapter.

In California, in the company of the eucalyptus, we survey a prime example of what has been called a "transported landscape."[25] We also advance into more recent times, moving the study firmly into the second of my two chosen periods. Though dealing primarily with a nonnative tree that arrived and spread through cultivation during the same period as the English sparrow and various agricultural plants and their associated pests, the emphasis is on the twentieth century's final third, where we remain for the rest of this book. Having previously dealt with negative reactions that arose within a generation of the arrival of the offending biota (sometimes after a few years), in this investigation of the national identity politics of the eucalyptus I concentrate on later manifestations of disapproval and hostility.

In many respects, the trajectory of the eucalyptus in California conforms to the rise and fall that characterize the English sparrow's American reputation. Both were introduced in the 1850s to tremendous acclaim—the bird to eradicate a menacing tree pest and the tree to relieve a timber famine. Yet the enormous hopes invested in them were soon dashed. An additional feature in the social and cultural scenery of late twentieth-century California, though, was a vigorous lobby for native nature. Since the early 1970s, the nation's strongest native plant movement has been located in California, which also has a higher proportion of foreign-born residents than any other state (a quarter, whereas the national figure is a tenth). Furthermore, some of the most acute expressions of antipathy toward immigrants stem from the West Coast. For California's native plant proponents, the eucalyptus remains a permanent and unwanted alien, representing a transported landscape whose delivery was never accepted: in California but not of California. For other Californians, though, the eucalyptus has become an integral and thoroughly desirable feature of both cultural and ecological landscape: in *and* of California; indeed, many Californians are blithely unaware of its Australian provenance.

In this respect, the tree's fortunes differ from the bird's. The eucalyptus has retained far more American friends than the benighted house sparrow. This doubtless reflects, to a greater or lesser degree, their relative aggressiveness. Whereas the sparrow's spread knew no bounds, the eucalyptus has been less mobile. It has tended to stay put, with relatively few examples of spontaneous expansion, and certainly not at the expense of California's treasured redwoods and giant sequoias. Nonetheless, the tree has an almost peerless capacity to polarize communities in northern California. As Judith Larner Lowry of the small coastal town of Bolinas reflected in 2002, "The question of the removal or preservation of our local eucalyptus has become a bloody battle bringing a poisonous disharmony to the town."[26]

In the early decades of the twentieth century, public attitudes and government policy toward immigrants of all kinds were dominated by the ethic of restriction. In the floral and faunal sphere, this ended the era of naïve and complacent introduction. The object lessons supplied by a series of backfiring transplantations were subsequently reinforced by advances in the appreciation of ecological relationships, specifically the disruptive impact of introduced species on host communities. This recognition was paralleled by growing support for tighter controls over human immigration in the 1910s and 1920s, based on a racialized science of humankind biased toward Anglo-Saxons and others from northwest Europe, which ended the era of open door immigration. The increasing acceptance, thereafter, of an influential new anthropology pioneered by Franz Boas (a German Jewish immigrant) and underpinned by cultural pluralist and relativist ideals signaled the demise of traditional concepts of racial hierarchy.[27]

The outcome of the spread of these notions of racial equality, though, contrasted sharply with the results of a developing understanding of inter-actions between nonhuman organisms. A stricter admissions policy for flora and fauna reflected the more sober and cautious attitude to nonnative species. On the other hand, the replacement of a racially based, constrained notion of U.S. citizenship biased toward "old-stock" Americans with a racially equalitarian ethos engendered a new kind of open door immigra-tion policy. The open door policy that held sway before the introduction of early twentieth-century quotas on the size and national sources of intake was open door in the sense that the numbers admitted were unlimited and that entrants could, in theory, come from almost anywhere (with the specific exceptions of China and Japan). Numbers continued to be regulated after 1964, but the abolition of national quotas and the revocation of excluded categories in that year threw the door truly wide open for the first time in terms of immigrants' national and racial origins.

Attitudes to nonhuman immigrants have clearly diverged from attitudes to the human variety since the 1920s. Flora and fauna are tolerated less; a wider range of people are tolerated more. Another major point of differ-ence since the early 1960s lies in the mode of entry. Whereas most people have arrived through legal channels, the vast majority of their floral and fau-nal counterparts have come in unofficially. Regardless of an enhanced eco-logical understanding and public awareness of the potential dangers non-native flora and fauna pose, and despite tougher government regulations, the power to restrict entry to official channels has been limited at a time when the international movement of goods, peoples, and other organisms has intensified. In fact, the rate of influx and the degree of intermixing since the 1960s has been the highest since the initial colonization of the Americas.

Chapter 5 is set against this backdrop of an increasingly borderless world, a world that is further undermining old certainties about nations, national cultures, national identities, and national nature. Pitched at a more general level than previous chapters, it examines the most recent debates over the treatment of flora and fauna from elsewhere and their relationship with par-allel debates over human immigration (with, as ever, an eye to earlier episodes and historical precedents). My central finding is that, for all the colorful and arresting accusations of botanical xenophobia and eco-nativism, ties between conservation and prejudice, between the desire to preserve an "American" nature and to defend old-stock America, once sub-stantial, have largely dissolved.

THE NAMING OF STRANGERS

We employ a variety of terms to designate flora and fauna that have been relocated from one place to another (or have relocated themselves): *immi-*

grant, alien, stranger, foreigner, nonnative, nonindigenous, invader, and *exotic.* Yet sensitive issues arise when we try to define the national citizenship of flora and fauna and to decide what to call those that fail to qualify for this status. Because these terms have strong human connotations, making it hard not to think about people as well, some reflections on terminology are essential before continuing. President Jimmy Carter's executive order on the problems associated with exotic organisms, the first in U.S. history (May 24, 1977), encapsulated traditional notions by defining exotic species as "all species of plants and animals not naturally occurring, either presently or historically, in any ecosystem of the United States," and native species as "all species of plants and animals naturally occurring, either presently or historically, in any ecosystem of the United States."[28] "Occurring . . . historically" is generally understood to refer to a time before the arrival of Europeans in the Western Hemisphere. A native species, therefore, is one that was already present when Europeans first showed up, with their flora and fauna, somewhere that eventually became part of the United States. (For cultural nationalists, it often means a good deal more: a biotic citizen of a terrestrial Eden.)

Despite its powerful popular and scientific orthodoxy, a distinction between native and nonnative based exclusively on this historic watershed—and on the absence of direct human intervention implicit in the phrase "naturally occurring"—is problematic. This is so partly because of our incomplete knowledge of the pre-Columbian complement of species.[29] We also easily forget that Native Americans themselves were invaders. Who knows for sure what seeds accompanied those who migrated across the Bering land bridge from Siberia some 14,000 years ago at the tail end of the last great glaciation, whether carried deliberately or stuck to hair, clothes, or feet?[30] Once settled in the Americas, the invaders' descendants undoubtedly shifted plants around both by design and unintentionally. Plants also came up from the south. Without the introduction of various Eurasian crops, remarked Frances Jewett, "we might today be living principally on Indian corn, squash, pumpkins, and beans."[31] Yet these crops cultivated by the native peoples first encountered by European colonists were not indigenous to the eastern seaboard. They came from Central America. Corn may not have arrived in southern New England until the eleventh century, and considerable effort was required to develop new strains adapted to the region's shorter growing season.[32]

The first wave of American immigrants decimated megafauna so extensively, argues environmental scientist John Terborgh, that the large species inhabiting the national parks of the western United States today "are not even true Americans." And were it not for the ecological vacuum created by this early American bout of overkill (allied to extreme climatic change), they "might not be here at all." "Signature" big mammals of the parks—grizzly bear, moose, elk, and buffalo—all "invaded" across the land bridge once Clovis culture was superseded, in the absence of sufficient large animals to hunt, by gathering economies.[33] The distinction between native species and the rest also looks messier when it is appreciated that 18,000 years ago, when ice blanketed much of North America, the ice-free zone to the south that more or less corresponds to the present-day continental United States was inhabited by a cosmopolitan faunal mixture of indigenous North American types and immigrants from Eurasia and South America.

Even within historic (as distinct from geological) times, further complications arise from differences between national and ecological units. Common names often underline the "foreign" character of nonnative plants in the United States: English and German ivy, Scotch broom, Australian pine, Andean pampas grass, European gorse, Chinese tallow, Russian thistle, and Canada thistle.[34] Among introduced animals, we find the English sparrow, German carp, and Argentine ant.[35] (By the same token, Britain has American water weed, American mink, and American gray squirrel.)

The nonnative species that feature as this book's main case studies are all nonnative in that they come from another part of the world. Not all nonnatives, though, are foreign in this sense. A species native to one part of a national unit can be nonnative elsewhere in that unit. The American bullfrog *(Rana catesbeiana)*, an East Coast species, is as nonnative in California as it is in Britain. The striped bass, historically present in the Chesapeake Bay, is as nonindigenous in California as the German carp. Sixty percent of nonnative fishes in the United States are in fact internal transfers, many of them, some biologists feel, just as bad as real foreigners—or worse.[36]

The black locust highlights the limitations of standard terminology in floral terms. The northern limits of this tree's native ecosystem stretch from Pennsylvania across to southern Indiana, its southern boundary runs from Georgia to Louisiana, and it extends as far west as Iowa, Missouri, and Oklahoma. But the tree was taken to California during the Gold Rush and has since been planted across the nation for windbreaks and erosion control.[37] Beyond its native territory, however, the black locust is nonnative in a strict botanical sense.

A tree can even be a stranger within a single state. Midwestern landscape designer and native flora enthusiast Jens Jensen discovered this when commissioned in 1935 to design the Lincoln Memorial Garden on a patch of old farmland near Springfield in central Illinois. Jensen's original idea was to gather together the native trees of Illinois, Indiana, and Kentucky, the three states in which Lincoln had lived. Yet even the less ambitious plan to assemble trees typical of those areas of Illinois where Lincoln had dwelled ran into difficulties, for this meant bringing species from the state's warmer, swampy southern reaches (such as bald cypress) and from the colder northern zone (like white birch) into the tallgrass prairie/savannah/forest complex of mid-Illinois. These northern and southern transplants have not flourished in the Lincoln Memorial Garden.[38]

An animal may also be nonnative within an American state. The Olympic Peninsula is geographically isolated from the rest of Washington, so quite a few mammals historically present not more than a hundred miles to the east in the Cascade Mountains have been absent here. In the 1920s, sport hunters introduced the mountain goat from British Columbia, Alberta, and southeast Alaska to an area of the Olympic Mountains that acquired national park status in 1938. In the early 1980s, the Park Service began removing the goats, which it identified as highly detrimental to the park's fragile native alpine vegetation.[39]

Direct human intervention is not required to produce a homegrown exotic. Altered conditions triggered by human actions can give natives the opportunity to expand their range. The brown-headed cowbird (also known as the buffalo bird, because it formerly fed on insects and seeds thrown up by bison hoofs) was originally confined to the Great Plains. Since then, this most infamous of North American brood parasites has spread eastward and westward in association with forest clearance and livestock rearing.

Just as a national unit (or single state) may contain a variety of ecological communities, an ecological community can transcend national frontiers. Caribou in the North American Arctic have dual citizenship. The creatures of the Sonora Desert are equally oblivious to the southern U.S. border, and the Mexican gray wolf has been reintroduced to its native Arizona. Adopting this more sophisticated approach based on the ecosystem as a unit, a major international conference in 1996 avoided the tendentious language of nationality and defined foreign species as those "that occur in places different from their area of natural distribution."[40] Similarly—and therefore in contrast to President Carter's previous announcement—President Clinton's executive order (13112, on February 3, 1999) on invasive species defined a nonnative (alien) species, "with respect to a particular ecosystem, [as] any species . . . that is not native to that ecosystem."[41] In many ways, however, *nonnative* is one of the least controversial of the terms applied to species from elsewhere.

THE ALIEN MENACE: HUMANIZING NATURE
AND NATURALIZING HUMANS

Of all the names for the unequivocally "foreign" species whose American histories I explore, by far the most common—witness the National Safety Council's alert—is *alien*. *Alien* has also been the standard appellation for human immigrants over the past two hundred years or more. This French (originally Latin) word for "other" or "another" has for centuries denoted a person of a different race or nation. It has also been applied more specifically to a person who is not native to the country in which he or she resides (a resident foreigner, in other words). In the United States, *alien* gained popular currency in New England's Federalist circles in the 1790s, with reference to the alleged threat to national tranquility posed by Irish and French immigrant radicals who supported the Jeffersonian opposition. California's Alien Land Law of 1913—the first of many in western states— aimed to prevent the unwanted from rooting themselves in American soil by barring land purchase or lease by Japanese and other Asian noncitizens.[42]

Alien has subsequently acquired other pejorative trappings now largely inseparable from prevailing understandings. Making my way through the "aliens" queue on my first visit to the United States in 1976, I tried to joke with a stolid official of the U.S. Immigration and Naturalization Service about the unflattering, even insulting, connotations of the term. Undergoing a similar interrogation to ascertain his "alien desirability," British novelist H. G. Wells referred to "the provocation to answer impertinently."[43] I also resisted the provocation, though I was not asked whether I was a polygamist or an anarchist. Yet I expressed the view that *alien* denied me and my fellow non-Americans our terrestrial humanity by lumping us together with the Martians.

Though Wells did not use the term *alien* in *The War of the Worlds* (1898), this influential current usage was prefigured in all its essentials in his novel about a Martian invasion of England. The Martians were accompanied by seeds, which sprouted with remarkable vitality into blood-colored plants that ran amok, choking native vegetation and smothering rivers and buildings. Science fiction writers on both sides of the Atlantic started using *alien* explicitly after 1945, an early example being the "monster" plant (a "horrible, alien thing") in British novelist John Wyndham's *The Day of the Triffids* (1951). In science fiction films of the early Cold War era, alien biota often functioned as allegories for the communist menace. In *Invasion of the Body Snatchers* (1956), vegetative "pods" from outer space germinate in California's greenhouses, producing a strange disease that turns people into zombies. Public hysteria over that other red menace—the imported red fire ant *(Solenopsis invicta)*—in the American South in the late 1950s was stoked by the movie *Them!* (1954), in which ten-foot, atomic mutant ants from test sites in New Mexico wreaked havoc, winding up in Los Angeles sewer systems and storm drains.[44]

These thick layers of human association that encrust the term *alien* help explain why human and nonhuman immigration are often closely twinned in the popular mind; why debates about the impact of nonnative biota are frequently conducted within the wider context of discussion of the acceptability of certain human immigrants; and why the personhood imparted to nonnative flora and fauna by the transfer of imagery and terminology from debates over human immigration is such an emotive issue.

My discussion of how notions of biological belonging are produced and of the relationship between a nature of fear and a broader culture of fear takes its cue from a spate of recent references to "ecological nativists" and allegations of "biological nativism."[45] *Nativism* denotes an extreme, defensive-aggressive form of nationalism based on a perception of immigrant menace. The term was coined around 1840 in the context of Protestant "Know-Nothing" opposition to Irish Catholic immigrants. It is more commonly associated, though, with the anti-immigrant sentiments of Anglo-Saxon Protestant Americans between the 1890s and 1920s, when it had acquired connotations of the racial superiority of Anglo-Saxons (also referred to as Nordics or Teutonics).[46] Nineteenth-century nativists characterized their creed as "Americanism." Yet their fears, resentments, and suspicions reflected a rigid conception of Americanism and American nationhood. The liberal (or pluralist) ideal urged the United States to enlarge its population and character by accepting diverse European (and sometimes non-European) contributions, locating strength and greatness in breadth of demographic composition and respect for diversity.

Still, the conservative form—often dubbed "one-hundred percent" Americanism—demanded protection of the nation's existing, British- and continental northwest European–derived complexion by barring nonconforming elements (notably Asiatics, Jews, and Catholics). The pluralist sense of nationhood, being fluid and open-ended, confidently anticipated future developments, even though the hundred-percenters harkened back to the past perfection, purity, and security of a completed pattern and sealed identity. The ultimate expressions of nativism during the late nineteenth and early twentieth centuries were efforts to restrict the entry of "undesirable" immigrants—and in some cases to exclude groups entirely.

Today's defenders of nonnative species routinely level the charge of nativism at those who bemoan the impact of certain foreign flora and fauna on their native counterparts. Drawing on an influential article by Michael Pollan, Jonah Peretti refers to Nazi Germany's enthusiasm for native plants and hostility to exotic species in a subsection titled "The Disturbing Historical Legacy of Purist Biological Nativism." Banu Subramaniam cites Nancy Tomes's work on the intersection of early twentieth-century "germ panics" and antipathy toward mass immigration from southern and eastern Europe.[47] But this historical consciousness is exceptional. Claims for the greening of hate are usually confined to the present or to the past decade.[48] My intention is to test the validity of allegations of ecological nativism in the context of the late nineteenth and early twentieth centuries as well as recent times.

The culturally loaded language of the menacing stranger in which the debate about relatively recent arrivals such as the zebra mussel, tiger mosquito, and Asian long-horned beetle is often conducted (witness references to "unwelcome aliens," "conquering hordes," and "isolated terrorists") usually furnishes the basis for allegations of intolerance. Accordingly, the distinctive styles of thought and expression that move back and forth across the hallowed divide between humans and the rest of nature by seeing the latter in human terms and naturalizing the former is one of this book's overarching themes. As well as being particularly alert to rhetorical and other linguistic evidence of intersections of human and other immigrants and to their larger meaning, I also locate links of a more material nature, notably between efforts to combat exotic species and attempts to restrict the influx of people. In pursuit of these ends, I examine various written media, including government publications, scientific periodicals and reports, natural history magazines, botanical literature, environmentalist writings, investigative journalism, and the popular press, as well as, albeit to a lesser extent, the archival records of government agencies and prominent individuals. These individuals expressed some powerful ideas in a striking fashion, but they also represent a wider group and outlook.

OUR FELLOW IMMIGRANTS

Comparing floral and faunal immigrants to human immigrants is just one aspect of a wider tendency in Western thought. Anthropomorphism (or humanization)—our habit of bestowing human characteristics, positive and negative, on natural entities, animate and inanimate—is endemic to the way we think and express ourselves and to how we go about positioning ourselves within the wider biotic world. Equally incorrigible is anthropomorphism's opposite—naturalization—which refers to our proclivity for endowing people with the attributes, positive and negative, of natural entities (animate and inanimate).

Witness the terminology shared by those who study flora and fauna and those who deal with the human world. Botanists, zoologists, and historians alike refer to natives, immigrants, colonists, and aliens. Botanists investigating processes of plant succession and historians and social scientists studying human migrations and power struggles speak a common language of invasion, immigration, competition, conquest, colonization, and pioneering.[49] Meanwhile, botanists and zoologists as well as lawyers and sociologists mull over questions of nationality and citizenship.

These common interests and the shared terminology of humanization and naturalization are hardly surprising. Many nonhuman animals maintain kinship and social relations, demonstrate personalities, and exhibit tribalism and territoriality. Moreover—and more directly pertinent to the subject of this book—people, plants, animals, and microbes frequently move into new places as part of what Crosby calls a "mutually supportive" biotic "portmanteau" or "team." Joseph Hooker, Britain's leading nineteenth-century botanist, recognized this on arriving at Boston in the summer of 1877. There to greet him in New England were over two hundred and fifty "Old England" plants that were mainly "fellow emigrants and fellow colonists with the Anglo-Saxon." Having crossed the Atlantic in the Anglo-Saxon's company, they had "like him, asserted their supremacy over and displaced a certain number of natives of the soil." His foothold was complemented by their root-hold (to use one of Hooker's phrases).[50] From his vantage point at the metropolitan center, Hooker employed the phrase "his fellow emigrants." Nearly a century later, from his internal, American perspective, Robert Froman adapted this phrase. The title of his popular treatment of introduced flora and fauna in the United States neatly captures the sense of collective enterprise that engaged Hooker: *Our Fellow Immigrants.*[51]

It may appear easiest (and most natural) to compare ourselves to the more closely related lifeforms represented by various members of the animal kingdom—however small in size. Yet people are also frequently compared to plants, and plants, in turn, are regularly likened to people. Botanical analogies came effortlessly to a farmer like J. Hector St. John de Crèvecoeur. Referring to America's regenerative effect on immigrants in the late eighteenth century, the French aristocratic immigrant remarked that "in Europe they were as so many useless plants, wanting vegetative mould and refreshing showers; they withered and were mowed down by want, hunger, and war; but now, by the power of transplantation, like all other plants they have taken root and flourished." "Men are like plants," he announced in a classic statement of environmental determinism, "the goodness and flavour of the fruit proceeds from the peculiar soil and exposition in which they grow."[52]

Crèvecoeur thought exclusively in terms of benign transplantation. Others have seen a kinship between people and plants in their role as invaders. As Crosby commented, the American exploits of European plants such as white clover, plantain, and dandelion "tempt the botanist to use such anthropomorphic terms as aggressive and opportunistic." He certainly succumbed himself, writing of hundreds of European weeds that "packed up, weighed anchor, set sail for the colonies, and prospered there." Over the centuries, rural folk and agriculturalists have denounced these unwanted plants—regardless of nationality—as savage, filthy, unruly, and criminal. Nineteenth-century Euro-American botanists were virtually incapable of thinking about plants and people as separate categories. In particular, they realized that foreign weeds were much like themselves and correlated the demise of native peoples with that of native flora. That a comparatively small number of European weeds had emigrated to the United States (as of the early 1830s) was a blessing, judged Lewis David von Schweinitz, a Moravian churchman from Pennsylvania who had botanized as far west as mid-Indiana. "Otherwise," he remarked, "our native vegetation would have been swept from the scene, as has been the human race of aborigines [and] our native plants would have stood as little chance of maintaining their ground against a phalanx of vegetable colonists from Europe, as our straggling aborigines did against the columns of emigrants from that part of the world, were these vegetable colonists as prone to establish themselves."[53]

Though botanists use the same terms as historians and others who study human immigration and colonization, they do not necessarily use or interpret them in the same way. Prominent early twentieth-century American plant ecologist Frederic Clements employed *invasion* and *colonization* in a strictly scientific sense. He defined *invasion* as "the whole movement of a plant or group of plants from one area into another and their colonization in the latter." The *colony* was thus a plant community almost invariably the result of invasion, usually composed of plants exhibiting pioneering qualities.[54] Like many plant ecologists of his generation, Clements was deeply influenced by the work of Danish botanist Eugene Warming. *Oecology of Plants,* Warming's major book, contained a chapter titled "The Peopling of New Soil," which examined the history of invasion and colonization of fresh sites by "successive immigrants": namely, newly emerged sand dunes along the Danube; alluvial deposits at the mouths of rivers such as the Rhone; lava fields following volcanic eruptions in Iceland; talus slopes and naked ground resulting from landslips and glacial retreat in the Alps; and burned-over grasslands like the Brazilian *campos.*[55]

To the historian, though, Warming's chapter title evokes images of the Virginia Company (or reminds us of the "planting" of the northern counties of Ireland with lowland Scots as an integral part of British conquest). Warming was well aware of the urge to draw parallels. Writing of the ceaseless struggles between and within plant communities, he reflected that " 'situation wanted' is the cry in all communities, whether these be human or vegetable." Generally, however, Warming not only resisted but expressly advised against making the connection.[56]

An influential group of American social scientists had no such qualms. A biologically grounded urban sociology flowered at the University of Chicago in the 1920s. The Chicago school's groundbreaking work in what they called *human ecology* borrowed explicitly from Clementsian botany. Clements's work was imbued with the notion of plant *society,* which Roderick McKenzie referred to directly when commenting on changes in a neighborhood's ethnic/racial composition: "Just as in plant communities successions are the products of invasion, so also in the human community the formations, segregations, and associations that appear constitute the outcome of a series of invasions." Alluding to "foreign races and other undesirable invaders," he explained that these invasions produced spatial units with distinctive functions and characteristics, "which may be termed 'natural areas' . . . to use the term of the plant ecologist."[57]

In his pioneering sociological-historical study of the Jewish ghetto from its medieval European origins to its contemporary American manifestation, Louis Wirth explained how the analysis of a cultural community across time and place provided the opportunity to transform "history into natural history." Ernest Burgess, who explained that "the immigrant colony in an American city possesses a culture unmistakably not indigenous but transplanted from the Old World," insisted that the sociologist could learn more from Warming's *Oecology of Plants* than from any other source.[58] In the nineteenth and early twentieth centuries, in the United States as well as other parts of the English-speaking world, habits of thought that consciously compared people with plants and animals and plants and animals with people, often in the form of sustained analogies, were thus a distinctive feature of the scientific and popular mind.[59]

Metaphors are commonly used to naturalize humans and humanize non-human nature. Their task is to encourage us to compare otherwise unrelated things.[60] The metaphor's effectiveness (Wayne Booth calls this its "good weapon" value) relies on common assumptions about the objects of comparison.[61] Citing the example "man is a wolf," linguist Max Black points out that the accuracy or truthfulness of this "system of associated commonplaces" is less important than that "they should be readily and freely evoked." The "current platitudes" tied to particular animals emphasize certain traits that can be readily suggested through the connection. "The wolf-metaphor," he explains, "*organizes* our view of man" by transferring the received qualities of the "subsidiary" subject (the wolf) to the "principal" subject (man). Within Western thought, the wolf analogy has almost invariably been applied to people for defamatory purposes. But whether figurative uses of language carry pejorative, positive, or essentially neutral meanings usually depends on context and user. Black explains: "There are . . . many contexts (including nearly all the interesting ones) where the meaning of a metaphorical expression has to be reconstructed from the speaker's intentions (and other clues) because the broad rules of standard usage are too general to supply the information needed. . . . the tone of voice, the verbal setting, the historical background, [help] make clear what metaphor [is] being used."[62]

Here's an example involving bees. "Forth from Europe's teeming mother-hive" Nordics "swarmed" around the world, reflected Lothrop Stoddard, a leading early twentieth-century Nordic supremacist.[63] His choice of animal was particularly apposite, since settlers took honeybees wherever they went (how else were they supposed to recreate the biblical land of milk and honey?). Stoddard's aim in linking Nordics with bees was to appropriate the associated commonplaces of energetic industry and sweet productiveness.

North American aboriginals just as readily associated bees with invading

Europeans. The bee's characteristics they sought to communicate, however, had to do with menace, not promise. The dangers associated with bees and wasps also dominated metaphorical applications when nativists wanted to bad-mouth non-Nordic immigrants. Playing on deep-seated antipathy to stinging insects, they applied traditional allusions to "hordes" of rapidly multiplying insects to unsavory immigrants. In an influential work of pseudo-scientific racial theory (from 1916), a leading wildlife conservationist, Madison Grant, reported of his hometown, New York City, that Anglo-Saxons were "literally driven off the streets . . . by the swarms of Polish Jews."[64]

The impact of these nativist analogies was heightened by America's connection with prelapsarian purity—a place of new beginnings uncontaminated by the past. A sign in a late nineteenth-century California eatery read: "John's Restaurant. Pure American. No Rats. No Greeks."[65] No trespassers in Eden, in other words. Nativists also sought to accentuate the alien menace through analogies with disease. "I would quarantine this Nation as I would against the bubonic plague," proclaimed Texas Democrat Martin Dies at a congressional hearing on immigration restriction in 1912.[66]

Human undesirables were not just compared to pathogens. They were often blamed for maladies. "They no longer come, like the hordes of old, on horseback, fantastically dressed in skins, brandishing spears," remarked Cornelia James Cannon in 1923. "But they come in far greater numbers, vermin infested, alien in spirit." William Deverell sees a distinction-blurring policy of "aggressive cleanliness aimed at both rats and Mexicans" in measures to eliminate bubonic plague after a 1924 outbreak in a Mexican quarter of Los Angeles.[67] Implicit in these analogies was the reconfiguration of a political entity, the nation, as a biological entity—the human body.[68] And, as we shall see, this host of negatively naturalizing images was complemented by a welter of anthropomorphic metaphors that unfavorably humanized undesirable faunal and floral immigrants.

Metaphors that naturalize people and humanize animals and plants are equally pervasive today. Subramaniam calls these rhetorical parallels between human immigrants and the floral and faunal varieties "striking," especially in the popular media, where, she argues, they constitute a distinctive genre of media sensationalism. Mark Sagoff explains why, in his view, environmentalists conflate human and nonhuman immigrants:

> Those of us who support a liberal immigration policy concede that some newcomers have been undesirable. . . . However, from the premise that a person is no good *and* an immigrant, it does not follow that a person is no good *because* he or she is an immigrant. One still has to show a connection between the characteristic of being a foreigner and the characteristic of being a nuisance. To make this connection in the ecological context, those who seek funds to exclude or eradicate non-native species often attribute to them the same disreputable qualities that xenophobes have attributed to immigrant groups.[69]

Subramaniam goes further. The rising tide of recent fear over exotic species is not only comparable to a recent upsurge in hostility toward immigrants in its outward manifestation (and it is more than just a question of pro-native species ecologists trying to "sex up" their grant applications, as Sagoff implies). She believes that these two phenomena are directly related, even inseparable: "The battle against exotic and alien plants is a symptom of a campaign that misplaces and displaces anxieties about economic, social, political, and cultural changes onto outsiders and foreigners."[70]

Are these links really substantive as well as rhetorically conspicuous? Instead of dwelling on rhetorical-metaphorical continuities between past and present and then drawing inferences about persisting nativism, I am more struck by the break with the past since the 1950s. Those who detect an ecological version of nativism in attitudes to nonnative species—and who see an umbilical cord between this manifestation of intolerance and the more familiar human version of xenophobia—have not shown much interest in historical evidence. Yet their analytical line is more applicable to the past than to the present. During the nineteenth and early twentieth centuries, the wider meaning of humanizing and naturalizing metaphors in the debate about immigration, human and nonhuman, was much clearer than it has been since the 1950s. It would be rash to approach the function of metaphor between the 1840s and 1920s as largely decorative and to dismiss linguistic analysis as nothing more than a tortuous parlor game for underemployed cultural theorists and historians who have been seduced by the linguistic turn. You do not have to be an expert in semantics, argues immigration historian Roger Daniels with reference to what he calls the "hydraulic metaphors" of floods and tides, "to understand that one result of the habitual use of such language is to stigmatize immigrants as the 'other,' rather than as the ancestors of us all."[71] With reference to the period between the 1840s and 1920s, this observation's validity is unquestionable.

The applicability of this observation to my second period of study is not, however, so clear-cut. My case for material discontinuity despite the appearance of rhetorical continuity—a central concern of the final chapter—draws on the notion of the "faded metaphor," a term coined in 1885 by German linguist Philip Wegener. What Susanne Langer refers to as "constant figurative use" generalizes the sense of words that had a crisper, more literal meaning in a previous social and scientific context.[72] Once that context changes, however, the color is drained out of those metaphors that naturalize people and humanize animals and plants.

STRANGERS ON THE LAND

As well as being dubbed a "little foreigner" and an "avian alien," the English sparrow was also stigmatized and marginalized as a "little stranger" and "stranger in a strange land." Eucalyptus trees in California have also been caricatured (more recently) as "strangers in our midst."[73] Yet this popular synonym for *nonnative* does not fully explain this book's subtitle. My inspiration comes primarily from John Higham's seminal study of hostility toward immigrants, *Strangers in the Land: Patterns of Nativism in American History, 1860s to 1920s.* In a new preface to the second edition, Higham touches on the themes of immigrant promise and immigrant menace by emphasizing the perennial tension in American society and culture between the desire for openness and flexibility and the demand for stability and security. A transplanted midwesterner of Protestant old stock who grew up in the cosmopolitan New York City borough of Queens, Higham characterizes nativism as an "ideological disease," an exclusionary "habit of mind [that] illuminates darkly some of the large contours of the American past; it has mirrored our national anxieties and marked the bounds of our tolerance."[74] Since the 1840s, anxious and frustrated Americans have identified a host of threats, internal and external, to the well-being of their values and the nation itself, among them popery (1840s); Jews, alcohol, exposed female ankles, salacious movies (1910s and 1920s); the Soviet Union's "evil empire," "environmental extremists" (1980s); and, most recently, the "axis of evil" (Iraq, Iran, and North Korea).

An American anthropologist, Anthony Wallace, coined the term "revitalization movement" in the 1950s to describe efforts to restore stability to the national body politic during times of severe sociocultural stress and dislocation. He identified nativist attempts to eradicate disruptive alien elements as a distinctive type of revitalization movement.[75] Like other anthropologists of the time, Wallace formulated these ideas exclusively with reference to non-European peoples. Other American scholars of the fifties and sixties, however, felt that revitalization movements and purification drives were most fruitfully examined within a Euro-American context. In a lecture in England in 1963 on arch-conservative dissent in the United States, historian Richard Hofstadter identified a "paranoid style" of thought and expression that saw conspiratorial threats to nation, culture, and way of life wherever it looked. He singled out "frustrated nationalisms" as the common ingredient linking all manifestations of the paranoid style, from the anti-Catholic hysteria of the 1840s to his era's anticommunist "witch hunts."[76]

During the immigration debate of the early 1990s, an advocate of restriction, Lawrence Auster, denounced the overwhelming tendency to regard past efforts to limit immigration to the United States as a pathological, parochial, and irrational reaction. And he credited *Strangers in the Land* with a powerful role in shaping this prevailing (liberal) wisdom. The problem with the traditional view handed down by the likes of Higham, Auster argued, was that it largely ignored "the huge and unsettling impact" of immigration on the host society during decades such as the 1850s and

1920s. He noted (with evident satisfaction) that Higham himself eventually acknowledged the scale and depth of this impact. What Higham once dismissed as "nativist hysteria," Auster announced, "he now admits was a normal reaction to social upheavals caused in part by massive immigration; he further admits that when those problems were eased by a reduction in immigration, so was the 'hysterical' response."[77]

Regardless of Auster's political agenda, he accurately assesses Higham's shifting stance. As early as 1956, Higham acknowledged that the demise of mass immigration in the 1920s following the enactment of quotas "relieved the worst fears of old-stock Americans, and . . . also facilitated assimilation by depriving the ethnic minorities of constant, large-scale reinforcements."[78] In addition, impressive economic growth after 1945 supplied a wealth of opportunity for old-stock Americans and immigrants alike, removing root causes of tension and accelerating assimilation. From their early twentieth-century zenith, nativism and the ideology of Anglo-Saxon (Nordic) supremacism declined steeply in influence—not least through association with the excesses of Nazi racial theory and policies and the subsequent efforts of civil rights campaigners at home. Already by 1933, racial thinking that had been mainstream a decade earlier was dismissed as Nazi propaganda, and Boazian notions of cultural and racial egalitarianism were winning hearts and minds. (Besides, even during nativism's heyday in the late nineteenth and early twentieth centuries, the United States was by far the most immigrant-friendly of nations.)

Then, in 1958, Higham reflected that *Strangers in the Land* had exaggerated nativism's influence, leading to undue emphasis on "subjective, irrational motives" of hostility toward immigrants and a failure to appreciate material considerations; he referred to the latter as "*the objective realities* of ethnic relations" (my emphasis). Nativism, he admitted, "now looks less adequate as a vehicle for studying the struggles of nationalities in America." To dismiss "as nativist any kind of unfriendliness toward immigrants," he declared, was a "bad habit . . . to be resisted." In his preface to the book's second edition, he remarked that, were he to write *Strangers in the Land* again, he would "take more account of aspects of the immigration restriction movement that can not be sufficiently explained in terms of nativism."[79]

Recent commentators have identified a "new," revived nativism over the past few decades that closely resembles the "classic" nativism of the previous period.[80] As suggested, this coincides with a tendency to appraise criticism of nonnative species of flora and fauna in similar fashion to Higham's original explanation of anti-immigrant sentiment in *Strangers in the Land*. "Some have expressed the concern," noted the project director for the congressional report of 1993 on injurious nonindigenous species, "that it may be a form of racism to believe that certain species don't belong in some places—

something like xenophobia—a fear of foreigners just because they're foreigners."[81]

This viewpoint, as previously intimated, has a certain logic when applied to the past. After all, the Americans most acutely aware of immigrant menace in the late nineteenth and early twentieth centuries were also those most exercised by the fate of native species at the hands of foreign flora and fauna. These old-stock Americans of British and other northwest European origin had enshrined themselves as the nation's native constituency and, sharing their status anxiety with other native species, compared their own shrinking numbers with dwindling faunal and floral populations.

We must take a much harder look, though, at nativism's role in shaping American responses to nonhuman immigrants. With Higham's second thoughts in mind, I query the emphasis on subjective irrationalities concerning national origins and what Subramaniam refers to as "changing racial, economic, and gender norms."[82] This approach to the subject of attitudes to nonnative species marginalizes the material problems of an ecological nature associated with certain nonnatives and slights the frequently sound ecological (not to mention economic) case for promoting native species, especially during the twentieth century's last quarter and the twenty-first's early years. (How we react to new species, in other words, depends largely on their degree of aggressiveness.) Had his interests extended to floral and faunal strangers, Higham would most likely have referred to these considerations as the "objective realities of ecological relations."

I also revisit the notion of exceptionalism that often dominates discussion of the impact of nonnative species on host ecosystems and American responses to them. The American histories of the eucalyptus and English sparrow are not the only ones that supplement their homeland stories. The eucalyptus was also transplanted to Algeria, Brazil, India, Italy, South Africa, and Spain. The sparrow was added to the fauna of other colonies of white settlement such as Australia, New Zealand, and South Africa, where initial hopes were also soon challenged and eventually overwhelmed by perceptions of menace. The English sparrow was a disputed creature at home too (though in Britain, obviously, it was simply called the sparrow). Also, prior to the early 1900s, many British settlers in Australia loathed a tree they considered uncouth and scruffy. Moreover, as John MacKenzie suggested, the world's biotic traffic was not as "one-way"—from Eurasia to the rest of the world—as Crosby had insisted. "How often," rejoined Crosby, "have American species swamped and driven to the verge of extinction native species in Great Britain?"[83] Not as infrequently as Crosby implies, it turns out. The most controversial immigrant fauna in Britain are all deliberate introductions from North America: gray squirrel, mink, muskrat, signal crayfish, and ruddy duck.

There was no equivalent among the English or Italians, Hofstadter reflected during the anticommunism climate of the Cold War in the 1960s, to the "one hundred percent" American. He also noted how the notion of being, doing, or investigating things "un-English" or "un-Italian" was foreign to those nations.[84] Higham, who had expressed a similar distaste for the excesses of Americanism during an earlier bout of American intolerance known as McCarthyism, did not reflect on other national experiences. Yet *Strangers in the Land* also gave the (dubious) impression that nativist efflorescence had been unusually virulent in the United States. Fear of the outsider has, however, erupted into xenophobic activity at various points in African, Asian, Australian, and European history. Nativist feelings shaped an influential immigration restriction movement in Britain in the 1910s, for example.

Those who speak of ecological nativism likewise give the impression that antipathy toward exotic species and the simultaneous championing of native biota have been particularly robust in the United States. This view usually emerges by default: commentators simply neglect to reflect on other national experiences. Sagoff, though, directly compares American intolerance with a more relaxed European "cosmopolitanism" that "tolerates porous borders" for immigrant flora and fauna. He sees this as a reflection of different New and Old World conceptions of nature. Whereas Americans are dedicated to the "idea of pristine nature," as enshrined in the related concepts of wilderness and indigenous species (native plants and animals, by implication, being biotic citizens of a terrestrial Eden), these notions, he claims, lack cultural, spiritual, and historical meaning for Europeans, who prefer their nature to be a blend of the nonhuman and the cultural. The alien organisms Europeans worry about and are keen to exclude from their countryside and farms, he explains, are genetically modified crops (mostly born in the United States).[85]

Pictures of saboteurs snapping the stalks of genetically modified corn planted in trial plots were certainly a familiar sight on British television screens and newspaper front pages a few years ago. But parties of native plant enthusiasts can also be found bashing away at the riotous growth of Himalayan balsam along British riverbanks.[86] The "Today" program, BBC Radio's flagship morning news broadcast, regularly reports heated controversy over the alleged misdeeds of species like the American gray squirrel, American mink, American ruddy duck, Argentine ant, and Spanish bluebell (as well as plans to protect the natives they beleaguer). Meanwhile, the American bullfrog has made it onto the U.K. government Environment Agency's "dirty dozen" list of "worst invasive nasties."[87] Whether or not wilderness carries the same cultural cachet in Britain or enjoys the same historical resonance (and the growing popularity of John Muir in his Scottish homeland and the emergence of the John Muir Trust as the fastest growing organization on Britain's landscape conservation scene suggests that it may be acquiring greater purchase), the juxtaposition of native and nonnative species is far from alien to British conservation debates. Since its establishment in 1983, the Trust's overriding aim has been to "conserve and protect wild places with their indigenous animals, plants and soils."[88]

Few animals are more reviled in the British popular, sporting, and conservationist press than the gray squirrel and the mink. Integral to the vilification of the gray squirrel (introduced between the 1870s and 1920s to enrich Britain's impoverished mammalian population) has been the metamorphosis (with a little help from Beatrix Potter's Squirrel Nutkin) of its alleged victim, the smaller native red squirrel, from forester's scourge to national icon.[89] Debates of the 1970s and 1980s over the mink—a semiaquatic fur farm escapee (originally introduced in 1929) whose naturalization in the late 1950s is usually blamed for the decline of the otter and the water vole—were no less saturated with metaphors of the vicious, fast-breeding, all-conquering alien than many concurrent American debates over invasive exotics. Moreover, British wildlife managers and popular science feature writers are equally fond of the suggestive imagery of otherworldly menace. "Forget little green men—the real alien invasion is taking place in our very own countryside," announces an article on threatening nonnative species in the official news publication of the British government's Environment Agency. Discussion about the characterization of species on the basis of nationality and the use of appropriate terminology that does not offend certain groups of people is often equally heated in a nation not conventionally considered to be the product of immigration but whose population has become increasingly diverse through rising immigration levels over the past three decades. Periodic allusion to the reception of foreign species elsewhere will improve our understanding of the Americanism of American reactions to nonhuman immigrants.[90]

At a 1988 international conference in Honolulu, Hawaii, on the ecology of biological invasions, an American biologist voiced his unease over "a kind of irrational xenophobia about invading animals and plants that resembles the inherent fear and intolerance of foreign races, cultures, and religions." James Brown felt that he had encountered examples of this prejudice among fellow scientists at the meeting itself but offered this remark with specific reference to the "disfavor, if not . . . outright loathing," with which the majority of North American birdwatchers, conservationists, and biologists regarded the English (house) sparrow and starling.[91] My explorations of the humanization and nationalization of nature through the construction of biological belonging and non-belonging begin with one of these two birds. The English sparrow is so small, unremarkable, and ubiquitous that few Americans—with the exception of those belonging to Brown's three categories—would give it a second glance or thought. Yet its modest size and unprepossessing appearance are belied by the remarkable insight the bird provides into enthusiasm for exotics and its eventual replacement by nostalgia for natives. Nor do the bird's unexceptional physical features prepare us for its impressive position in the debate over the role of fear and prejudice in shaping attitudes to faunal arrivals.

Chapter 2

The Avian Conquest of a Continent

The sparrow is an exotic species to America, and following the law of introduced species, has become a pest.

A. H. ESTABROOK, "The Present Status of the English Sparrow Problem in America," 1907

It has been branded as thief, wretch, feathered rat, etc. etc., but whatever may be said about it, the bird certainly is important.

EDWARD HOWE FORBUSH AND JOHN BICHARD MAY, *Natural History of the Birds of Eastern and Central North America,* 1939

TRANSATLANTIC FLIGHTS

Visiting New York City's Central Park in May 1903, Clinton G. Abbott conducted a quick survey of foreign birds. He spotted five species in twenty minutes: the European goldfinch, European chaffinch, European greenfinch, European starling, and European house (English) sparrow. He hailed goldfinches as "cheery little songsters" and admired the chaffinch's plumage, tunefulness, "pleasant disposition," and tidy nests. But he did not like anything about the other three. The positive attributes of goldfinch and chaffinch were also insufficient to atone for the undesirable features of all five feathered foreigners.

The worst offenders, in Abbott's view, were the starling and sparrow. The starling *(Sturnus vulgaris),* successfully released in the park as recently as 1890, was "already a very abundant permanent resident" across the entire city. This spectacular growth suggested that it would soon replicate its status in Britain, where it was "second only to its compatriot, the House Sparrow, in dominion over the land." He predicted that all cavity-nesting American birds would eventually suffer from the "persecutions of this pugnacious bird." His opinion of the longer established English sparrow was no higher. Ornithologically speaking, he concluded, "we must surely speak of the European invasion of America."[1]

Introduced to northeastern seaboard cities in the early 1850s, by 1880 sparrows could be found most places east of the Rockies, and isolated colonies had been recorded in San Francisco. Attracted by kernels of grain in empty boxcars, they often traveled large distances "hobo" fashion, establishing beachheads in Midwest railroad hubs. Though the Great Plains and the mountains and deserts beyond stalled their progress, the bird occupied the continent with considerably less effort than its human counterparts. In 1889, Walter Barrows (Assistant Ornithologist, Division of Economic Ornithology and Mammalogy, Department of Agriculture) announced that "the marvelous rapidity of the Sparrow's multiplication, the surpassing swiftness of its extension, and the prodigious size of the area it has overspread are without parallel in the history of any bird."[2]

The "conquest" of the continent by this "avian alien" was virtually complete within a decade of the official announcement of the human frontier's closure in 1890.[3] As Abbott had predicted, the starling also maintained its brisk momentum. Eventually it even outstripped the sparrow, despite its compatriot's forty-year head start and the absence of further introductions from Europe after 1891.[4] An avian Daniel Boone was taken west of the Alleghenies in 1916. By 1925, starlings had expanded north to Montreal, south to Florida, and west to the Mississippi, reaching the California coast in the mid-1940s; "Manifest Destiny for starlings," reflected the author of an article marking the bird's American centennial.[5]

A century and a half ago, there were no English sparrows or starlings in the United States. Today, about a hundred and fifty million English sparrows and a further two hundred million starlings span the nation from Alaska to Florida. Though these numbers pale beside the size of the passenger pigeon's former population (billions in its heyday), their current ascendancy evokes the once unrivaled hegemony of a now extinct native. And the potential for fruitful comparison goes further. When the last pigeon died in captivity, conservationists had already begun to convert a bird hitherto notorious as the farmer's scourge into a peerless national icon of tragic faunal loss. The other, less familiar side of this story is how the English sparrow and (to a lesser extent) the starling acquired an equally prominent symbolic status as icons of bioinvasive success.

In *Flight Maps,* Jennifer Price chose the story of the pigeon's fabled superabundance and stunning decline as a springboard for her ruminations on the meanings of nature for contemporary Americans.[6] Students of environmental history can readily name the last pigeon and rattle off the date and location of her death (Martha, 1914, Cincinnati Zoo). By contrast, the sparrow and starling languish in obscurity.[7] This oversight is surprising enough in view of their dominant position within the American bird population, but especially so given their peerless notoriety among imported birds that have adversely affected American avifauna.[8]

Price believes that urban Americans missed the connections between the pulsating creatures whose dense, massed ranks darkened rural skies like thunder clouds and the dish before them in fancy New York City restaurants like Delmonico's. Unable (or unwilling) to see how they were implicated in the pigeon's rapid descent, these well-heeled urbanites increasingly defined nature as a "Place Apart" and a "Place Out There."[9] Yet, as the pigeon's numbers dwindled in the late nineteenth century, the sparrow's burgeoned. And this demographic upsurge was most notable and noticeable precisely in those urban-industrial environments that Americans increasingly called home. Affluent New Yorkers might have had pigeon pie on their plates in the 1870s, but they had live sparrows on their window ledges, under their eaves, in their backyards, in their streets, and in their parks—joined increasingly, after 1890, by starlings. These ever-present imported birds bridged the widening physical gulf between the natural world and urban consumers.

Whether they were considered a natural part of that natural world is a separate issue. Moreover, permanent residents were not the same thing as naturalized citizens. The study of sparrows and starlings reveals a dense layer of meaning beneath those unearthed in Price's imaginative journeys—a meaning that resides at the heart of this book. Her nature is simply American. "Why save the birds?" she asks, and answers, "for their beauty, economic value, potential as role models, and status as God's creatures—but, mostly, for womanhood." Why save the birds? Another vital answer, I would wager, is "for their Americanism." The tender new sympathies toward (native) birds whose emergence she traces in the context of the women's crusade against the plumage trade was paralleled by growing hostility toward sparrow and starling. In fact, prominent individuals Price frequently mentions who were in the vanguard of (native) bird protection (notably Frank Chapman, Olive Thorne Miller, and Mabel Osgood Wright) also spearheaded the assault on the English sparrow.

Price's flight maps do not include the sparrow's and starling's transatlantic passages and startling American stories. Yet one of the most illuminating ways in which Americans have known nature is through the notion of nationality, which has often been used as a conceptual tool to sort the sheep from the goats, or, rather, the English sparrows from the American sparrows—to which, it should be emphasized, English sparrows are not related (most ornithologists classify them as finches).

Contemporary observers often quibbled over which bird's invasion was the biggest and the most momentous in its consequences. What is clear, though, is that the sparrow provoked greater and more impassioned discussion than the starling. Because the sparrow controversy has a novelty and degree of emotion lacking from its starling sequel, responses to the sparrow constitute this chapter's main meat.

FLYING FEATHERS

"Without question the most deplorable event in the history of American ornithology," declared William Dawson in 1903, "was the introduction of the English Sparrow." This may sound absurd to those acquainted with the

Figure 1. English sparrow (male). From Walter B. Barrows,
*The English Sparrow (Passer domesticus) in North America, Especially
in Its Relations to Agriculture* (1889). The original wood engraving
appears in William Yarrell, *A History of British Birds,* vol. 1
(London: John van Voorst, 1871–85), 521.

passenger pigeon's fate. Yet Dawson insisted that the notorious extinctions
of the pigeon and the great auk (also the wild turkey's near eradication)
were mere "trifles" compared to the frightful repercussions for various
small native birds of the "invasion of that wretched foreigner."[10] A dramatic
remark of this sort from a century ago serves as a welcome corrective to the
unreflective tone of current literature on bioinvasion, which frequently inti-
mates that today's level of concern is unmatched.

In the final third of the nineteenth century, few issues grabbed the attention of American ornithologists, naturalists, and outdoor enthusiasts quite
like the "sparrow question." Lined up against the bird in the interests of
homeland biosecurity were two powerful, closely related interest groups: the
federal government's economic ornithologists and entomologists and the
American Ornithologists' Union (AOU). Founded in 1883, the AOU was
the leading citizens' organization for bird study and protection. Many sci-

entists in the Department of Agriculture's Division of Economic Ornithology counted among the AOU's leading members. The sparrow's supporters, though strong initially at local and civic levels—and the loudest voice until the early 1870s—did not enjoy a federal presence. Most Americans with an interest in birds and the natural world felt aroused and took sides, however, and this engendered a debate of such acrimony that it was often referred to as the "sparrow war."[11] The controversy was particularly turbulent in New York City, home to the nation's foremost sportsman's magazine, *Forest and Stream,* a weekly founded in 1873. *Forest and Stream* received an enormous volume of correspondence on sparrows, and the flow of letters to the editor of the *New York Times* and the number of features there are also astonishing.

A ditty penned in 1883, "The Sparrow Must Go," summarized the case against a feathered reprobate whose descent from paragon to pest was almost as swift as the passenger pigeon's ascent in the opposite direction; by 1900, most Americans had forgotten that the latter had recently been the cereal farmer's bête noire.

> Steals wheat.
> Eats few moths
> Makes too much noise,
> Picks off blossoms,
> Eats early lettuce,
> Drives off useful birds,
> Disfigures buildings,
> Befouls gutters,
> Can't sing.[12]

What interests me most, though, is how old-stock Americans projected attributes associated with nationality onto the bird to supplement these objections of a palpably material nature, whether economic or ecological. Michael Brodhead (writing in 1971) noted the common ground, rhetorically speaking, between the expression of antiforeigner feeling and hostility toward the sparrow in the late nineteenth century.[13] Yet he discounted its importance. "The parallels between the movement to restrict foreign immigration and the 'sparrow war,'" he concluded, were "merely coincidental."

This argument has some merit. To observe that reactions to human and other immigrants are frequently expressed in more or less identical language does not mean that they are more or less identical in nature. Similarly, to note that objections to particular nonnative species and a specific group of immigrants are registered essentially in the same breath is not to say that the response to the former explains hostility to the latter (or vice versa). Nor were those instrumental in the movement for immigration restriction and the leading lights in the anti-sparrow campaign necessarily the same people. Furthermore, many of the English sparrow's champions, like the bird's opponents, were Anglo-Saxon Protestant members of the cultural establishment and upper socioeconomic echelons.

Nonetheless, Brodhead's focus on the sparrow war as "one of the first great scientific controversies among professional scientists" in the United States underestimates its value for the study of human immigration. He overlooked the significance of the rhetorical strategy of negative humanization that the sparrow's enemies adopted to inflame public opposition. And he failed to appreciate the extent to which supposedly dispassionate scientific arguments were themselves entangled with attitudes to human immigrants.

The sparrow's archenemy from the start, Elliott Coues, an eminent army surgeon and naturalist, presented the division of views in the sparrow war in terms of informed science versus uninformed public sentiment—the AOU embodying the objective field observation he claimed to represent.[14] The sparrow's defenders counterattacked in identical fashion, accusing the bird's opponents of bias unrelated to any clear and present danger to wheat, blossoms, early lettuce, genteel ears, park benches, or useful native birds. In another important respect, though, the two warring parties shared the same outlook. In common with most late nineteenth-century Americans (and Britons), they firmly believed that birds were part of the "book of nature" that demonstrated qualities of "good" and "bad" comprehensible in human terms. Though poor natural science, representing birds as miniature humans (regardless of nationality) was an enormously popular device in nature writing. Books and articles claiming to supply "accurate and reliable" information in "popular and accessible" form teemed with moralistic asides.[15]

Reactions to the bird divided into the two camps of Americanism—pluralist and conservative—identified by Higham in the late nineteenth and early twentieth centuries. William Rhodes, a Canadian colonel from Quebec who was instrumental in the first introductions to Maine (in 1854), spoke for the pluralists who believed that being in North America—and behaving itself—meant that a particular species was, de facto, of North America. He pronounced the English sparrow "fond of citizen life, and in every way suitable to be an inhabitant of the New World."[16] Others, for whom national nature self-evidently meant native nature, hotly disputed its eligibility as a member of American avian society. They hankered after something Henry James referred to (in another context) as a "close and sweet and *whole* national consciousness"—as distinct from the "hybrid farce"—to quote fellow novelist Owen Wister—into which American identity had degenerated with the mass immigration of the unsuitable.[17] "Patriotism or prejudice," many bird watchers frankly admitted, prevented them from including the bird on their lists. "And who," they continued, "will presume always to decide between these two feelings, one of them so given to counterfeiting the other?"[18]

For these ornithologists, there was an implicit link between the decision to exclude the English sparrow from their lists and to deny its identity as an American bird, as distinct from a bird that happened to live in the United States. Just because the English sparrow was well ensconced in the United States and had produced many new generations there did not mean that there should be an avian equivalent of citizenship based on *jus soli*. Though they never articulated this view explicitly, champions of native nature who sought to exclude American-born English sparrows from citizenship rights adhered tacitly to the opposite principle. According to the principle of *jus sanguinis*, national citizenship is determined by the citizenship and nationality of one's parents, regardless of place of birth. English sparrows, in other words, were fated to forever remain English sparrows.

Like James and Wister, the Americans most concerned about the English sparrow's impact were themselves of British descent. As such, they might have been expected to welcome (on the basis of *jus soli* and *jus sanguinis*) the "little Saxon" as a fellow creature from the Anglo-Saxon world in an Anglo-Saxon nation at a time of dire warnings about the contraction of the nation's English stock. But these British Americans who had enshrined themselves as the nation's native element were also the constituency most exercised by the fate of indigenous fauna through habitat loss, excessive hunting, and the influx of nonnative species. Perceiving a community of interest with their fellow natives, they compared their own shrinking numbers with the dwindling populations of birds the sparrow allegedly displaced. For them, a crisis of ecological identity complemented the crisis of racial identity. In the book of nature's avian chapter, they cast the English sparrow as a generic foreigner that embodied the distasteful features of human immigrants from non-British sources. But the English sparrow's role in the larger history of American immigration and race and ethnic relations is ultimately greater and more complex. Because the history of ethnic tensions in the second half of the nineteenth century is more than a simple case of old-stock Anglo-Americans feeling threatened by immigrants from Italy, Poland, and Japan, the English sparrow remained a flexible symbol lending itself to other constructions. Most revealing (and perhaps most surprising), the bird served old-stock Americans as a vehicle for venting anti-English feelings.

How, though, did the English sparrow come to be in the United States in the first place? Across the former British "settler" colonies, today's environmentalists privilege native forms. Indigenous creatures are lionized as more appropriate ecologically as well as more beautiful and more culturally and historically authentic. By the same token, exotics are often heavily stigmatized. This nostalgia for natives and the replacement of an inclusive notion of nature by an exclusive one makes the nineteenth-century passion for exotics difficult to appreciate. Yet, whether in North America, South Africa, Australia, or New Zealand, immigrants were intent on habituating familiar species. The English sparrow's North American acclimation is a chapter in an international success story.

Settlers wanted to recreate their homelands by transplanting creatures as well as customs. The author of the U.S. government's seminal English sparrow report of 1889 referred to the homesick immigrant's longing for the bird's "familiar chirp."[19] The perception of more practical value, however, was often intertwined with sentimentalism. The mandate of the Cincinnati Acclimatization Society (founded in 1873 by a German immigrant) was to "introduce to this country all useful, insect eating European birds, as well as the best singers."[20] A clutch of comparable outfits shared this ambition to translate non-European ecosystems into their own language.

Some native-born Americans also wanted to "author" ecosystems. As well as the desire to redress the depletion of native game supplies, a consumerist ethos of maximum possible choice governed the activities of the Pacific representative of the U.S. Fish Commission. "The wishes of all should be met if possible," declared Livingston Stone in 1875, adding that, "if some like shad, they ought to have shad; if some like catfish, they ought to have catfish, and so on with the rest."[21] Of the twenty-one species the commission imported to California between 1871 and 1896, however, only two were from overseas: brown trout and carp.[22] The rest were native to the East Coast, a salutary reminder that nonnative does not necessarily mean non-American.

The major material value native-born white Americans pinned on the English sparrow differed markedly from that attached to shad, catfish, German carp, Hungarian partridge, or "English" pheasant. No one was anticipating a splendid day's sport or salivating at the prospect of a tasty sparrow pie. Each spring in the 1850s and 1860s, canker worms plagued urban trees from Boston to Washington, D.C.[23] These native caterpillars munched heavily on new leaf growth, afflicting all species, it seems, except the exotic ailanthus, but particularly elms. Branches teemed with fat, leaf-bloated caterpillars, which hung at the ends of long threads, brushing against the cheeks of hapless pedestrians, dangling over hat brims, slipping down necks, and crawling up backs and sleeves. Others fell directly to the sidewalks, where passing feet mashed them into a sickening mush. By full summer, barely any leaves remained. With parks, squares, and avenues effectively shadeless and surrendered to the worm, summer in the city became unbearable.

With harassed citizens begging for relief, public-spirited individuals, civic bodies, and municipal authorities merrily recruited English sparrows. The first batch that survived (from Liverpool) was released in Brooklyn's Greenwood Cemetery by the directors of the Brooklyn Institute in the spring of 1852. Eugene Schieffelin, a prominent figure in Manhattan society, whose immigrant grandfather had made a bundle in the wholesale pharmaceutical business, took over the initiative. Between 1860 and 1864, the future founder of the American Acclimatization Society (est. 1871) released five to six pairs annually near his house on worm-infested Madison Square. The degree of interest in English sparrows gripping many American cities in the 1860s and early 1870s ("fever" and "craze" were terms skeptics regularly employed) was reflected in the staggering prices the birds commanded on the domestic market—50 cents per pair.

Demonstrating that humanizing analogies are not inherently derogatory, renowned nature poet William Cullen Bryant celebrated the sparrow's arrival at his country estate near New York City in 1859:

> We hear the note of a stranger bird
> That ne'er till now in our land was heard;
> A winged settler has taken his place
> With Teutons and men of the Celtic race;
> He has followed their path to our hemisphere—
> The Old-World Sparrow at last is here.

Bryant welcomed the "bane" of the "swarming, skulking, ravenous tribe" of army worm, Hessian fly, and canker worm, from whose "busy beak" there would be no escape.[24] A delighted *New York Times* correspondent also thought in terms of an ennobling reenactment of the nation's foundational experience. He described a Manhattan release site (Union Park, 1866) as "the Jamestown, so to speak, of these little colonists."[25]

Bryant's optimism appeared well founded. After a few summers, hardly any caterpillars were left. Though it eats grain and fruit when it can, the English sparrow is a generalist forager that consumes whatever provides the most energy per unit of time and effort expended. With such a superabundance of caterpillars, the winged settlers gorged on them. Susan Fenimore Cooper (whose gifts as an observer of birds are less known than her father's novelistic talents) characterized them in 1868 as "public pets of New York, on account of their usefulness in clearing the trees from insects."[26] Deploying the birds for partisan purposes a few years later, the *Times* (which represented the Republicans) published glowing tributes to a model "public servant" that brought deliverance from evil. Shortly after the trial and conviction of the Democrat boss of the notorious Tweed ring, the *Times* commented: "With the most hideous corruption prevailing in almost every other department of the public Municipal Government, the administration of this one has been singularly pure and efficient."[27] This immediate record of achievement won over many neutrals and doubters. Even a prominent critic like Thomas Gentry conceded that the bird had initially performed a valuable service.[28]

The bird's major sponsors puffed out their chests, one of them bragging in 1868 that the house sparrow (as he insisted on calling it) would soon "become one of our most common and familiar favorites."[29] Yet this confidence proved misplaced. The bird certainly took to American cities like a duck to water. "At the end of four years," Coues reflected, "each sparrow of the original immigrant batch had become a great-great-grandfather, and had lived to see his descendants all settled, naturalized, married and full of canker-worms and prosperity."[30] But this immigrant success story never became a firm favorite.

By the mid-1870s, observers were noting the return of the canker worm. Other objections reinforced complaints that the sparrow had become derelict in its duty, "forgetful that in no other way can he pay his passage money."[31] What unsettled and repelled many middle-class Americans of British ancestry were the bird's apparently natural urban connection, its excessive fecundity and display of other traits associated with undesirable immigrants, its conduct toward native birds, and its foreign origins.

A close relationship with the city counted heavily against the bird at a time when many old-stock Americans viewed swelling cities with distaste and fear. Antiurban sentiments typical of an influential sector of the Anglo-American establishment were committed to print by Frank Bolles, whose father served as solicitor and judge advocate general of the U.S. Navy in the Grant administration after the Civil War. The well-connected Bolles lived in Cambridge, Massachusetts, but regularly retreated to his family's country place in the mountains of New Hampshire.[32] He wrote several outdoor books, including *Land of the Lingering Snow: Chronicles of a Stroller in New England from January to June* (1891), was a frequent contributor of articles on birds to *Atlantic Monthly* magazine, and involved himself in forest conservation campaigns in New Hampshire. Bolles was also a member of one of the AOU's forerunners, the Nuttall Ornithological Club (est. 1873), a Cambridge-based group (whose select, elected membership included a Harvard sophomore, Theodore Roosevelt) that roundly denounced the sparrow at a special meeting in February 1878.[33] Writing at a time when he was secretary of Harvard University (effectively President Charles W. Eliot's right-hand man) and a member of Nuttall, Bolles's invective also expressed the close relationship between notions of human and avian fitness and belonging that was characteristic of Anglo-American thinking at the time:

> City-bred man without knowledge of lake and forest, mountain and ocean, is an inferior product of the race; but disagreeable as he is, the city-bred bird is worse. The English sparrow . . . is a bird of the city, rich in city vices, expedients, and miseries. The farmer's son who takes to drink and the East end makes a hard character. The sparrow who has taken to a similar form of existence is equally despicable.[34]

Bolles died of pneumonia two years later (1894) at the age of thirty-seven. But others continued to think and write in the same vein about urban America and its new residents. In the early 1900s, Henry James recorded the "sense of dispossession" that haunted him on the streets of New York City, surrounded by the "inconceivable," "immeasurably alien" immigrant.[35] Wister, one of Theodore Roosevelt's Harvard chums and fellow big-game hunter and conservationist, also lamented urban deterioration. The author of the prototypical western novel, *The Virginian* (1902), contrasted densely populated places like Manhattan's Lower East Side with the "clean cattle country" of Texas, where the untamed Anglo-Saxon could breathe free and stretch his powerful limbs astride a horse on hallowed ground uncontaminated by Poles, Italians, and Jews. The American city, according to Wister, had become "debased and mongrel with its hordes of encroaching alien vermin."[36]

Vermin were synonymous with filth and cleanliness was synonymous with virtue in the nineteenth-century moral text of nature. And their critics considered English sparrows among the dirtiest of birds. They complained that this grimy "bird of the street and gutter" lived in slovenly conditions in any available cavity—furnishing these "lodgings" and "tenements" with "any rubbish."[37] Nesting materials blocked drainpipes, gutters, and gas lights, polluted water supplies, and posed a fire hazard.[38] Droppings fouled ledges, window casings, porches, awnings, and park benches. They besmirched statues and headstones in cemeteries. The unsanitary sparrow's detractors also accused it of transmitting hog cholera and poultry lice.

Some of these objections were entirely reasonable. Critics failed to realize, though, that explosive urban growth was creating hospitable conditions. Canker worms were easy pickings. But the birds quickly located a more reliable food supply: the wholly or partially undigested grains—ideal for fledglings—that studded the horse manure liberally littering city streets.[39] The birds also descended on copious quantities of edible refuse. Yet those who claimed to represent the reasoning voice of scientific ornithology turned the bird's adaptability into a character issue. "Lazy little louts" and "vagrants," they preferred begging and scavenging to an honest day's work.[40]

Coues reported that sparrows "fell into city ways, and lost their British timidity and got finally to thinking they had been sent for to run the town."[41] Yet standard colloquialisms evoked the bird's venerable urban heritage and brash assertiveness. Among the common names Coues listed were "tramp," "hoodlum," and "gamin."[42] The latter, a synonym for "street Arab," is an obsolete word for a grimy street urchin who commits petty acts of cruelty and thievery (such as raiding fruit trees) and spends the rest of his time dodging the police. "These rowdy little *gamins*," Coues complained, "squeak and fight all through the city."[43] Another popular American term—"little cockney"—was an English import. "Cockney"—denoting a person born in London's East End—evoked urban crudity and inferiority, and those who spoke the Queen's English dismissed the cockney dialect and accent as the snarl of the guttersnipe.

If anything, the "London sparrow" was more incorrigible than the street Arab. Lord Lilford (Thomas Littleton Powys), one of the founders of the British Ornithological Union (est. 1858), fretted that "whilst the latter vagrant may be caught up, partially reclaimed and sent to school, the former sets the police and School Boards at defiance, and manages to lead a happy and carefree life." Other refined Victorians alluded to fast-talking, chirpy, quick-witted people, especially Londoners, as "cockney sparrows." This urban essentialism was encapsulated in the engraving from William Yarrell's *History of British Birds*—reproduced in Barrows's report—of the bird perched on a ledge against the backdrop of a city skyline.[44]

Coues and Gentry expected urban immigrants of all stripes to make it on their own. Yet Gentry explained that Philadelphia's sparrows had frequently "fared much better than their poor human brethren," thanks to a "gullible" public that accommodated them in thousands of bird boxes, often sturdy and spacious constructions of iron with thatched roofs and wide eaves. Central Park's commissioners dispensed cracked corn at public expense.[45] Gentry was concerned about what people would learn from this particular page of nature's book, for these quasi-pets "set the unwholesome example of consuming what they do not earn."[46]

The "immigrant finch" was thus an especially notorious character in the book of nature's avian chapter. Even a person closely involved in some of the initial introductions conceded that it was a "little blackguard—fond of low society and full of fight, stealing, and love-making."[47] The moralist's greatest fear was that this absence of "domestic ethics" set a perilous example to the working class—especially adolescent boys whose animal instincts needed curbing at the best of times.[48] Goodness (and hygiene) were associated with reproductive restraint. But in its squalid nest, the sparrow outstripped the breeding rate of native birds (and other imports) by typically raising three to four broods during a breeding season that often stretched from late January to early November. A particularly fertile pair might raise an annual total of twenty to thirty young. According to a widely quoted, mind-boggling statistic from the Barrows report, one pair in New York City could well produce, in ten years, no less than 275,716,983,698 offspring.[49]

Henry Van Dyke, a Presbyterian minister, prominent nature writer, and leading literary critic, divided the bird world into "real birds and English sparrows," not least because of the latter's courtship rituals.[50] Stopwatch in hand, one student of sparrow sexuality clocked fourteen successive bouts of intercourse at a rate of five seconds per act, with mere five-second intervals.[51] The sparrow's male enemies considered these outdoor orgies highly distressing for metropolitan ladies who ventured beyond the private sphere. Outraged, Coues dashed off a short poem about sex and the city:

Sparrows to right of them—
Sparrows to left of them—
Sparrows in front of them—
Copulate freely.[52]

Fears that a tightly woven racial, social, moral, economic, and sexual order was jeopardized by mass immigration and burgeoning cities were thus projected onto these "disgusting exotics," whose *furor amatorius* caused the more fearful to anticipate the worst: common ownership of wealth and "free love."[53] "Respectable" women were equally anxious. In "A Ruffian in Feathers," Olive Thorne Miller, a prolific author of popular bird essays and books, related the stormy and "ignoble" domestic life of various pairs observed in a Norway spruce with an opera glass through the window of her Brooklyn home. Exuding pity for battered sparrow wives, she documented their courtship, setting up home, housekeeping, infant raising, marital quarrels, and "divorce," followed by the prompt installation of a "coquettish" young replacement by a "domestic tyrant . . . a bully, so self-willed and violent."[54] It was impossible to read Miller's accounts, reflected the editor of *Birds,* without agreeing with John Greenleaf Whittier: "Then, smiling to myself, I said— / 'How like are men and birds!' "[55]

The English sparrow's brutish qualities were usually juxtaposed against American avian assets. Though many commentators on both sides of the controversy noted the sparrow's bustle, Fletcher Osgood, a New Englander who regularly contributed bird essays to *The Auk* (the journal of the AOU), emphasized its profoundly un-American indolence. By contrast, diligence and purposefulness distinguished the native red-eyed vireo. The robin's "soldier-like erectness" was employed in the single-minded pursuit of cutworms. "Dear" native finches were devoid of the English sparrow's "impudence and pugnacity." Various species of native sparrow—the chipping sparrow, tree sparrow, field sparrow, and song sparrow—all were useful, clean living, and tuneful. The most effective way to exacerbate hostility, though, was to emphasize the English sparrow's origins.[56]

THE STRANGER FINCH

Often simply identified as "this foreigner," the English sparrow was sometimes tagged with the more pointed designations "little Britisher," "English stranger," "the Englishman," or "little John Bull." Though positive applications were not excluded, a degree of hostility to England frequently informed these labels.[57]

British–American relations were fraught after the Civil War. Northerners did not quickly forgive or forget the partiality for the Confederacy of the British ruling class and certain segments of the public. The two nations had verged on war in 1861 after a Union warship's seizure of a British vessel carrying Confederate diplomats to London on a mission to secure material aid for the rebels. In his correspondence with Charles Darwin, Harvard botanist Asa Gray remarked on Britain's desire to see the United States "fall to pieces" and the British belief that the Yankees were itching to swallow up Canada.[58] The threat of war passed. But northerners remained livid over the construction of Confederate blockade runners and armored raiders in Merseyside shipyards.

The clash of interests with Britain in Central America as the United States exerted its own economic authority in the region culminated in the 1895 furor over the American role in adjudicating the long-simmering border dispute between Venezuela and British Guiana. A *New York World* cartoon depicted Britain as a large pig with its body spread over a globe, one of its fore trotters resting across the United States and the other across Central and South America.[59] "The conduct of the English sparrow in this country," the *Washington Post* had noted a couple of years earlier, "very much resembles that of the human members of that all-conquering nation."[60] The British themselves took pride in the bird as an imperial symbol: "At any given portion of the habitable globe, within ten minutes of the unfurling of the British flag, [the British sparrow] perches authoritatively on the flagstaff. . . . Bold, active, and vivacious, its distribution is as wide as that of the Englishman."[61] Anglophobic Americans were thus predisposed to see the bird's American exploits as another example of Britain's hogging of the world.

In *Strangers in the Land,* John Higham argued that, despite these international conflicts, a feeling of cultural and racial kinship "exempted" English immigrants from anti-English feeling. This assumption that Anglophilia was a basic ingredient of the American upper-class outlook at the time of the sparrow war is supported by the reverence of patrician sport hunters for the aristocratic English creed of the fair chase. John Reiger sees *Forest and Stream* as a "vehicle for importing the British concept of sportsmanship" that also carried news of the American progress of eminently English sports like polo and cricket.[62] Yet many sparrow defenders suspected that naked Anglophobia motivated detractors. "I cannot account for the bitterness of some writers against this plucky little bird," declared a Chicagoan ("Norman"), "unless it is that he is a Britisher." Norman identified the sparrow's enemies as those who "invariably decry everything coming from England: dogs, guns, gentleman sportsmen, even breeders who visit our dog shows." Disclosing that he was born in Britain, Norman contrasted American intolerance with British tolerance. Over there, he insisted, the denizens of city streets and country seats were united in gratitude to the bird for the worms, slugs, and grubs it consumed.[63]

Even so, the most direct analogies between the sparrow and other Britons were drawn by the bird's champions—whose ranks included British immigrants kindly disposed to a fellow countryman.[64] In the fall of 1884, Professor John W. Robson of Abilene spoke to the Kansas Horticultural Society about the bird. Robson, who had observed it for twenty years in its native haunts, explained that, on reflection, he was unhappy with his talk's title—"The English Sparrow." Illinois issued naturalization papers to a "larger British biped" after five years residence, he argued, and Kansas granted citizenship after just nine months. Yet "Jack Sparrow," despite residing in the United States for a quarter-century and having produced many generations of "native born" sparrows, was still lumbered with the pejorative designation "English Sparrow." Making the case for the acquisition of faunal citizenship after a well-defined and relatively short period of permanent residence as well as on the grounds of *jus solis,* Robson saw no reason for continuing to withhold "all the rights and privileges of free American citizenship and also . . . the use of his proper name—the House Sparrow." The house sparrow, in Robson's view, was both in and of the United States.[65]

Among Robson's audience were undoubtedly farmers who disliked the bird because it preyed on their crops. So he reminded his listeners that the press and many leading citizens had hailed the sparrow's introduction (to save shade trees from ruin) as a glorious act of patriotism. Then he invited them to ponder the useful work the bird continued to execute as part of an urban sanitary corps. In his effort to create an Anglo-American fraternity of sparrows, he rode roughshod over the niceties of ornithological taxonomy, presenting them as "English cousins" to native sparrows.

Objections based on the bird's alien origins and bad character, which Robson associated especially with Coues, told him more about Coues's nativism—the "extreme hatred in your heart against all bipeds of foreign birth"—than about the bird's true nature. He interpreted the intensity of Coues's antipathy as an expression of the flag-waving Americanism of the second-generation immigrant eager to obliterate all traces of foreign ancestry, a bombastic effort to establish his credentials as a "Native American" that was necessary because "[you] just barely escaped being the subject of Queen Victoria because your parents emigrated to this country, and to cover this fact you became a bitter 'Know Nothing.'"

Robson was in fact completely mistaken about Coues's family background. Both his parents were Americans with long lineages: his great-grandfather had immigrated in the 1740s and his mother was also of colonial stock. Moreover, Coues was too young (born in New Hampshire in 1842) to have joined the Know-Nothings, an anti-immigrant movement of the late 1840s and early 1850s, principally opposed to Irish Catholics, which represented the original face of American nativism.[66] But he did think of himself as "Native American" at a time when a term now reserved for indigenous peoples referred to Anglo-Saxon Protestants of British origin.

Those who bestowed Native American status on themselves did not automatically extend this to floral and faunal Britons. Domestic animals and plants such as cows, pigs, horses, wheat, and apples had painlessly acquired U.S. biotic citizenship without debate centuries earlier. Instead of perceiving a kinship with more recently arrived species like English sparrows, however, many Americans of British stock consciously identified with native birds, whose plight they attributed directly to these particular British avian immigrants.

That Americans of British stock had a complex, often ambiguous relationship with things British is further illustrated by their attitudes toward human indigenes. Notwithstanding their appropriation of native identity, sparrow critics like Coues remained aware of the continent's original human inhabitants. As the last flickers of American Indian resistance were extinguished, growing numbers of British Americans bemoaned the impact of energetic Europeans on aboriginal species, human and nonhuman. Anticipating Crosby's notion of ecological imperialism, Coues saw the sparrow as part of a larger European biotic takeover, warning that "we are repeating the history of the white weed and the Norway rat." The ultimate manifestation of this process was the elimination of "aboriginal" peoples. The aboriginal survivor, he noted, "sadly likened" floral and faunal usurpation "to the invasion of his country by the pale faces."[67] The American Indian's recession did not bode well for native avifauna in the face of the sparrow's remorseless advance, and the likes of Coues could not resign themselves to another chapter in the saga of European seizure.

The hardening of American opinion against the sparrow following the 1889 Barrows report prompted the British consul in Baltimore to report home to the foreign secretary a month after its publication: "I have the honor herewith to transmit a Report on 'Adulteration of Butter and Lard,' 'Deleterious Canned Provisions,' and 'Sparrows.'" [68] The consul referred to the "universal" but largely unfounded "ill-will" toward what he also called the house sparrow, which Americans vilified for "refusing to eat American insects" and hounding insectivorous native birds.[69]

Nomenclature remained a sore point for English commentators. Provoked by a 1912 Department of Agriculture farmer's bulletin on the bird, one editor protested that its identification with England was "bringing disgrace on things English." Yet the bird was "no more 'English' than Welsh or Irish or Scottish or French or German," in view of which he advised that the English would be "much obliged if our American friends would recognise this fact, and call it the European sparrow, or the Old World sparrow—for he is found also in Asia."[70] British visitors agreed that the bird was a bad ambassador. Reflecting on his first North American trip in 1881, the Duke of Argyll, a keen ornithologist, described the pleasure of a new floral and faunal experience—a reaction shaped by the hegemony of "Sparrowdom" back home. "With very few exceptions," he explained, "every bird one sees is a bird one has never seen alive before." He soon realized, though, that he had not shaken off Britain entirely because misguided Americans had transplanted "our old and forward little friend . . . the London sparrow."[71]

The maligned sparrow also attracted the attention of a prominent Canadian American nature writer of English immigrant stock. Ernest Thompson Seton, born and raised in northeastern England, wrote a yarn called "A Street Troubadour: Being the Adventures of a Cock Sparrow" in 1901. The heroes of the tale are two English sparrows, Randy and Biddy, who are thoroughly at home exploring Manhattan's "brick wilderness." Seton recounted their rough courtship in Fifth Avenue's gutters, their constant brawling, and efforts at setting up home. The pair abandon a birdhouse for an unlikely site on top of an electric lamp in Madison Square Park before finally settling on a notch in one of the park's elms. A drawing depicting the birdhouse Randy and Biddy had vacated is topped by a sign that reads "To Let: No English Need Apply."[72]

Nevertheless, immigration from Britain was already easing off by the 1880s; immigrants like Thompson Seton's parents were not the ones by whom old-stock Americans felt pressured. The most visible immigrants east of the Mississippi were southern and eastern Europeans, and their West Coast counterparts were Japanese and Chinese. Before restrictive quotas were imposed on Europeans from outside the continent's northwest regions in the early 1920s, measures excluding Japanese and Chinese were already in place. In her widely read beginner's guide to bird study, Neltje Blanchan stressed the difference in attitude toward feathered undesirables and their human counterparts from Asia during the heyday of sparrow "mania." Not that she opposed foreign birds in principle. She regretted the failure to establish the skylark in Cincinnati, cheered the goldfinch's success in New York City, and looked favorably on the starling's progress. The English sparrow, though, was a horse of a different color. To highlight its misdeeds, she wielded "yellow peril" imagery, beginning to catch on as shorthand for American fears of invasion—military and demographic—from China and Japan. "As the 'yellow peril' is to human immigration," she warned, "so is this sparrow to other birds." Yet enthusiasm for the bird during the 1870s and 1880s had been so strong that, had a "sparrow exclusion act" been mooted, "it is doubtful if a single senator who lent his voice to secure the Chinese exclusion act would have given it his support."[73]

Blanchan did not mention it, but a "sparrow exclusion act" of sorts had recently been enacted, in 1901. American colonial acquisitions in the Caribbean and Pacific in 1898 heightened federal scientific awareness of the threat to the biotic security of the contiguous United States posed by casually or deliberately introduced organisms and the challenge mainland species and those from other countries presented to islands like Puerto Rico and Hawaii. For Theodore Palmer, assistant chief of the Department of Agriculture's Division of Biological Survey, existing regulations to keep human and livestock diseases at bay and to restrict entry of certain immigrants provided ample precedent for the exclusion of potentially noxious animals.[74] Pressure on these grounds from Palmer and his boss, C. Hart Merriam, contributed to the Lacey Act of 1901. Better known as the first federal wildlife conservation measure, it also confronted the excesses of acclimatization by empowering the secretary of agriculture to bar foreign species "injurious" to agriculture and horticulture. And no species had been more instrumental in fostering disenchantment with the "open door" policy that had held sway since Columbus appeared in the Western hemisphere than the English sparrow.

The main task of the economic ornithology section set up within the Department of Agriculture's Division of Entomology in 1885 (at AOU urging) was to categorize species as "good" or "bad" according to what they ate.[75] The priority for study was the English sparrow. To determine whether it was an eligible "naturalized resident" or an illegitimate alien, economic ornithologists distributed a long and detailed survey.[76] The information received in some 3,300 replies was incorporated into a devastating 350-page critique, released in 1889. Among the testimonies recorded by its author, Walter Barrows (a prominent AOU member), were those of first-generation English immigrants with firsthand experience of the sparrow in its native haunts. Jabez Webster of Centralia, Illinois—a nurseryman who was sufficiently assimilated to refer to the avian casualties of the sparrow's advance as "our native birds"—related his return visit to Britain after more than two decades. He reported that "intelligent agriculturists and horticulturists everywhere" were amazed that Americans had imported such a damaging and valueless bird; during his Cambridgeshire boyhood, farmers had hired him and other youth to scare them off ripening grain.[77]

Like Blanchan, Webster did not object to importing British birds in principle (indicating that the objective realities of economic and ecological relations were not invariably or automatically subordinate to the subjective considerations of ethnic and racial unsuitability). They weighed up each species according to its merits. But the English sparrow would "never make a good citizen, being a grain and fruit eater."[78] This first U.S. government study of an introduced "problem" species confirmed—on the basis of the widest sample of stomach contents to date—that the bird consumed relatively few insects—of which relatively few, in turn, were noxious. Barrows's findings also indicated that its impact on native birds aroused the strongest public feelings. Of the 767 submissions discussing this aspect, only 42 either largely or wholly absolved the bird of blame.[79]

THERE GOES THE NEIGHBORHOOD:
DISPOSSESSING THE RIGHTFUL TENANTS OF LAND AND SKY

Despite the acclimatizer's partiality for foreign species, the superiority of native birds had long been an article of faith for the cultural nationalist. Eco-jingoists among the post-revolutionary generation of thinkers and writers chastised their peers for neglecting familiar local materials in their obsession with the exotic. Alexander Wilson, a Scottish immigrant, was in the vanguard of the dispute over the respective merits of American and European avifauna. His main target was Count Buffon, an equally eco-jingoistic French zoologist who had never been to the Americas but insisted that every faunal specimen there was a greatly degenerated descendant of a European form. Thus the American thrush was a miserable younger relative of the European song thrush, its voice as awful "as are the cries of all birds that live in wild countries inhabited by savages."[80] Yet Wilson praised the bluebird for its lovely voice, pleasing manners, and prodigious consumption of nasty insects. He regretted that "no pastoral muse has yet risen in this western, woody world, to do justice to his name, and endear him to us still more by the tenderness of verse, as has been done to his representative in Britain, the Robin Redbreast."[81]

This chauvinistic thrust was on display during a "literary war" (Benjamin Spencer's term) that broke out in 1805 in which the nightingale and skylark were "singled out for literary slaughter."[82] Thirty years later, Bryant would welcome the English sparrow with open arms. But in 1832 he had rebuked his brother for enthusing over the skylark because it was "an English bird, and an American who has never visited Europe has no right to be in raptures about it."[83] The outcome of the literary war was inconclusive. And nightingales and skylarks were certainly not crossed off the shopping lists of acclimatization societies. In 1850, Susan Fenimore Cooper expressed regret that these two birds were "strangers" to the United States, reiterating in 1868 that "the voices of those two noblest of the singing-birds of the old world would indeed form a charming addition to our native choir."[84]

After the Civil War, though, Wilson's feelings became more widely shared as part of a growing appreciation of the nation's contracting component of native nature. The most popular of American nature writers, John Burroughs, hailed the robin as "one of the most native and democratic of our birds; he is one of the family and seems much nearer to us than those rare, exotic visitants." And Blanchan welcomed the native song sparrow's tune as "ever the simple, homely, sweet melody that every good American has learned to love in childhood."[85] Within Osgood's "Christian ornithology," the scrupulously clean white doves that graced buildings like Boston's Trinity Church served as the sparrow's moral opposite. And because its "chaste and noble conjugal lives have passed into a proverb," the dove's urban presence was vital as a noble example to unruly urbanites.[86] Now these wholesome and uplifting natives found themselves elbowed out and forced to "emigrate to other quarters."[87] The sparrow's worst crime, according to the most influential wildlife conservationist of his generation, William T. Hornaday, was to crowd out "its betters" (giving a new twist to the expression "flight to the suburbs").[88] Not even in a "more retired neighborhood," though, were native birds safe from "molestation."[89]

The English sparrow thus found itself in a no-win situation. If it stayed in the city, this bolstered the allegation that it was clannish lowlife. But if the "detested stranger" entered the more wholesome suburbs or—even worse— infiltrated productive farmland, pinching the "choicest rural sites" such as the cliff dwellings of swallows, then it was denounced for not knowing its proper station.[90] "Banish to the city the little pests." A woman who lived on an estate on the Hudson immediately to the north of New York City saw this as her duty. Assuming the pseudonym of a native bird ("Tanager"), she identified herself as a direct descendant of John James Audubon—the naturalist whose *Birds of America,* a magisterial celebration of the magnificence of American birdlife published in 1838, exposed the folly of European taunts such as Buffon's. Then she harked back to the American struggle for independence, alluding to the longer history of conflict between tyrannical conservatives and freedom-loving liberals: English sparrows were "as much the enemies of our birds as ever Tories were of Whigs."[91]

These "sturdy little foreign vulgarians," grumbled Coues, were depriving "our" American birds of "certain inalienable rights to life, liberty, and the pursuit of happiness after their own fashion." Gentry explained that the "plucky little natives"—who, "like their human brethren, become strongly attached to the homes of their nativity"—initially gave a good account of themselves in defending home turf. Turning the tables on those who accused native birds of intolerance and the sparrow's opponents of nativism, he claimed that the bird was motivated by an "indubitable hatred of native species."[92]

Most native bird champions believed that "real Americans" of the feathered sort were fighting a losing battle.[93] Superior strength or other virtues, in their view, had nothing to do with the sparrow's displacement of natives. Nor did it occur to critics that the growth of cities through immigration and the shift from country to town might have something to do with the sparrow's success. It all boiled down, they believed, to the weapon of fecundity. In Eurasia, a pair of house sparrows produced between three and five fledglings annually. While expanding across North America, though, the average was twenty-four. Demographic swamping explained the success of the bird's "alien hordes."[94]

Swamping was also a key word in the nativist's verbal arsenal. And *horde*— with its Asiatic roots and connotations of savage bands wreaking havoc while roaming at will—was a common term for undesirable immigrants. Contemplating the consequences of high immigrant reproductive rates for America's "superior" classes, a leading nativist was reminded of the English sparrow. Prescott F. Hall, a lawyer, was chairman of the Committee on Immigration of the American Genetic Association and cofounder of the Boston-based Immigration Restriction League (est. 1894), the first organization to campaign for a restrictive policy overtly based on race. Like the League's other executive committee members, Hall was Harvard-educated and, in the words of Thomas Gossett, "conservative and wealthy" (Higham characterized them as "haughty Bostonians").[95] Members of the nation's British stock, Hall maintained, were voluntarily checking their reproductivity, fearing a bleak future for their children in a nation overwhelmed by aliens.[96]

In this context of so-called race suicide, the most aggressive nativist organization of the 1920s inverted the received meaning of "strangers in the land." "The Nordic American today," complained Hiram Evans, Grand Imperial Wizard of the Ku Klux Klan, "is a stranger in large parts of the land his fathers gave him. Moreover, he is a most unwelcome stranger, one much spit upon."[97] Evans underscored the Nordic's victim status by deploying military metaphors of "alien invasion."[98] Arriving in steerage, a former secretary of the New York State Immigration Commission believed, was a more "stupendous army" than any wartime deployment.[99] This sense of terror becomes relevant to this study of nonhuman immigrants because it was entwined with anger over the beleaguered condition of native birds, highlighting an area of overlap historians of immigration and historians of wildlife preservation have been slow to appreciate.

"Strangers," lamented Coues, "whether human or faunal, were in possession of the native's former haunts."[100] And the sparrow's lifestyle assisted its cause, the detractors maintained. Bluebirds, for instance, were "too refined . . . to long live neighbors to such low-lived little beasts."[101] "The English sparrow stands to me," remarked Bolles, "as the feathered embodiment of those instincts and passions which belong to the lowest class of foreign immigrants. The Chicago anarchist, the New York rough, the Boston pugilist, can all be identified in his turbulent and dirty society."[102] If native birds found the odds stacked against them in the festering cities, so did native Americans of the Anglo-Saxon sort.

Madison Grant, a prominent wildlife preservationist from New York City, explained that "the native American" was "gradually withdrawing . . . abandoning to these aliens the land which he conquered and developed" because "he cannot compete in the sweat shop and in the street trench." In the intellectual bible of the immigration restrictionists and Nordic supremacists, *The Passing of the Great Race*, Grant argued that " 'survival of the fittest' means the survival of the type best adapted to existing conditions of environment, which today are the tenement factory. From the point of view of race it were better described as the 'survival of the unfit.' " Since Nordics thrived on fresh air in the great outdoors, the "cramped factory and crowded city quickly weed him out."[103]

Grant was the conservative conservationist par excellence who, an obituary writer explained, was "always trying to preserve something worth saving."[104] An independently wealthy patrician lawyer of Scottish colonial ancestry, he was secretary and president of the New York Zoological Society and also occupied these posts in the big-game hunter's fraternity and leading wildlife preservationist organization, the Boone and Crockett Club. He served as a trustee of the American Museum of Natural History and a counselor of the American Geographic Society as well. All these positions he held for decades. Additionally, he founded the American Bison Society (est. 1905) and played a leading role in organizing the National Parks Association (est. 1919). Though he had no scientific training, Grant was also a prominent "scientific" racial theorist, serving as president of the Eugenics Research Association and vice-president of the Immigration Restriction League for a quarter-century. Gossett hailed him as "one of the most powerful racists this country has produced." (Higham agreed.) Yet his discussion of Grant's views and influence did not mention his conservationism. (Nor did Higham.)[105]

This overlap of interests was not unusual. Francis Walker, a political economist who served as commissioner general of the Immigration Service in the late 1890s while president of MIT, linked forest conservation with immigration limits as urgent national priorities:

> Today all intelligent men admit that cutting down of our forests, the destruction of the tree covering of our soil, has already gone too far; and both individual states and the nation have united in efforts to undo some of the mischief which has been wrought to our agriculture and to our climate from carrying too far the work of denudation. In precisely the same way it may be true that our fathers were right in their view of immigration, while yet the patriotic American of today may properly shrink in terror from the contemplation of the vast hordes of ignorant and brutalized peasantry thronging to our shores.[106]

Robert De Courcey Ward, a professor of climatology at Harvard and cofounder of the Immigration Restriction League, went further. He criticized conservationists for neglecting the most precious of depleted "national" resources: "The conservation and improvement of the American race is infinitely more important than all other conservation. The real wealth of a nation is the quality of its people. Of what value are endless acres of forests, millions of tons of coal, and billions of gallons of water, if the Race is not virile, and sane, and sound?"[107]

In his prefaces to the first and second editions of *The Passing of the Great Race,* Henry Fairfield Osborn, Ward and Grant's close friend and associate, emphasized the need for the "conservation" of the "best spiritual, moral, intellectual, and physical forces of heredity" and of the Nordic race. And in his introduction to Grant's second racial history, *The Conquest of a Continent*, Osborn spoke of the "precious heritage" "which we should not impair or dilute by permitting the entrance and dominance of alien values and peoples of alien minds and hearts."[108] A biologist and eugenicist who directed the American Museum of Natural History between 1908 and 1933, Osborn was not just referring to the peerless Nordic achievement represented by the nation's economy, culture, and political democracy. He also had in mind the (equally besieged) patrimony of the American land with its remnant native species.

Some nativists-cum-conservationists seized on the English sparrow as a resounding object lesson. To bolster his case for staunching the influx of non-Nordics, Hall drew on distaste concerning the sparrow's fecundity. As World War I ended and the United States faced the resumption of European immigration at prewar levels, the "new" immigrants' unsavory nature was compounded in his eyes by their lower-class complexion. In his view, population pressure that propelled emigration largely reflected this social stratum's high birthrate. He also claimed that the English working-class reproductive rate had been boosted by the "vacuum" resulting from an earlier epoch of mass emigration. In a strained analogy, which implied that quantities of sparrows comparable to those of their human counterparts had quit England—and under their own steam—Hall remarked that "there are just as many sparrows in England today in spite of the unfortunate spread of these birds in the United States."[109]

Another active campaigner for immigration restriction attracted to the sparrow analogy was Charles M. Goethe, a leading entrepreneur, land developer, and benefactor from Sacramento, California. Goethe was a founding board member of the Sierra Club, a pioneer member of the California Audubon Society, a major player in the Save-the-Redwoods League (est. 1918), and a member of the National Park Service's Educational Advisory Board. He, too, believed that the conservation of natural resources and human assets went hand in hand.[110] As president of the Immigration Study Commission, a group he formed in the early 1920s, Goethe lobbied for legislation to curb immigration from Mexico and later the Philippines. An enthusiastic eugenicist as well, he was the moving force behind California's Sterilization Law of 1913. His distinctive philosophy of conservation is most clearly displayed through his participation in the Save-the-Redwood League (after his death in 1966, the League named a grove in his honor in Prairie Creek Redwoods State Park). The pioneering generation of redwood conservationists connected the perfect human type with the finest product of floral evolution, which towered over its inferiors just as Wister's racial aristocrat, the Nordic cowboy, lorded over the huddled, cowering Slav and

Italian. And they believed that the American Nordic, like this arboreal master race, was in danger of being toppled despite his overweening superiority.

To illuminate the underappreciated threat to California from growing Mexican immigration in the late 1920s, when he was president of the Immigration Study Commission, Goethe compared the "peon problem" (which, ultimately, was a threat to Nordic racial purity) to the English sparrow problem. Whereas most native birds were valuable members of American society ("songsters, insect destroyers, weed-seed eaters"), this "songless immigrant" descended on grain and "in a new favorable environment, it multiplied, like the peon." By 1919 the sparrow had spanned the nation from Boston to Los Angeles; it even established a colony at Furnace Creek, Death Valley, which it entered in the wake of muletrains hauling out borax. Having "swarmed" into southern California's towns, Goethe alleged, it was pushing aside native birds just as the "old Type American" was being "displaced with Mexican slums inhabitants" in border cities.[111]

Price's account of the late nineteenth- and early twentieth-century native bird protection crusade did not make the connection. Yet, as Goethe's remark indicates, the sparrow controversy became inseparable from the larger debate over the thinning ranks of native birds as well as the controversy over the undesirable immigrant's swelling numbers. Native bird protectionists identified a string of guilty parties: pot hunters, market hunters (particularly those working for the plumage trade), stylish ladies, specimen collectors, callous city lads armed with slingshots, blacks (in the South), immigrants (in the North), and, not least, English sparrows. For Osgood, the sparrow's routine "murdering" of native broods exemplified its "innate wickedness."[112] By the mid-1880s, however, protectionists had latched onto the millinery trade as the greatest threat to American birds. So had farmers and horticulturists who appreciated their role as pest controllers. (The British consul at Baltimore, keen to take the heat off the house sparrow, also identified the hat makers as chiefly responsible for the plight of native birds.)

Hornaday and Osborn did not entirely absolve the Anglo-American "lady of fashion" whose hats were festooned with bird parts or even entire bodies (and whose only redeeming feature was the opportunity for urban birding that this headgear inadvertently provided). And the *Times* reported that native birds had "vanished forever" thanks to milliners *and* the sparrow.[113] Yet for patrician New Yorkers, lower-class whites, foreigners, and blacks posed a bigger menace to their feathered kin. As Osborn (currently president of the New York Zoological Society) lamented in his foreword to Hornaday's seminal 1913 book on the urgent need for wildlife conservation, every New Englander was poorer "when the ignorant whites, foreigners, or negroes of our southern states destroy the robins and other song birds of the North for a mess of pottage."[114]

The struggle to conserve native race and native nature thus found a common enemy. But these conservationists did not always approach human and nonhuman undesirables in the same way. Whereas Hall and Bolles made explicit connections, Grant showed no interest in English sparrows (or in any other bird, for that matter—big-game animals were his thing, and he wrote engagingly and reliably about the moose, Rocky Mountain goat, and caribou). Others combined hostility to English sparrows with profoundly racist views of black Americans and Chinese immigrants without employing a strategy of linkage.

A prime example of non-linkage is the stance of Robert Wilson (R. H.) Shufeldt. In 1883, when he was a captain in the U.S. Army's Medical Corps, this prominent ornithologist, who wrote extensively on bird anatomy (particularly osteology), railed against "that miserable and noisy little foreigner, the so-called English sparrow," found in "alarming numbers" from Boston to New Orleans. He wagered that the day was not far off when "we shall have seen enough of his dappled brown coat, so constantly and impertinently intruded upon us, at the expense of our own avian favorites."[115] Shufeldt, a resident of Washington, D.C., retired from the army with a disability in the 1890s. In the early twentieth century, he began writing venomously and hysterically about black racial inferiority, the threat of miscegenation, and the need to curb black reproduction as well as learnedly about avian palaeontology. In his two notorious books on race, *The Negro: A Menace to American Civilization* (1907) and *America's Greatest Problem: The Negro* (1915), he held up blacks as the ultimate aliens in the United States and argued for their mass deportation. He also denied that he was prejudiced against African Americans, citing an analogy with birds: "One might as well charge a naturalist with prejudice against a vulture and with favoring a blackbird," he ventured; both were black, but whereas the former's habits were repulsive, the latter was a charming, refined, and gentle bird. But allusions to the English sparrow are absent.[116]

The Negro was also identified as a menace to American birds. Southern blacks who shot for the pot, a white sportsman explained, were highly adept at hunting because, as members of a primitive race, their eyesight was sharper than that of whites, who had dulled their vision with too much reading.[117] Hornaday viewed southern blacks (and poor whites) who shot and ate doves as particularly execrable, placing their "cheap and ignoble pastime . . . on a par with the 'sport' of hunting English sparrows in a city street." Arch-conservative conservationists like Hornaday also spoke of blacks and undesirable immigrants in the same breath. "You might just as well cut down four twenty-inch trees and let them lie and decay, as to permit one woodpecker to be killed and eaten by an Italian in the North, or a negro in the South," he reflected on the high economic value of this and other native birds as consumers of insects that afflicted trees and crops, not least nonnative pests such as the codling moth and boll weevil; he quoted H. W. Henshaw, chief of the Biological Survey, who described the Baltimore oriole as the boll weevil's "deadly enemy".[118] Though Hornaday chronicled the barbarities of southern blacks and the infamies of "lower class" Austrians and Hungarians, he reserved most of his ire for the "steady stream" of Italians who were "pouring" into America and "rapidly filling up" the country.[119] Citing a recent British article by Hubert D. Astley, Hornaday warned in 1913 that they were importing beastly attitudes toward defenseless songbirds—in striking contrast to the noble sentiments of the more civilized, nature-loving Germans. He instructed American game wardens and judges to pay particularly close attention to Astley's gruesome account of a "slaughter of the innocents" near Lake Como: "File it for use on the day when Tony Macchewin, gun in hand and pockets bulging with cartridges, goes afield in our country and opens fire on our birds."[120] Drawing on Astley's testimony, he imaginatively reconstructed the fate of a linnet that nested in hospitable Germany, then headed down the Italian peninsula to warmer climes and met a horrendous end. Hidden in a hilltop tower (roccolo), a fowler ("lowbrowed, swarthy, ill kept") lured the innocent into a net and jabbed a sharpened twig through its eyes.

Hornaday drew a defiant line between America's shores and the savagery beyond: "Antonio shall not come to this country with the song-bird tastes of the roccolo and indulge them here!" He rejected the anticipated charges of nativism and racism by insisting that he was "strongly prejudiced against the people of any race, creed, club, state or nation who make a speciality of any particularly offensive type of bird or wild animal slaughter," adding that "and I don't care who knows it." Then he took aim at the republican hunting ethos (central to the "now-accursed land-of-liberty idea") for instilling the belief in "every foreigner who . . . lands on our liberty-ridden shore" that "*now, at last,* he can do as he pleases!" The first thing the male immigrant did, Hornaday explained, was to buy a gun and go after wildlife that was up for grabs. To make matters worse, those most avid and depraved of immigrant hunters—Italians—were "spreading, spreading, spreading. If you are without them to-day, to-morrow they will be around you." In a backhanded compliment, he warned that the Italians—"strong, prolific, persistent and of tireless energy"—stole a march by toiling while Americans slept. The list of transgressions and usurpations, in his view, was long. Not content with preying on homes and jobs, the Italian "invades your fields, and even your lawn," to take a potshot at all kinds of native songbirds, however tiny.[121]

Hornaday advocated state bans on the ownership, possession, or discharge of firearms by aliens and a proscription on their use for hunting by any naturalized alien from southern Europe resident in the United States less than ten years. In holding these views, he was by no means out on a limb. They were mainstream. "It is difficult to overstate," remarks Louis Warren, "the degree to which conservationists despised Italians for killing songbirds and insectivorous birds." The state of Pennsylvania, whose western reaches housed a growing population of Italian-born coal miners and quarry workers, had in fact already acted.[122]

When discussing undesirable human immigrants, Hornaday never directly alluded to the English sparrow (nor did it occur to him that Italian pot hunters might well be killing English sparrows for their stews and spaghetti sauces as well as small native birds). One reason may have been the readily available parallel with an even more alarming group of alien creatures that were not yet "American residents" (or of English origin). "Toward wild life," he remarked, "the Italian laborer is a human mongoose. Give him power to act, and he will quickly exterminate every wild thing that wears feathers or hair."[123] English sparrow and Indian mongoose were often twinned, though, in the public mind, the bird serving as a stark warning to those tempted to import the fierce little carnivore to the mainland from Hawaii or Puerto Rico, where it was already a fearsome presence.[124]

Protecting America's avian heritage against English birds and Italian hunters was not an isolated cause for Hornaday. It was part of a seamless patriotic crusade that included defending the nation's British racial stock, political institutions, and ideological traditions. Hornaday's previous admiration for German tenderness toward birds evaporated as he led the assault on all things German as president of the American Guardian Society after the United States entered World War I.[125] As chief counselor of the National Educators Conservation Society, he proclaimed that "our American institutions are man-made; our national resources are God-given; the perpetuation of the former depends on the conservation of the latter."[126] A culture of fear and a nature of fear dovetailed neatly under wartime exigencies. This organization's purpose was to "weed out" and "root out" aliens among teachers, deemed unfit to instruct because they corrupted young minds with "vicious and pernicious ideas" from Europe, not least the "exotic menace" of bolshevism.[127] To shield Americans from the threat of foreign infection, Hornaday also joined the Committee of One Thousand of the League for Constructive Immigration Legislation.[128]

How, though, could American birds and farmers be shielded from the menace of a foreign bird that already enjoyed protected status itself in many parts of the country? In twenty-two states and territories, the protection granted to many small native birds that were deemed innocuous or beneficial (as insect eaters) extended to the English sparrow (with many references to sparrows simply conflating the English sparrow with a clutch of native sparrows). Farmers in the Northeast were advocating extirpation by 1884, and West Coast fruit growers soon chimed in.[129] Gentry wanted to "strike" in the name of science and patriotism until "the last foe expires."[130]

As an incentive, some farmers emphasized the bird's culinary merits: "The sooner . . . young America is let loose . . . to convert them into pot-pies the better."[131]

The Model Bird Law of 1886, formulated by the AOU, sought to rectify the legal position by extending protection to all native birds not specifically classified as game—whether insectivorous or not. Specifically excluded were the English sparrow and categories of natives such as granivorous flock feeders and raptors.[132] Shoot the "bad" bird whenever you can, recommended Mabel Osgood Wright, founder of the Connecticut Audubon Society (and author of genteel books such as *The Garden of a Commuter's Wife*).[133] Few, if any, believed that total eradication was possible. A substantial reduction was considered achievable, however, through "energetic persecution," including the use of poisoned grain and the incentive of bounty payments.[134] By 1902, ten states had adopted laws modeled on the AOU's, which permitted the year-round destruction of nests, eggs, and fledglings as well as the killing of adult birds. "We have as much right to kill a bird that is generally considered obnoxious, as we have to kill mice, rats, fleas, mosquitoes, bedbugs, and the like," insisted eugenicist-naturalist Arthur Howard Estabrook, who, in 1907, called for all Americans to work together to "clean out the species till not one is left."[135] The lofty status the bird had once enjoyed seemed a distant memory as it joined the ranks of the unmitigated pests. The descent from savior to scourge was complete.

STANDING UP FOR POOR JACK

Like those who spoke out for immigrants from southern and eastern Europe, the sparrow's supporters counterattacked with accusations of prejudice and defamation. Thomas Mayo Brewer, the bird's leading proponent, marshaled his observations of birdlife on Boston Common, on whose edge the physician and publisher resided. Brewer, who belonged to the same ethnic group and socioeconomic class as Coues, conjured up images of a happy, vibrant nation founded by immigrants and defined by immigration; the northeastern city was a site of touching fraternity between native sparrows and their "European cousins." And, like Robson, he passed off the latter as their closest avian relatives. As for the familiar complaint that sparrows drove off bluebirds, well, it was more a case of an intolerant native refusing to extend hospitality to the innocent newcomer.[136] Meanwhile, Robson accused Coues of keeping quiet about the American jay's bullying of small, insectivorous native songbirds.[137] And insofar as native populations were declining in some areas, the sparrow's supporters stressed that the fundamental inimical changes were rapid urbanization and industrialization, forces in full swing long before the sparrow flew into town. Nicholas Pike, one of the directors of the Brooklyn Institute responsible for the original introduction in the fall of 1850, pointed this out in 1884: There were fewer native birds in Brooklyn now because "whole streets and avenues of houses are now standing where not many years ago were thick woods where I went gunning."[138]

The English sparrow's champions thus interpreted hostility toward their bird as ethnic discrimination by other means. Facile stereotypes similar to those applied to human groups were distorting perceptions of the bird, insisted the sparrow's supporters. What impression would a foreigner visiting England for the first time form if the first natives he encountered happened to be swarthy? To reinforce his point that allegations against the bird were mostly unsubstantiated, this is the question J. C. Atkinson invited his readers to ponder in the early 1890s, when the bird's stalwarts had their backs against the wall. According to Atkinson (a Briton), the visitor might record that "the English are singularly dark in complexion; indeed, they might be described as tawny rather than fair!" In other words, these Anglo-Saxons might be mistaken for southern Italians like the swarthy fowler whose cruelty Hornaday deplored. Flimsy generalizations comparable to this one about the complexion of the English, Atkinson concluded, had rendered the humble sparrow the most mud "bespattered" of all birds.[139]

Atkinson deplored the relentless humanization that had transformed the English sparrow into a "scientific burglar" and murderer without conscience.[140] But the case for the sparrow at this time was most memorably put by American poet George Horton. His maudlin ode, "To an English Sparrow," freely conceded that the immigrant's singing was inferior to that of native songsters. But where were those fickle "visitors sweet" of June when most needed in the depths of winter? Wielding the humanizing metaphors that Atkinson frowned on (when the bird's opponents used them, that is), he thanked the "brave, saucy Briton" for its nerve and loyalty: "you stayed." This cheerful tenacity gave him the opportunity to present its reputation as a "fighter" in a more sympathetic light.[141] In fact, the survival instincts of the "tough little Britons" with their "bull-dog courage" threatened to melt the hearts of their harshest detractors—perhaps a concession to a stubborn and forgiving sense of shared racial solidarity with nonhuman creatures from Britain.

Though bird conservationists derided the likes of Horton and Atkinson as sentimentalists and "so-called humanitarians," the English sparrow presented them with a considerable moral dilemma; the selective incitement of violence against it sat uncomfortably with efforts to expose wanton cruelty against other (native) birds and nurture tenderness toward them. During the sparrow war's opening salvos, Henry Ward Beecher, the prominent clergyman, had sought to exploit what he saw as this glaring inconsistency. In a style that anticipated Hitchcock's film *The Birds* (1963), he warned Coues of the feathered wrath that would descend if he did not make his peace with a bird that had won its right to be considered American:

> On some day unawares he shall be surrounded by swarms of sparrows, darkening the sun, and multitudinous as the locusts of Minnesota. Each bird shall nip him. He shall grow small by degrees and beautifully less, until the last thread of his garment and the last hair of his head shall be borne away in triumph to line the nest in which a valiant sparrow shall give its now native country another brood of these vigorous workers![142]

By the second decade of the twentieth century, debate pivoted increasingly on whether the bird was receiving a "square deal in our Land of Liberty." The bird's vilified, persecuted, and peripheral status reminded Harvey Whipple of Ishmael. Whipple did not elaborate, but the allusion was to the firstborn but illegitimate son of Abraham and his wife's maidservant, Hagar, who, it is prophesied in Genesis, "will be a wild donkey of a man; his hand will be against everyone and everyone's hand against him, and he will live in hostility toward all his brothers." Ishmael is banished to the desert on the birth of Abraham's second (and legitimate) son, Isaac, and the Ishmaelites were a group of nomadic bands fathered by Ishmael's twelve sons. Yet in referring to the English sparrow as "the Ishmael among birds," Whipple may also have been referring more pointedly to a group of notorious outcasts and undesirables much closer to home: the "Ishmael clan" was a roving band of thieves and beggars (supposedly descended from a transported convict) that operated in the Indianapolis area.[143]

In any event, Whipple repudiated the bird's reputation as a social vagrant and parasite, holding up the "alien" sparrow as being "plain and unpretentious like the great bulk of humanity."[144] Simplicity and lack of affectation were democratic qualities usually celebrated in connection with native birds. But it was the English sparrow that commended itself to Whipple as the antithesis of the exotic and inspired his fanfare for the common bird, the feathered equivalent of Whitman's leaves of grass.

For this constituency, the desire to cleanse the nation of English sparrows violated the essential American creed of equal justice for all. "Under the constitution," cautioned one of Blanchan's correspondents, the sparrow was "entitled to his attorney and his day in court."[145] Her own views had mellowed considerably between the publication of *How to Attract the Birds* in 1902 and American entry into World War I. By 1917, she felt, native birds had had sufficient time to adapt to "the ways of these foreigners in their midst, just as, happily, we humans have had to learn to live tolerantly and peaceably with Jews, Italians, Slavs, and many other European immigrants whose virtues were not at first appreciated."[146]

Instead of worrying about the sparrow's impact on American birds and its suitability for biological citizenship, Blanchan now fretted about the effect on American children of sparrow hatred and the official endorsement of eradication campaigns. Coues had regarded the very youngsters he sought to mold into native bird guardians as potential recruits in the sparrow war. The main character in *Citizen Bird,* co-written with Mabel Osgood Wright in 1897, is a naturalist who opens the eyes of his niece and nephew and their friends to the delights of American birds, all of which he encourages them to cherish—with one notable exception. Even the northern shrike, despite its reputation as the "butcher bird" (it impales insects and small birds on thorns and sharp twigs before eating them), deserves respect because it exacts revenge on a foreign intruder that evicts the "industrious native birds who are good Citizens." Another boy in *Citizen Bird* (Nat), explains why he had never appreciated birds before. "It was all those Sparrows in the city that made me think all wild birds must be ugly."[147]

In the fall of 1916, the New York City–based League of American Sportsmen (whose official organ was "devoted to game protection, nature study, and all legitimate outdoor and indoor sports") raised the chilling prospect of all those English sparrows—not properly of America—as the sole representatives of birdlife in America. The league's founder and president, George O. Shields (who is credited with coining the term "game hog"), already had a record of stalwart service in the defense of American avifauna. Every Sunday in the early 1900s, he had mounted armed patrols in the woods and thickets on the northern fringes of New York City (especially the Bronx) and Westchester County to prevent the indiscriminate killing of native songbirds by Italian immigrants. Though some poachers eluded him by vanishing into a "human rabbit-warren of the Italian boarding-house species," he made a string of arrests (and, amazingly, was never wounded).[148] Turning his attention to this other foreign threat, Shields advocated nationwide extermination of English sparrows to forestall the nightmarish scenario of their unchallenged supremacy in the skies of America. In support of his drastic proposal, Shields cited the successful local campaign launched in 1915 in San Diego (where the "British intruder" had arrived as recently as 1913) and the statewide "war" the California Game and Fish Commission had declared against the bird. Meanwhile, in New Jersey, an official sparrow-killing day, in which Boy Scouts would take the lead, was proposed in 1916.[149]

Precedents of this sort were precisely what alarmed Blanchan. Alluding to the German invasion of Belgium, she wondered whether the human race was "good enough to withstand the brutalizing effect of wantonly torturing and killing even a sparrow." Bear in mind, she entreated, that the sparrow was often the only bird American children fated to grow up in large cities ever saw. Authorization to persecute it could therefore "Prussianize" these young Americans, who then "might just as well grow up in Berlin."[150]

American callousness and cruelty toward (native) birds—the qualities

Blanchan identified as Prussian—had been contrasted with the "love and protection" the English showered on their birds in an earlier essay on the demise of American birds. Deploring in equal measure the depredations of the English sparrow ("little pirate") and man ("the real 'bird of prey'"), the American author recommended following the British example that united peer and peasant. "Even the *gamin* of London," Eugene Rolfe reported, "is fain to share his crust with the birds of the park."[151] He did not point out, though, that many of those fortunate birds in London's parks were his confounded English sparrows. By the 1890s, as a prominent British naturalist explained, the "little brown-coated crowd" had "conquered London"—and won the affection of working-class cockneys who identified with these unpretentious daily companions.[152]

Rolfe was mistaken on another matter as well. He was seemingly unaware that the sparrow war in the United States was the western front of a transatlantic phenomenon whose British front had opened two decades earlier and also peaked in the 1890s. Interested British parties kept a close eye on American developments, and a report Coues had prepared for the federal government in 1879 was in considerable demand.[153] No longer available, it was reprinted in Britain in 1885 together with specially commissioned pieces on England's sparrow problem. Also included was an abbreviated version of Olive Thorne Miller's account of "a ruffian in feathers."[154] Another British book about the house sparrow, subtitled *The Avian Rat*, urged readers to "save the bread of the people from these feathered robbers." Denouncing the bird as a parasite that failed to live in a "natural manner," the authors even queried its British identity. A bird of indeterminate origins, it had "no natural location" in Britain.[155] Another observer of birdlife, a benign Oxford don, remarked that this "noisy and quarrelsome" bird was "growing sootier every year."[156]

British sparrow critics took the opportunity for an occasional dig at the Irish. In her reminiscence of a long quiet life amidst the rural serenity of Hampshire, novelist Charlotte Yonge almost felt sympathy for the "poor despised [but "unconquerable"] creatures, whom some one has well named the Irishmen of birds, with their noise and their squabbles, their boldness and ubiquity." Meanwhile, the author of a bird book remarked that they bickered and rioted "with as little object seemingly as an Irish 'row.'"[157] But pejorative references to nationality were a lesser feature of Britain's sparrow war, which concentrated on crop damage. This is hardly surprising, given that the British population was far more ethnically and racially homogenous than that of the United States and immigration was not the same defining historical experience. Yet—as Barrows was fully aware—the British war was no less passionately fought.[158] Many Britons also issued bloodthirsty calls for extermination, not least because of the sparrow's alleged impact on certain other birds, notably house martins. Letters to the London *Times* protesting wholesale "murder" by "sparrow clubs" expressed revulsion at the annual dinners of these "ornithocide" societies, which distributed cash prizes (between the cheese and dessert courses) to members who had killed the greatest and second-highest number.[159] Nor was the hounding of the sparrow in nineteenth-century Britain anything exceptional within Europe. French and German authorities railed against the bird as well—as they had done, on and off, for centuries. In fact, as Harvard botanist and physician Charles Pickering reminded his audience at a meeting of the Boston Society of Natural History as early as April 1867, house sparrows had been the "acknowledged enemy of mankind for more than five thousand years." He proceeded to explain that "when writing was invented the Sparrow was selected for the hieroglyphic character signifying enemy."[160]

The ferocity and duration of the sparrow war in Britain and the long pedigree of hostility toward the bird in its other European homelands brings the late nineteenth-century American controversy into sharper focus. As well as reminding us not to neglect material considerations (the objective realities of economic and ecological impacts) as we seek to extract maximum cultural value from this animal story, a comparative perspective underlines the malleability of the sparrow's symbolic identity. Insofar as distaste for the bird tells us something significant about disapproval of certain groups of people, the bird's immigrant identity appears sufficient, at first, to explain American opposition. Yet some of its sworn enemies were perfectly happy to import the skylark and nightingale. A closer look indicates that the lower-class and urban identity invariably bestowed on the sparrow was also a major sticking point. This emphasis on social status and place of residence rather than nationality per se—to the extent that these categories can be separated at a time when so many immigrants were working-class urbanites—is supported by parallel experiences in Britain. British commentators often appraised their own bird in identical fashion to American observers of similar social rank. Gentry, for instance, cited a British source to support his view that the insubordinate sparrow had no respect for private property, stealing food from its faunal betters.[161]

This observation underscores the vital point that the assignation of pejorative human qualities to animals is by no means restricted to nonnative species. Because they fed on "useful" and "good" native creatures, Hornaday detested predatory natives like the wolf, coyote, and mountain lion as much as the English sparrow. In fact, the most notorious victim of negative humanization in North America (and Europe) has probably been the indigenous wolf. Nor was the English sparrow the only bird available for unflattering comparisons with undesirable immigrants. Native species that grain farmers considered a nuisance were also fair game. Hinton Rowan Helper, the prominent North Carolinian slavery critic, argued that the Chinese he encountered in Gold Rush California had no more right to be there than "flocks of blackbirds have in a wheat field," for "as the birds carry off the wheat without leaving anything of value behind, so do the Confucians gather the gold."[162]

Moreover, hostility toward the English sparrow eventually subsided. Though opposition in California was in full swing during World War I, the eastern front had grown much quieter. As early as 1884, Robson had urged "anti-sparrow men" to abandon their "foolish prejudices" and drop their "cruel crusades" because "you can not extradite him, for like yourselves and numbers more of his countrymen, he has come here to stay." And most critics east of the Rockies knew full well, long before 1900, that though they might chalk up the occasional local victory, they were never going to win the national war. That Brewer's death in 1880 had left "poor Jack without a prominent, zealous defender" (to quote Robson) and that Coues remained an indefatigable critic until shortly before he died in 1899 made little difference.[163] As a war-weary Coues explained when he finally admitted defeat in 1897, "I could whip all my featherless foes, but the Sparrows proved too many for me, by a large majority." Osgood was equally resigned. Like the common (Norway) rat, the sparrow was "doubtless destined always to be with us in some numbers."[164]

Nonetheless, the sparrow's enemies derived some consolation from evidence that the bird's onslaught was running out of steam in areas of initial colonization. Data from Pennsylvania's state parks in the early 1890s prompted euphoric headlines such as "The English Sparrow: Indications that his Victorious March is Nearing its End." By 1916 gleeful reports from the Northeast, the Midwest, and the central Rockies suggested that numbers were falling. Meanwhile, anguished reports of confrontations with native birds were harder to spot in the ornithological and popular press, and the Biological Survey received significantly fewer complaints.[165]

The sparrow's decline in urban areas reflected the switch from horse-drawn transportation to electric trolleys in the 1890s and, thereafter, to motorized vehicles. Fewer horses meant fewer piles of manure and pools of spilled grain. To fend off winter starvation in the 1920s, sparrows quit cities in droves. This was no solution, for the shift from stable to garage was paralleled in the countryside, where the Fordson tractor brushed aside horse power.[166] Once again, though, the sparrow demonstrated its adaptability. Many commentators during the 1930s (including the chief of the Biological Survey) noted its habit of pecking at the mashed insects stuck to the radiator grills of parked cars.[167] Still, their numbers were reduced substantially. Sparrow critics who figured out what was happening realized that the automobile would accomplish far more than any planned extirpation—directly as well as indirectly. Sparrows, despite their streetwise reputation, loomed large among auto-inflicted fatalities in the 1920s. Urban populations began to diminish as automobile numbers increased, to the extent that in 1927 the *New York Times* inquired, rather melodramatically, "Where is this feathered street arab of yesterday?"[168]

Still, the bird remained a "bad denizen of the air" in the eyes of the federal government's economic ornithologists, who remained concerned in the 1910s and 1920s that its wrongdoings would tarnish the reputation of the forty or so species of native sparrow—all "better behaved" than their "pesky" "English cousin."[169] And in view of the bird's continuing spread, the ongoing expansion of cities and agricultural production, and the remorseless arrival of additional foreign insects, the Biological Survey reassessed its economic status half a century after the Barrows report. The heat of the sparrow war having long since cooled, this much shorter update in 1940 was also the most detached study so far—though, like many bird books, it retained the appellation "English sparrow" in deference to popular usage. The report's author reiterated that American agriculture and native birds would have been far better off had the sparrow never arrived. But he did not regard it as a significant problem anymore.[170] There was a further explanation for the waning of antipathy, however. The misdeeds of another, more recently imported British bird had diverted public attention.

THE COCKNEY COUSIN

The editors of *Forest and Stream* had regularly reported public dismay over the sparrow's poor performance as an agent of biological control and its negative impact on native birds since the mid-1860s. Nevertheless, at the height of the sparrow war, in 1877, they claimed to speak for "all naturalists and sportsmen" in supporting the American Acclimatization Society's renewed efforts to import the English titmouse, chaffinch, robin redbreast, and skylark.[171] "Ship them all home," a Brooklynite had recommended a few months earlier, referring to English sparrows. Yet in the same breath he urged the society to bring back nightingales and starlings.[172]

When the first starlings were released in Central Park in 1877 (unsuccessfully on this occasion), *Forest and Stream* hailed it as the bird that would really do the job the sparrow was supposed to have done.[173] The first "English" starlings that established themselves in the park were among the sixty that disembarked in March 1890 from a liner Edwin Way Teale subsequently dubbed the "*Mayflower* of the starlings."[174] The instigator, Eugene Schieffelin, was a Shakespeare buff as well as an avid acclimatizer, and his two passions apparently dovetailed in his consuming desire to import every bird mentioned in the bard's works.[175]

Through nesting site competition and aggressive disposition, the starling has been implicated in the decline of various native species; like the English sparrow, the starling is nonmigratory, whereas migratory natives must fight afresh for nest sites each spring.[176] As starlings expanded beyond the

Figure 2. European starling. The caption accompanying this draw-ing by George Miksch Sutton, state ornithologist for Pennsylvania, reads: "he waved his wings ecstatically whenever his mate appeared, and puffed out his long, lanceolate throat-feathers as he sang." From *Bird-Lore* 29, 4 (July–August 1927), 252.

Northeast within a decade of arrival, Page explains, "bird people began to look upon the starling with the same wariness with which the American Indians no doubt observed the Pilgrims."[177] The removal of the statutory protection it had enjoyed across the Northeast since 1890 triggered a public debate over the bird's merits on the letters pages of the *New York Times* and *Forest and Stream* during 1914 and 1915. Portraying the starling as the sparrow's evil twin, one correspondent demanded that the authorities promote insectivorous natives instead of "those two cockney aliens."[178]

Yet the alignment of forces in the starling debate (it was never referred to as a "war") differed from that of the earlier sparrow controversy. Hornaday rejected any comparison because this "cheerful immigrant" was a peerless consumer of noxious insects—especially the dreaded Japanese beetle, which most native birds seemed to avoid. In recognition of this sterling service, he recommended the reinstatement of protection for a bird that was "not a quarrelsome little bully."[179] Reports that starlings ate English sparrow eggs and fledglings, dispensing a kind of rough justice by evicting them from the nesting holes they themselves had "stolen" from bluebirds, was a firm plank in the pro-starling platform.[180]

Another leading sparrow opponent and starling supporter was Frank Chapman. A former banker, he was curator of birds from 1908 to 1942 at the American Museum of Natural History (whose eaves hosted the first nesting starlings). Chapman was also the editor of *Bird-Lore,* the Audubon Society's journal. Adopting the comparative framework of reference characteristic of some commentators, he likened the starling to other species permitted entry "with thoughtless hospitality"—notably the house sparrow, San Jose scale (a plant pathogen), and gypsy moth. Nonetheless, he was reconciled to the starling's eventual spread across the entire continent, which made whatever Americans thought of the bird largely irrelevant. Echoing Robson's attitude to the English sparrow, he reasoned that "Nature has accorded him his 'papers' and he exercises all the privileges of citizenship."[181]

Chapman then examined the implications of the standard emphasis on the starling's foreign origins. "Now whatever we ourselves may be," he explained, "whether our forbears came over in the Mayflower or on the Mauretania, there can be no doubt that our birds are Americans." This native status automatically enhanced their value for many Americans, for it meant that they were not just birds but American birds. "As such, they are not only the products but expressions of their environment," Chapman explained. "When, in early March, a moving nebulous blur resolves itself into a flock of redwings, they are less birds than the Spirit of Spring." By the same token, if they were not American, their value was automatically downgraded: "But if the hurrying smudge becomes a passing troupe of starlings," he pointed out, "we regard it with disappointment or indifference. It has no seasonal significance." The starling, in short, was just a bird—perhaps less than a bird—burdened rather than uplifted by its cultural baggage.[182]

This distinction based on nationality struck Chapman as unfair as well as arbitrary. If viewed "merely as a bird"—and from this angle being just a bird rather than an American bird or a foreign bird was an advantage—the starling's virtues were more readily perceived. The sight of a huge flock moving in unison (which reminded many commentators of the passenger pigeon's former massed ranks) rendered subjective considerations of national origin petty for the utterly captivated Chapman. Smoothly assuming multifarious forms, these avian artists performed "a dance in the clouds to the music of the winds,—a pure expression of a *joie de vivre,* which raises the industrious plodder of our lawns to an ethereal realm where nationalities are unknown and the glorious heritage of flight is the universal emblem of bird life."[183]

Though more concerned with the bird's reputation as a devourer of crops, and concluding that "judged by food habits alone, it is not a bad citizen," a Bureau of Biological Survey researcher acknowledged in 1928 that "partiality for our native birds naturally causes antagonism to the starling." A press release accompanying her earlier report on the bird's spread and status also pointed out that, though "its food habits are in some cases more beneficial than those of many of the [native] birds it supplants," "many people look upon the bird as an undesirable alien." [184] The starling, like the sparrow, was not often viewed simply as a bird that inhabited a realm without nationalities.

Ten years later, in one of her first publications, Rachel Carson entered another plea for tolerance. She was struck by the starling's indifference to its peerless unpopularity among birds. Its notoriety was like water off a duck's back to the "cheerful" bird as it went about its business of eating nasty insects like the Japanese beetle—for which, in her view, it deserved the farmer's gratitude. It was also with "complete indifference to angry protests" that the unruffled bird swooped into cities in winter in search of warm roosts—"going out each morning, a faithful commuter-in-reverse, to earn his bread" in the fields beyond. Carson's jaunty, highly anthropomorphic piece, like Chapman's, toyed with the analogy of citizenship in the human world. Her stance mirrored Blanchan's revised position on the English sparrow. Since the starling, like its fellow British import, was here to stay, and no more of a bully than other native birds (including the "gentle" and much loved house wren), it was time to recognize that the bird's "successful pioneering and his service in insect destruction entitle him to American citizenship." Also like Chapman, she was mesmerized by the spectacle of a large flock in flight. She described how "they wheel and turn above the buildings [of Washington, D.C.], patterning the evening sky with intricate designs." "Leaderless, apparently animated by the pure joy of flight," she pronounced their performance to be "one of indescribable beauty."[185]

In this way, Carson inverted the usual notions of beauty and ugliness in avian society, in which beauty was a commodity so often wedded exclusively and irrevocably to native nature, and ugliness an attribute automatically associated with foreign nature. Chapman and Carson had cast off these cultural blinkers to see the starling clearly for what it was and not from where it came.

THE SUCCESSFUL AND EXEMPLARY SPARROW

Whether the starling and sparrow met with approval or disapproval, the evidence for their widespread naturalization was incontrovertible by the 1920s. Around this time, scientists began to formulate explanations for these roaring American success stories. Ever since Darwin chronicled the impact of exotic animals (mostly livestock) on the Galapagos in the 1830s, successful bioinvasion has been most readily associated with oceanic islands.[186] Island fauna often consist of a few highly specialized species that have evolved in isolation. As such, they are highly vulnerable to takeover. By contrast, major continental landmasses support a wide range of native species. Given that a host of birds similar to the English sparrow and starling already inhabited the United States on the eve of their arrival, their expansions are particularly striking.

Their American triumphs challenge the still powerful Darwinian orthodoxy that more diverse ecosystems are inherently more stable. Many environmentalists today believe that native creatures are automatically the most perfect biotic forms because they represent the end product of natural selection. In connection with the English sparrow, University of California zoologist Joseph Grinnell anticipated the views of evolutionary biologist Stephen Jay Gould: natives are better suited than other species only at a particular time under particular circumstances. Because it was equally at home in Boston and Death Valley in the early twentieth century, and just as comfortable at sea level as at ten thousand feet in the Colorado Rockies, the sparrow served this prominent native bird conservationist as a prime illustration of a universal law of nature: "When a species native to a large area is successfully introduced into a new small area the related species which is native in this area and with which the former comes into competition is soon supplanted."[187]

Grinnell was identifying the characteristics of species that have since become known as "generalists." The invader's attributes, in other words, are as important as the qualities of the species whose territories are invaded, if not more so. Since many of North America's invasive species are European, it seems that a long experience of invasions in Europe has created a class of species predisposed to invade. As Grinnell theorized in 1925, "It looks as though the environment of large compass, where the long-time inhabitants have been subjected to the widest range in the rigors of existence, has developed species of the greatest hardihood, and particularly of the greatest degree of aggressiveness."[188] More recently, as invasion biology began to assume the dimensions of a collective and more systematically theorized pursuit, invasion biologists who attempted to enumerate the qualities of the "perfect" or "ideal" invader and to identify "high risk" species more or less echoed Grinnell's findings.[189] Accomplished avian invaders were credited with qualities such as "toughness," meaning that they range extensively in search of food and nesting sites, feed opportunistically, and readily locate unoccupied habitat or displace existing occupants.[190]

Invasion biologists have also established that the European birds most successfully naturalized in North America are human commensals, those already accustomed to habitats dominated by cultivation and human presence.[191] Major European landscape traits for centuries, these were more recent features of North America—features to which native birds had not had time to adapt by the mid-nineteenth century. The English sparrow, though, was preadapted. As its Latin name *(Passer domesticus)* suggests, it has been living around people since Eurasia's first settled agricultural communities started cultivating grains. As for the advantage of shaking off your old enemies by moving abroad (a phenomenon now dignified by the name "Enemy Release Hypothesis"), English sparrows in North America typically carry thirty-seven species of mites, fleas, and lice in contrast to sixty recorded on their European counterparts.[192]

Mightily impressed by the scale of the sparrow's success, an early twentieth-century animal behaviorist pinpointed a related advantage enjoyed over native American birds. James Porter's experiments required "the hungry animal to overcome some simple difficulty in order to obtain food." The results corroborated zoological opinion that the English sparrow was the most intelligent of small birds—how (and how quickly) it learned from experience was compared to the mechanisms of the higher vertebrates. Porter was particularly struck by its "persistency" in trying to access food through a maze. He surmised that the "native wildness" it had retained, combined with adaptability to human presence, had rendered it "one of the creatures best fitted to survive in the struggle for existence under whatever conditions man may afford or enforce."[193]

The casualties in that struggle for existence, Porter agreed, were often native birds, whose status was that of what has since become known as "naïve victims"—species with no prior experience of new species or of those "functionally equivalent" to themselves.[194] Even before 1900, the sparrow had acquired a larger meaning as the epitome of the dangers of species transplantation—"ecological roulette" or "species pollution," as this phenomenon is now often, more emotively, dubbed.[195] Comparisons with the rabbit's ill-fated introduction to Australia were standard by the

1890s, while others who remained supportive of introductions on a limited scale felt obliged to reassure skeptics that they would not be repeating the "blunder of the English sparrow."[196] In a lengthy essay about the pitfalls of species transfer, chief government entomologist Leland O. Howard, despite his primary interest in insects, took the "ubiquitous" English sparrow as his leading faunal example.[197] For Chapman, the havoc the sparrow wreaked among native birds was the penalty for meddling with the hallowed "laws of Nature." Using artistic license to make this point (which was more applicable to the starling's introduction), the naturalist-uncle in *Citizen Bird* instructs his young listeners that English sparrows—these "bad Citizens and criminals"—happen to be in the United States because (to quote one of the boys), one man "thought he was so smart and mixed things up."[198]

In 1920, with species like the English sparrow very much in mind, Scottish zoologist James Ritchie observed sagely that "man in transporting creatures for his own purposes often seems to forget that their nature, and not his desires, will remain their guiding law."[199] Immigrant promise can turn to menace and an introduced species prove troublesome in ways never anticipated—though, as Ritchie intimated, an elementary grasp of nature's willful and unpredictable nature would indicate that we should never be surprised when this happens. The sparrow saga also shows that this is particularly likely to happen when a nonnative organism is deployed to check a native pest.

A relocated species does not necessarily change its spots—or feathers. What sometimes happens, though, is that the very characteristics that earmark it as a desirable introduction—fecundity and flexibility—are reconceived, rendering it an "undesirable alien."[200] In other words, some Americans opposed the sparrow's introduction for the very reason other Americans supported it, namely, that the canker worm would be devastated by an unknown enemy accustomed to broadly similar forms of prey at home because the pest had not developed defensive mechanisms against exotic predators.[201] The problem was that the worm's vulnerability to outsiders was shared by desirable native biota.

In view of its impact on these non-target species—not least those native birds that preyed on the target pest—the English sparrow fulfilled the worst expectations of those who disapproved of biological forms of pest control involving nonnatives. Solutions involving nonnatives often contain the seeds of other problems. Insofar as sparrows did a good job of eating canker worms, they created an opportunity for other pests. As explained by Charles V. Riley, the Department of Agriculture's entomologist, the niche the worm vacated was filled by the likes of the (white-marked) tussock-moth, rusty-vaporer moth, and web-worm, which the canker worm had previously kept down. And the English sparrow had compounded this royal mess by driving away the "better" native birds that would have industriously kept their numbers down. To cap it off, as Riley concluded after dissecting more than six hundred stomachs, the English sparrow largely disdained to eat these very hairy caterpillars (canker worms being smooth), and when it did eat insects it mostly ate harmless or beneficial species.[202] To make matters worse, the depredations of the tussock-moth were by no means confined to the spring months. So, by the late 1880s, the press was again lamenting the evils of a great tree pest.

Leaving aside the question of how well the sparrow carried out its allotted task of pest control, there was clearly a material basis to objections in terms of economic impact and also on ecological grounds. Sometimes the English sparrow was treated primarily as a bird, pure and simple—as Chapman wanted the starling to be treated—rather than as a feathered person. What remains unresolved, though, is whether the cost to the farmer and gardener in terms of what the bird ate was greater than the value of the crops saved thanks to the insects it also consumed. Even harder to gauge is whether the sparrow was more prejudicial to the interests of native birds than deep-seated changes associated with industrialization and urbanization. What is clear, however, is that the readily available sparrow became a very convenient scapegoat on which to heap the wickedness of the undesirable human immigrant. It proved much harder, however, to banish the heavily laden creature—like the goat in the Old Testament book of Leviticus—to the desert of no return. The English sparrow was not budging. Moreover, as Grinnell had pointed out, it appeared to like Death Valley as much as New York City.

Barrows had likened the English sparrow's "phenomenal invasion" to that of a "noxious weed transplanted to a fertile soil."[203] And so great was the bird's notoriety that word sometimes spread from zoologist to botanist. The bird's infamy served as a telling point of reference for a prominent native plant champion concerned about the impact of foreign flora. Having seen how effectively Japanese honeysuckle, an escaped ornamental, had colonized Maryland's woods by the 1930s, Jens Jensen (a Danish immigrant) predicted that introductions like this would "become the sparrows of the plant world."[204] The sparrow's opponents rarely drew parallels with plants— whether deliberately or inadvertently transplanted. But they occasionally alluded to other, smaller nonnative biota like the San Jose scale and gypsy moth. Though plant pathogens like this scale differed from the sparrow in the mode of their initial arrival (surreptitious), these afflictions came in the good company of desirable foreign plants. And this moth was bred with the best of intentions.

After the American Society for Environmental History's annual conference in Tucson, Arizona, in April 1999, I was waiting in the hotel lobby for a taxi to the airport in the company of some departing Russians. Had he encountered any trouble entering the United States? I asked one of them. No, he replied. The immigration official had just wanted to know if he was bringing in any plants. With growing concern over the threat to U.S. agriculture from invasive overseas pests—and in view of the disintegration of the Soviet Union and the communist peril—it had become possible for a Russian plant to be regarded as a greater menace than a Russian person. Leaving alien fauna for foreign flora (and their fellow-traveling insects), we find that late nineteenth- and early twentieth-century efforts to distinguish between the desirable and the dangerous were equally influenced by the perception of promise and menace in human immigrants. At the same time, the primary botanical and zoological identities of plants and insects were never completely submerged beneath thick layers of human-imposed cultural meanings.

Chapter 3

Plants, Insects, and Other
Strangers to the Soil

*There were on the planet where the little prince lived—as on all planets—good
and bad plants. . . . If it is only a sprout of radish or the sprig of a rose-bush, one
would let it grow wherever it might wish. But when it is a bad plant, one must
destroy it as soon as possible, the very first instant that one recognizes it. Now there
were terrible seeds on the planet that was the home of the little prince; and these
were the seeds of the baobab. The soil of that planet was infested with them. A
baobab is something you will never, never be able to get rid of if you attend to it
too late. It spreads over the entire planet. It bores clear through it with its roots.
And if the planet is too small, and the baobabs are too many, they split it in pieces.*
ANTOINE DE SAINT-EXUPÉRY, *The Little Prince*, 1943

FLORAL MENACE AND FLORAL PROMISE

The fractious relations between the United States and Britain that flavored
American attitudes to the English sparrow also spiced responses to floral
pests from Britain. The Civil War did not interrupt Charles Darwin and Asa
Gray's regular correspondence on botanical matters. In the early 1860s,
though, they often spent more time discussing politics than plants. British
partiality for the Confederacy (see "The Stranger Finch" in chapter 2) —
aggravated tension between the scientists' countries, and this colored their
exchanges. Though Darwin appreciated the American newspapers Gray
sent him, he also expressed annoyance at their "digs at England." "When
you receive this [letter] we may be at war," he wrote in December 1861 after
a Union warship's seizure, from the British mail packet *Trent*, of Confederate agents en route to London. The British government demanded their
release. "I fear there is no doubt we shall fight," Darwin ventured, "if the two
Southern rogues are not given up."[1]

Diplomatic maneuvering averted military conflict. Yet the Civil War continued to cast a long shadow across their letters. One Darwin wrote in
November 1862 was therefore notable for its departure from the distrac-
tions of war and the subject of deteriorating British–American relations.
Plants replaced politics for once. Darwin wondered whether Gray was familiar with an American work he was currently reading: Susan Fenimore
Cooper's *Journal of a Naturalist in the United States*. This book was first pub-

lished in the United States in 1850 as *Rural Hours* by the famous novelist's daughter, an accomplished botanist. But the mold within which the Darwin–Gray correspondence had been conducted since sectional tensions over slavery came to a head in the United States in the late 1850s was not broken entirely. There was more plant politics than plants in Darwin's letter. Unable to break free from the nationalistic sparring that had become such an ingrained feature of their botanical intercourse, Darwin recommended that Gray read Cooper's "capital account of the battle between *our* and *your* weeds."[2]

Journal of a Naturalist in the United States was an intimate diary of meticulous observation around the illustrious Cooper family's seat in rural Otsego County in upstate New York. Her entry for June 6, 1848, was devoted entirely to the topic of the impudent and tiresome weeds that sprouted up everywhere and required so much effort to keep in check. Like the English sparrow, these weedy plants were human commensals, as successfully preadapted to environments modified by agriculture as the avian Cockney was to a heavy human presence. By the same token, most native plants appeared less equipped to deal with these relatively novel agricultural conditions—just as native birds proved less adaptable to an urban setting. "It is remarkable," Cooper reflected, "that these troublesome plants have come very generally from the Old World; they do not belong here, but following the steps of the white man, they have crossed the ocean with him." The great majority of the most familiar weeds that were "choking up" fields, gardens, paths, and homesteads, she emphasized, were "strangers to the soil." Among those she listed (around paths and buildings) were balm, burdock, catnip, celandine, chickweed, comfrey, May-weed, purslane, nettles, and tansy; (in gardens) burweed, mulleins, and teasel; and (in meadows) buttercups, dandelions, thistles, wild garlic, and yarrow. What these besieging plants all shared, which set them apart from the native products of the American soil, was "a certain impertinent, intrusive character." By contrast, she observed, most of the American flora that had taken root in Europe had been deliberately introduced—beneficial crop plants such as maize, potatoes, and tobacco. And, adding insult to injury, relatively few weeds had accompanied their eastward migration, chiefly evening primrose and silkweed.[3]

Darwin could not resist the desire to twist the knife of national chauvinism in a little deeper, however jocularly. "Does it not hurt your Yankee pride," he inquired of Gray, "that we thrash you so confoundedly? I am sure Mrs. Gray will stick up for your own weeds. Ask her whether they are not more honest, downright good sort of weeds." Gray, rather surprisingly, had not seen Cooper's book, but he reported back that his wife "allows that our weeds give up to yours." American weeds, she agreed, were "modest . . . retiring things; and no match for the intrusive, pretentious, self-asserting foreigners." Gray routinely sent Darwin seeds and on this occasion enclosed those of one of the select handful of native weeds mentioned by Cooper that could match the disorder that Eurasian "throngs" visited on American soil: the bur cucumber, a vinelike gourd with painful prickly seeds that grows up to hundred feet a year and infests grain fields. *Sicyos angulatus,* Gray explained mischievously, had been "corrupted by bad company" and was therefore "as nasty and troublesome" as any foreign import.[4]

The asymmetry between the preeminence of Eurasian weeds in North America and the weak presence of North American weeds in Eurasia has engrossed botanists on both sides of the Atlantic since Darwin and Gray's exchanges.[5] Alfred Crosby mentions Canadian water weed as one of very few irksome plants Britain received from North America in exchange for a wealth of British weeds.[6] An isolated first appearance in 1842 caused little stir. By 1859, however, "the American weed"—which undergoes no growth surges in its home environment—had rendered sections of the River Thames impassable. The plant's most infamous exploits, however, were on the River Cam. By 1851, the College Backs at Cambridge were so clogged up that normal river life ground to a virtual standstill (disrupting, not least, the hallowed "amusement" of college rowing).[7] "Thoroughly established, and injuriously abundant," was a leading botanist's verdict in the late 1860s.[8]

Because it popped up simultaneously at various locations and in such large quantities, some Britons thought water weed must be a "true native."[9] Most commentators, though, were suspicious of claims to aboriginal status. The local expert in the Cambridge area, William Marshall of the nearby town of Ely, consistently personified the plant: "If you were some fine morning to find that a strange person, of foreign aspect, had intruded himself into your house, I imagine the questions which would most naturally occur to your mind under such circumstances would be,—Whence came the fellow, how did he get here, and how am I to get rid of him?" Locals promptly pronounced the plant "a furreigner." But Marshall, to his credit, was reluctant to jump to conclusions. After all, "our present unwelcome visitor" might be an "obscure" local character from the "back streets of your own town."[10]

Nonetheless, Marshall eventually satisfied himself that the plant in the Cam was "an unmistakeable foreigner, greedy and rapacious," and he targeted North America—especially the United States—as the source. He resented that the stranger was "'fixin' himself in John Bull's rivers, for all the world as if he had as good a right to occupy them as the aborigines themselves."[11] "Smothering our native water-plants," he lamented, "it takes exclusive possession of ditches and drains."[12] He interpreted this success as a striking example of colonial revenge:

Like the imported European horses and oxen in the South-American pampas, or Capt. Cook's pigs in New Zealand, or the Norway rat in our own farm-yards, or the Oriental black-beetle in London kitchens, or (more remarkable still) like the exotic mollusk, Dreissena polymorpha [zebra mussel], which has now spread itself through the canals of this country, we may conclude it has fairly established itself amongst us, never to be eradicated.[13]

Novelist Charles Kingsley was also resigned to its invincibility. In an essay extolling the pleasures of trout fishing in the chalk streams of the counties that surround London, the author of the children's fantasy classic *The Water-Babies* explained that their quieter stretches were choked with native weeds at the best of times. An already dire situation threatened to deteriorate immeasurably, however, when "our Transatlantic curse" showed up. Having reached the Thames, it was poised to devour every mill and trout stream in the land, thereby jeopardizing "peaceful, graceful, complete English country life."[14]

Kingsley's paranoia and hysteria were misplaced. The plant burgeoned for a few years and high numbers were maintained for another three to ten years. Then colonies slowly shrank over a seven- to fifteen-year period, after which the weed vanished almost completely. "Our own native weeds far more than hold their own against it," a relieved observer reported in the early 1900s.[15] That was more than Mrs. Gray had been able to say about the capabilities of her own weeds in the United States—not that Britain was the only source of the weedy foreign flora that vexed her (and Susan Fenimore Cooper). Nor were the agriculturally dominated environments in the United States on which Darwin and Gray's comments focused the only sites they occupied with such apparent ease.

Transgressive flora also shot up in American cities. Thirty years after Darwin and Gray's jousting, an urban example of mobile nature captured the attention of a leading native plant advocate. One of Alice Eastwood's first articles was about the freshly arrived floral residents of Nob Hill, then, as now, one of San Francisco's most sought-after areas, where she lived in a garret. During the rainy season, as she walked to work in Golden Gate Park (where, since 1892, she had held the post of curator of botany at the California Academy of Sciences), Eastwood collected specimens of the plants which, brought in as seeds by winds, birds, and animals, had thrust up between recently laid cobblestones. They survived even on heavily trodden thoroughfares but thrived especially in her neighborhood, where streets were so steep that cable cars were the only traffic; in this respect, new conditions appear to have been as important to their success as preadaptation and enemy release. A "wilderness of plants" sprang up in these linear places, so thick and tangled they almost blotted out cobbles and cable car tracks. Of the sixty-four species Eastwood identified, she reckoned that fifty-five were "foreigners."[16] "True" California plants, like lupine ("content to remain at home and . . . never yet . . . called weeds"), were tentative immigrants to the urban floral commons engulfed by riotous nonnatives less discriminating in their living requirements.[17]

Eastwood was an immigrant herself, born in Toronto to a Canadian father and a Scots-Irish mother. She acknowledged that the bright exuberance of these floral squatters relieved urban dreariness and squalor. But she shared the racial anxieties of William Hornaday and Madison Grant, frowning on the makeup of the city's human population the floral composition of Nob Hill's streets reflected. "This spontaneous vegetation," she remarked, "indicates by its cosmopolitan character the final results of civilization." Given her belief in the importance of regional floral distinctiveness, this homogenizing exotic presence deeply disturbed her. "The tendency," she noted, "is to reduce mankind as well as plants to one dead level. In time, the tribes and races that persist in their individuality will either become exterminated or be driven to inaccessible places." Like responses to the English sparrow, these feelings were shaped by the Euro-American sense of an inundating "yellow peril" that was particularly acute in San Francisco; she contrasted spacious, sparsely populated Nob Hill with the seething masses below in Chinatown. "Whether the type that persists is to be Oriental or Occidental," she mused, "time alone can decide."[18]

As the stories of Nob Hill's floral wilderness and American water weed in Britain indicate, foreign origins can coat unwanted plants with an additional layer of objection. At the same time, when they are faced with an undesirable foreigner, Americans and Britons can peel off one of the layers of villainy that cloak a home-grown pest, and its own struggle with the newcomer may seem almost admirable. After all, they may be weeds, but, as Darwin pointed out, they are *our* weeds. The essential point, though, is that foreignness itself rarely lies at the core of antipathy.

Aldo Leopold, for example, complained that Iowa's agricultural authorities had designated many "uncommon and lovely" native plants as dangerous weeds.[19] More than ten natives currently appear on the State of California's noxious weed list, and California natives—among them the state flower, the California poppy—constitute nearly a third of the nation's most common agricultural weeds. Perceptions of flora and responses to them are not dictated by notions of nationality. What plants do is usually the crux, not what they are.

Leopold's sympathies extended to a "tough immigrant" on Iowa's hit list—chicory. He admired this naturalized European because it was the sole representative of the "botanical melting-pot" sufficiently brave, during hot and dry spells, to "decorate with ethereal blue the worst mistakes of realtors and engineers." Nevertheless, among the weeds of the United States, immigrants such as chicory are more numerous than natives such as the

California poppy and *Sicyos angulatus,* whose seeds Gray sent Darwin. Because there are more of them, these overseas arrivals have aroused more annoyance and anger than their native counterparts. The sense of righteous indignation is encapsulated in the disparaging common names food-growing Americans attached to them: devil weed, wind witch, and cheat grass.[20]

Nineteenth-century botanists in the United States (and Britain) perceived a hierarchy within plant society that closely mirrored the human social scale. Weeds, regardless of nationality, generally occupied the nether ranks. *Weed* is not a biological term; it has no biological definition. Roughly synonymous with the equally unscientific *pest,* it simply means unwanted plant. A plant becomes unwanted—vegetable vermin—by being in the wrong place. And "out of place" has traditionally meant growing in the productive environment of field and orchard, competing with "useful" plants that feed families and the nation. Yet these "good" plants mostly come from other parts of the world too.

Donald Culross Peattie, botanist and nature writer, once described the U.S. Department of Agriculture's plant introduction gardens as acclimatization stations for the production of "Americanized new plant citizens."[21] Claire Shaver Haughton's *Green Immigrants: The Plants That Transformed America,* celebrated—according to the book's back jacket blurb—the plants "that have played a part as surely as human immigrants in the building of our nation."[22] By reminding us that analogies between human and plant immigrants are not inherently derogatory, these two remarks serve as a useful antidote to recent allegations of botanical nativism against the opponents of invasive exotics—allegations that are based, not least, on the extensive use of anthropocentric rhetoric. The above quoted summary of Haughton's book also brings to mind historian Oscar Handlin's famous declaration: "Once I thought to write a history of the immigrants in America. Then I discovered that the immigrants *were* American history." If Handlin had turned his attention to immigrant plants, he might have rewritten that statement to read: "Once I thought to write a history of introduced plants in American agriculture. Then I discovered that the immigrant plants (and livestock) *were* American agricultural history."[23]

Lacking the ability to self-generate through seed dispersal, agricultural plants rely on humans to sow their seeds and provide a nurturing environment through plowing, weeding, and fertilization. In fact, many crop plants would die out if we stopped husbanding them. Scientifically speaking, therefore, it is misleading to refer to domesticated crops as naturalized plants. In a broader cultural sense, however, food crops such as apples and various cereal grains were quickly and effortlessly naturalized during the colonial period. Very few Americans these days think about the origins of the fruit in the pie that has become a byword for Americanism; not one student in a group of about sixty very bright freshmen I met on a recent visit to the

United States seemed aware that the apple, like so many other common American fruits and vegetables, had been brought from Europe. The cow was an equally uncontroversial biotic immigrant—a prime symbol of Americanism purveyed abroad by countless cowboy movies and fast food restaurants. The distinction between being in America and of America was largely meaningless.

The majority of subsequent introductions were as uncontroversial as those of the colonial era. They displaced native plants insofar as any crop plant does when an agricultural environment supersedes a hitherto uncultivated one. Because they depended on copious amounts of human care, however, these introductions did not readily intrude into uncultivated environments of their own volition. Current efforts to publicize the threat invasive nonnatives pose in so-called natural areas recognize the qualitative difference between a crop plant and an invasive plant by routinely acknowledging the enormous agricultural contribution of introduced species.

Though crops themselves were not invasive, by the late nineteenth century confidence in the promise of floral immigrants was increasingly tempered in government circles and beyond by consciousness of potential threats to the existing agricultural order in the shape of dubious traveling companions: insects and diseases. Various scares thrust the problem to the forefront of government attention in the early 1900s. The first quarantine measures, enacted at state level from 1881 and by the federal government during the 1910s, were the functional equivalents of various immigration restrictions imposed between 1875 and 1924. Debates about the promise and perils of plant introduction also echoed discussions over the merits of the nation's time-honored "open door" immigration policy. Would further unrestricted plant immigration yield a harvest of disorder and degradation instead of conferring richer bounty? Like the sparrow war, disputes over plant immigration provided a springboard for impassioned discussion of fundamental national principles.

This does not mean that views on foreign plants and their accompanying pests always synchronized neatly with attitudes to human immigrants. A belief in an unhindered plant importation policy did not preclude support for immigration restrictions. Nor did belief in regulating people rule out enthusiasm for unhindered floral entry. The study of "good" plants and "bad" insects also reinforces a central point made with reference to the English sparrow and American water weed: that the tendency to dissolve the boundary between nonhuman and human threats and to nationalize faunal and floral "pests" is not a peculiarly American trait. Moreover, the United States was actually slow to protect its agricultural interests. That Americans maintained a welcoming stance for so long, and that opposition from government plant explorers and the horticultural industry to restrictive measures was so robust, may surprise those conditioned by Higham's initial emphasis on the virulence of American nativism and those who believe that American criticism of immigrant flora and fauna essentially became a reductive vehicle for its expression.

Peattie, who worked with tropical plants in the Department of Agriculture's Office of Foreign Seed and Plant Introduction in the early 1920s, embraced new species that enriched agricultural production, like the navel orange, as "cherished immigrants."[24] Yet yields might also be imperiled by otherwise useful nonnative plants that hosted diseases or injurious insects (not to mention the plants known as weeds that competed with crops). As Beverly Galloway, chief of the Bureau of Plant Industry from 1901 to 1912, reflected in the wake of the Department of Agriculture's introduction of the first quarantine measures for foreign plants in 1912, "Willingly or unwillingly, knowingly or unknowingly, consciously or unconsciously, man is the direct and indirect agent for the transportation of things that may make him or things that may break him."[25]

Whether the plant immigrant's promise or its peril was emphasized and the response was warm or wary often depended on the kind of natural scientist involved. Whereas botanists were generally enthused by exotic potential, their entomologist colleagues—housed within a different branch of the federal agricultural bureaucracy—were more cautious. It was the latter who supplied the major impetus for biosecurity measures. Philip J. Pauly has interpreted these tensions between botanists and entomologists as part of a wider ideological clash between ecological "cosmopolitans" and "nativist" proponents of American ecological "independence."[26] During this chapter's coverage of Haughton's green immigrants and those that tagged along with them, I consider the analytical value of this distinction to the study of connections between the reception of immigrants human and nonhuman.

I examined the origins and meanings of the term *nativism* in chapter 1. Henry Ridley used the term *cosmopolitan* to describe plants "found in any part of the world where the climate and environment were suitable to their growth," in other words, plants that lack what Ronald Good called a "peculiar element."[27] *Cosmopolitan* stems from eighteenth-century Europe, where, Robert Darnton explains, a refined transnationalism distinguished "persons of quality from the unwashed masses, whose mental horizon did not extend beyond the territory that could be viewed from the tower of their local church: hence . . . *campanilismo* to denote the narrow-minded." Yet *cosmopolitan* could also serve as a term of disapprobation; Darnton cites its definition in the dictionary of the Académie Française: "COSMOPOLITAN. Someone who does not adopt any fatherland. A cosmopolitan is not a good citizen." He also draws attention to the less than flattering meaning that appeared in the *Encyclopédie:* "One sometimes uses this term in joking, to signify a man who has no fixed abode or a man who is not a foreigner anywhere."[28]

In the late nineteenth- and early twentieth-century United States, biological nationalists produced ecological versions of the dichotomous terms *cosmopolitan* and *campanilismo*. They adopted the uncomplimentary eighteenth-century interpretations of cosmopolitan internationalism Darnton quoted and placed a positive spin on its parochial opposite. Though they did not use the term *campanilismo*, it was central to their worldview, functioning as the virtuous antidote to a rootless cosmopolitanism that converted floral citizens of particular places through species transfer into plants of no fixed abode, at home everywhere and strangers nowhere.

STRANGE FRUITS: THE ENRICHMENT OF NATURE

Those who implemented the cosmopolitan ethos of floral introduction were called plant hunters. Plant hunting is best known as a British imperial undertaking. Among the flood of swashbuckling nineteenth-century schoolboy novels unleashed by Mayne Reid, an English writer whose favorite literary territory was the American West, one title has a peculiar ring: *The Plant Hunters, or, Adventures among the Himalaya Mountains*. Reid identified a potential credibility gap and sought to bridge it. The opening lines of his tale about the adventures of a young Bavarian botanist in the Indian "Alps" report the following imaginary exchange between his juvenile readers:

> "A plant-hunter! What is that?"
> "We have heard of fox-hunters, of deer hunters, of bear and buffalo-hunters, of lion-hunters, and of 'boy-hunters'; of a plant hunter, never."
> "Stay! Truffles are plants. Dogs are used in finding them; and the collectors of these is termed a truffle-hunter. Perhaps this is what the Captain means?"

At this point, the author interjects:

> No, my boy reader. Something very different from that. My plant-hunter is no fungus-digger. His occupation is that of a nobler kind than contributing merely to the capricious palate of the gourmand. To his labours the whole civilized world is indebted—yourself among the rest. By his agency England—cold cloudy England—has become a garden of flowers. . . . Many of the noble trees that lend grace to our English landscape . . . are the produce of his industry.[29]

The boy reader was soon immersed, as usual, in the scintillating details of barbaric places and the obligatory thrills and spills as the hero barely survives a string of hair-raising encounters with murderous beasts. Plants rarely get a look in.

Nonetheless, Reid deserves credit for reminding his readers (and today's historians) that plant hunting was a characteristic activity of empire. It was a curious form of imperialism, though, in terms of its consequences for the existing floral residents of the imperialist nation of Britain. Various exotic trees, Reid told British boys, "already share the forest, and contest with our native species, the right to our soil."[30] Yet this was hardly the alarmed voice of an ecological nationalist dismayed at the onslaught of ecological imperialism; sentiments of that sort were reserved for American water weed. The cosmopolitan rationale of Frank Kingdon-Ward, the last of the illustrious early twentieth-century British plant hunters in Asia, echoed Reid's. Without "invasion" by "alien plants," he explained, England "would be a poorer and duller place," its landscape as hard to imagine as London without its house sparrows.[31] Kingdon-Ward's choice of noun to characterize the arrival of these thoroughly welcome floral foreigners from the lands Britain was colonizing sounds rather odd to today's ears. In the recent and current literature on the global movements of flora and fauna, *invasion* usually denotes a hostile takeover by biota acting more or less autonomously. By contrast, Kingdon-Ward and Reid described a process that takes place under human tutelage and whose impact on the indigenous floral population is deemed thoroughly beneficial.

This British story of cherished green immigrants has a lesser known but no less consequential American counterpart. Before Columbus brought seeds and cuttings along on his second voyage to the West Indies, North America was home to less than 1 percent of the world's total complement of cereals, starches, fruits, and vegetables. The work of introduction, which, as Howard Hyland notes, constitutes a perpetual agricultural revolution, continued informally throughout the colonial period.[32] The enterprise received official encouragement when the United States joined the ranks of nations in the early 1780s, and in 1827 consular officials were formally instructed to look out for plants "as may give promise, under proper cultivation, of flourishing and becoming useful."[33]

No late eighteenth-century public servant took a stronger personal interest in plant relocation than Thomas Jefferson. In other respects, he displayed a fervent biological nationalism and green *campanilismo,* notably his staunch defense of the merits of native wildlife in the face of European scientific scorn. But Jefferson the avid horticulturist was particularly proud of his cosmopolitan accomplishments in the field of plant introduction. In fact, when he compiled a list of his contributions to his nation, they overshadowed his better known public achievements. Referring to his procurement of a cask of upland rice from Africa and olive trees from Europe for South Carolina and Georgia in 1789/90, Jefferson announced that "the greatest service which can be rendered any country is to add a useful plant to its culture, especially a bread grain."[34]

The work of floral enrichment received a further boost in 1838 when the commissioner of patents secured congressional funding for the collection of useful seeds overseas and their free distribution at home. When the Department of Agriculture was established, in 1862, the introduction, testing, propagation, and distribution of new plants featured prominently in its organic act. The pursuit of foreign plants was institutionalized in 1898 when the Section for Foreign Seed and Plant Introduction was set up within the department.

Today, the only crops of significant commercial value native to the territory that became the United States are cranberry, blueberry, pecan nut, sugar maple, sunflower, and tobacco—a fact that offers eloquent testimony to the great service that has been duly rendered by a string of public-spirited Americans. With the exception of tobacco, the plantation staples of the southeastern states—rice, cotton, and sugar cane—are all naturalized exotics. A government radio broadcast in 1927 indicated that 90 percent of the foodstuffs on display in a typical American grocery store were of immigrant origin.[35] A note attached to the copy in the National Archives of a speech the secretary of agriculture, Henry A. Wallace, delivered in 1939 to mark the centennial of the government's plant exploration work announced that the United States was a "'melting pot' for plants and trees as well as for persons."[36]

The national origins of the vegetables raised in American backyards mirrored the crop profile on American farms. The author of a 1949 *National Geographic* article recounted an exchange with a friend, who told him: "So far, I've grown only American vegetables. . . . Next year I want to go in for foreign things." Sizing up the onions, lettuce, broccoli, carrots, spinach, eggplants, peas, and asparagus in his friend's vegetable patch, the author (principal horticulturist in the Department of Agriculture) replied, "The foreign plants in your garden outnumber the native ones by about five to one." Taken aback, the friend retorted, "What do you mean, 'foreign'?   I bought the seed for all these right here in town, and I've always eaten most of these things. They're common."[37] Having become so firmly embedded in American soil, their original identities had ceased to bear any meaning long ago.

No American public servant since Jefferson deserves more credit for transforming the foreign into the common than David G. Fairchild. In his capacity as agricultural explorer in charge at the Section for Foreign Seed and Plant Introduction from 1898 until 1928, Fairchild brought the navel orange to Florida and California from Brazil and oversaw the introduction of Italy's seedless grape and China's dry land pistachio. His most notable contributions, however, were the introduction of the Chinese soybean and—departing, for a moment, from this chapter's main focus on crops— the tree that became an essential prop of Washington, D.C.'s monumental landscape, adorning the Tidal Basin: the Japanese flowering cherry tree.[38] In his view, the introduction of such plants was as important as the invention of the telephone and typesetting machine. In 1933 the Committee on the Marcellus Hartley Fund of the National Academy of Sciences recognized Fairchild's role in enhancing the agricultural "wealth of the nation" by awarding him its Public Service Medal for distinguished services to the application of science to the public welfare.[39]

Fairchild was eager to dissociate his plant explorers from the popular image of the botanist as effete aesthete preoccupied with the self-indulgent scholarly study of wild plants of no practical benefit. In the context of agricultural expansion west of the Mississippi and the nation's new role as an imperial power in the more conventional sense after the Spanish-American War, he announced that

> the rapid development of any new country, is due to the discovery of soil and climatic conditions suited to the growth of introduced food plants, and seldom to the development of an endemic species. . . . So thoroughly has this fact been recognized by all colonizing nations that they have established botanic gardens in their new colonies, one important function of which is to secure and distribute exotic economic plants throughout the colony.[40]

The Fairchild section's initial activities concentrated on two areas: tropical plants suitable for introduction into recently acquired Caribbean and Pacific islands, and cereal grains for the arid and semiarid West, where Fairchild and his team criticized stubborn efforts to grow ill-suited crops from the temperate northeast United States and northwest Europe.[41] When the Bureau of Plant Industry was established in 1901, the Section for Foreign Seed and Plant Introduction become part of it and a major part at that.[42] Summarizing the Bureau's achievements on its tenth anniversary, its chief, Beverly Galloway, highlighted the contribution of hardy, drought-resistant grains and forage plants from the Russia steppes to farming on the northern Plains.[43] Farmers in Minnesota and North Dakota initially dismissed Russian durum wheats as fit only for goose feed, and millers rejected them as too hard. Yet these spring wheats turned out to be perfect for making pasta, for which demand was growing with increasing Italian immigration. Within fifteen years, along with hard red winter wheat from Karkhov (Ukraine), these Russian transplants had become the foundation for what Galloway hailed as a "new cereal empire in the North-west."[44]

The recognition that parts of the United States were more akin to lands beyond western and southern Europe in terms of climate, physical environment, and flora generated strong interest in Chinese as well as Russian plants. The floral resemblance between China and the American South was so close, according to the Bureau of Plant Industry's leading China expert, Frank N. Meyer, that somebody "suddenly transported from either region to the other would not always exactly realize where he was."[45] No wonder Fairchild was concerned lest American entry into World War I disrupt the Dutch immigrant's activities in China gathering "good things to eat and to look at."[46]

In 1923, to commemorate its twenty-fifth anniversary, Fairchild publicized his agency's attainments in a widely distributed special feature. Durum wheat was just one of many "useful foreign aliens."[47] Sudan grass from northern Africa (introduced 1909) proved an immediate success as an annual hay crop on the southern Plains and—with alfalfa from Turkestan— quickly secured a position as a major forage crop across the Southwest and Southeast. After 1920, cotton cultivation in the Southwest was based on an Egyptian strain. Rice cultivation was reinvigorated across the South and extended into southern Louisiana and Texas with upland strains from Japan. Meanwhile, dates from Algeria and avocados from Central America were transplanted to southern California.

Far from being an arcane activity of scant interest to the cotton-wearing and rice- and avocado-eating public, plant hunting by the Department of Agriculture's "plant explorers" during its early twentieth-century heyday appealed enormously to Americans fascinated by the encounter between representatives of white civilization and the non-Western world. Metropolitan journalists grafted the plant hunter—and the botany of desire—onto their nation's frontier and imperial narratives as Reid had done in a British context half a century earlier.[48] The glamorous coverage of top plant hunters like Meyer was typified by an article in the *Washington Post* titled "Millions Added to Nation's Wealth by Food Plants Sent by Agriculture Agents from World's Far Corners." To capture the heady tone of W. J. Voss's article, his voluble subheading is worth quoting in full: "Little-known corps of Washington experts, risking lives in savage lands, already has added scores of valuable fruits and vegetables to America's natural production— some that have brought riches cited—romance and thrilling incidents recalled by veterans stationed here—some of the tragedies service has suffered." Captions such as "Hardy Explorers Brave Perils of Wild Lands to Benefit America" lionized the descendants of Daniel Boone and Davy Crockett and reassured an anxious post-frontier nation that Americans had not gone soft.[49] In *Plant Immigrants,* the Department of Agriculture's official record of introductions, plant hunters described the exhilaration of bringing exotic fruits back from "a perfect virgin field untrodden by any botanist or agricultural explorer" (in this instance, the hills of northern Siam).[50] To early twentieth-century cosmopolitans, the possibilities of the beckoning floral frontier seemed boundless. Nor were there limits to how much the United States could absorb; its agricultural frontier remained very much open. As the botanist in charge of seed and plant introduction and development at the Bureau of Plant Industry announced in 1905, "There is always room for something better."[51]

DETERMINING DESIRABILITY

The open-minded and open-armed floral cosmopolitanism of early twentieth-century America had its human counterpart. The notion of cultural pluralism complemented the idea of natural pluralism. Horace Kallen, a Jewish immigrant from Germany who arrived in Boston as a youth, coined this phrase in a two-part article in *The Nation* (February 1915) that protested against calls for the abandonment of America's open door immigration policy and objected to the slogan "100 percent Americanism." In a book that popularized this new version of Americanism, the Harvard-educated philosopher explained that he wanted cultural pluralism to replace the melting pot ideal, which (unlike the green cosmopolitans, who applied the term more loosely) he rejected because it fused distinct identities into a composite nationality. Instead of amalgamation or assimilation to Anglo-American norms, Kallen celebrated difference and referred pointedly to the American *peoples*. Through "spontaneous self-rooting," he explained, cultural pluralism had made itself integral to the spacious American nation.[52]

Kallen's polycentric vision was a sociological expression of the new scientific ideas on race and culture recently promulgated by a fellow German Jewish immigrant, anthropologist Franz Boas. Boas immigrated to the United States in 1887 and acquired citizenship four years later. Appointed as Columbia University's first professor of anthropology in 1899, he occupied this post until 1937. *The Mind of Primitive Man*, which became his most influential work, was a robust rejection of the twin notions of racial purity and racial superiority that dominated the thinking of the American scientific establishment. Boas brushed aside the Anglo-Saxon American's fear that immigrants from southern and eastern Europe as well as other parts of the world would degrade the quality of the nation's stock through genetic pollution. Notions of a "mongrel nation" and the "impending submergence of the northwest European type," he insisted, were "imaginary."[53] The implications for existing notions of culture were no less far-reaching than for concepts of race, for the received wisdom hinged on the belief that only the "highest" race (Anglo-Saxons) possessed culture and was capable of cultural achievement.

These profoundly novel contentions were directly relevant to U.S. immigration policy. Boas had already deconstructed time-honored notions of culture and race in a report prepared on the ability of the "new" immigrants to assimilate American society for a congressional commission appointed in 1907 (the [Dillingham] Immigration Commission). *Changes in Bodily Form of Descendants of Immigrants,* published in 1911, argued for the plasticity of human types: environmental influences, specifically the experience of living in the United States, modified any inherited mental and physical traits, tending toward the production of a more generalized American type. Boas's contribution to the Immigration Commission's final report was directly at odds with the overall view the investigators reached, which endorsed the need for racially based immigration quotas. *Changes in Bodily Form* and *The*

Mind of Primitive Man thus served as the intellectual touchstones for the emerging cultural pluralist case against restriction.

The approach of Boas and Kallen flew in the face of a race-conscious immigration policy desirous of preserving the nation's "native" (i.e., Nordic/Anglo-Saxon/Teutonic) profile by guarding the gates more rigorously. A biology infused with an anthropological rationalization for racism based on Nordic preconceptions and presuppositions instructed that Nordics were more intelligent than the Europeans it identified as Alpine and Mediterranean as well as non-whites. According to this prevailing scientific orthodoxy, fundamental considerations of racial inheritance determined human characteristics. Even the most nurturing of environments could not mitigate bad or inferior traits.

One of the leading biologists steeped in these Nordic ideals during their halcyon days in the 1920s was Vernon Lyman Kellogg, who breezily dismissed Boas's emphasis on nurture in 1916. Trained as an entomologist, Kellogg held an academic post at Stanford University between 1894 and 1920, where he conducted breeding experiments with silk worms, beetles, and honeybees and published some of the pioneering research on population genetics. He also published popular and more technical works on evolution, Darwinism, and insects. His acclaimed textbook, *American Insects,* embraced all species found in the United States, which meant that troublesome overseas bugs such as the gypsy moth, Hessian fly, cottony cushion scale, San Jose scale, and elm leaf beetle were included as well as infamous invasive natives like the locust, canker worm, chinch bug, army worm, and Colorado beetle.[54]

During World War I, Kellogg entered government service, directing the American Commission for Relief in Belgium and the food relief program in Poland. In 1919 he helped found the National Research Council and served as its permanent secretary until 1931. Kellogg was also a prominent eugenicist; he belonged to the eugenics commission of the American Breeders Association and held office in the Save-the-Redwoods League. He publicized the currently influential application of biology to human society (witness also the Chicago school of sociology's stance) in an article on the selection of immigrants billed as "A Biologist Looks at the Immigrant." The effective study of a whole range of urgent human problems, Kellogg argued, required a new breed of biologist-sociologist to ensure that a robust knowledge of basic biological laws and the scientist's unparalleled dedication to the pursuit of unprejudiced facts was applied to societal questions.[55]

From the standpoint of self-styled "original" Americans like Kellogg, immigration was the most pressing of these problems. The National Research Council's Committee on Scientific Problems of Human Migration, part of the division of Anthropology and Psychology, formed in 1922 to finance racial studies supporting immigration restriction, issued a major report in 1924. And the region they identified as the least desirable source of immigrant was the Far East. The analogies the English sparrow's opponents drew suggest how readily anxiety about the "yellow peril" could be conflated with an avian "brown peril" and mixed up with responses to unwanted fauna. On the other hand, plant hunters like Meyer targeted East Asia as the most promising source of desirable floral immigrants. This highlights the danger of drawing convenient yet glib parallels between attitudes to human immigrants and the floral and faunal varieties. Botanical cosmopolitans were not necessarily cultural pluralists.

Meyer's main stomping ground was China. "So much of China has he successfully transplanted to this country," proclaimed Fairchild in a testimonial after his untimely death in June 1918 (he fell overboard and drowned in the Yangtze River).[56] Meyer's enthusiasm for Chinese plants was not matched, though, by fondness or respect for the Chinese themselves.[57] In his letters to Fairchild during the early 1900s, he often commented on tensions between Chinese and Westerners in the wake of the Boxer Rebellion. Given that the "Chink" population was growing at a terrific pace, Meyer reported to Fairchild (during a particularly tense phase in relations between Chinese and resident foreigners) that "the yellow peril is not such a chimera as some people think."[58] Writing for *Plant Immigrants* from the city of Jingmen in the province of Hubei during World War I, he forecast that "if the white races do not soon stop committing suicide, these people [sustained by the miracle food, the soybean] will, by . . . 2000, constitute one third of the earth's inhabitants."[59]

Meyer was no more fond of weeds than any midwestern farmer. Yet the worst weeds he encountered in China were of the human sort. His letters were laced with derogatory remarks conveyed in the language of plant breeding. "The whole race," he sermonized, "has become too weedy for lack of healthy contact with outside people during all of these past centuries." Since the "rabble and coolie classes" were breeding fast and indiscriminately, "crowding out the more intellectual classes," he could envisage no future for a country "alive with human weeds."[60]

Illustrations sometimes accompanied the inventories of introduced species that dominated the pages of *Plant Immigrants*. But not just plants were depicted. A picture of the Chinese persimmon, for example, was accompanied by a photograph of equally exotic-looking natives.[61] This twinning tactic also appealed to the popular media of the 1920s and 1930s. A picture of the chaulmoogra oil tree, which provided a widely touted cure for leprosy from the Burmese jungle, with two locals standing beside it appeared in *Florists Exchange*. The caption read, "A Potential Plant Emigrant to the U.S. in its Native Home."[62] The message was clear: We want your plants but we don't want you. Fairchild's strong objection to racial mixing— expressed in response to the "half castes" (a mix of Dutch and Singhalese) he encountered in Ceylon—can be set against his enthusiasm for plant hybridization. He knew it was impossible to restrict people to their original geographical locales. But he was determined to confine them to their "proper genetic spheres."[63]

At the zenith of government-sponsored plant immigration in the 1920s, a journalist commented that fruit and vegetable species arriving in the United States had been "uprooted from the old-world soil." A quarter-century later, historian Oscar Handlin used the same metaphor. The "new" immigrants of the twenties were the "uprooted" who were "replanted . . . in [the] strange ground" of northeast cities.[64] Handlin had no interest in foreign fruits and vegetables, not even the seeds the uprooted brought with them.[65] It is unlikely, though, that the journalist was oblivious to the human parallels and connotations. Nevertheless, we may still be inclined to write off references to the "uprooted" and the "plant immigrant" as weary clichés of the kind to be expected from the daily press and periodicals like *National Geographic*. Yet, as indicated, references to "plant immigrant" appear just as frequently in government reports and scientific writings. And, like those who admitted human immigrants, government entomologists divided immigrant plants into the categories of desirable and undesirable. Moreover, many analogies in newspapers and journals were neither facile nor merely figurative touches. They were designed to do a job—to sharpen an argument by blurring the distinction between human undesirables and other pests.

Fear of infection provided a particularly tangible link. To some, undesirable immigrants constituted a virus in themselves. In the article in which he entered the English sparrow controversy, Prescott F. Hall of the Immigration Restriction League compared attempts to confine the non-Nordic to its native "habitat" ("where its own multiplication in a limited area will, as with all organisms, eventually limit its numbers and therefore its influence") to efforts to "isolate bacterial invasions, and starve out the bacteria by limiting the area and amount of their food-supply."[66] More specific were the objections of Newton A. Fuessle, a Chicago journalist and novelist whose fiction works included *The Flail*, a story about a German immigrant's self-loathing and desperate efforts to acquire American traits. The imperative for tighter controls on plants to keep out piggybacking diseases and insects struck Fuessle as being comparable to efforts to protect public health by barring immigrants afflicted with scarlet fever, yellow fever, and smallpox.[67]

Immigration restrictionists had other viruses in mind too. One advocate of radical change in immigration policy was Cornelia James Cannon, a regular commentator on social affairs in leading journals such as *Harper's*, *Atlantic Monthly*, and *North American Review*. She was also the author of *Red Rust*, a best-selling novel about a Swedish immigrant family that settles on a farm in her home state of Minnesota. Cannon was gloomy about the prospects for democracy in the United States given the growing influx of those she deemed of inferior intelligence and overall quality to the nation's old stock. Army intelligence tests had confirmed, she contended, that Poles, Italians, and Russians were disproportionately represented among the less mentally able. Unfortunately, in her view, the American nation was far too eager to naturalize these disparate, incongruous strains of newcomers whose markedly inferior qualities would never improve, regardless of the length of their American residence. "As we keep out certain plants and animals lest they bring in physical disease," Cannon remarked in another article, "we are equally justified in excluding those who may bring in social disease." Her reasoning matched the thinking of those who recommended caution in view of the unexpected consequences of floral and faunal introductions. "Our civilization is complicated enough and full enough of obscure pitfalls of misunderstandings to make us wary about introducing any more unassimilable elements than we can help."[68] The people, plants, and animals she had in mind could never be of the United States—a legitimate part of its polity—as well as in the United States.

The sort of immigrants of whom Cannon approved were Nordics like the hard-working, ambitious, and readily assimilated Swedes she saluted in *Red Rust*. Matts Swenson, the novel's hero, despite a lack of formal schooling, is innately intelligent and, thanks to his can-do attitude ("Man did not need to accept the world as he found it"), becomes an accomplished plant breeder. His achievements are of value not only to his community of New Sweden but to the entire farming nation because, out of his desire to work for a "better America," he confronts and vanquishes the biggest scourge facing midwestern farmers: (nonnative) wheat rust. By crossing a hardy Swedish variety with a native wheat strain, Swenson hopes to engineer a vigorous, high-yielding hybrid for the inauspicious wheat-raising region of northern Minnesota, recently rehabilitated from its wilderness condition. Then, one July, the year after he has rescued his crop from grasshoppers, the dreaded red spots appear on the stalks and leaves of his hybrid grain, whose growth is immediately "arrested as if in response to a signal from some malign, invisible spirit." Mercifully, however, two stalks in his experimental plot that have already developed fully ripened ears are unaffected. Here is the perfect wheat, the veritable "king of wheats," immune to the depredations of this heart-breaking blight.[69]

The fundamental problem, as the restrictionists saw it, was that there were precious few Matt Swensons landing at Ellis Island. For many of them, unsavory immigrants were a fundamental biological problem regardless of their medical or social condition or intelligence level. Isaac Frederick Marcosson, a prolific author who wrote on a range of subjects (including the emergence of the petroleum industry and the company that owned the world's richest copper mine, in Butte, Montana), wanted to "weed out undesirables" from the "ignorant horde." To strengthen his case, he quoted an unnamed eugenicist who contrasted lackadaisical policy toward immigrants from southern and eastern Europe with the tight legislation governing livestock importation. He concluded that "we should take the same care to secure high quality in our human breeding stock."[70]

Also struck by the difference between policies applied to people and those pertaining to other organisms was journalist W. J. Voss. His lengthy 1922 *Washington Post* article on plant exploration and plant explorers (cited earlier) was shaped by the introduction a few months earlier of the first numerical quotas based on national origin. These quotas were set to privilege areas that had contributed the nation's "old stock" that now called itself the nation's native stock. Voss's opening gambit was to focus attention on the "one part of the Federal machinery of government that doesn't care a whit about immigration restrictions and limitations of 3 per cent on newcomers to these shores."[71] The first explanation he offered as to why this particular branch of government was out of line with the new ethos of restriction was that "these visitors to America are not yet coming in such great numbers that their entrance needs to be limited." The real reason, though, was that the immigrants he was writing about were plants. And the branch of the federal government he had in mind was the Office of Foreign Seed and Plant Introduction.[72]

"Department of Agriculture, Office of Foreign Plant Introduction, Washington, DC, USA." This was the address written on the neatly sewed cotton packages which, heaped into a pile, were pictured in *Plant Immigrants* in 1923. Carefully bundled in sphagnum moss, waxed paper, and sheets of newspaper, the plant specimens these packages contained were pronounced "ready to start for the land of their adoption," a journey which, in the case of a shipment from Ecuador containing potato tubers and cuttings of papaya and black cherry, could take over a month.[73] Plant and human immigrants shared more, however, than just an arduous journey. Contrary to Voss's observations, plants, like people, were also subjected to ever more exacting inspection.

In addition to those barred on racial and national grounds, a succession of restrictive statutes (since 1875) had disqualified various classes of immigrant on social, political, moral, and medical grounds. The efficacy of these statutes depended on the quality of inspection. During his presidency, Theodore Roosevelt sought to procure a "higher grade of our common citizenship" by revamping U.S. Public Health Service inspection procedures at New York City's Ellis Island, the major port of entry since 1892.[74] He increased the number of medical personnel and the range of tests they carried out. Touring Ellis Island toward the end of Roosevelt's presidency,

Henry James noted that the immigrant was "marshalled, herded, divided, subdivided, sorted, shifted, searched, fumigated."[75]

Though these safeguards were designed to separate the "sound and desirable" from the "unsound and undesirable," a doctor at Ellis Island explained that the "patriotic duty" of working for a "cleaner and better" America was made more difficult by what had become the predominant immigrant type by 1913—one that lived "on a low plane."[76] Markedly inferior "hordes" had replaced the "best of Europe's blood" in the "land of the alien."[77] The 1917 Immigration Act sought to reverse a continuing decline in immigrant quality by extending the list of excluded medical, moral, and social categories and banning all southeast Asians not already specifically excluded. Together with more stringent inspections facilitated by dramatically curtailed immigration during World War I, supporters credited the 1917 act with substantially reducing the entry of "defective aliens." Nevertheless, the American Genetic Association's immigration committee, certain that postwar immigration from war-torn Europe would rebound to prewar levels at the very least, urged additional legislation on openly eugenic grounds.[78]

Customs inspectors sometimes intercepted plants, seeds, and fruit that immigrants tried to smuggle inside loaves of bread.[79] The stricter examination of plants themselves, however, matched the progressively tighter regulation of human immigrants between the 1880s and the early 1920s. Investigating (well before "9/11") the American tradition of exaggerating the nation's vulnerability to foreign attack, John A. Thompson referred to an "exotic flowering of alarmism."[80] Plant pests were far from his mind. Writing a month before the United States declared war on Germany, however, an economic zoologist had interpreted American vulnerability to outside assault in broad fashion. J. G. Sanders, an entomologist with the Bureau of Plant Industry, was one of the scientists who inspected the original shipment of Japanese cherry trees when they arrived in Washington, D.C. He remained on high alert, urging a wholesale embargo on foreign plants and plant products because "unknown dangers," liable to run amok when liberated from the usual domestic restraints, "lurk in every shipment of plants to America."[81] By the early 1920s, government botanists in the business of plant introduction were also much more sensitive to the potential risks from the diseases and insects that often accompanied plants than they had been when introduction was institutionalized in the late 1890s.

A century later, environmentalists and invasion biologists who fret over the impact of troublesome introductions on native species often complain that only those unruly nonnatives that jeopardize farming interests by attacking domesticated plants have ever been taken seriously. Early twentieth-century unease was undeniably driven by economic considerations. Nonetheless, this threat to agricultural production prompted some of the first expressions of concern over the invasiveness of certain alien biota and galvanized some of the earliest remedial efforts.

SHUTTING THE DOOR ON PLANT PLUNDERERS

Recently, the American public has become familiar with rogues' galleries of nonnative nonhumans. Playing on the outlaw's role in the region's history and folklore, the Bureau of Land Management publicizes the top ten "most wanted weeds" of the western rangelands it manages. Meanwhile, the Nature Conservancy distributes "least wanted lists" of invasive insects and plants injurious to wildlands (the nation's "meanest environmental scoundrels"). "Not Wanted: Zebra Mussel Outlaws" is the headline for these "threats to the West" announced by the State of California's Department of Water Resources, which calls on members of the public to volunteer for a posse. Yet these depictions were anticipated by early twentieth-century roll calls of "plant plunderers" such as the Hessian fly, gypsy moth, cottony-cushion scale, Japanese beetle, and boll weevil.

Various exotic plant pests had been well established in the States for more than a century. The codling moth (from the proverbial "worm in the apple"), bud moth, and pear slug—whose collective damage to orchards overshadowed the losses stemming from the five fruit flies native to the United States—had been arriving inadvertently since early colonial days.[82] The Hessian fly, the most notorious of grain pests, was first spotted in fields near New York City in the late 1770s. This tiny midge (also known as the gall gnat) reputedly arrived in the wheat straw bedding of troop ships bringing George III's (equally nasty) Hessian mercenaries to quash American revolt, prompting Jefferson's quest for European strains of resistant wheat in 1803.[83] In 1900 it inflicted losses valued at $100 million on the nation's wheat crop; it also infested barley, rye, and oats. Resentment against this long-resident foreigner and other harmful insects, regardless of nationality, boiled over soon after entry into the war. Leading entomologist Stephen Forbes insisted that the United States was already under occupation by fifty billion allies of the kaiser. Insofar as their impact on food production weakened the American war effort, the Hessian fly was demonstrably "still Hessian," and the widely distributed native chinch bug and army worm were effectively "pro-German."[84]

Since the mid-nineteenth century, however, the number of arriving pests had increased with the growing popularity of acclimatization, expanding mercantile relations, and improved transportation methods that multiplied the opportunities for "free travel."[85] The first horror story featured the foliage-munching gypsy moth *(Lymantria dispar),* accidentally released in Medford, a Boston suburb, in 1869, by a French immigrant. With the United States facing a cotton shortage after the Civil War, Etienne Leopold

Trouvelot (an amateur entomologist and astronomer as well as an illustrator) wanted to plug the gap with silk. Because the common American variety of silkworm did not relish cooler climes, he aimed to produce a tougher silkworm, which would eventually replace the mulberry silkworm (*Bombyx mori*), by crossbreeding it with gypsy moths imported from France.[86] Fletcher Osgood, one the English sparrow's leading critics in New England, attributed the modest rate of initial expansion of these "dark and bristly invaders" partly to the sterling work of insectivorous native birds not yet "mobbed out by the English sparrow." But the gypsy moth's proliferation eventually gathered pace, the "terror" first striking the Medford area twenty years after their original escape (Trouvelot having since returned to France).[87] Contemporary reports echoed lurid accounts of the canker worm's depredations forty years earlier. The pest's caterpillar larvae, recorded a Medford resident in the summer of 1889, hung "so thick on the trees that they were stuck together like cold macaroni." Another eyewitness recalled the "constant shower of excrement" that rained down from the trees. There were so many of them, remembered a horrified resident, that "one could slide on the crushed bodies on the sidewalks."[88]

No equivalent to the English sparrow was available for an experiment in biological control. Instead, the Commonwealth of Massachusetts instigated the first state-sanctioned war of extermination against an alien creature.[89] A ten-year, $1.2 million campaign was launched in 1890 to rid Massachusetts of a nonnative species which, like many of its fellow invaders, was relatively innocuous in its homelands. Though the multipronged physical and chemical assault appeared successful at first, the gypsy moth's movements proved impossible to contain. Like the English sparrow, the moth sometimes traveled under its own steam. However, just as the bird had sometimes hitched a ride in boxcars, the moth also covered considerable distances in its caterpillar form by dropping onto passing vehicles. By 1912 this "winged calamity" had spread to neighboring Vermont and eventually reached New York State, where its larvae embarked on a spree of destruction that has become a regular feature of eastern woodlands.[90]

Galloway noticed that alien insects, restrained at home by predators and competitors, "may after introduction here sweep like fire through our fields or through our forests."[91] Yet not all injurious insects were nonnative. Swarms of grasshoppers descended from their homelands farther west in the foothills of the Rockies like a biblical plague on ripening wheat in Minnesota in the early 1870s. The government entomologist, Charles Valentine Riley (who had revealed in the late 1880s that the English sparrow ate hardly any noxious exotic insects, one of which was the elm-leaf beetle [*Galerucella luteola*], a quarter-inch, reddish yellow fiend that skeletonized leaves as efficiently as the native canker worm), explained that "armies" of this "ravenous horde" swept "clean a field quicker than would a whole herd of hungry steers" during the worst invasions on record, in 1874. Some authorities contended that the American locust (as the grasshopper was also known) was descended from its Old World cousin, having immigrated across the Bering land bridge with the first Americans. Riley, though, insisted that it was a truly indigenous American.[92] So did Kellogg.

The Colorado (potato) beetle *(Leptinotarsa decemlineata)* was another homegrown pest whose nefarious exploits were openly couched in terms of invasion. Before miners brought potato cultivation to the zebra-striped beetle's traditional territory in the Southwest when they flocked to gold strikes in the Colorado Rockies in the late 1850s, it subsisted on the wild solanum (sand or buffalo bur). But on encountering the cultivated variety, the beetle took a shine to it and began a remorseless eastward march across the plains, reaching the Atlantic within fifteen years (1874).[93] Only the English sparrow, some believed, was a greater "outlaw."[94] By general consensus, however, the worst native scourge during the early 1880s was the chinch bug, a "terror" spreading eastward and northward from the South and West, attacking the roots of fodder grasses and crops.[95] As New York's state entomologist warned, invading armies of this one-sixth-inch-long, black-and-white beetle could sweep over and utterly destroy a wheat or corn field in two or three days.[96] The chinch bug remained invincible. Despite Matts Swenson's triumph against wheat rust, the Midwest's crop scientists could not rest on their laurels. Cannon concluded her novel *Red Rust* on a challenging note: other enemies remained at large, notably the chinch bug.[97]

Notwithstanding this formidable array of ruinous native pests, which Kellogg described as "hateful," the *American Cultivator* concluded that "most noxious insects come from foreign countries."[98] By the 1890s attention was firmly focused on the "foreign-born." Leland O. Howard, chief of the Department of Agriculture's Division/Bureau of Entomology between 1894 and 1927, reckoned that thirty-seven of the seventy-three pests of "prime economic importance" had been introduced, and another six were of "doubtful origin." He identified the blossoming trade in ornamental plants, an offshoot of the post-1865 consumer spending boom, as the likeliest entry route.[99] For quarantine advocates like Howard, another scale insect, of oriental origin and reputedly arriving with Chinese flowering peach trees, underscored the recklessness of the cosmopolitan ethos. First detected in the early 1880s on the San Jose, California, property of an ardent tree importer (by Kellogg's closest colleague at Stanford, John Henry Comstock), the "San Jose" scale began its eastward march in the 1890s.[100] San Jose's citizenry resented the speed with which the bug's common name spread, bringing the town into disrepute. Kellogg also pronounced it "ill-named." *Aspidiotus perniciosus,* in his view, should have been called "pernicious scale" or "Oriental scale." Once again, the "yellow peril" served as a point of orientation. In 1915, Forbes characterized the scale's onslaught as a Japanese invasion "far more successful, and probably more destructive also, than any which Japan could possibly make by means of dreadnoughts and armies of little brown men."[101]

American flora succumbed to foreign pests like San Jose scale in much the same way that the continent's indigenous peoples had capitulated to pathogens like smallpox: lack of exposure translated into lack of resistance to what Crosby termed virgin soil epidemics. Predictive powers were weak, however. The effects of pathogens were understood only after the fact, when a rearguard action, at most, could be fought.

In 1904 the most notorious plant disease in American history was diagnosed among the Bronx Zoo's American chestnuts. Contemporaries traced the infection to a batch of Japanese chestnuts imported in the 1890s to round out a private collection of the chestnuts of the world.[102] Regardless of individual responsibility, by the mid-1920s, when this fungal pathogen had destroyed virtually all New York's and Pennsylvania's native chestnuts, the blight had come to epitomize the "menace" of introduced plant disease.[103]

A flurry of other plant pests arrived thick and fast in chestnut blight's wake. According to one authority, the European corn borer *(Ostrinia nubilalis)* had gained entry around 1910 in hemp imported for a rope walk near Boston.[104] Further specimens arrived in bales of corn stalks New England broom makers imported from Italy.[105] By 1923 all broomcorn was steam-sterilized on arrival, and there was a total ban on summertime entry at some ports. The moth spread westward regardless, launching a major incursion into the American corn belt in 1926.[106]

Though the competition was stiff, the plant pest that many considered the most obnoxious entrant after chestnut blight was the Japanese (fruit) beetle, first detected in 1916 at a New Jersey nursery. Previously restricted to the Japanese archipelago, where it was rarely thought of as a pest, this beetle probably entered as a grub in the rootballs of Japanese iris.[107] As well as ruining many fruits, in the grub and adult stages it decimated ornamental shrubs, roses, shade trees, and flowers of all sorts as well as major vegetable crops.[108] Appearing before a congressional appropriations committee in 1919 to request additional funding for control measures, Howard described it as "very striking in its oriental appearance," quite unlike any American beetle.[109] In a tirade calculated to whip up public fear and loathing of "the shadowy menace of innumerable slinking foes to our plants that have not yet crept in," but which were "lying in wait" in unknown foreign places for the "opportunity to attack American fields and orchards," Fuessle dubbed the Japanese beetle "the real yellow peril."[110] By the end of 1923, this powerful flier had left a swathe of devastation across 2,500 square miles of New Jersey and Pennsylvania.

The Japanese beetle also left its mark on lawns. Freshly hatched grubs devastated rootlets so extensively that withered turf could apparently be rolled up by hand like a carpet. The most infamous turf destroyer, however, was the larva of the Asiatic (Oriental) beetle, first spotted at a nursery near New Haven, Connecticut, in 1920.[111] Another Far Eastern pest that entomologists reckoned a quarantine policy could have kept at bay was citrus canker, a bacteria that slipped into the Gulf states with Japanese nursery stock circa 1910.[112] This pathogen produces lesions on fruits, twigs, and leaves that can result in defoliation, points of access for rot fungi, and "premature fruit drop," not to mention cosmetic damage.[113] Highly susceptible citrus groves in Florida were incinerated in a bid to contain the infestation that had caused land values to plummet and engendered the fear that the state's orchards would meet the same fate as the Northeast's chestnut forests.[114] Even when they recognized that this influx of pests simply mirrored the predominant flow of people and commerce, those who pondered the havoc they wrought resented the corresponding incongruity in the "accidental interchange" of insect pests between Eurasia and America.[115]

Nevertheless, not every dreaded foreign insect was Eurasian. Having rested unnoticed for centuries in its Guatemalan mountain home, the most infamous crop pest in American history arrived circa 1894. As irrigated agriculture in the Southwest eliminated the arid lands that had served as a natural barrier to its northward spread, the boll weevil crossed the Rio Grande. Also thriving on narrow-row planting and heavy doses of fertilizer, the beetle had infested most of the southern cotton belt by the 1920s.

Government resolve to curb the depredations of other alien insects was strengthened by the wartime need to maximize food production. In 1916 an outbreak of grain rust extracted losses of 180 million bushels on spring wheat; Cannon evoked the devastating results for rural communities in *Red Rust*. Government plant pathologists linked grain rust (also known as black stem rust) to leaf rust on European barberry, a shrub the first English colonists had brought to New England for hedges. Federal authorities mobilized an ambitious eradication program in partnership with thirteen north-central states in 1918. By 1926 more than twelve million bushes had been poisoned with salt, kerosene, and sodium arsenite or simply uprooted; thousands of schoolchildren participated in this foretaste of today's "weed war" initiatives.[116]

Fighting these assorted plant pests (especially insects) was elevated to a solemn and urgent patriotic duty in a string of pronouncements by government entomologists and in numerous exhortative newspaper and magazine articles.[117] "No tribute levied by pirates or robber barons ever approached this sum in magnitude," exclaimed a contributor to the *Literary Digest* in 1923 with reference to the toll exacted by the gypsy moth, Hessian fly, Japanese beetle, European corn borer, and assorted scale insects. In fact, raiding by these "crop criminals" was reckoned to pose a more insuperable challenge than that formerly presented by notorious "human plunderers" like the Barbary pirates of North Africa, who preyed with impunity on American shipping in the Mediterranean in the late eighteenth and early nineteenth centuries.[118]

Advocates of precautionary measures chided government officials and the public for their tardiness, compared to their counterparts in other countries, in waking up to the menace these pests posed. It was increasingly unrealistic, they contended, to expect to be able to enjoy the benefits of new foreign plants without encountering these associated dangers. If national quarantine measures had been imposed a few decades earlier, contended economic botanist George H. Dacy in 1923, many pests firmly ensconced as "permanent American citizens" would have been denied entry.[119]

Echoing resentful contemporary commentators who felt that the United States was being unduly victimized by Old World pests, historian Alfred Crosby asserted in the 1980s that Europe had suffered remarkably little from biotic exchanges.[120] Yet the first significant action against nonnative pests at a national level had been taken by Europeans in response to the exploits of two American insects. After discovering a Colorado beetle infestation in a shipment of potatoes from the United States, Germany barred American potatoes in 1875. It was the arrival of an American vine louse, however, that provoked the most stringent measures. Phylloxera is barely a twenty-fifth of an inch in length when full grown, and then only visible if the vine roots were dug out at the height of the growing season. The tiny aphid was first detected in the Bordeaux region in 1859. By 1884 it had crippled over a third of French vineyards, and the rest were all affected to some degree.[121] The bug (which worked slowly, taking two to three years to kill off a vine completely) penetrated German vineyards in 1874 and by 1890 had spread as far east as Russia's Crimea. The first official reaction in France and Germany was to prohibit further imports of American vine stocks.[122] Then Germany set up a Reich Phylloxera Commission, a paramilitary offensive that Sarah Jansen characterized as "extermination squads . . . turning vineyards into scorched wasteland."[123]

Having visited blighted French vineyards in 1871, Riley certified the vine louse's American identity. The future chief entomologist of the United States (1878–79 and 1881–94) also demonstrated that American vintners' minimal success with European rootstocks was due to the latter's lack of resistance to "this insidious little root-louse." The analogy with native peoples suddenly confronted by European diseases was at the forefront of Riley's mind. "Many diseases that are comparatively harmless among civilized nations," he reflected, "acquire greater virulency and play fearful havoc when introduced among savage or hitherto uncontaminated peoples." Though the roles of victims and perpetrators were reversed in this instance, the basic principle remained the same. Through long exposure to this "microscopic plague," many American grape varieties had acquired relative immunity to damage from a louse whose population was also contained by various natural enemies. (Diseased tissue on native roots was confined to the annually renewed bark.) California's vineyards, founded on European rootstocks, proved equally vulnerable when phylloxera turned up there with French rootstocks in the 1880s.[124] For once, it was the turn of a European plant to assume the role of naïve victim.

Riley's solution to the European vineyard crisis was a new, resilient generation of stocks produced by grafting European vines onto American rootstocks.[125] This ultimately proved to be the salvation (in California too), but it was resisted by powerful French and German interests who clung to a policy of attempted eradication. Big French growers, worried about loss of reputation if their renowned wines became Americanized, tried to thwart the grafting proposal that the "Americanists" supported. The large concerns preferred insecticides (which small growers could ill afford) to "Americans."[126] Grafting offended French notions of national purity and ran up against deep-seated notions of *terroir* rooted in a belief in the fundamental unsuitability of nonnative flora to local conditions.

Jansen believes that Germany's anti-phylloxera campaign also served as a psychological rallying point for fears concerning "alien" threats to national integrity, which included the spreading pestilence of Americanization. American origins thus rendered the louse particularly terrible, regardless of any Anglo-Saxon racial traits Germans shared with millions of Americans (and the United States' popularity as a destination for German emigrants). In the later nineteenth century, the United States symbolized the new, transnational mass culture of lowbrow, homogenizing modernism whose vulgarity, invasive vigor, and seductiveness appalled Europe's cultural establishment.[127]

The European reaction to phylloxera was not an isolated incident. In 1898, Germany banned American fruit in response to San Jose scale's progress across the United States—the first stage in what became effectively a pan-European embargo (of varying degrees of severity) on all or certain types of American fruit. Various French and British colonies followed suit. So did thirty-five American states. Pressure from horticultural interests in California secured a quarantine law in 1881 for all plants and fruits entering the state.[128] By 1908 nearly forty states had enacted similar laws, among them Illinois.[129] The aim, explained Stephen Forbes, Illinois chief entomologist, in humanizing language conditioned by the outbreak of the war, was to ensure that "no indifferent noncombatant may give aid and comfort to the enemy" (i.e., "food and lodgment on one's premises").[130]

Meanwhile, in 1906, at the federal level, the Bureau of Entomology had initiated the strict inspection—and fumigation and destruction when necessary—of all plants imported under the Department of Agriculture's auspices. Given that the Bureau of Plant Industry was the nation's leading importer of plant materials, this was a significant advance. Under this authority, government entomologists and mycologists subjected two thousand ornamental cherry trees that arrived by train from Seattle to rigorous inspection in January 1910. This consignment was a gift (urged by Fairchild) from the city fathers of Tokyo to their counterparts in Washington, D.C. "Incorporating exemplars of oriental horticulture into the landscape of official Washington," Pauly explains, was intended to provide "symbolic compensation" for the recent American ruling (the so-called Gentleman's Agreement) that no more Japanese immigrants would be admitted.[131] But scientists supervised by the Bureau of Entomology's chief and assistant chief, L. O. Howard and Charles L. Marlatt, detected crown gall in 45 percent of the specimens, and the roots were generally infected with fungous mycelium. Moreover, five trees had been girdled by the fungus *Pestalozzia (Pestalotia)*, and it was not known whether this was an "indigenous" or exotic species (indeed, it has still not been positively identified).[132] The inspectors also found root gall worm and various scale insects and wood borers. This created an extremely delicate diplomatic situation in early 1910. In an official communication to the Japanese ambassador, secretary of state Philander Knox explained that Howard and Marlatt had "no choice but the painful duty" of ordering immediate incineration (on the Mall) because of the tremendous losses alien insects and plant diseases had already imposed on American trees and crops.[133]

Philip J. Pauly, a historian of science, wishes to highlight—as a corrective to recent high levels of enthusiasm for native species in the United States—the wider sociocultural context of "illiberal prejudices" that shaped early twentieth-century attitudes toward indigenous and exotic biota. He argues that Marlatt, the leading proponent of national quarantine measures, seized on the diseased cherry trees as a golden opportunity to press for legislation.[134] Whatever his political agenda and personal views, Marlatt's report to secretary of agriculture James Wilson was certainly grounded in practical objections.[135] The problem, Marlatt explained, stemmed largely from the age and size of the trees. Young ones would have been less risky.[136]

Daniel Simberloff, an American biologist specializing in the study of biotic invasions, has challenged Pauly's perspective on the cherry tree incident.[137] He argues that Pauly's underlying thesis—that public and scientific attitudes toward nonindigenous species were "heavily colored by ethnic prejudices"—while suggestive, is largely unproved.[138] My investigations in this chapter and the preceding one on imported birds serve to corroborate the general thrust of Pauly's claims—reiterated in his rejoinder to Simberloff—that the contemporary climate of opinion regarding immigrants influenced public attitudes toward harmful exotics in the late nineteenth and early twentieth centuries.[139] How strongly attitudes to immigrants influenced responses to the likes of the English sparrow and the

Japanese beetle is much harder to judge.[140] And, like Simberloff, I wonder whether Pauly overstates the extent to which scientists as well as lay persons were affected by racial neuroses and ethnic bias.

After all, Japanese officials responded to the rejection of the first shipment of cherry trees by following Marlatt's advice closely. They ensured that the trees for the second shipment were carefully cultivated and youthful specimens that were scrupulously inspected and fumigated prior to export. That Marlatt did not repeat his protest suggests that his objections to the initial gift may have been more mundane than Pauly allows. Nativism shaped the *expression* of attitudes to floral and faunal immigrants, but it was by no means responsible for the attitudes themselves (and nativism certainly did not rely for its virulence on the presence of pesky nonhuman immigrants like the English sparrow and the Japanese beetle). Pauly's approach also diverts our attention from a range of issues that complicate the picture and undermine the juxtaposition of ecological cosmopolitans and advocates of ecological independence: the cosmopolitan's appreciation of native species, the ability of the native species champion to discriminate between harmful nonnatives and other immigrant species, and, not least, the material (economic and ecological) grounds for objecting to certain nonnative species.

Even at a time of widespread antipathy toward certain immigrant groups, there are limits to the meaningful association between opposition to plant pests and prejudice against people. Looking at attitudes to Mexican immigrants of various sorts enhances our appreciation of these boundaries. The headaches the boll weevil gave American cotton growers were compounded after 1917 by those inflicted by the pink boll worm. Probably native to India, this moth arrived in Texas in 1915 in a Mexican shipment of Egyptian cottonseed. The Europe-bound cargo was scattered during a storm while awaiting transshipment in Galveston. In an attempt to bring deliverance from weevil evil, all railroad boxcars potentially contaminated with cottonseed from Mexico and all raw cotton headed for Texan crushing mills was intercepted at the border during the late 1910s and throughout the 1920s. At the five main border stations, boxcars were disinfected in fumigation sheds big enough to hold several freight cars. Despite these measures, Marlatt emphasized the standing threat of further insect invasions represented by the "uncontrolled entry" of laborers headed for Texan cotton districts. So migrants' mattresses, pillows, and quilts—all stuffed with raw cotton—were fumigated too.[141] Entrants themselves were bathed—sometimes in gasoline—and their clothes disinfected.

Charles Goethe, the prominent California conservationist and eugenicist, had hitched his objections to Mexicans in southern California to his hostility to the presence of English sparrows. And comparisons between the boll weevil and Mexican immigrants commended themselves to immigration restrictionists like the illustrious retired soldier, Frederick Russell

Burnham. Burnham had begun his military career on the Arizona frontier, serving under Kit Carson and John C. Fremont and building a peerless reputation as a scout in the Indian Wars of the Southwest. Then he placed his scouting talents at the disposal of British forces in southern Africa before and during the Boer War (receiving the rank of major in the British army). Burnham became a close friend and mentor of Robert Baden-Powell and was pivotal in the American Boy Scout movement. An avid conservationist too, he supported the conservation program of his friends Theodore Roosevelt and Gifford Pinchot, was a founding member of the Save-the-Redwoods League, campaigned for state parks in California, and lobbied for bighorn sheep reserves in Arizona. By the late 1920s, Burnham was nearly seventy and living in Los Angeles; he had owned a cattle ranch at Three Rivers, the southern gateway to Sequoia National Park, since 1908.[142] "Every year, like that other importation from Mexico, the boll-weevil," he lamented in an essay contributed to a collection coedited by his close friend Madison Grant, "this creeping blight [Mexican immigration] goes further afield and robs more of our own people of the chance to live on a civilized plane."[143]

No matter how indignant some Californians felt about Mexican immigration, though, it was not regarded as an urgent national problem.[144] Moreover, given the relative paucity in California—as elsewhere in the Southwest—of intruding creatures from south of the border, the scope for faunal analogies was restricted. And even the exceptions—the beaver and muskrat—are doubtful examples of invasive nonnatives.

A species migration from Lower (Baja) California and Sonora was stimulated when the foundations of an hydraulic empire were dug out in southern California's Imperial Valley during the 1910s. Irrigation channels attracted beaver and muskrat, whose infestation of 300 miles of mainline and feeder canals undermined their banks and breached levees.[145] These water-loving rodents also displaced rodents such as the wood rat and kangaroo rat, which prefer dry lands. But, as a University of California zoologist reflected, the northward-moving Sonora beaver (a recognized subspecies) and (pallid) muskrat of the Colorado Delta "do not need passports in crossing the International Boundary."[146] Animal passports bearing information about vaccinations are increasingly common for cats and dogs traveling across borders with their owners (the European Union introduced one for member countries in 2004). Even if there had been such a thing as a passport requirement or immigration papers for wild animals in the 1920s, however, it is by no means clear that the beaver and muskrat leaving Mexico for the United States would have required this documentation. A passport was certainly superfluous on biological grounds. The Sonora beaver had been heavily trapped on the American side, and the muskrat's California population was hitherto confined to a few small pockets along the Colorado and on the eastern slopes of the Sierra Nevada. But both species were endemic ("native") to both sides of the border. In terms of species distribution, this particular national frontier has little meaning. The beaver and the muskrat that inhabit the U.S. Southwest and northwestern Mexico highlight once more the arbitrariness of definitions of native and alien species based on the political criterion of national units.

The low profile of troublesome animals from other parts of the Americas among the fauna in the United States at this time was complemented by the relative absence of unwanted plants from the rest of the Western Hemisphere. According to official figures for 1895, of 108 foreign weeds identified as particularly problematic in the United States, only fifteen originated in Mexico or points farther south. Besides, their impact was largely restricted to the states on the Gulf of Mexico, where weeds from Europe were equally prevalent.[147] The situation regarding the national origin of insects was similar, nationally and regionally. And these European plant and insect pests were the ones that provoked further government action. These measures did not command universal support, though. Some parties considered the cure far worse than the disease.

THE MENACE OF PLANT QUARANTINES

In 1909, state inspectors in New York discovered a brood of notorious defoliators—European brown-tail moths—in shipments of fruit seedlings and roses from France. In response, the Bureau of Entomology entered into a series of voluntary agreements with state authorities for the inspection of commercial plant imports not covered by existing quarantines; these applied only to the Department of Agriculture's importations. The United States remained the only major nation without national legislative protections, which, according to Marlatt, turned it into the "dumping ground for the plant refuse of other countries." Deploying imagery identical to—and interchangeable with—the imagery that saturated corresponding debates about human entrants as the rate of arrival swiftly climbed back to prewar levels by 1921, he stressed that "unwelcome immigrants" such as the boll weevil, San Jose scale, Japanese beetle, brown-tail moth, and European corn borer had taken advantage of this excessive "freedom of entry." Though resigned to "these undesirable immigrants we must lodge and board forever," he was determined to "shut the doors if we can to their brothers and sisters and cousins and aunts!"[148]

The Plant Quarantine Act of 1912 finally authorized a national policy to "ward off foreign scourges."[149] To enforce measures against "any tree, plant, or fruit disease or any injurious insect new or not theretofore widely prevalent or distributed within and throughout the United States" (to quote its congressional sponsors), the act set up the Federal Horticultural Board under Marlatt's chairmanship.[150] Initial policing efforts were directed at detecting "bad bugs from overseas" (to quote *Illustrated World*) prior to departure. Under the terms of the act, nursery stock could be imported only from countries that operated an inspection service.[151] An additional safeguard was reinspection of packing case materials and storage holds by federal officials ("plant disease policemen") at ports of entry.[152] Nevertheless, insects and plant diseases continued to enter via nursery stock, even from the two exporting countries with the best inspection services. Between 1912 and 1919, 148 and 245 different kinds of noxious insect—many entirely new—were intercepted on stock from Holland and France, respectively.

The thirty-seventh quarantine measure applied since 1912 is the best known. Plant Quarantine Number 37 (PQN37, effective June 1919) extended permit requirements and other regulations to the private importation of a whole range of horticultural and ornamental plant materials. Where it really broke the mold, however, was in excluding entire categories of materials known as "florists' stock." These could now be legally imported only through the Department of Agriculture, whose stated aim was the "practical exclusion of all stock not absolutely essential to the [nation's] horticultural, floricultural and forestry needs."[153]

Marlatt and his fellow entomologists had fought hard for PQN37, insisting that "our plants" deserved the same protection American people and livestock enjoyed from their human and faunal counterparts. Galloway, however, criticized it as "non-specific and sweeping."[154] He and his colleagues at the Bureau of Plant Industry supported the inspection and surveillance measures embodied in the previous thirty-six quarantines but balked at the thirty-seventh's replacement of the principle of selection by the principle of exclusion. They also perceived a bias against non-European plants. Galloway felt that Marlatt's call for the total exclusion of balled plants from Asia and Africa was unwarranted without the same unconditional ban on European plants.[155]

This clash between botanists and entomologists, increasingly embedded in separate professional and institutional spheres, was reflected in Frank Meyer's response to the insect invasions that aroused so much anger during the 1910s. Since the spring of 1907, at Fairchild's request, he had been making a note of the insect pests attached to his plant quarry.[156] But he did not really think it was the plant explorer's job to worry about incidentals like potentially perilous insects. Nor was he equipped to detect them. "Upon reading that some of these pests are very dangerous," Meyer wrote in 1917 to the acting explorer in charge at the Division of Plant Exploration and Introduction, "I cannot help but think what millions of harmful creatures must have been introduced during all these years, on live plants, that must have come from the Orient."[157] He was mightily relieved that he had accomplished so much before the imposition of draconian regulations.[158]

Meyer altered his mode of operation reluctantly, poking fun at what he saw as the paranoid mood fostered by overzealous entomologists who were cramping his style. "Good heavens! What are we going to do nowadays?" he asked Fairchild in 1917 with reference to the bamboo mite infesting the bamboo plantation at Brooksville agricultural station in western Florida. "I find that on account of these constant findings of new diseases, my aspect toward looking at plants is undergoing a radical change. Instead of seeing beauty first, I do not dare to do it, but look first for parasitic pests."[159]

Anxiety over alien intrusion and the narrow outlook of *campanilismo* pervaded other, seemingly unrelated aspects of American life during the postwar decade. Despite its popular image as the go-getting, risk-taking, modernizing "jazz age," defined by Model-T Fords, flappers, F. Scott Fitzgerald's *The Great Gatsby*, bathtub gin, daring music, risqué movies, and extravagant expenditure on dashing new consumer goods, some historians believe that widespread suspicion of the alien constitutes the twenties' basic temper. This mood of fanatical bigotry, exemplified by the reborn Ku Klux Klan and the racist pseudoscience of Madison Grant, culminated in the drive to curtail the immigration of elements that threatened a racially (and religiously) constituted Americanism.

Another aspect of this "nervous generation," overlooked by political, cultural, and social historians alike, was the "bulb war."[160] During the final quarter of the nineteenth century, the planting of expansive suburban lawns with daffodil, tulip, iris, and crocus bulbs had been the last word in floricultural style. Just as the English sparrow war had engrossed the reading public a quarter-century earlier, strident treatises on the menace of the narcissus bulb fly and the dangers of quarantines appeared alongside more familiar period pieces on short skirts and the new consumerism in journals such as *Literary Digest* and *Atlantic Monthly*. Preceding an *Atlantic* article on the growing addiction of automobile ownership was a piece by Marlatt on pestiferous foreign plants.[161]

The most fearsome of these pests—also deplored in their native northern Europe—were the European earwig, bulb mite, stem nematode, eelworm, and narcissus (daffodil) bulb fly (large and lesser). Between fifty and seventy-five tiny maggots of the narcissus fly might live in a single bulb.[162] Together, they could do a lot of damage. Alluding to a renewed effort to impose an effective quarantine on narcissus bulbs from Holland and France, Oliver Peck Newman painted a picture of purity defiled and vulnerability exploited. A former president of Washington, D.C.'s Board of Commissioners (the city's governing body), he attacked the "voracious appetite of . . . insect boarders from foreign lands. . . . Sneaking into an originally virgin country . . . these little foreigners have everybody in America who raises fruit and vegetables working two hours a day to feed them!"[163] Exclusionists tasted their first success with the imposition of a ban, from January 1926, on commercial bulb imports.[164]

In the coterminous debate over human immigration, the prime opponents of restrictive measures were entrenched business interests wanting to maintain their supply of cheap labor. Similarly, those least amenable to the constriction of horticultural imports were the commercial concerns whose priority was an uninterrupted supply of inexpensive bulbs. Importers were doubly opposed to the ban since the desire to nurture a domestic bulb industry capable of providing an adequate and disease-free home supply complemented the stated objective of excluding diseased foreign bulbs. In their view, PQN37 and the bulb embargo of 1926 were an indirect effort to erect an impregnable tariff barrier. Their position on the economy of nature was just as laissez-faire as their approach to the human economy. Anticipating the stance of today's defenders of exotics, they felt that restrictive measures disregarded the "fundamental principle of Nature that plants and animals shall have their enemies and parasites." And, adopting the lofty tone of the biological cosmopolitan, they emphasized the mobility of nature and the futility of efforts to impose "artificial barriers of rules or regulations to prevent the movement of such organisms across imaginary political boundary lines." Instead of dwelling on these matters, however, horticultural importers (understandably) stressed the embargo's wider political and economic implications. For the Merchants' Association of New York, quarantines epitomized the evil of business overregulation. Creeping bureaucracy was a far bigger menace than foreign creepy-crawlies. American horticultural interests objected to the open-ended approach, embodied in PQN37 and the 1926 bulb ban, of presumed guilt (now dubbed the "clean/white list" approach). Like Galloway, they wanted the more limited and defined approach of innocent until proven guilty—the "dirty/black list" ethos, in today's parlance.[165]

Representing the American Association of Nurserymen at congressional hearings in 1910, William Pitkin protested that the number of disease-carrying imported plants was trivial. This argument did not impress the House agriculture committee's chairman, who quickly drew a human parallel. "If we were inspecting human beings coming into this country, we might find a million healthy and then find another one with the smallpox." Pitkin was unmoved. Attending Federal Horticultural Board hearings some years later, he again mocked the overblown fears of "scientific friends" in government circles that the plant world's "dangerous criminals" would "enter this country and . . . spread destruction over the face of this fair land."[166]

The Committee on Horticultural Quarantine (est. 1920), representing a range of interests including Harvard University's Arnold Arboretum, various state horticultural societies, and the Garden Club of America, took the lead in lobbying for the relaxation of restrictions. The committee's chair-

man was J. Horace McFarland, a noted conservationist, national park advocate, and founder of the American Civic Association in 1904. For those, like
McFarland, who were closely associated with the "City Beautiful" movement,
bulbs were not just so-called foreign novelties. Daring to see beauty in
plants first (rather than potential pests), he regarded them as a fundamental ingredient of wholesome and desirable urban and vernacular
landscapes.

In McFarland's view, Marlatt was a "zealot" wielding inordinate influence
over agricultural policy despite his botanical ignorance. Lashing out at
Marlatt's "horticultural dictatorship," McFarland characterized PQN37 as
"probably the most unsettling and autocratic action ever taken by the
American Government outside a declaration of war."[167] Fellow committee
member Stephen F. Hamblin, director of the Harvard Botanical Garden,
interpreted the measure as isolationist. He found it highly incongruous, if
not downright hypocritical, that a nation that had always gained enormously from "availing herself of the best of all the world in men and plants
and culture," now assumed it would "benefit through refusal to admit plants
save under regulations so stringent as to be generally prohibitive." He called
on Americans to remember their debt to the plant immigrant, stressing
that, if the thinking behind PQN37 had held sway a century earlier, the
nation would lack more than half its profitable agricultural products, not to
mention the plants that "make her gardens beautiful."[168] McFarland also
reminded his readers that "America is of polyglot origin. This is as true of
plant life as of society." Had the quarantine mentality prevailed during the
nation's formative years with regard to people, he added, then the nation's
founders would have been kept out, "or if admitted might have been given
such 'precautionary treatments' as to leave them little or no vitality."[169]

Critics of PQN37 and the bulb embargo found other human analogies as
well. Hamblin favored a renewed attempt to make a success of inspection at
source, but undertaken by American officials representing a "horticultural
consulate." He based this stance in part on the conviction that the exclusion
of human undesirables had become much more effective thanks to inspection at the point of departure by U.S. consular officials.[170] With such
remarks, however, the potential scope for analogies was by no means
exhausted. Procedures followed upon arrival on American soil provided
especially thick and fertile ground for cross-reference.

A HORTICULTURAL ELLIS ISLAND

Whether or not American screening procedures abroad were efficacious, a
standardized processing system for plants was in place at home by 1920.
The first destination for a plant immigrant was the inspection house at the
headquarters of the Division of Foreign Seed and Plant Introduction in

Washington, D.C. Here, the arrival was unpacked, given an identification number, and scrutinized by Federal Horticultural Board pathologists and entomologists.[171] A few months after the first immigrant quotas came into force in 1921, Marlatt published an article on federal plant protection policies in *National Geographic Magazine*. An accompanying photograph bore the caption, "A Search for Fungi and Insects at a Horticultural 'Ellis Island.'" Taken at the inspection house, it depicted four open crates containing the roots, packed in straw, of lily-in-the-valley plants from Holland. Four inspectors were examining bunches of roots. Another picture caption read, "Examining Plant Immigrants to See Whether They are Healthy." This picture showed inspectors in white lab coats poring over specimens, the small print explaining that "more than 10,000 naturalized plant citizens of the United States have been brought from every quarter of the world by plant explorers of the Department of Agriculture."[172]

If found free of disease or potentially dangerous insects, the plant immigrant's initial "home" was a Department of Agriculture plant introduction field station (garden). P. H. Dorsett, acting chief of the Division/Office of Foreign Seed and Plant Introduction, dubbed this facility the "Ellis Island" of plant immigration. At these processing centers, Galloway explained, "our new friends are placed on probation, as it were, so that we can keep an eye on them."[173] After a lengthy trial period at one of these field stations, each plant immigrant had acquired a bulky personal file.[174]

References to the human world were more than just an occasional feature of descriptions of how plant immigrants were received. Often involving sustained comparison, they were routine, even mandatory. In carrying out their meticulous work, Galloway believed his inspectors had gone significantly beyond "our colleagues who have looked after the human immigrants that have come to our shores for we have a record of every one of the 70,000 different lots that have come in, know how they have behaved, and whether they have made good."[175] In an article justifying elaborate inspection and certification procedures to a skeptical business audience, an official insisted that "no human import at Ellis Island gets more thorough examination."[176] Outlining the functions of plant introduction gardens in 1924, Galloway also noted the recent overhaul of immigration policy: "Not many years ago our gates were wide open to immigrants from nearly every country. We welcomed all such people with open arms and they were soon swallowed up in the thinly-populated, open country and the rapidly growing cities." Of late, though, with the nation rapidly filling up, the public and government had of necessity become "more circumspect about all these strange folk."[177] The aim, to paraphrase Theodore Roosevelt, was to produce a higher grade of plant citizenship.

The Johnson-Reed Act of 1924 had moved beyond percentages of foreign born as the basis for quotas to percentages based on the national origins of the entire population. Alluding to this law, designed to preserve the Anglo-Saxon Protestant complexion of the nation's "basic strain" more effectively than its predecessor of 1921, Galloway remarked that "our bars are now set up and those who now get by are subject to the closest kind of scrutiny." "As it was and is with people," he emphasized, "so it was and is with plant immigrants." He was keen, though, to distance himself from any appearance of opposition based on national origins. "It is not so much the plants themselves that have caused this change in our attitude," he explained, "but the things that may come with the plants."[178]

In 1928, Knowles A. Ryerson, the Bureau of Plant Introduction's new head, reemphasized the desirability of painstaking inspection and a lengthy naturalization process. The total number of official introductions had risen to over 77,000 since his bureau's establishment in 1898, the annual rate was currently running at between three and four thousand, and, not least, pests and diseases were intercepted almost daily. Fairchild's successor explained that though no "quota" was enforced regarding national origins, "as is the case with human immigrants, certain plant groups are much more desirable than others. The past history, family connections and relations, and information on desirable or undesirable behavior are as expressly sought by officials responsible for plant immigration as is the case with persons desiring entrance to this country."[179]

Biologically viable and approved plants were then assessed for economic potential. Focusing on the introduction garden's hybridization function, Galloway explained that scientists could "take raw materials in the shape of plant emigrants and in the melting pot of the breeder's garden develop new crop plants."[180] The long-term economic success of a successfully acclimatized crop plant was by no means guaranteed, however. Americans needed to be persuaded to eat them. As Galloway remarked in his "abbreviated Who's Who" of plant immigrants, quite a few "have their little day or hour and are never again heard from." Conversely, there were those that "sink out of sight for a time and later achieve great prominence."[181] Others were fated to languish in obscurity forever. Galloway was particularly interested in "struggling plant immigrants" that had not won public acceptance easily. The tomato and potato, now thoroughly assimilated into the nation's diet, were prime examples of those that "have made good."[182] Yet they had encountered indifference or suspicion at first.[183] It is a shame that Galloway did not flesh out his analogy more fully with examples of the tomato's and potato's equivalents among human immigrants.

THE REDISCOVERY OF NATIVE VALUE

The story of the bulb war underscores the value of Pauly's distinction between ecological cosmopolitans who chafed against restrictive measures and advocates of ecological autonomy determined to keep out pests. And there are good reasons Pauly chooses Fairchild as a potent symbol of the former camp. Fairchild decried quarantines as a costly, overbearing "racket" and prime example of "smothering" government protectionism—objecting vehemently to the automatic suspicion under which, he believed, all foreign plants now labored. [184] Fairchild felt just as strongly about trees imported for gardens and more natural environments beyond their confines as he did about crops destined for the more heavily modified agricultural environments of field, pasture, and orchard. His sentiments when visiting a five-acre walled garden in France were reminiscent of Frank Chapman's when the ornithologist mulled over the reasons for undervaluing the starling's beauty. The garden near Orleans contained barely a single native plant. But this was scarcely a problem, because "beauty depended upon the selection of the species and not on any mystical feeling that is supposed to come from the fact that they are native. Many Chinese and Japanese species are as much at home in America as in their own habitat. The drooping Japanese flowering cherry . . . that I planted in a place in the woods of Maryland, went wild there and in a generation one would come to think of it as native."[185]

Fairchild constantly defended exotics, whether in France or the United States. Like Hamblin, he thought that exclusion ran counter to the prevailing logic of globalization. "The whole trend of the world," he explained in 1917, "is toward greater intercourse, more frequent exchange of commodities, less isolation, and a greater mixture of the plants and plant products over the face of the globe."[186]

Yet the dichotomization of the worldviews of Fairchild and Marlatt can be taken only so far. Fairchild's enthusiasm for things exotic was not entirely unqualified. He thought that European plane trees on the grounds of a temple near Yokohama, Japan, were completely out of tune with "choice native" trees. He was also capable of learning from his errors. His enthusiasm for fast-growing tropical legumes that built up humus and controlled erosion was dampened by the aggressiveness of a plant he brought from Java, *Mimosa invisa* (commonly known as giant sensitive plant or prickly mimosa), at Chapman Field, the Department of Agriculture's plant introduction garden in southern Florida (since 1923). This thorny, creeping perennial (native to Brazil) proliferated with "such a fury" that Fairchild got scared, doused it with gasoline, and torched it. This sobering experience alerted him to the need to monitor potential invasives before they were distributed beyond heavily controlled sites.[187]

Fairchild's encounters with the infamous vine that "ate the South" also left him somewhat chastened. He first came across kudzu about 1900 while touring Japan, where this wild, semiwoody perennial was fed to livestock. In his autobiography he recalled a visit to a "kudzu enthusiast" in Chipley, Florida, who was renowned for singing its praises as a forage crop in the early 1900s, despite his neighbors' distrust.[188] "Whenever I think of that night's talk with the kudzu pioneer," recalled Fairchild, "I have a special feeling of pride in what might be called our American willingness to try something new, whether it be a new forage crop, a new food, or any one of a thousand new, machine-made gadgets." Fairchild, who confessed that "perhaps I have an undue passion for the new," retained his faith in kudzu for quite some time, despite its proclivity to spread at will. By the late 1930s, however, he was expressing his growing reservations in print. The seeds he brought back from Japan and planted on his property in Florida "'took' with a vengeance, smothering everything they got onto, and pretty soon we became alarmed. Feeling that the kudzu was too much for us, we began to cut it out."[189]

Most telling, though, and perhaps most surprising in view of his reputation as a peerless cosmopolitan, is that Fairchild's belief in the superiority of many exotics did not entirely blind him to the value of the unimproved status quo of native plants and the landscapes to which they belonged. His shifting attitudes to imported palms and native palms illustrates this ambivalence. A mandatory motif in the boosterist tracts that fueled Florida's real estate boom of the mid-1920s was the "graceful palm, latticed against the fading gold of the sun-kissed sky," to quote one of the decade's leading commentators.[190] The member of the palm family most likely to be found on the inauspicious, swampy lots speculators conned the gullible beneficiaries of "Coolidge prosperity" into buying was the native palmetto, or cabbage palm. Their young heads of tender leaf buds, when cooked, were a tasty food (as the common name suggests), and the palmetto's timber was valuable for building cabins and (in earlier centuries) forts. In fact, *Sabal palmetto* is so integral to local identity that South Carolina, nicknamed the Palmetto State, subsequently adopted this palm as its official state tree in 1939. It also features on South Carolina's state seal.

The cabbage palmetto was not, however, the elegant palm silhouetted against the Florida sunset in 1920s evocations of the good life (often in tandem with an orange tree). The signature palm of the beckoning state was the palmyra palm from Asia *(Borassus flabellifer)*. Regardless of any other merits the cabbage palmetto might possess, Fairchild believed that the palmyra easily overshadowed its American cousin in aesthetic and ornamental value. In terms of "stateliness," there was no contest between the humble native and the leggy palm he first saw in Ceylon in 1926.[191] Transplanting the tree, he insisted, would "add tremendously to the charm" of southern Florida's landscapes, rendering them "more tropical than they are now." Propounding the palmyra's flagpole qualities, he explained that it was "no more than six inches across at the base yet attained a lofty sixty feet"—ideal, in short, for small residential lots as it thrust up well above roofs without taking up much room on the ground.[192] American "snowbirds" from the Northeast who were migrating down to the Sunshine State in droves in the twenties created a steady demand for the palmyra.

Part and parcel of Fairchild's apparently insatiable cosmopolitan appetite and his rapturous praise for exotic beauty was his denigration of native flora. A generation more attuned to the value of indigenous species might find somewhat callous his perception of deficiencies in the native landscape of coastal southeast Florida, where he made his home. "Essentially, this is a land of pine and palmetto," he explained. "The shade and the beauty and the fruitfulness which mark it today are provided by plants which came from other parts of the world."[193] Yet Fairchild was not completely insensitive to indigenous floral charms. He ensured that a list of native flowering plants was drawn up in 1915 before clearing the site chosen for the plant intro-duction field station at Miami, and that a small patch was set aside as a rep-resentative sample of the original floral community, which was dominated by an understory of palmetto and an overstory of Cuban pine.[194]

Having done so much to beautify southern Florida with exotic orna-mentals during the century's first two decades, Fairchild eventually became aware of the cost of improvement. As most of his obituary writers pointed out in 1954, Fairchild was in the vanguard of lobbying in the late 1920s and early 1930s for an Everglades national park to preserve a "virgin wilderness of tropical plant and animal life under the very eaves of the greatest civi-lization of Anglo Saxons that has ever gathered under the coconut palms."[195] As first president of the Tropic Everglades National Park Association, he presented the case for protecting what remained of south-ern Florida's original mangrove swamp and hammock grassland to an unconvinced audience at the annual meeting of the American Forestry Association in 1929. He summed up the terrifying scenario of a future United States as densely populated as China (if not with Chinese immi-grants), extolled the remnant native charms of this "strange and fascinating region . . . unlike any other" in the United States, and propounded the virtues of the humble palmetto and other native palms. (The cabbage pal-metto's rehabilitation was completed in 1953, when Florida, following South Carolina's lead, adopted it as the official state tree; since 1970, it has also featured on the state seal.) On the eve of the Wall Street crash, Fairchild was bemoaning that the Sunshine State's only attractive feature that had not been ruined was its climate.[196]

Fairchild finally returned home, so to speak, in 1946, when invited to make his selection for the "My Favorite Tree" guest column in the journal of the American Forestry Association (the nation's oldest conservation orga-nization, founded in 1875). After mentioning a string of exotic also-rans, but discarding them as unsatisfactory, he recalled that he had seen his first grove of California coastal redwoods *(Sequoia sempervirens)* fairly late in life, at a time when he was still besotted with exotic Asiatic promise: "A feeling of utter paralysis overtook me and the passion for planting trees, my puny little trees, anywhere, became distasteful."[197] Though the redwood is only really found in California (there is a tiny patch in the most southwesterly corner of Oregon), it is arguably more American than any other tree in the United States insofar as it has no relatives, near or distant, in any other country. In the humbling presence of these magisterial, uniquely American trees, the globe-trotting ecological cosmopolitan was converted into a plant patriot of the first order for whom floral beauty was indeed a function of a mystical feeling that comes from the fact that something is native as well as deriving from the majesty of shape and sheer size.

The coastal redwood is the tallest of tree species. The three hundred feet a mature specimen regularly attains is higher than many campaniles (bell towers). A large perspective is required to take in the king of the vegetable kingdom from base to crown. This image of Fairchild as a late recruit to the green *campanilismo* of the "See America First" school transports us gracefully into the company of trees. It also clears the ground for the redwood's closest rival in terms of how far you can see from its top on a clear day: the eucalyptus, the Universal Australian.[198]

Chapter 4

Arboreal Immigrants

On National Arbor Day in 2001 (April 27), the National Arbor Day Foundation announced the results of a four-month online poll to select America's National Tree. More than 444,000 votes were cast. The oak won by a clear margin, not least because it comes in sixty varieties that are more widely distributed around the nation than the representatives of any other nominee. Despite its exclusively Californian identity, the redwood that had wowed Fairchild in his twilight years was a respectable runner-up. Another tree with a distinct, if broader regional stamp—the cabbage palmetto that had made so little impression on Fairchild at the height of his floral cosmopolitanism—ranked sixth (though with fewer than a sixth of the votes cast for the oak). Not a single nonnative tree featured among the twenty-one tree taxa that were candidates.[1] To be a contender for the accolade of National Tree, it was clearly insufficient for a tree to be imposing in appearance and of historical, heritage, economic, and aesthetic value. National obviously meant native.

Thomas Pakenham, British historian of empire and author of books about "remarkable" individual trees, recalls his astonishment when he learned that a pagoda tree outside a sea captain's house on Martha's Vineyard—the world's biggest specimen outside the tree's native China and Japan—was absent from the Register of American Champion Trees. The reason, he explained, "was as astonishing as the tree." He went on to explain that the pagoda was not registered "because it was neither native nor naturalised. It was an alien, a non-tree or un-tree." The pagoda, though in the United States, was clearly not of the United States. "Good heavens," Pakenham exclaimed, concluding that "America must be bursting with great trees . . . if it can tell a giant Pagoda tree to go back to China."[2] The

United States was indeed bristling with tremendous trees of its own (as Fairchild finally realized). And, despite Pakenham's surprise, the American habit of thinking about the natural world's ecological and cultural value largely in terms of native nature has deep roots.

Native is often synonymous with *natural* as well as *national*. Critiquing the slavish imitation of English norms in late nineteenth-century American landscape design, prominent Boston landscape architect Charles Eliot, Jr., juxtaposed existing "natural beauty" with the desire for "foreign beauty." Though "supremely beautiful in England," he insisted that in the United States (except for a few temperate places akin to the "Old Country"), "the beauty of it cannot be had and should not be attempted."[3] Do organisms imported from abroad disfigure a landscape or ecosystem and detract from their natural (and cultural) value? Or do these transplants enhance our natural (and national) heritage? These two questions prompted by Eliot's views about what is fit and proper in nature and about what constitutes beauty in landscape lead to two more. Do naturalized exotics have as much right to be protected as natives after a lengthy period of residence in a new country, especially if many people have come to regard them as an intrinsic part of local or national patrimony? In a world of nature which, for better or worse, is mixed up regarding the geographical origin of species, how appropriate are policies based on notions of original identity and authenticity?

I begin this chapter with an investigation of the late nineteenth-century antecedents of recent and ongoing debates about the relative cultural and biological virtues of native and nonnative trees.[4] My essential departure point is botanical historian Edgar Anderson's notion of the "transported landscape," which commends itself as a more appropriate term than "mobile nature" for the more fixed (if not inanimate) biotic forms represented by trees.[5] Britain's experience again serves as a useful reference point because of British horticultural influence in the United States, but also in view of the substantial role of deliberately transported and transplanted American flora in the British landscape, which contrasts starkly with the low profile of weedy plants from North America. Coverage of the late nineteenth-century debate over the desirability of American plants for American places indicates that views on native and nonnative trees are far more complex than the caricatured positions often read back into the past by recent critiques of native plant advocacy.

The light that a renowned novel set in the early 1900s sheds on a famously indomitable arboreal immigrant—the ailanthus—serves as a prolegomena for my main case study: the eucalyptus. The Universal Australian does not fit the asymmetrical flow of floral traffic between Eurasia and the white settler colonies Crosby identified as a central feature of biotic interchange in the half-millennium since the 1490s.[6] In 1895 a prominent eucalyptus booster in California (seemingly oblivious to the transformative role of wild oats in the nineteenth century) claimed that the tree had done more to "change radically the appearance" of large areas of the state "than any other one thing."[7] Over the past thirty years, however, it has become highly contested there, taking us into the more recent of this book's two major periods and the heart of debate over the desirability of certain human and nonhuman immigrants.

THE GLAMOR OF A FOREIGN NAME

The native oaks of Britain and the United States were greatly admired by J. C. Loudon, a leading British horticulturist of the mid-nineteenth century. He pronounced them "the most beautiful of trees." Yet exotic trees had already become a mandatory ingredient of the "polite" British landscape enclosed within private estates. Loudon himself was one of the trendsetters who insisted that, notwithstanding the oak's charms, "no residence in the modern style can have a claim to be considered as laid out in good taste, in which all the trees and shrubs employed are not either foreign ones, or improved varieties of indigenous ones."[8]

The most sought-after of these arboreal exotics were hardy North Americans. Britons were ruthlessly condescending toward American artistic achievements at this time. "In the four quarters of the globe," Sydney Smith famously inquired, "who reads an American book? or goes to an American play? or looks at an American picture or statue?"[9] Yet no one asked "who plants an American tree?" David Douglas returned from the Pacific Northwest in the late 1820s with Sitka spruce, sugar and ponderosa pines, and the fir that bears his name. The seeds, cones, and seedlings of the giant sequoia, which grows only on the western slopes of the Sierra Nevada, were carried by another plant hunter from Gold Rush California to English estates. Alongside American oaks, maples, magnolias, and poplars, these conifers quickly Americanized the landscape of the elite.[10]

This enthusiasm for North American trees was part of a broader botanical cosmopolitanism. Loudon advocated unfettered free trade in plants and a transnational dialogue in floral matters to complement the current assault of laissez-faire doctrine on mercantilist thinking in the commercial sphere.

> The time for believing that the exclusive possession of any benefit contributes to the prosperity or happiness of nations is gone by; and the principles of free and universal exchange and intercourse are found to constitute the surest foundation for the happiness of nations. This is so obviously true in matters of botany and gardening, that it cannot for a moment be doubted. . . . it is desirable for the advancement of civilisation and human refinement, that all the trees and shrubs of temperate climates should be distributed throughout all those climates.

Loudon looked forward to the homogenization of the plant world "at some future period, when the civilisation of the whole world is comparatively equalised."[11] Few reservations—let alone fear of "invasion" or "takeover"—marred this exuberant worldliness. In the United States, the fruits of arboreal cosmopolitanism were displayed in the heart of the nation's capital. By the 1870s the grounds of the Capitol boasted splendid specimens of Norway maple, whose presence was deemed to demonstrate "taste and culture."[12] Nonetheless, an arboreal variety of *campanilismo* asserting the national ownership of nature sometimes clashed with this green cosmopolitanism. The Royal Horticultural Society's John Lindley quickly changed the name of the transported giant sequoia from *Sequoia gigantea* to *Wellingtonia gigantea* to honor the recently deceased (in 1852) British military hero, who "stood as high above his contemporaries as the California tree above all the remaining forests."[13] This appropriation irked many Americans. A woman from Cambridge, Massachusetts, asked Asa Gray if, when in England, he deferred to the new English name. No, he replied, very earnestly. "It is too bad," she fretted, "that a name prompted by narrow national feeling should be allowed to supersede an older botanical name."[14] And even in its nineteenth-century golden age—witness the above-quoted views of Charles Eliot, Jr.—the acclimatizer's desire to improve on nature's existing arrangements did not go wholly unchallenged on either side of the Atlantic. Some horticulturists believed that high Victorian cosmopolitanism had lost touch with the wider, authentic national landscape. Spearheading British protest, William Robinson ridiculed the "passion for the exotic," thanks to which "our own finest plants are never planted, while money is thrown away like chaff for worthless exotic trees like the Wellingtonia." Many beautiful natives, he lamented, are "strangers to our own gardens."[15]

Positions were rarely clear-cut, though. Robinson's vision of floral harmony and fitness was not restricted to the view from the tower of a village church. Wild did not just mean native. As indicated by the subtitle of his best known book, *The Wild Garden: The Naturalization and Natural Grouping of Hardy Exotic Plants with a Chapter on the Garden of British Wild Flowers,* published in 1870, Robinson welcomed tough nonnatives from other temperate climes (especially North America).[16] This transnational northern bias was just as evident in his writings as a specifically British pride.

These debates were no less pervasive in American gardening circles.[17] Few issues of the weekly *Garden and Forest: A Journal of Horticulture, Landscape Art, and Forestry* appeared without reference to questions of national origins during its decade-long existence from 1888 to 1897. Reflecting the human immigrant's higher profile in the United States, analogies between foreign plants and peoples were more common in its pages than in its British counterparts. "Among many distinguished tree foreigners who have taken out naturalization papers in the United States, some of whom are living in eastern Texas, is Paulownia imperialis," noted a Texan contributor in 1895. Commonly known as the empress or princess tree, *Paulownia imperialis* is native to Japan and China and serves as the former country's imperial tree symbol. The Texan warned, though, that a tree that was handsome enough when planted as an ornamental had "quickly run wild." Then he made the familiar leap from floral to human world. "Foreign plants as well as foreign people," he continued, "are rapidly taking possession of many parts of the country." Like the English sparrow's opponents and those who wanted to keep out noxious insects, he highlighted the discrepancy between the exclusion of human immigrants from southeast Asia and the persisting open door policy toward other, nonhuman immigrants: "We are loath to admit the Chinaman, but we freely admit the China tree to naturalization." He went on to list some of the Chinese trees, in addition to paulownia, that were being extensively planted and thriving in his part of the country: *Melia azederach* (chinaberry tree/Persian lilac), ailanthus (see the next section), and sterculia.[18] Expressing a botanical version of the Sinophobia characteristic of many Anglo-Saxon Americans of this era, he predicted that "the new forests of the south are likely to be largely of Mongolian extraction."[19]

A woman from New Jersey wrote that foreign plants were engaged in a "strenuous, and often victorious, fight for life with our native species." She referred to the "direct attacks of foreign plants, which crowd them and rob their roots of food and moisture," and to "aggressive foreign species [making themselves] perfectly at home," singling out Japanese honeysuckle for a special reprimand.[20] Articulating the same sentiment as the champions of native birds who objected to the acclimatizer's fetish for avian exotics, a resident of Larkspur, California, complained bitterly that "no matter how insignificant the flower or straggling the growth of a plant may be, if it comes from Australia, New Zealand, Japan or China, it meets with a ready sale here, while plants like the beautiful native evergreen Blueberry cannot be found in any nurseryman's catalogue."[21]

Defenders of the foreign—who included *Garden and Forest* founder and editor Charles Sprague Sargent—often struck back. In an issue of a comparable British journal, *The Garden,* its editor, William Robinson, had rejected the view that "the true use and first reason of a garden is to keep and grow for us plants not in our woods, and mostly from other countries than our own." In Sargent's rebuttal, direct human analogy featured again, but more positively than it had for the Texan who feared a Mongolian floral takeover. In Sargent's hands, it was a device for celebrating the nation's commitment to floral cosmopolitanism and green multiculturalism:

> Here in America she [Nature] does not confine herself to growing plants which were originally American. She takes up vegetable immigrants as hospitably as our civilization takes in human immigrants, and assimilates them as

quickly and naturally. Who would suspect the White Willow in New England, or the Pawlonia in the woods of Maryland, to be an exotic? And who sees anything inharmonious or strange in the aspect of the Ailanthus-trees which, mingling with the native Elms, shade the rustic streets of Nantucket?[22]

In an editorial response to a letter from Frederick Law Olmsted, the most famous landscape designer of his generation, Sargent advocated a middle way between indiscriminate devotion to exotics and a strict natives-only policy. A compromise position commended itself not least because "native" was a political term geared to the nation-state that made little sense in terms of botanical communities at a subnational level. A broad-leaved magnolia from the southern Alleghany Mountains, he pointed out, would be just as out of place in the northern regions of the United States as "any tree from any foreign land" could possibly be.[23]

Olmsted had been provoked into writing his letter by a short editorial three months earlier in which Sargent had taken a harsher view of exotics than usual. "Combinations of plants other than those which nature makes or adopts," Sargent remarked, "inevitably possess inharmonious elements which no amount of familiarity can ever quite reconcile to the educated eye." He singled out Brooklyn's Prospect Park—an Olmsted creation—as a model of bad practice because one section featured flowery foreign shrubs in close proximity to "natural woods" and "native shrubbery." Sargent did not object to forsythias and lilacs in a garden. Among the wild natives, though, they "look not only out of place, but are a positive injury to the scene." He concluded that "all attempts to force nature . . . by bringing in alien elements from remote continents and climates must inevitably produce inharmonious results."[24]

This declaration really riled Olmsted, whose views on natives and exotics were as complex as Sargent's. A leading proponent of native landscape protection in the form of national parks, he encouraged design in keeping with local climatic and environmental conditions, which, in California, involved a reaction against the fashionable English norm of lush greensward. Yet, like Robinson, Olmsted did not oppose introductions from climatically and physically comparable regions. Flora from the Mediterranean, not surprisingly, was his choice for California.

On this occasion, though, in his response to Sargent, he vigorously defended the place of foreign plants in the American landscape. Denouncing the emerging "taboo" on trees "from over sea," he invited the journal's readers to picture an old clearing in the Northeast progressively colonized from a range of sources. The result of this mixture of seeds from an adjacent "aboriginal" woodland, an abandoned local homestead and those that birds brought from more far-flung gardens, was "a remarkable variety of trees and bushes of foreign ancestry" in addition to the natives.

Olmsted then introduced a hypothetical man—who could have been from New Zealand or the moon (he believed it made no difference). Having no knowledge of the vegetation of Europe, Asia, or North America, this man walks through the area and is invited to rank, in descending order, the most "incongruous, unblending, unassimilating, inharmonious and apparently exotic" of the plants he encounters. Olmsted doubted that the trees and bushes of "foreign ancestry" would invariably appear higher on the man's list of conspicuous elements than any of the native species. (Given the ubiquity of Eurasian plants in New Zealand, however, a New Zealander was unlikely to have been entirely unfamiliar with the plants that colonized a Northeast clearance.) Olmsted emphasized that some of America's commonest plants—barberry, privet, Cherokee rose, dandelion, buttercup, and mint—originated overseas. Yet few Americans, in his view, considered them inharmonious.[25]

Some participants in the debate over the merits and desirability of plants native and nonnative suspected that a consciousness of foreign origins not merely influenced but determined the stance of many critics. That naturalized flora such as the Cherokee rose and ailanthus "do not look out of place in the landscape," editorialized Sargent in response to Olmsted, "confirms our idea that fitness comes not from similarity or dissimilarity of form or color or texture, but from mental association."[26] Yet the evidence in the pages of *Garden and Forest* suggests that a preference for natives was frequently based—as in Britain—not on mere mental association on but their superior capacity to withstand climatic rigors—particularly a hard Northeast winter.[27]

Questions of "fitness" based on national origins also arose in connection with commercial crops. A Sargent editorial in 1888 addressed the problems of raising fruit on the prairies. He quoted from an address by C. L. Watrous, president of the American Association of Nurserymen, who explained that soft fruits derived from native stock (raspberries, blackberries, strawberries, and gooseberries) had coped with extremes of heat and cold, whereas apples, cherries, and plums—still largely of "foreign ancestry"—had succumbed to climatic vagaries. The berries, Watrous argued, were "so thoroughly emancipated from their taint of foreign ancestry as to be thoroughly reliable throughout all the regions indigenous to their wild relatives." He also looked forward to the day when all varieties of apple in the Pacific Northwest would be "descendants of the native Crab Apples, indigenous to the glades and thickets of the prairies, which have through ages unmeasured and immeasurable by any standard of ours, by variation and natural selection, adapted their race to every vicissitude of their climate and soil, as none of foreign ancestry ever can."[28]

These various positions on the virtues of native and nonnative species were rarely backed by experimental evidence. They were usually based on casual observation. Yet native superiority, Watrous explained, was a demonstrable quality of trees: "The best authorities now agree that American trees are the best for America." Transplanting trees to unfamiliar conditions, he believed, greatly strained their "vitality." The American horticulturist should learn to "test the favorites of distant regions with no more than hopeful distrust, and to prove them well before proclaiming them . . . as worthy of confidence." Beware "the glamor of a foreign name" was his advice.[29]

Olmsted was far more sanguine. "Two hundred years hence," he wagered, "are not Japanese honeysuckle, 'Japanese ivy' and 'Japanese box' likely to be equally bone of our bone in scenery?" He regretted that a "picturesque" nonnative shrub like broom—one of the most invasive plants in California today—had yet to make much of a mark. He was equally relaxed about the ecological impact of other exotics, hailing another of today's most notorious weeds of the American West, waxen woad, as the personification of "cosmopolitan toughness." Olmsted also embraced tamarisk—currently the bane of the Southwest's riparian environments (including George W. Bush's Texan ranch): "May we not (as artists) think that there are places with us in which a landscape composition might be given a touch of grace, delicacy and fineness by the blending into a body of low, native tree foliage that of the Tamarisk . . . that would not be supplied in a given situation by any of our native trees?" That paulownia, English elm, horse chestnut, Norway maple, and ailanthus were "elbowing places for themselves in the midst of our native forests" left him unperturbed.[30]

THE TREE THAT GREW IN BROOKLYN
(AND NEARLY EVERYWHERE ELSE)

Of the tough green cosmopolitans with sharp elbows Olmsted enumerated, the most famous and infamous is the ailanthus. This is a tree that grows in Illinois and would certainly have flourished in the Lincoln Memorial Garden—where Jens Jensen tried in vain to cultivate representatives of indigenous trees gathered from the length and breadth of the state. This East Asian tree arrived at the eastern seaboard via western Europe in the 1780s. Initially a great novelty confined to opulent estates, ailanthus became a sought-after street tree in early nineteenth-century industrializing areas because it was untroubled by air pollution, wind, ice, compacted soil, diseases, and insects.[31] Olmsted was suitably impressed, planting it in Central Park. Forty-niners flocking to the gold diggings brought the tree to California, where it also arrived directly from China with "coolie" laborers.[32]

In the first issue of *Garden and Forest*, Sargent extolled its multiple virtues: "For hardiness and rapidity of growth, for the power to adapt itself to the dirt and smoke, the dust and drought of cities, for the ability to thrive in the poorest soil, for beauty and for usefulness, this tree . . . is one of the most useful which can be grown in this climate."[33] The second mentioned quality, its speedy upward thrust of as much as a meter a year, probably explains its common name, "tree of heaven."[34] The tree also appeared, miraculously, to be devoid of any insect.

Others were less impressed by a tree they cast as the arboreal equivalent of the English sparrow. The ailanthus's abundant winged seeds (shaped like airplane propellers) are wind dispersed over considerable distances, germinating within a few days in light or dark, even from the proverbial sidewalk crack. Searching roots invade sewers, springs, and wells and crack house foundations. Moreover, the male tree emits an odor while flowering that some find extremely unpleasant (hence the alternative name "stink ash"). Some even claimed that it made them ill.[35]

The critic with the highest profile was Andrew Jackson Downing, the nation's most prominent landscape gardener prior to Olmsted (he died in 1852). As editor of *The Horticulturist* in the late 1840s and early 1850s, Downing frequently extolled the virtues of "neglected" American plants. In one of his last editorials (August 1852), "Shade-Trees in Cities," he tore indignantly into the (misnamed) tree of heaven—unable to resist unflattering human analogy:

> We look upon it as an usurper in rather bad *odor* at home, which has come over to this land of liberty, under the garb of utility, to make foul the air, with its pestilent breath, and devour the soil, with its intermeddling roots—a tree that has the fair outside and the treacherous heart of the Asiatics, and that has played us so many tricks, that we find we have caught a Tartar which it requires something more than a Chinese wall to confine within limits.

Having enumerated its manifold vices, Downing made no bones about the fact that his ultimate objection was "patriotic." For "this miserable pigtail of an Indiaman" had distracted Americans from "our own more noble native American trees."[36]

Nonetheless, appreciative voices had been heard sporadically since the 1850s, when the calamity the canker worm visited on New York City's shade trees was the talk of the town. Of all the city's trees, native and nonnative, the ailanthus alone was unaffected by the pest that spurred the introduction of the first English sparrows. In fact, it appeared to be happily immune to the predations of any insect. Supporters reveled in the temerity and tenacity of a tree that was mocked as the "fragrant stranger."[37] "I don't think the Ailanthus runs any danger of being abolished, tho' a foreigner (if it is a foreigner)," remarked "Philo-Ailanthus" of Philadelphia—referring to its alleged prehistoric presence in part of the Americas; fossil records indicate a western American presence before the last ice age. As well as being the place where the tree was first introduced, Philadelphia was the site of the most violent recent nativist backlashes against Irish Catholic immigrants.

"Philo-Ailanthus" was thus disposed to argue in the same vein as John Robson, the English sparrow's champion in Kansas. The tree, he concluded, "is too well naturalized now, and only '*Know Nothings*' will seek to deprive it of its rights and us of its comforts."[38]

Another wave of support for a tree that one woman addressed as a "gamin of the streets" gathered force in the 1920s.[39] In the face of what they described as prejudice and persecution, supporters in New York City (not all of whom had identifiably non-British names) rallied behind this "plebeian weed" for much the same reason the English sparrow had secured some American respect. The kernel of their case was that the "lusty" tree exuded cheerful resilience under adverse conditions.[40] Here, embodied in a single tree species, was the invasive alien and nature's life force incarnate.

The ailanthus was an Ishmael among trees. In 1944 a rehabilitator characterized it as the "most maligned tree of all time." Like the English sparrow's champions before him, he celebrated its rugged individualism and indifference to extremes of heat and cold. It "asks little," he explained, and "needs no coddling." "We have learned," he added, "that this is the tree that grows in Brooklyn."[41] This was a reference to a best-selling novel published the previous year, whose title encapsulated the tree's capacity to flourish in the most inauspicious of locations. *A Tree Grows in Brooklyn*, Betty Smith's classic 1943 tale of a young female immigrant, posits an intrinsic relationship between tree and immigrant poor. The novel tells of the coming of age of a working-class Irish Catholic girl in the decade before American entry into World War I. Born and raised in Brooklyn (like the author), Francie Nolan hopes for a better life, attending evening classes while working in a factory making artificial roses out of wire and paper. At the novel's close, she is bound for college. The story ends with Francie packing up her belongings the day before she and her family are due to leave the modest house where she has lived her entire life, their neighborhood having been slated for a model housing project.

"There's a tree that grows in Brooklyn," Smith explains in the novel's scene-setting preamble, which serves as a passable summary of the natural history of a tree with an uncanny ability—like the English sparrow and Francie herself—not only to survive but to thrive.

> Some people call it the Tree of Heaven. No matter where its seed falls, it makes a tree which struggles to reach the sky. It grows in boarded-up lots and out of neglected rubbish heaps. It grows up out of cellar gratings. It is the only tree that grows out of cement. It grows lushly . . . survives without sun, water, and seemingly without earth. It would be considered beautiful except that there are too many of it.[42]

The tale begins late on a Saturday afternoon in the summer of 1912. The long-awaited appearance of the declining sun in her family's small backyard reminds Francie of a famous poem by Henry Wadsworth Longfellow, learned at school, which celebrates the glories of the "murmuring" hemlocks and pines in the twilight of the "forest primeval."[43] Yet only one tree stands in her yard and it is neither hemlock nor pine. This solitary tree is an ailanthus, a tree that grows prodigiously—"but only in tenement districts." Eleven-year old Francie sits on the fire escape engulfed by the tree's umbrella-like foliage and feels as if she is dwelling in Longfellow's forest. Smith reports that the appearance of small, advance specimens of ailanthus in the yards of more affluent neighborhoods presaged their future as tenement areas, as ever-growing numbers of immigrants pushed outward from the inner cores and the middle classes quit the pressurized areas, stimulating suburban growth. "The tree knew," Smith remarked. "It came there first. Afterwards, poor foreigners seeped in and the quiet brownstone houses were hacked up into flats, feather beds were pushed out on the window sills to air and the Tree of Heaven flourished. That was the kind of tree it was. It liked poor people."[44]

In Smith's novel, the tenement dwellers embrace the tree of heaven as part of the boisterous, spontaneous, grubby, and common yet also beautiful and irrepressible life of the city, which includes "scratching curs," "scavenging cats," "sooty sparrows," and the (nonnative) white clover (*Trifolium repens)* that grows among the rank grasses of abandoned lots and makes lovely bouquets. As she prepares to leave her home, Francie observes that their ailanthus has been felled because "housewives complained that wash on the lines got entangled in its branches." But the tree, undismayed, had simply sprouted from its stump, the trunk crawling along the surface "until it reached a place where there were no wash lines above it. Then it had started to grow towards the sky again." She contrasts this unquenchable life force with the fate of "Annie," a fir tree her family had tried to raise in their yard (perhaps as part of their efforts to assimilate to American norms in the culture of nature as well). Despite lavishing water, manure, love, and hope on this native representative of Longfellow's forest primeval, "Annie" had languished in a sickly state and died long ago. "But this tree . . . that men chopped down . . . this tree that they built a bonfire around, trying to burn up its stump—this tree lived!" These qualities Francie admires—which bring to mind the southern African baobab—were precisely those that made others shudder. "It lived! And nothing could destroy it."[45]

Though synonymous with urban squalor and dereliction, the ailanthus also thrives in more salubrious surroundings. It does not fare well in dense forest, but it was growing wild in clearings in Virginia by the 1880s. This attracted a new form of resentment. And the ailanthus is better known today as the "tree from hell" than the tree of heaven. Many environmentalists also dismiss this floral counterpart to the English sparrow as a "trash" tree.[46] In California it has invaded the lower reaches of riparian areas subject to nat-

Figure 3. Avenue of Blue Gums, San Jose, California. Lantern slide (undated, but pre-1920). Courtesy of the Frances Loeb Library, Harvard Design School.

ural disturbance from varying seasonal stream flow. A more high-profile and controversial "trash" tree in California, though, is the eucalyptus, recently dubbed the nation's largest weed.[47]

THE STRANGE CAREER OF THE UNIVERSAL AUSTRALIAN

After his botanizing voyages to Australia and New Zealand in the early 1840s, Britain's premier botanist, Joseph Hooker, reflected that fast-moving exotics from northwest Europe "wander from the cultivated spots and eject the native, or, taking their places by them, appear, like them, to be truly indigenous." He then noted the "total want of reciprocity in migration."[48] The eucalyptus was a potential exception. The display of sections from a huge tree at London's Crystal Palace exhibition of 1851 raised hopes for its naturalization in the mild climes of southwest coastal Britain. Eucalypts generally succumbed, however, to Britain's damp and cool climate.[49] Realistic expectations were moribund by 1900.

This lack of success endorsed Robinson's views on delicate exotics. In England, he reflected, eucalyptus "never present the graceful and stately port which they show in countries that really suit them, such as parts of Italy and California."[50] Parts of Italy and California really did suit eucalyptus, particularly the variety known as the (Tasmanian) blue gum *(E. globulus)*. What commended the tree in Italy was its widely touted antimalarial property. Vapor from the oil in its aromatic leaves and the gum-like secretions exuded from the trunk that gives the eucalyptus its generic common name was thought to purify the air by absorbing or neutralizing noxious, disease-causing gases.[51] The abundant leaf litter was also believed to disinfect the soil, while the tree's adventurous roots sucked up excess moisture.

The swampy Roman Campagna was so badly afflicted with malaria in the late 1860s that its Trappist monks retreated into Rome at night. Thousands of blue gums were planted there in the 1870s, which played an indirect sanitary role by reclaiming the wetland, thereby shrinking mosquito breeding grounds. French officials in Algeria and Tunisia had taken the lead, however, after severe outbreaks of malarial fever in the early 1860s. Eucalypts (mostly red gum, *E. rostrata*) were so common in Algeria by the mid-1870s, claimed French tree expert Jules Planchon, that a foreigner unaware of its "exotic origin . . . would suppose it to be an indigenous tree."[52]

Of the many species of genus *Eucalyptus* (around 750), the vast majority are Australian.[53] So, as Planchon saw it, Australia was finally giving something back in return for the many beneficial European transplantations it had received. Though aware that many English plants had become "miserable herbs" there, his overall view was that European biota had redeemed wastelands that barely supported "a few miserable" natives. The tree that had taken "possession of Moorish ground" in the 1860s provided "the rare example of a truly Australian tree having become a citizen of the world by right of utility and beauty." The gum tree swayed over the Mediterranean's native vegetation with a "sovereign power."[54] And this was a foreign onslaught of which southern Europeans seemingly approved. "Australia is invading the ancient Provence. The antipodean forest is gradually taking the place of the indigenous species of the Old World," declared a satisfied Frenchman.[55] The manifest destiny of this singular Australian gift, its boosters believed, was to colonize not just Europe's warmer parts but the rest of the world's too. By the early 1990s, eucalypts beyond Australia covered an area equivalent to the state of Washington. One of its new homes was California.

Just as French visitors to Algeria and Tunisia were under the impression that the eucalyptus was local, many Californians have also assumed it to be a California native. "Say," an American serviceman [presumably Californian] had reportedly drawled in Sydney during World War II, "You got some of our eucalypts here."[56] Environmental historian Joseph E. Taylor III told a similar story half a century later. "Drive through California's Central Valley or along its coast," he observes, "and you will eventually encounter a road named 'Blue Gum' or a grove of eucalyptus trees." "As a boy," he continued,

"I took these as natural and timeless facets of my environment." Only later did he realize they were a relatively recent addition.[57] For some Californians, the redwood is their green icon. For others, California without eucalypts is not California.

Californians who regard the tree as an unwelcome stranger often attribute its presence to a hare-brained impulse comparable to that which brought the starling to New York City. But utility and beauty, the promise of goodness, explain its arrival in California as well as Italy and North Africa. Initially, many Britons who had settled in Australia were astonished by the gum tree's widespread popularity abroad. They considered it ugly, ragged in appearance, irregular in shape, peculiar in smell, and, not least, a poor provider of shade.[58] But acclimatizers in other countries saw merits to which Australian colonists were often blind. "One of the worst features of the settlement of new countries by Americans," exclaimed C. F. Reed, president of the State Board of Agriculture, in the board's annual report for 1869, "is the useless and criminal destruction of timber. In our State this reckless and improvident habit has been indulged in to an unprecedented extent."[59] Californians were thus greatly enamored of what chief forester Gifford Pinchot described as the eucalyptus's "phenomenally rapid growth."[60] Some specimens reputedly grew 40 feet within four years in the 1860s and 1870s. This prompted many Americans (including residents of redwood country) to view the gum tree as an emerging rival to the coastal redwood, to which the world's tallest hardwood was frequently compared in terms of height.[61] Moreover, as Asa Gray conceded, some eucalyptus specimens even outstripped the redwood in this department—though, as Abbot Kinney remarked, "those of an ultra patriotic humor" might still insist that the genus *Sequoia* was unsurpassed in solid stem height and cubic wood content.[62]

Californian promoters whipped up an enthusiasm for the "miracle" tree that Kenneth Thompson describes as "almost a mania"[63]—and which certainly resembled the previous decade's sparrow "craze" on the East Coast. During the 1870s, the state's zealous periodical press was rife with anticipation. Eucalyptus "apostle" Alfred Russell Heath celebrated them as "a race of trees apart [that] in their variety, utility and adaptability have no compeers on earth."[64] As native hardwood supplies were depleted nationally in addition to redwood locally, foresters and entrepreneurs increasingly regarded the tree's astonishingly durable timber (especially sugar gum's) as a worthy successor to hickory, oak, and ash for the manufacture of tools, furniture, telegraph poles, pilings, bridges, mine supports, barrels, railroad ties, and paving blocks.[65] One promotional article depicted three paving blocks hewn from red gum that had been exhibited at the Los Angeles chamber of commerce. Two were from the streets of Sydney. Despite having been pounded by feet for twelve years, they were virtually indistinguishable from the third, freshly cut block.[66]

For Alfred James McClatchie of the California State Board of Forestry (est. 1885), eucalyptus afforestation in the Southwest was an essential tool for conserving what remained of ancient native forests elsewhere in the nation.[67] Planting was also promoted as a way to overcome the treeless nature of the southland, which, as the first Spanish colonists had noted more than a century earlier, was characterized by a prairie-like mix of flowering forbs and grasses. Many Americans who visited California or settled there in the late nineteenth century regarded the state as severely deficient in natural tree cover. "We lack forests; we must make them," announced F. D. Cornell.[68] Though its oak was unsurpassed in "stateliness," Sargent believed that, due the relative paucity of native species, California would "doubtless always be obliged to depend somewhat on other parts of the world for ornamental trees."[69] East Coast forestry expert Robert Douglas, addressing an 1888 meeting of the American Horticultural Society in Riverside, California, applauded the state's decision to set up experimental stations to test the usefulness of new tree varieties. Revealing the bias of landscape tastes shaped by temperate zones, he asserted that a visitor from the East, surveying California "from the window of a sleeping-car, would see a very discouraging prospect" of unpromising desert and hills, the latter's southern aspects being "generally destitute" of native trees. By contrast, the redemptive eucalypts could thrive here, also greening hilltops and other "almost impossible places."[70]

Half a century from 1890, predicted a visiting German forester, it would be "inconceivable" that the nation's "beautiful fruit-garden" had once been treeless. Surrounded by tremendous forests of blue gum and acacia, "the visitor will be inclined to doubt that he is really in America."[71] Writing just before substantial public interest in California's native plants emerged, Viola Lockhart Warren insisted that the eucalyptus was California's most distinctive natural feature. She, too, painted an unflattering portrait of southern California's prairie and chaparral, from which the blue gum brought deliverance.[72]

McClatchie's 1902 USDA bulletin about the eucalyptus in the United States was primarily concerned with "usefulness." He was only incidentally interested in ornamental value, which, in his view, had been "disappointing" anyway.[73] That ornamentalism could constitute usefulness did not occur to him. Nevertheless, this turned out to be the overriding use in California, for commercial hopes were soon dashed. The tree's growth rate certainly matched—even exceeded—expectations.[74] Unfortunately, timber grown at such an accelerated pace tended to be brittle and to split when cut. It was also prone to warp and shrink when sawn. Even worse, eucalyptus ties failed to hold railroad spikes. And the wood was often too hard to work.[75] Not least, with the spread of irrigation in the late nineteenth century, land once written off as good for nothing except eucalyptus plantations was coveted for fruits and vegetables.[76]

For Ian Tyrrell, the feature of the tree's history in California that stands out within a global framework is the greater importance there of "aesthetic considerations." He focuses on the "ornamental crusade" to make California a true terrestrial paradise, whose ample legacy could be seen along countless suburban streets as well as the campuses of Bay Area universities such the University of California at Berkeley, Mills College (Oakland), and Stanford (Palo Alto).[77] Yet Californian proponents usually discussed this particular virtue as part of a broad-based evaluation of the tree's appeal. They spoke of timber, fuel wood, shade, shelter, sanitary, and ornamental/ aesthetic values more or less in the same breath (at least until the collapse of the commercial planting boom circa 1912). "Beautiful, profitable, inspiring"—this is how one booster summarized its attractions.[78] McClatchie also regularly cited the "combined merits of attractiveness and usefulness," the tree's mission being "the clothing of the naked unproductive portions [of the Southwest] with garments of beauty and utility."[79] Tyrrell's emphasis on Californian exceptionalism notwithstanding, the state did not have a monopoly on ornamental plantings. There were plenty of eye-catching eucalypts in southern France too; in recognition of the tree's contribution to the landscape of Cannes and its environs (in tandem with its palms, grape vines, and orange trees), the region was dubbed "Californie."[80]

For cultural historians, though, this picturesque American branch of the tree's history is particularly enthralling. In an article celebrating the affluent city of Santa Barbara as a showcase of refined arboreal taste, Charles Shinn, editor of *California Horticulturist and Floral Magazine,* pointed out that the absence of "fine" California conifers was "as striking as the presence of fine exotic species." He regretted that the Monterey cypress ("coarse and stiff," though "admirable" enough in its "native grove" at Cypress Point) had been widely planted in the public squares of many other towns twenty years earlier.[81] Shinn himself had no great love for the blue gum. But ornamental deployment began in 1876 when Kinney fringed Santa Monica's streets with them in his capacity as "road master" (local highways chief).[82]

Kinney appreciated the tree's value as part of a "scientifically managed" program of afforestation to ensure a sustained "crop" yield. He also appreciated its "sanitary influence," citing the rehabilitation of the Roman Campagna.[83] What attracted the beautifiers of residential subdivisions to the tree, however, was its "noble" growth through regular shedding of lower limbs. An expert at the State of California's Santa Monica Forestry Station (established by Kinney) characterized one variety growing there, the lemon-scented gum tree *(E. citriodora),* as of a "general appearance at once suggesting the words graceful and elegant."[84] By the mid-1870s, eucalypts were already so widely planted that visitors and residents alike could not help but comment on their essential place in the landscape. An Ohioan dubbed it a "great favorite." The Archduke of Austria, visiting Los Angeles in the 1870s,

Figure 4. Albert Johnson's "One-Tree Woodlot"—an enormous blue gum at Watsonville, California—yielded seven cords of wood in 1935. Courtesy of the Forest History Society, Durham, N.C.

thought the blue gum merited "special mention" since it was "planted in masses everywhere." Tourists in Pasadena remarked on square blocks planted for firewood "rising plume-like" to heights between 60 and 100 feet.[85]

Not everyone approved of the tree. Despite his positive view of many non-natives, in his 1865 plan for a burial ground near Oakland, Frederick Law Olmsted had warned against using the shallow-rooted eucalyptus, which also tended to dispossess other trees. A quarter of a century later, he noted that it had become a "marked (not generally an agreeable) feature" of the state.[86] Fast growth and quickly resprouting stumps prompted references to "the Australian Weed" as well as the "wonder" tree. Others simply disliked its looks and smell. The rot of disenchantment and disapproval had begun to set in.

Lawrence Clark Powell, librarian of the University of California at Los Angeles, gave a talk at Mills College in 1955 about the manuscripts of Scottish German novelist Norman Douglas. Since the Mills campus was

renowned for its groves, Powell selected Douglas's "diatribe" against eucalypts as a suitable opening gambit. In his celebrated 1915 travel guide to the
southern tip of Italy, based on a trip in 1911—in a style reminiscent of
Andrew Jackson Downing's denunciation of the ailanthus—Douglas lashed
out at an avenue of eucalyptus in Policoro (in the region of Basilicata),
planted in the 1870s. "I never lose an opportunity," he remarked, "of saying
exactly what I think about this particularly odious representative [of the
gum tree] . . . this eyesore . . . this reptile of a growth with which a pack of
misguided enthusiasts have disfigured the entire Mediterranean basin."
The "intruder" ought to be "expelled without mercy" because

> A single eucalyptus will ruin the fairest landscape. No plant on earth rustles in
> such a horribly metallic fashion when the wind blows through those everlast-
> ingly withered branches; the noise chills one to the marrow; it is like the sibi-
> lant chattering of ghosts. Its oil is called "medicinal" only because it happens
> to smell rather nasty; it is worthless as timber, objectionable in form and
> hue—objectionable, above all things, in its perverse, anti-human habits. What
> other tree would have the effrontery to turn the sharp edge of its leaves—as
> if these were not narrow enough already!—towards the sun, so as to be sure
> of giving at all hours of the day the minimum of shade and maximum of dis-
> comfort to mankind?[87]

A comparable, homegrown form of mockery emerged long before the
bubble of expectation finally burst in California in the 1910s and 1920s.
The most hyperbolic example appeared in the first volume of the San Francisco *Argonaut*, in 1877:

> There is a craze all over the state about the eucalyptus. . . . Eucalyptus will
> frighten away fevers and murder malaria. Its leaves cure asthma. Its roots
> knocks [out] ague as cold as jelly. Its bark improves that of a dog. A dead body
> buried in a coffin made from the wood of the blue gum will enjoy immunity
> from the exploring mole and the penetrating worm. Blue gum is good for the
> bite of a mad cow. . . . In point of beauty, it is about as desirable as the scaf-
> folding of a factory chimney. This absurd vegetable is now growing all over the
> State. One cannot get out of its sight. . . . [it] crops up everywhere in inde-
> pendent ugliness. It defaces every landscape with blotches of blue and embit-
> ters every breeze with suggestions of an old woman's medicine chest. Let us
> have no more of it.[88]

Others simply focused on the monotonous effect it created. Shinn complained that a huckster had sold hundreds of thousands of seeds to university officials at Berkeley. So, "instead of the garden art [Olmsted's lost plan]
that every educated Californian wanted to see, Berkeley became for years a
wilderness of tall, crowded Eucalypti, and all its natural beauties were
obscured." And when the town itself also succumbed to the "Eucalyptus
craze," its appearance "soon rivaled the University in its stiffness."[89]

Southern California's suburbanites also turned against it. Initially entranced by its elegance and shade, they soon noticed that it generated prodigious amounts of litter (leaf, bark, twig, and limb) and that its thirsty root systems sometimes traveled a hundred feet. Residents faced blocked drains, cracked and buckled sidewalks, damage to septic tanks, and destabilized house foundations. Falling limbs were also hazardous to human life and automobiles. The tree was simply too big and unruly, some concluded, for residential plantings.[90] By the 1910s, Santa Monicans were chopping down Kinney's gums. A small voice heralded more vociferous recent objections rooted in the tree's alien status. Praising madronia (madrone, *Arbutus menziessi*) as a timber and ornamental tree, Sargent criticized the California tendency to overlook magnificent native materials and "ransack the world for exotic trees" to "beautify" the state. Yet madrone, redwood, and sequoia were "world-wide wonders . . . which ought to be the pride of every true Californian."[91]

Despite commercial failure in California, the eucalyptus became the leading plantation tree in Brazil, India, Ethiopia, Portugal, and Spain, acclaimed as a quick fix for lands denuded of native cover.[92] Australians, who had come to revere the gum as their national tree, welcomed this overseas success. In his preface to Robert Zacharin's international history, *Emigrant Eucalypts*, J. H. Willis expressed the hope that this account of "expatriate" eucalypts would instill pride in "the beneficent part being played by Australian vegetation outside its homeland."[93] According to Zacharin, nothing induced more "rapid nostalgia" in the Australian abroad than encountering a eucalyptus unexpectedly and "crushing their leaves and inhaling the aromatic perfume."[94]

Australian artist Stan Kelly, who painted every variety in Australia, was concerned that success abroad would lead to declining appreciation at home of a species that composed 95 percent of Australia's forest cover. In *Eucalypts*, his collection of plates celebrating a tree genus that is "truly Australian," he reminded his readers that "in spite of the ubiquitous appearance of . . . blue gums in California, they were from Australia."[95] But Zacharin was not in the least bit bothered that his nation's peerless symbol was often mistaken for a native elsewhere. "In California today," he remarked in the late 1970s, "the Australian gum typifies California to a host of people quite unfamiliar with the redwood, sugar pine and others of her splendid native forest trees." His glowing account insisted that long-term residence and worthy contribution had earned the tree American arboreal citizenship. No praise was too high, for the eucalyptus held more than dual nationality. In his view, it was the great exception to a generally poor global experience with exotics (Australia itself having suffered particularly).

In the whole of nature there are very few species of either animal or plant which have a record of doing nothing but good wherever they have found a new home. One only has to think of the sparrow and the rabbit, the black-berry and the thistle. But the Australian gum-tree—so totally naturalized in so many countries that the inhabitants now regard them as native plants—has no blemish on its reputation. Its products enrich those who cultivate it and the lands where it grows are healthier and more useful.[96]

Since Zacharin's paean, the tree's allegedly spotless reputation has become increasingly tarnished. In 1983, villagers in the Indian state of Karnataka stormed nurseries and wrecked seedlings, sometimes substituting the native tamarind. Gum trees might be good for pulp, but Thai villagers called it the "selfish" tree; it dried out the land and excluded native trees that had supplied vital everyday products. Livestock found its foliage and bark unpalatable.[97] In 1990, Spanish villagers on the Bay of Biscay uprooted thousands of seedlings the night after they had been planted, and Portuguese olive farmers clashed with police in plantations. Small farmers and environmentalists accused the tree of desiccating water supplies, erod-ing soil, banishing wildlife, and consuming the traditional landscape of pas-ture lands, vineyards, and olive groves.[98] Nicknamed the "capitalist tree" and the "fascist tree," the eucalyptus came to symbolize the corporate agro-forestry and neocolonialism that appropriate communal lands and foster a cash economy at the expense of subsistence lifeways that coevolved with native flora.

THE TARNISHED TREE:
CALIFORNIA'S RAGING EUCALYPTUS CONTROVERSY

The Californian reputation of a tree Powell described as being "as symbolic of the Golden State as the orange" was hardly flawless when Zacharin penned his rhapsody in 1978.[99] It had been ridiculed as a spectacular com-mercial flop and deplored as a visual blight. Its antimalarial properties had been disputed, and it had been denounced as a threat to human life and property. Yet it was a generally accepted feature of suburban, agricultural, and substantially natural landscapes. Moreover, the bulk of commentators prior to 1980 were approving as well as accepting.

This applied to visitors from abroad as well. In *California Coast Trails,* his 1913 account of a horseback ride from Mexico to Oregon, Joseph Smeaton Chase described the night he slept out on a deep bed of blue gum leaf litter at Aliso Cañon near Laguna Beach. The British naturalist and world traveler paid tribute to the blue gum as somehow more Californian than the state's native trees. Anticipating Zacharin, Smeaton Chase felt that the Universal Australian ran against the grain of experience with nonnative biota:

The landscapes of California have been greatly enriched by the acclimatization here of the eucalyptus. It is not often that the presence of an imported ingredient adds a really natural element to the charm of the scenery; but the eucalyptus, especially the *globulus* variety that has become so common throughout the State, has so truly native an appearance that it seems as if its introduction from Australia must have been more in the nature of a homecoming than of an adoption. The wide, treeless plains and valleys which once lay unrelieved and gasping under the summer sun, and inspired similar sensations in the traveller, are now everywhere graced by ranks and spinneys of these fine trees, beautiful alike, whether trailing their tufty sprays in the wind, or standing, as still as if painted, in the torrid air.[100]

Others agreed that the eucalyptus gave California a little extra something. As a tree specialist typically explained in the 1920s, it imparted a "unique, exotic flavor totally lacking in other parts of the United States."[101] The penchant of a group of southern California–based landscape artists for the tree at this time earned them the label "Eucalyptus School." And though critical of the ill-founded scramble to blanket the state with the tree, Raymond Dasmann did not include it as one of the forces responsible for the "destruction" of California in his famous early 1960s tract. On the contrary, this "graceful" "permanent resident" contributed "beauty to many areas."[102]

Since 1978, however, the debate over the tree's desirability in California has taken a fresh turn. In 1928, Merle Armitage, art critic for the California magazine *West Coaster* and coiner of the rather patronizing term "Eucalyptus School," described this popular genre of landscape art as "harmless." Whether the school's members actually painted gum trees (Douglas Parshall's "Eucalyptus and Clouds" and Orrin White's "Eucalypti" are the best known examples) or other outdoor scenes, their canvases were pleasant enough in a decorative sense. Yet sophisticates brushed them off as bland, superficial, and unsophisticated, and many art critics dismissed them as unimaginative representational renditions of natural objects.[103] Whether the tree itself was harmless was rarely debated. Nowadays, though, many Californians perceive the tree the artists celebrated as downright harmful.

Growing emphasis on its harmful qualities has been partly fueled by growing awareness of the fire hazard it represents, especially on the eastern side of San Francisco Bay. Yet the critique has also assumed the air of an ecological decolonization movement that seeks to reverse what Planchon's promotional essay (translated by the Department of Agriculture in 1875) had referred to as the "colonization of the Eucalyptus."[104] This recent furor has involved the various units of the Golden Gate National Recreation Area in Marin County, but it pivots on a state park—Angel Island.

Fire and eucalyptus enjoy an intimate evolutionary relationship in Australia. Regular outbreaks keep down competitors, improve conditions for regeneration, and recycle nutrients. But American plant ecologists call it a "dirty tree" because of the prodigious quantities of litter it produces, whose flammability is enhanced by high oil content (fire fighters call them "gasoline trees"). An entrepreneur planted large tracts of blue gum between 1910 and 1913 on the grassy hills above Berkeley and Oakland. Nothing came of it commercially, but the trees flourished. In December 1972, an exceptionally hard freeze killed off many of them. The shedding of frost-burned outer branches, leaves, and bark massively compounded the amount of litter, leaving up to 50 tons per acre strewn across 3,000 acres of private and public lands. In some spots, the debris rose waist high.[105]

The summer and fall of 1972 were unusually dry, hot, and windy. Governor Reagan declared a state of emergency in the spring of 1973. President Nixon, a fellow Californian, was reluctant, though, to match this with a federal decree. Congressional hearings in May 1973, at the onset of California's long dry season, considered bills requiring Nixon to furnish federal pre-disaster assistance to Alameda and Contra Costa counties to help with the cost of removing highly combustible litter and felling hazardous dead trees (also for reforestation with natives better adapted to climatic extremes).[106]

The pungent tinder box did not ignite on that occasion. In October 1991, however, fire swept through the Berkeley and Oakland hills, incinerating about 3,000 houses and claiming twenty-five lives. Regardless of how it actually started, most experts and lay persons agreed that the "Australian imports" were largely to blame for the scale of devastation. Congressional testimonies in 1973 had emphasized that objections were entirely expedient: Senator Cranston, for instance, freely acknowledged their beauty.[107] In the fall of 1991, though, a storm of vilification raged through the area in the conflagration's aftermath. To prevent a repetition, many demanded the razing of what they dubbed "trash" trees, "immigrants," and "mongrels."[108] "With this tree, it seems you either love it or fear and hate it," reflected the garden editor of *Sunset Magazine,* a self-confessed eucalyptus enthusiast, on the fire's first anniversary. "And I've noticed," he continued, "that those who fear the tree seem almost irrational about it."[109]

For another self-styled "eucalyptophile," who dubbed these feelings "eucalyptus phobia," this phenomenon was most evident a few miles to the west.[110] Angel Island, the largest in San Francisco Bay, is an 800-acre state park immediately north of Alcatraz island. It had served as a garrison post since the Civil War but is best known as the processing point for East Asian immigrants between 1910 and 1940—hence its popular title, "Ellis Island of the West."[111] Most arrivals were Chinese; the bulk of the 175,000 Chinese who arrived in the United States between 1910 and 1940 landed here. Many of the mostly male Chinese were "paper sons"—those who claimed to be related to someone already an American citizen. An arrival in this category was often detained under high security for many weeks, sometimes years, while his claim's legitimacy was ascertained. Desperate to vent their feelings, detainees engraved poetry on the detention center's soft redwood walls.[112] These poems communicated frustration, dejection, humiliation, pain, and anger. As well as referring to the abominable food and the status of inmates as inferiors to cattle and horses, they compared the detainees' confinement on a lesser Alcatraz to the plight of zoo animals and caged birds. Vengefulness was expressed in the desire to "level" the immigration station.[113]

Recent oral testimony confirms that detainees had plenty of time to gaze at the scenery beyond the barbed wire.[114] When the immigration station opened at China Cove, the local press announced that it boasted "lots of sunshine and a splendid marine view."[115] Yet a poem that one of the first detainees sent to a Chinese newspaper in San Francisco a few months later recorded that "the trees . . . are gloomy outside the prison. . . . the scenery evokes my emotions. Everywhere is desolation."[116] Those gloomy trees were undoubtedly eucalypts. And, ironically, they are the features of the detainee's landscape that have since been leveled, whereas the detention station has been preserved.

Having served as a prisoner of war and internment camp during World War II, Angel Island hosted a Nike missile base in the late 1950s. In 1958, however, thirty-seven acres were designated a state park. Then, in 1962, when the base was "deactivated" and the military departed, the entire island became a park. The quarantine station where arrivals were fumigated and disinfected had been ripped down after closing in 1950. Now, the immigration station and the detention barracks at China Cove were slated for demolition. The site on which they stood was earmarked as a picnic site. In 1970, though, a park ranger, inspecting the condemned barracks with a flashlight, discovered the calligraphy on its walls.[117] After a campaign by San Francisco's Chinese American community, these buildings were restored and opened to the public in the mid-1970s; National Historic Landmark designation followed in 1997. The old barracks now house a museum featuring the original engravings.

As the poems on the redwood walls testify, the eucalyptus groves already loomed tall and somber when the first Chinese disembarked at China Cove. American coastal traders who used "Isla de los Angelos" in the early 1800s knew it by the more prosaic name of Wood Island; enormous live oaks clothed the lower slopes down to the water's edge. When Richard Henry Dana's hide boat visited in 1835, its crew cut a prodigious supply of fuel wood. Extensive cutting (also for construction) left various sites around San Francisco Bay exposed to sharp ocean winds.[118] Many remaining trees were cleared for pasture. Those left standing fed the stoves of the ships that clogged the bay during the Gold Rush. By 1900 the island was characterized by prairie dotted with occasional surviving groves of native buckeye, California bay laurel, coast live oak, bigleaf maple, and toyon.[119]

To furnish windbreaks for vegetable gardens, picnic areas, and encampments, to control erosion, and to supply shade, the island's military authorities planted blue gum between the 1870s and the late 1930s—along with nonnatives from other parts of California and the United States such as Monterey pine, Monterey cypress, sequoia, Douglas fir, Norfolk pine, and black locust, as well as another overseas nonnative, Portuguese cork.[120] Then, in 1979, the California Department of Parks and Recreation (CDPR) issued a general directive for the removal of invasive exotics from state parks and their replacement by noninvasive natives. In line with this recommendation, the Angel Island State Park Resource Management Plan (also formally adopted that year) included a proposal to "control and/or eliminate aggressive introduced plant species that are not a part of either the natural or historic environment but are extending their ranges and crowding out native species."[121]

The blue gum is not a particularly virulent invader. Studies in southern California a few years earlier by Australian geographer J. B. Kirkpatrick had suggested that eucalyptus regeneration was modest, with self-sown seedlings rarely found more than 20 meters from the parent tree. Spread was mostly restricted to roadsides and abandoned farmlands—in other words, open ground with plenty of light. Kirkpatrick also emphasized that its fruits had no special mechanisms for dispersal by birds or other animals. The tree, he concluded, lacked "invasionary prowess." With naturalization quite uncommon, he was confident that it was "unlikely to be a troublesome exotic weed anywhere."[122]

Northern California's moister coastal areas are a far cry from southern (and central) California's water regime, however. In this part of the state, there is sufficient moisture for propagation from seed, especially on sites benefiting from summer fog drip. Dispersal takes place by wind (up to 60 feet away from a 131-foot tree).[123] The original twenty-four acres of blue gum planted on Angel Island now covered nearly ninety acres, the initial plantation and spread having mostly replaced native grasslands.[124] David Boyd, the state park system's senior resource ecologist for the northern California region, drew the same distinction between *natural* and *foreign* that Charles Eliot, Jr., had a century earlier. Blue gums were "completely unacceptable" where "natural values" were uppermost. Publicizing removal plans, Boyd was keen to shift attention to the end (restoration) rather than the means (removal).[125] The parks and recreation department planned to replace eucalypts with live oak, bay, and madrone, coastal shrubs such as sagebrush, chamise, manzanita, and coyote brush, and perennial grasses.[126] This project—the most thorough effort to date to restore the pre-European ecology of a California state park—was supported by the Marin chapters of the California Native Plant Society, Sierra Club, and National Audubon Society as well as the local National Park Service, the Tamalpais Fire Protection District, and the Tamalpais Conservation Club.[127]

The case against the blue gum illustrates how qualities perceived as virtues a century earlier were redefined as drawbacks, whereas the environmental defects the tree was recruited to remedy have been reconceived as assets. Just as those who wanted to introduce the English sparrow were often unimpressed by the quotient of native birds, eucalyptus crusaders deplored the plainness and emptiness of native grasslands and meadows. Now, the new generation of eucalyptus critics wanted to revive the simplicity and integrity of this former scene. For the acclimatizers, the alien feature was the bare California landscape. Today, for many Californians, the eucalyptus itself has become the alien presence. Blue gum boosters once sought to enhance the landscape by adding the tree. Nowadays, opponents seek to improve ecological communities by removing it. Formerly seen as the perfect method for greening the desert, the trees are now accused of creating a "green desert."[128] Successful and beneficent colonization has been reappraised as regrettable invasion. "The tree that captured California" (captured in the sense that it captivated and enchanted) is how *Sunset* magazine hailed the blue gum in the 1950s. "The tree that destroyed California" was the subtitle of a 1997 protest poem by Robert Sward of Santa Cruz, one of the gum tree's most fervent critics.[129]

"Anyone who has had to live with blue gum and other related oversize eucalyptus trees knows they just don't belong," wrote a member of the public supportive of removal on Angel Island. "They are non-native, dirty and dangerous."[130] They were also dismissed as plain useless. A member of the citizens' advisory committee that helped draft the master plan that recommended removal reported as follows on a visit to the groves slated for logging: "I didn't see another soul. People don't go there. . . . And why would they? These are not your landmark Eucalyptus to be saved elsewhere within the park. They are much too close together. The place is dark, silent as the tomb, devoid of sight or sound of birds, insects, mammals, wild flowers."[131]

Another supporter of removal, whose family had come to rue the eucalpyts they had extensively planted with such high hopes nearly a century earlier, warned that "they will in time take over the entire Angel Island."[132] Annoyed by the postponement of removal to facilitate further study, a resident of nearby Tiburon commented that it was "almost as though a Committee to Save the Rabbit might have prevailed in Australia in the 19th Century."[133] Many proponents also reminded the plan's critics that state parks occupied little more than 1 percent of California and that there was hardly a shortage of eucalpts elsewhere in the state.

Attitudes to the eucalyptus had not shifted wholesale, though. Like the

English sparrow, the tree retained some support. In fact, this recent backing has been much stronger than persisting enthusiasm for the bird. A leading advocate, the *San Francisco Chronicle,* chose Arbor Day to publicize National Park Service plans (issued through press release on March 3, 1986) to log off 600 acres on its Marin County lands. Sharing the outlook of the tree's original proponents, the *Chronicle* denounced native plant enthusiasts who wanted to impose a bland, treeless landscape.[134] In the wake of the second public hearings (held in October 1986, on a drastically scaled-back project to determine the feasibility of a more ambitious removal program), disconcerted individuals formed a small citizen's lobby, Preserve Our Eucalyptus Trees (POET). POET's mission was to protect eucalypts across the state, especially those on public parklands.[135] Their motto can be summed up as "Don't Nuke the Eukes."[136]

POET member David Haase informed Boyd that, as a cab driver in San Francisco, he had discussed the matter with "hundreds of passengers from the Bay Area, California, the United States and abroad." He explained that when he told his fares about the removal plan for Angel Island, "the near unanimous response I've gotten is, 'unbelievable,' 'that's stupid,' or 'you're kidding.'" "I and others don't care whether the tree's DNA molecules are originally from here or from somewhere else," he concluded.[137] For eucalyptus defenders, this intrinsic value of all trees regardless of origin was only marginally behind the aesthetic argument. POET and Sierra Club member Flora Davis wanted to know how the supplanting of trees by grassland could be regarded as environmentally progressive at a time of alarming global deforestation.[138]

POET, which quickly became the formal voice of organized opposition, pressed for a proper assessment of the environmental impact of proposed clearances in accordance with the California Environmental Quality Act. Among POET's submissions to CDPR was a petition with 118 signatures collected (allegedly) during a single hour on Angel Island on August 1, 1987. Bowing to pressure from state senators, CDPR agreed to delay logging (scheduled for early September) to allow further study and the opportunity for public review of a draft report (including public hearings). A $25,000, 290-page "Focused Environmental Study," conducted by U.C. Berkeley's Department of Forestry and Resource Management, was published in July 1988.[139] Whereas many exotic grasses were "beyond eradication," the consultants judged that eucalyptus control and eradication were feasible, endorsing the project as a "responsible and cost-efficient means" of removal.[140]

These findings were subjected to intense public scrutiny, not least the material that addressed the project's impact on the island's aesthetic character. The author of this section of the study acknowledged that it was impossible to reach "universal agreement on what aesthetic criteria may best identify landscape quality." He insisted, though, that the native plant complex enjoyed a "visual fit" and "harmonious fit, both ecologically and aesthetically," with the physical landscape. The blue gum's "visual intrusion" violated this "subtle continuity" of the native landscape and its "aesthetic unity."[141] The Sierra Club's Bay Area chapter, the Marin Conservation League, the California Nature Conservancy, and the California Native Plant Society agreed. They signaled their support for phased removal starting with a twenty-four-acre patch near the summit of Mount Livermore, the island's highest point, in the fall of 1988.

Others were not placated. The study's authors, a local critic protested, had ignored the basic fact that "many people like and love the trees."[142] POET characterized the island as a recreational site rather than a preserve for native nature.[143] And many visitors agreed, echoing the sentiments of Smeaton Chase and the Eucalyptus School. "Anyone sensitive to the environment," one of them protested, "can hardly resist a tree that when the leaves are damp glistens in the light, when bathed in sunlight gives filtered shade, and in fog is a mystery of light and darkness."[144] Striking a similar note, a member of the board of directors of the Angel Island Association (a citizen watchdog group), who led a monthly "Tree Walk" to the Immigration Station at China Cove, rhapsodized over "the whisper of the trees, the pungent aroma, the soaring beauty of the trunks and branches."[145] Echoing the rationale of the first generation of eucalyptus enthusiasts, a letter to the *Chronicle* complained that the tree's "soothing, rustling sounds" had been sacrificed for open space with "large swaths abandoned to scrappy 'native vegetation.'"[146]

Emboldened by its success in forcing the National Park Service to shelve its removal project for the Golden Gate recreation area in favor of a more modest containment proposal, POET filed an injunction against the Angel Island plan in October 1988. The lawsuit demanded a full-scale environmental impact report that took into account alternatives to the intended action such as thinning and containment, as well as no action at all.[147] The court ruled in POET's favor. The draft environmental impact report, prepared by a firm of environmental planning and natural resource management consultants, was published in May 1989. Potentially negative impacts, its authors concluded, were "not significant," for eucalyptus groves supported precious little wildlife.[148] A final version, which addressed comments submitted during a mandatory review period (the great majority of them critical), appeared in July. Having weighed alternatives, it pronounced the existing project "environmentally superior."[149] Removal began in the fall of 1990, but the main phase occurred between November 1995 and July 1996. Seventy acres with 12,000 trees were cleared—making a total of eighty acres—which completed the program.

EUCALYPTUS EULOGY: THE NATURAL VALUE OF HERITAGE

Ecological arguments were not the sole preserve of native plant enthusiasts. POET mounted an ecological countercase to CDPR plans as well as an aesthetic one. Walter E. Westman, a forest ecologist serving as a consultant to POET, demanded to know why, of approximately one thousand nonnative and naturalized plant species in California, the eucalyptus had been singled out. What about the hundreds of invasive exotic grasses in state parks?[150] In his view, the blue gum's high profile rendered it an easy target. He also queried whether native grasses could form new cover quickly enough to ameliorate the post-felling problem of erosion, which would open the door for other nonnatives, not least thistle and broom, which are harder to eliminate and control than large trees.[151] He also queried how much of the pre-settlement landscape that park managers sought to restore had really been grassland and flowering forbs, suggesting that Native American fire strategies had contrived this apparently unmodified scenario.[152] A century earlier, the English sparrow's remaining champions had cited the irony of the bird conservationist's selective incitement of violence against this particular species. In similar style, opponents of removal on Angel Island highlighted what they saw as the paradox of environmentalist support for a form of agroforestry usually subjected to their most withering scorn: the clear-cutting of old growth—especially on public lands by a commercial company planning to export eucalyptus pulp chips to Japan.

Friends of the gum tree also seized on recent studies that questioned the tree's reputation as a "faunal desert" by indicating that 57 percent of the island's bird species were present in both eucalyptus stands and native oak woodland, while 8 percent were found exclusively among eucalypts.[153] It had also been known for a decade that migrating western monarch butterflies overwintered at eucalyptus sites throughout coastal California.[154] On this basis, some environmentalists distinguished between the blue gum and other exotic flora. A resident of Santa Cruz insisted that the tree's assistance to the monarch butterfly, which roosted in trees like a flock of starlings, had earned it a legitimate place among the state's flora.[155]

The tree's value in strictly ecological—or aesthetic—terms was never the overriding objection to its removal, however. Ultimately, the tree's advocates stressed its less tangible importance as a living connection with the past. "Those were old trees," reflected a visitor who had booked a campsite on Angel Island for the Fourth of July holiday in 1996, only to find himself in the middle of a logging site: "Older than all of us."[156] The tree's California history, emphasized POET, was "as old as the State itself."[157] Since introduced trees add cultural value to the land, according to this view, then it follows that their removal erases part of the historical archive's natural record.

The argument for protecting remarkable individual trees whose natural value is enhanced through association with a famous person or event differs little from the case for preserving a historic structure or other artifact. A tulip poplar planted by George Washington at Mount Vernon, for instance, is more highly valued than an identical specimen not blessed by an illustrious human connection. In the same way, the oak at Crockett, Texas, under which Davy reputedly camped on his way to join the Texan struggle for independence is no ordinary oak.

California is not as rich in arboreal monuments that bask in reflected human glory as states back east. Nonetheless, it has specimens of the world's oldest and biggest and oldest and tallest tree species—the giant sequoia and the coastal redwood, respectively—named after influential people—not least titanic Union army generals such as Grant and Sherman. And "heritage tree" programs are sprouting the length of North America's Pacific coast. The major criteria for designation as a heritage tree in addition to size, age, and rarity are botanical value and historical value. Of these, the final criterion is by no means the least important. On the contrary, a strong relationship to humans usually boosts their cause. John Rosenow, president of the National Arbor Day Foundation, emphasized the oak's "central part" in American history when he announced the results of the vote for America's National Tree in April 2001. William Penn, Andrew Jackson, and Abraham Lincoln, Rosenow pointed out, were all associated with oaks.[158] Few trees enshrined as heritage make it entirely on their own.

Given that nonnative trees can meet most, if not all, of the five criteria, heritage tree programs do not specifically exclude them—though some programs stipulate that nonnatives must be naturalized to be eligible. Among San Francisco's most famous trees are five blue gums on the site of the Green Eye and Ear Hospital. These were supposedly planted by Mary Ellen ("Mammy") Pleasant on the grounds of her mansion in the Western Addition area (now Octavia Street). A former slave and slave rescuer, Pleasant had moved to San Francisco in 1852 and initiated an abolitionist campaign. In the late 1960s, the hospital wanted to remove the gum trees as a hindrance to pedestrians and source of damage to parked and passing cars. But they were reprieved and became the main feature of a small memorial to the city's most famous nineteenth-century woman.[159] One of the "exceptional" trees of the Los Angeles area selected by a former secretary of the interior is a lemon-scented eucalyptus *(E. citriodora)* that John Muir planted at South Pasadena in 1889.[160] And, like the sequoia and redwood, the blue gum has a National Champion (currently growing in Petrolia, California).

Pakenham would doubtless approve. Yet the National Park Service and state park authorities in California are by no means insensitive to the historical value of nonnative trees—even those not dignified by a link with a

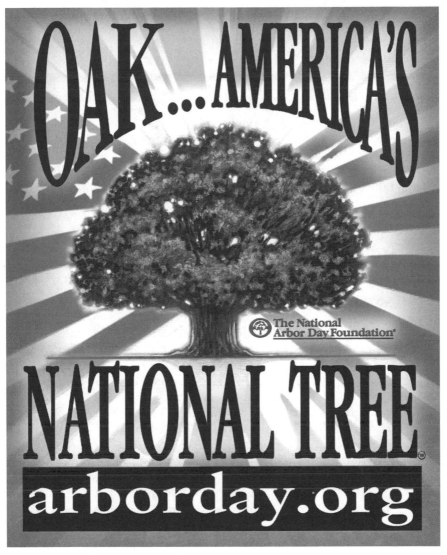

Figure 5. The oak emerged as clear favorite from a National Arbor Day Foundation poll in 2001 to select the American national tree. Courtesy of the National Arbor Day Foundation.

person of renown. The gum tree's stalwarts sought to portray the removers as deniers of history and themselves as loud affirmers of the past. As the eucalyptus removal project on Angel Island was drawing to a close, however, Donald W. Murphy, CDPR director, reiterated the state park mission to "preserve the state's extraordinary biological diversity, and to protect its most valued natural and cultural resources."[161] Those natural and cultural resources included some eucalyptus.

Removal plans on Angel Island exempted six acres near old buildings to preserve eucalypts "within reasonable proximity of the historic structures so that association between the cultural and natural features is maintained."[162] Elsewhere in California, the Etiwanda Windbreaks in San Bernardino—rows of blue gums planted to shelter orchards, fences, and houses from the withering Santa Ana winds that blow in from Cajon Pass—have been entered on the National Register of Historic Places.

City parks and university campuses host some of the oldest surviving eucalypts.[163] Blue gums planted on the Berkeley campus (west grove) in 1871 are reputedly the tallest (200 feet by the late 1980s) outside Australia.[164] Specimens flanking city streets also count among the state's most venerable. The 1996 proposal of state highway authority Caltrans to chop down about a hundred "nuisance" trees lining four-lane El Camino Real (State Highway 82) in Burlingame, San Mateo County, sparked bitter local controversy. Caltrans's maintenance chief in the Bay Area explained that large quantities of leaves and bark blocked storm drains in winter, contributing to road flooding. The trees had also been implicated in accidents by making it difficult for drivers to see oncoming traffic.[165]

Yet for a Burlingame councilman they are "sacred."[166] El Camino Real is California's oldest road, a lateral artery that linked the chain of Spanish missions and presidios. The embattled eucalypts were planted between Belmont and Millbrae in the 1880s, when El Camino was still a dirt road. They were to serve as "nurse trees" for young American elms and to provide shade for cattle herds driven north to San Francisco for slaughter. The native elms withered but the gums flourished.[167] Many have attained 120 feet. Certain residents of El Camino Real, echoing the complaints of their counterparts in Santa Monica, have been protesting since 1916 when a petition denounced the trees as a public safety "menace" during storms and a threat to sewers.[168] A Caltrans arborist explained that the trees were also in poor shape because of bad drainage and paved-over roots.

Whether or not ecological conditions were auspicious, a Burlingame planning commissioner retorted that they "were here first, and they give the area ambience. It's history."[169] Like the proponents of the cull on Angel Island, a Caltrans spokesperson defended removal by declaring that "it's not like we're chopping down an endangered species."[170] Yet Burlingame's eucalyptus defenders see them as living history in a literal sense, a vital and highly visible connection with their town's origins and founding fathers, regardless of their material drawbacks.

Overturning the accusation of monotony—and the charge that exotics en masse are producing an ecological McWorld—some Californians celebrate their blue gums as a source of distinctiveness in a world of creeping sameness. "Rather than destroy California," argued a Sierra Club member from Santa Cruz, "the Eucalyptus plays a rich part in its art, literature and history."[171] The most avid scholarly statement of the tree's desirability in California on historical and cultural grounds was issued in 1992 by Achva Benzinberg Stein and Jacqueline Claire Moxley. Reacting against the "environmental purism" of the 1960s and 1970s to which the eucalyptus allegedly fell victim, their strong sympathies are partly driven by aesthetics. Yet they also consider gum trees endearing "because there is precious little evidence of time and history in California's ever-changing landscape." By contemplating a big old gum tree, they contend, Californians can derive "a sense of some permanence and a scale that is larger than human."[172]

Just how shifting and unstable our sense of permanence can be—and how provisional and slippery our definitions of native and nonnative are too—was appreciated by a Californian who wrote to *Garden and Forest* in 1890 about lavatera, a small tree that flowers in midwinter together with acacias, eucalypts, and other Australian imports. Though he pronounced lavatera "unquestionably indigenous" to California, he felt that "a stranger would take it for an exotic from the southern hemisphere. Such was the impression it gave me when I first saw it."[173] Jake Sigg, chair of the California Native Plant Society's invasive exotics committee, underscored the role of personal perception and the transience of memory when seeking to reassure those distressed by the short-term disruption entailed by removal projects in the Bay Area. Within a few years, he contended, "no one will even know that eucalyptus trees grew in these places."[174]

GETTING BACK TO (LOST) NATURE:
RESTORING ORIGINAL CALIFORNIA

Stein and Moxley also addressed the question of landscape and memory with reference to California's eucalyptus. And, like Sigg, they used an argument based on the brevity—or absence—of public memory. But their objective was the exact opposite of his: to undercut the case for rehabilitating native species and bolster the case for retaining eucalyptus.

Scholars are becoming more attuned to the social, ethnic, and racial specificity of American landscapes. In particular, they focus on the "whiteness" of those "heritage" landscapes par excellence—the national parks and wilderness areas of the West.[175] One of the purposes of these places has been to preserve the physical conditions that possess the power to evoke a sense of what the continent was like when Euro-American explorers and pioneers first clapped eyes on the "new world." Just as the history and meaning of these sacred sites is primarily Euro-American, so too, traditionally, has been their clientele.

Stein's and Moxley's "defense of the nonnative" meshed with this critique of the exclusive vision of the relationship between nature, nation, and race embodied in conventional "heritage" landscapes. Given that California's population is becoming ever more youthful, immigrant-derived, and non-European, they held up the eucalyptus as a more familiar and fitting symbol of today's California than trees associated with the pre-eucalyptus landscape of which "most Californians have no memory."[176] For them, the accrued cultural value outweighs any negative environmental impacts. Accordingly, they were deeply troubled by any obliteration of these particular living reminders of the past.

This approach contrasted sharply with the position in countries such as India and Spain, where ordinary folk view the tree as another oppressive tool wielded by corporate interests. At pains to exonerate the tree from its eco-villainous reputation, Stein and Moxley brushed aside this grassroots backlash, attributing it to the novelty of plantations and trees that "seemed to interfere in [local] lifestyles." Their eucalyptus stands for tolerance, democracy, and pluralism in a state that has often been in the vanguard of American anti-immigrant initiatives and was consumed by another bout at the time of writing.[177] Roberta Friedman had concurred a few years earlier, offering the tree as the "embattled symbol of all transplants to this land, where bumper stickers read 'Welcome to California. Now go home.'"[178]

The reaction to the belated arrival of some of eucalyptus's habitual pests exemplifies the strong human attachment to the gum tree in certain parts of California. Various insects live on eucalypts in Australia. The freedom from their predations that eucalypts elsewhere enjoy helps explain their more rapid growth (an estimated 20 percent more stem wood). The dearth of leaf eaters translates into larger crowns and more foliage generally.[179] Kinney's late nineteenth-century observation that "no exotic enemy of moment has thus far appeared" held good until the 1980s, when the debate between friends and foes of the eucalyptus was sharpened by the arrival of its archenemy from back home, the longhorned borer. This "Australian killer with a taste only for eucalyptus," wrote Philip Taubman, lays its eggs in the outer bark, and its larval grubs then bore into the inner bark where they feed on cambium, which carries nutrients to the tree.[180] The borer showed up in southern California in 1984, probably in wooden pallets carrying Australian goods. Drought-enfeebled trees were especially vulnerable since moisture is required to manufacture the gum the tree normally secretes to smother its assailant. During 1995, 1,500 infected blue gums were felled in Ardenwood Regional Park at the southern end of San Francisco Bay. This invasive insect's assault allowed Stein and Moxley to present the eucalyptus as "another symbol for the threat of global environmental destruction."[181]

Since gum trees were deemed to lend character to the Bay Area's urban landscape, the insect's arrival and activities were widely reported. Its ravages on various prestigious university campuses received the most publicity. Two hundred and fifty of Stanford's red gums have capitulated since 1992, jeopardizing, in Taubman's view, the campus's "distinctive California accent," which derives from its "brilliant sunshine and eucalyptus fragrance."[182] Eucalypts planted by its founder in the 1880s and 1890s are an equally striking feature of the Mills College grounds. Mills's alumnae song, "Remember," bids its old girls to recall not only the good times and their bosom friends but also the elegant eucalypts. The college alerted alumnae to the dying trees by inserting a leaf in every fund-raising letter sent out to meet the costs of sick tree removal.[183]

This affection for the eucalyptus in California encourages us to think about the relation between our emotional attachments to trees and their position within our personal landscapes of memory. If you grew up around gum trees, then the gum tree seemed "right" for that place. The transported landscape was the one that belonged if you had no knowledge of its foreign origins or status as the Universal Australian and, moreover, the redwood had no place in your personal history. One wonders, though, how much affection and support for the gum tree are predicated on its relatively weak invasive prowess. If the Universal Australian had displaced those hallowed native trees associated with an older California—the live oak, the redwood, and the giant sequoia—would its critics have the field to themselves?

The clash of powerful feelings over the tree also prompts us to examine the relation between the world of nonhuman nature and the realm of human history. Nature and history were conceptual opposites around which debate over the tree's legitimacy revolved as much as the polarities of native and nonnative, if less overtly. Exempt from removal on Angel Island were trees with "historical value"—their historical assets being perceived to compensate for the absence (or shortage) of natural (i.e., native) value. Plans to recreate an approximation of "pre-settlement" ecological conditions, though based on a historically contingent vision of the natural world, were frequently presented as ahistorical by opponents of removal. "The island is not really a natural park," contended Clyde Wahrhaftig, an emeritus professor of geology at Berkeley. "It is a historical park, and the eucalyptus are part of that history."[184] In his view, native trees such as coastal live oak represented nature. The eucalyptus, however, stood for history (and, for him, history trumped nature). For others, the eucalyptus represented nature *and* history—and seeking to remove it tampered with both—for, as POET stressed, the tree had become a well-behaved part of the natural landscape. And who had the right to decide what is natural in nature?

If you thought in terms of a past deeper than the last century or so, however, then a live oak came with more historical value added than a relative newcomer like the blue gum. The tidy categories of nature and history were further disturbed by the fire threat many ecologists believed the gum trees represented for Angel Island's historic structures. For these reasons, the study of the blue gum in California offers a pungent opportunity for exploring not only personal visions of the natural world but also the porous relationship between nature and history and what it means to be within or outside these domains.

LANDSCAPES OF PURITY AND INTOLERANCE

An adjective eucalyptus supporters regularly used to describe removal projects in California in the 1980s and 1990s was *purist*—and the connotations were not positive. As they saw it, native species advocates had a vision of purity that required the wholesale elimination of alien impurities from the native flora. Ecological restoration, in other words, was a decontamination process akin to the sociocultural revitalization movements anthropologist Anthony Wallace had identified in the strictly human world. In an attempt to placate opponents toward the end of Angel Island's eucalyptus removal project, CDPR director Murphy reemphasized that only a tenth of the island had been affected.[185] Unmoved, the tree's champions sought to open up a wider front in the struggle against purification. The *San Francisco Chronicle* quoted an unnamed state parks ranger who wondered where on earth the zealous pursuit of environmental purity would lead—to a landscape consisting of nothing but poison oak and scrub oak?[186]

"We aren't against all eucalyptus," Boyd sought to reassure opponents of removal on Angel Island.[187] And California's ecologist restorers were perfectly capable of distinguishing between the dubious activities of invasive species in natural or seminatural areas and the positive contribution of crops of nonnative origin within the confines of the agricultural landscape. Nonetheless, critics portrayed eucalyptus removal as the thin edge of the wedge. At stake, they warned, was everything California had become through a powerful and far-reaching process of incorporation. A local journalist invited fellow Californians to ponder the larger implications of uprooting gum trees and accepting uncompromising native species zeal in a state whose agricultural economy was firmly rooted in transplanted species and a cosmopolitan ethos:

> Cotton came from India, oranges from Malay, almonds from Asia. Shall we reject them? . . . Must Golden Gate Park revert to sand dunes? Must Los Angeles expunge its palms? . . . Must Napa Valley uproot its vineyards? . . . Let's tell the purists to start their purification at home. Let's tell them to dig up everything non-native in their own yards. And of course they mustn't eat anything that wasn't already growing here when Junipero Serra arrived.[188]

As this feverish invocation of a wholesale floral purge indicated, the working definition of a native California plant (and animal) is one that was present in any part of the area that would become the state of California *before* May 14, 1769, when the first European settler, Father Junipero Serra, arrived in San Diego.[189] Applying this criterion strictly, a plant that an American Indian brought to the territory of present-day California on May 13, 1769—assuming this could be documented—would qualify as native. The journalist's rhetoric about floral repatriation was clearly groundless scaremongering. Nonetheless, restorationist references to "pre-settlement" environments and to an era before "modern people's influence" remain problematic in that they are politically and culturally shaped as well as ecologically grounded.[190] Native plant advocates counter the charge that the choice of 1769 is ecologically arbitrary by arguing that, although native peoples undeniably moved species around in "pre-settlement" times, their activities cannot compare in scale and impact with "modern people's" transfers.

This does not necessarily mean that all the state's nonnative "problem" plants are from outside California. Europeans also shifted flora from one part of California to another, thereby creating homegrown exotics. The eucalyptus's supporters did not mention it, but another invasive nonnative targeted for removal on Angel Island was the Monterey pine *(Pinus radiata)*. Though native to Monterey Bay—less than 150 miles to the south—this pine is just as foreign to the Bay Area. Visiting a new botanical garden in Rabat, Morocco, in the 1920s, David Fairchild had encountered this pine (successfully transplanted to Australia too). Its Moroccan presence served him as "a striking example of the illusion that . . . the cultivated plants of any region should be limited to the species that by fortuitous good fortune happen to be there at this particular geologic epoch."[191]

Monterey pine is almost extinct in its native region, limited to a few small areas in Monterey, Santa Cruz, and San Louis Obispo counties and a couple of islands in the Santa Barbara Channel. It tends to be overbearing, though, where introduced (not least in Australia, where it is infiltrating largely unmodified eucalyptus forests adjacent to plantations). The reasons for this planetary plant's success are the same as those that explain the blue gum's spread: release from the "biological burden" of competition from other tree species and diseases.[192] In fact, Boyd regarded it is a worse offender than the eucalyptus on Angel Island.[193]

Nor is Monterey pine an isolated instance. In the dunes of northwest California's Humboldt County, the Nature Conservancy organized an annual "lupine bash" in the early 1990s, the yellow bush lupine having been introduced at a Coast Guard signal station in 1908 from the southern part of the state. Meanwhile, in Monterey County, restorationists replant dunes with the same species; this lupine was once an integral part of the local scrub community, its historic range extending from the Sacramento Valley south to San Diego.[194]

California's ecological restorers were much more evenhanded than suggested by the champions of the eucalyptus, with their axiomatic charges of purgation, xenophobia, and worse. The friends of the gum tree often reduced the matter to a simple question of native versus nonnative. A typical opinion piece claimed that rationales for removal based on fire hazard and public safety were fig leaves, insisting that "the real reason the environmental purists want to wage genocide against the eucalyptus is that the trees aren't native to California."[195] Another protest against the resurrection of a "little piece of California's prehistoric landscape" (Boyd's phrase) by returning Angel Island to the ecological conditions of the 1790s, when the first Europeans arrived, dismissed "native vegetation" as "environmentalist buzzwords cynically invoked to subdue those plagued with post-colonial guilt and/or Anglo-Saxon self-loathing."[196]

Quick to connect plants with people (far quicker, in fact, than the native species advocates they accused of nativism), many "euk lovers" felt humbled by the tree's superior claims on American ancestry.[197] In the absence of formal criteria for bestowing floral citizenship on introduced species, a San Franciscan believed that any eucalyptus "planted (born) in California" over a century ago should be "accorded native born status"—an extension of *jus solis* citizenship to trees.[198] The champions of indigenous plants who cultivated the American garden never really recognized (let alone confronted) the paradox that their historically and ecologically correct vision of a pre-Europeanized, Edenic landscape consisting exclusively of native nature's specimens specifically excluded *them* too. But the gum tree's champions who labored in the global garden were fully alive to this irony and relished it at every possible opportunity. For Emil Schmidt, a native son of the Golden West, who grew unconventional eucalyptus varieties near Salinas, the logical conclusion of the "purist" approach would be to return California to its remaining native peoples.[199] Pursuing this standard refrain, Chris Womack of San Francisco, one of POET's founders, queried the lack of provision in the Angel Island environmental study for repopulation with aboriginal peoples.[200]

The most telling example, though, of the eucalyptus proponent's efforts to deflect discussion into a juvenile debate over national origins and literal restitution was a cartoon by George Russell in a Marin County newspaper (*Coastal Post,* July 18, 1988) which POET adopted in its 1988 campaign urging CDPR to study alternatives to eucalyptus removal. "We've plans to restore Angel Island to original conditions. . . . No non-native species will be allowed," says a park ranger to a featureless face. In the second part of the cartoon, the featureless face is revealed to be that of an American Indian, who responds with "Right." In an expression of continuing support for removal at the height of the controversy over removal, two Sierra Club members from Marin County registered their distaste for this strategy:

They excell [sic] in name-calling—for example declaring that those who support the State plan are "fascists"—and argue that, since most of the U.S. population is descended from immigrants, no one except a native-born Indian is justified in supporting eucalyptus removal. If they really wish to put an anthropomorphic spin on this debate, they might do well to remember that there has been much criticism of the way our native Indians were deprived of their heritage and their lands.[201]

Eucalyptus defenders routinely equated support for native vegetation with nativism. Jean Severinghaus insisted that removal was at variance with "an atmosphere supportive of cultural diversity, supportive of our California ethos of immigrants mixed with longer term inhabitants, supportive of all people's values, and not placing nativist values above others."[202] A similar reaction came from two academics with no particular interest in the eucalyptus controversy but who are sympathetic to the role of human processes in ecological systems and critical of what they see as an undue focus among environmentalists on wildlands as the only environment of real value. Sally Fairfax and Lynn Huntsinger, forest and range management policy specialists at the University of California at Berkeley, tell a story from the early 1990s about a seminar they attended in Berkeley's American Cultures Program (designed to raise awareness of cultural diversity). A topic that cropped up in this particular seminar was CDPR's eucalyptus removal campaign. "The chair of the Chicano studies program leaned back in his chair and asked, 'Isn't that just another one of these anti-immigrant things?'" In view of the prevailing climate of hostility toward immigrants in California at that time, Fairfax and Huntsinger ask, "Is it coincidental that we find it so easy to rally round stamping out alien invaders as an ecological moral crusade?"[203]

Stein and Moxley also underplayed material objections, attributing the impulse to protect vulnerable natives against aggressive aliens to "old nationalistic, racial, and xenophobic concepts." Others went further—and were more specific—in their deployment of emotive human analogies. Borrowing provocative terminology initially applied in 1992 to the brutalization, programmatic massacre, and deportation of Bosnian Muslim civilians by Serbian and Croatian soldiers and paramilitaries, a former executive director of the Angel Island Association protested that "this habitat restoration is like an 'ethnic cleansing' operation."[204] The ultimate weapon in their arsenal, however, was a reminder of the popularity of native species promotion in Nazi Germany.[205] Severinghaus characterized the "genocide approach to one particular species of tree" as "following in Hitler's footsteps."[206] Meanwhile, Boyd, who supervised the Angel Island felling operation, was accused of being a "plant Nazi."[207]

"Does the lay public," California ecologist Michael Barbour wondered in

1996, "privately make some unspoken link between wanting the landscape to be kept native and wanting the political borders closed to foreign human immigration?" And to the extent that Americans made this connection, how far was awareness of Nazi enthusiasm for native plants responsible?[208] With the final chapter I move into this territory, in an effort to understand the nature of recent relationships between an "ecology of fear" turning on antipathy to exotic flora and fauna and a wider "culture of fear" grounded in anti-immigrant feeling.[209]

Chapter 5

The Nature of Alien Nation

When you've finished your own toilet in the morning, then it is time to attend to the toilet of your planet. . . . You must see to it that you pull up regularly all the baobabs, at the very first moment that they can be distinguished from the rose-bushes which they resemble so closely in their earliest youth. . . . I do not much like to take the tone of a moralist. But the danger of the baobabs is so little understood. . . . "Children," I say plainly, "watch out for the baobabs!"

ANTOINE DE SAINT-EXUPÉRY, *The Little Prince*, 1943

A traveller in Europe becomes a stranger as soon as he quits his own kingdom; but it is otherwise here. We know, properly speaking, no strangers; his is every person's country.

HECTOR ST. JOHN DE CRÈVECOEUR, *Letters from an American Farmer*, 1782

THE NATURE OF FEAR AND THE GREENING OF HATE

He did not refer to the storm raging over the eucalyptus in northern California. The Universal Australian's champions there were precisely the sort of people Michael Pollan had in mind, though, when he criticized the growing emphasis on native plants in 1994. In his *New York Times* article, the prominent gardening writer coined the term "multihorticulturalist" to describe someone with a cosmopolitan, pluralistic vision of the plant world.[1] Likewise, the gum tree's critics in northern California were a prime example of those Pollan refers to as ecologically correct native plant purists. Emerging from beneath the broad canopy of California's eucalyptus to contemplate the bigger national landscape, in this final chapter I examine the sociocultural ramifications of the controversy over the ecological impact of nonnative species. This debate owes its wide reach, not least, to the habitual use of terminology heavily saturated with human connotations, which constitutes a distinctive manifestation of that hardy perennial known as anthropocentrism. By studying the language we use to convey our attitudes to nonnative species, I confront the charge of nativism that today's defenders of nonnatives routinely level at those who bemoan the impact of certain species of foreign flora and fauna on their native counterparts.

I also return, once again, to the question of the relationship between efforts to combat nonnative plants and attempts to restrict human immigration. The multihorticulturalist constituency, the most recent manifestation of the green cosmopolitanism of David Fairchild's generation, feels empowered by the trends of contemporary history. Fairchild believed that his internationalist stance made particular sense within a world that was fast becoming a global community. The processes of economic, cultural, and botanical integration he had praised at the beginning of the century were so far advanced by the 1990s that even he would have been taken aback. Despite the indifference of these globalizing tendencies to national borders and other fences, however, the wind seems to be in the sails of those who want to shore up those vanishing boundaries and reassert corroded traditional identities in order to recover a specific sense of place. I conclude with some reflections on the current debate about the role and status of nonnative species and the contribution the historian can make.

As the eucalyptus removal project on Angel Island underlines, the cause of native nature gathered unprecedented momentum in the early 1990s. Across the nation, local ordinances stipulated that landscape architects include a certain proportion of native species in their projects. In Minnesota, the nursery industry's lobbying narrowly defeated a 1991 bill that would have prohibited the sale of any plant not present in the state before 1800.[2] Pollan (the grandson of Jewish immigrants from Russia) strongly objected to what he saw as the wilderness ethic's intrusion into the garden by stealth under the guise of "natural garden" ideology, to which the native plant ethos was integral. Like members of Preserve Our Eucalyptus Trees, Pollan railed against the "ecologically correct" "obsession with native-plant purity" that dismissed immigrant plants as " 'flora non grata,' with 'invasive aliens' subject to deportation." In his view, this conflation of the wild, the natural, the native, and the national betrayed a profound antihumanism and stifling authoritarianism.[3]

Pollan's immediate target was Ken Druse's recent book, *The Natural Habitat Garden*, which articulated a new mission for gardeners: to "expand the realm" of indigenous flora and fauna "forced out" of their native range by nonnatives.[4] Having accused Druse of wanting to "close the border" against all nonnative plants, Pollan then took his argument a stage further. "The garden," he observed, "isn't the only corner of American culture where nativism is in flower just now." Native plant advocacy was flourishing within a social and political climate "rife with anxieties about immigration and isolationist sentiment."[5] To publicize the danger of what he referred to as "ideology in the garden masquerading as science," he drew attention to the horticultural and landscape gardening policies of the Third Reich that had been designed to purge German nature of pernicious foreign influences.

Pollan's portrayal of American native plant gardeners drew heavily on the recent writings of two German garden historians, Gert Gröning and Joachim Wolschke-Bulmahn. Their work during the 1990s (frequently coauthored) is highly critical of the turn to the native, which they also regard as a violation of the garden's primary purpose: the provision, through artifice, of beautiful places for human pleasure. In 1992, Gröning and Wolschke-Bulmahn emphasized that "associations of unwanted plants and unwanted persons" have not been restricted to Nazi Germany, and they found Nazi enthusiasm for native plants "particularly disquieting when one relates the phenomenon to more contemporary events." The current issues they alluded to were a German "mania" for native plants and an upsurge in antagonism toward certain foreigners in parts of Germany.[6]

To support their argument that native plant proponents "sometimes connect nationalistic and racist ideas about society" with their cause, thus "possibly promot[ing] xenophobia," Gröning and Wolschke-Bulmahn routinely quote a passage from a 1938 gardening book by Rudolf Borchardt, a German Jewish literary figure who lived in Tuscany for decades:

> If this kind of garden-owning barbarian became the rule, then neither a gillyflower nor a rosemary, neither a peach-tree nor a myrtle sapling nor a tea-rose would ever have crossed the Alps. Gardens connect people, time and latitudes. If these barbarians ruled, the great historic process of acclimatization would never have begun and today we would horticulturally still subsist on acorns. . . . The garden of humanity is a huge democracy. . . . It is not the only democracy which such clumsy advocates threaten to dehumanize.[7]

Pollan, who was equally impressed by Borchardt's celebration of a pluralistic and internationalist green democracy, selected this quotation as a concluding flourish for his 1994 article.

The association of unwanted people with other unwanted biota and the perception of close links between native species–loving environmentalists and xenophobes were also the main ingredients of a contemporary novel set in California—though the focus here was fauna rather than flora. The period flavor of *The Tortilla Curtain* by T. Coraghessan Boyle derives from racial tensions that culminated in the Los Angeles riots of 1992 and the passage, two years later, of Proposition 187, a package of prohibitive measures to curb "'undocumented" Mexicans. Delaney Mossbacher, the book's main character, is a freelance nature writer who contributes a monthly nature column to an outdoor magazine. He lives in an upscale hilltop community—the product of white flight—apparently safe from the Mexican hordes that break through the border (the thin and brittle "tortilla curtain" of the novel's title) and overrun the flatlands below.

To keep this alien menace at bay, Arroyo Blanco's residents install a security gate manned around the clock. For further protection, they encircle themselves with a seven-foot wall. Mossbacher initially opposes both gate and wall (erected, of course, by illegal immigrants), branding them as "intimidating and exclusionary, antidemocratic even." But he wrestles with, and eventually abandons his liberal humanism for blatant racial hatred when he discovers, on one of his daily rambles in Topanga Canyon State Park, that a pair of illegal aliens are hiding out in his beloved local retreat. Mossbacher is outraged by the desecrating evidence of makeshift occupation: "That was state property down there, rescued from the developers and their bulldozers and set aside for the use of the public, for nature, not for some outdoor ghetto . . . thoughtless people, stupid people, people who wanted to turn the whole world into a garbage dump."[8] Human and nonhuman menaces are conflated when a coyote snatches one of the Mossbacher family's little pet dogs. The wall is there to guarantee that "no terrestrial thing, whether it came on two legs or four, could get in without an invitation." Mossbacher tries to alert fellow residents to the danger of leaving out food for the coyotes and to get them to see the similarity between "illegals" and unruly local wildlife.[9]

There are few better examples of an invasive species that is both nonnative and native than the "unstoppable" coyote *(Canis latrans)*. This astonishingly adaptable canine is native in political-historical terms; it originates within the territory of the United States. It is nonnative, though, in the sense that it has spread from its historic range within the Great Plains to occupy every continental American state. A more straightforward instance of an invasive "foreign" species that crops up in *Tortilla Curtain* is the starling. Still smarting from his neighbors' indifference to coyotes, Mossbacher observes two of these birds pushing aside the native wrens and finches at his backyard bird feeder. This act of foreign aggression inspires him to write a series of articles on introduced species. His research informs him that the mangy starlings that infest the parking lot at his local McDonald's restaurant are descended from a flock released a century ago in his home town, New York City, by a "Shakespeare buff who felt that all the birds mentioned in the Bard's works should roost in North America."[10] The starling's infiltration of Mossbacher's backyard mirrors the pollution of his own perfectly organized and contented life by a disease-like Mexican creature.

Other invasive nonnatives conspire to further disrupt Mossbacher's ordered and stable existence. Tumbleweeds blow across his yard. Another invasive species from within the United States, the Virginia opossum, rifles cat food from the sack in his garage. And after a rain shower, he compares the shining wet blacktop of the highway into his deluxe community to the roads in Florida that vanished under a "glistening field of flesh when the Siamese walking catfish were on the move in all their ambulatory millions." This aquarium escapee (which made a fleeting appearance at the beginning of my book) is the ultimate alien nightmare: "unstoppable, endlessly breeding . . . gobbling up the native fishes like popcorn."[11]

If the degree of meaningful overlap Boyle portrays between hostility to nonnative species such as the starling and concurrent debates over immigrants is questionable, so is the closeness of the connection Pollan, Gröning, and Wolschke-Bulmahn draw between "natural gardening" in the United States in the early 1990s and native plant advocacy in Nazi Germany. A telling example of Gröning's and Wolschke-Bulmahn's paranoid style is how the latter quotes George Miller, the American author of a book that promotes landscaping with native plants in the American Southwest: "Plants are part of our great national heritage. The plants that have sunk their roots in Southwest soil since the last Ice Age can help us understand that our psyches and society are equally rooted to the earth." Wolschke-Bulmahn interprets this as "frightening evidence" of an American reincarnation of the Nazi's "blood-and-soil" *(blut und boden)* mentality.[12] But he has in fact torn Miller's statement from its context, which details a range of material benefits flowing from the use of native plants, such as superior wildlife habitat and lower maintenance costs (notably savings on fertilizer, pesticides, and irrigation). Miller also wants to preserve the heritage of the Southwest's native peoples as well as the ecological world encountered by the region's first Europeans.[13] Moreover, in his rush to roll nationalism, nativism, and native nature into a single malevolent entity, Wolschke-Bulmahn has misquoted Miller, who actually refers to local plants as an aspect of "our great *natural* heritage," not "our great *national* heritage" (my emphasis).[14]

The pursuit of heritage, David Lowenthal argued in 1991, "*differentiates; we treasure most the things that set us apart.*"[15] Cherishing what makes us different, though, does not require the denigration of what we are different from. Heritage is not the same thing as hate.[16] Love of nation does not demand hatred of other nations. Nativism is not equivalent to nationalism; it represents its darker side. By the same token, love of native plants does not require rejection of plants from other places. Yet the comparison between native plant advocacy and nativism is so reflexive for this latter-day generation of green cosmopolitans (Pollan's multihorticulturalists) and has such powerful resonance that Sara Stein, another American native species champion Pollan singled out for criticism in 1994, has felt compelled to distance herself formally from the "purists." Employing the same metaphorically charged language as multihorticulturalists, she identifies herself as a pluralist who accepts well-behaved naturalized foreigners ("responsible citizens"). "I haven't the personality for ethnic cleansing," she explains. "Much as I take pride in being botanically patriotic, I stop short of that degree of xenophobia."[17] The vast majority of botanical patriots do not go that far either.

The connection between botanical (and animal) patriotism and the more conventional variety has always been complicated—much more so than the likes of Pollan imply. And the influence of eco-jingoism has been more modest than many multihorticulturalists suggest.[18] This complexity is illustrated by the relationship between the old-stock Americans who called themselves Native Americans and the nation's native fauna and flora. Subramaniam objects to the appropriation, by the descendants of Euro-American immigrants in the United States, of "native" status—a designation she believes properly applies only to indigenous peoples.[19] This Euro-American seizure of native identity was indubitably a striking feature of opposition to the English sparrow in the late nineteenth century. What Subramaniam does not point out, though, is that campaigns against exotics deemed invasive—past as well as present—typically pit these neo-Europeans against fauna and flora of European origin on behalf of the indigenous nonhuman counterparts of those peoples who were truly Native Americans. The ignominious English sparrow came from England, not from countries like Italy or Poland—the sources of the newcomers the Anglo-American nativists despised (though the bird also inhabited these other countries).

Nor are the plants most heavily criticized by enthusiasts for native nature in today's California from the same regions that currently supply most of the state's human immigrants. They include English ivy (which Subramaniam cites as one of the nation's most vilified foreign plants), German ivy, Scotch broom, and (as we have seen) Australian eucalyptus.[20] On the current "red alert" and "to be kept a careful eye on" lists of the California Exotic Pest Plant Council (CalEPPC) are three quintessentially English species: hawthorn, foxglove, and holly.

Meanwhile, CalEPPC venerates the indigenous flora of North America's Southwest prior to European arrival. Weed whacking is not a natural extension of immigrant bashing (or a surrogate form). Just as immigration restriction organizations and xenophobes have no policy on nonnative plants, CalEPPC and the California Native Plant Society have no immigration policy.[21]

Subramaniam also overstates the extent to which ideological and political fanaticism has targeted nonhuman lifeforms of foreign origin. (She also gives the impression that antipathy toward invasive exotics is confined to the developed West. But, as the controversy over the eucalyptus demonstrates, "foreign" trees are perhaps even more unpopular in countries like India and Thailand than they are in California.) It is true that material and cultural features more or less accepted as part of a nation's fabric during peacetime can suddenly become objects of hatred as they are reidentified with their national origins when the nation in question becomes a wartime enemy. The desire to purify the United States of noxious German influences after American entry into World War I, for example, in which William T. Hornaday was so heavily involved, encompassed the renaming of foods and dogs. Sauerkraut was relabeled "liberty cabbage," while German shepherds and dachshunds were metamorphosed into Alsatians and "liberty hounds," respectively. More recently, in the context of French opposition to the

American-led invasion of Iraq, we have the attempted conversion of French fries into "liberty fries."

The world wars also illustrate how enemies are dehumanized through animalization, a process that facilitates beastly behavior toward the animalized. Examining American stereotypes of the Japanese as lice, scorpions, cockroaches, gophers, and malarial mosquitoes during World War II, Edmund Russell shows how "national and natural enemies" can be fused into a single menace.[22] What this xenophobic mentality lacked in both world wars, however, was an eco-jingoistic dimension. There was no backlash against German ivy in 1917. Nor were Washington's trademark Japanese cherry trees assailed after the attack on Pearl Harbor. It is not difficult, though, to imagine the anthropomorphic abuse that would have been heaped on the Hessian fly had it appeared in American wheat fields in 1917 rather than a hundred and fifty years earlier, or on the Asian tiger mosquito had it showed up early in 1942, in the wake of Pearl Harbor, instead of fifty years later. In the absence of war and of the simultaneous, if coincidental arrival of a foreign species, the chances that nonnative species will be singled out are pretty low, however powerful the antipathy toward certain racial or ethnic groups. Marauding anti-Oriental mobs in San Francisco during the 1880s did not exchange their cudgels for axes and displace their xenophobic wrath onto the Chinese tree of heaven.

Those who seek to curb the growth of invasive nonnative plants flatly reject the allegation that their beliefs and activities are reactionary, hate-filled, and militaristic. Addressing the alleged Nazi connection in the context of the use of native plants in restoration projects, one of the pioneers of the ecological restoration movement issued a swift rebuttal to Pollan in 1994. According to William R. Jordan III, the ideas and policies that cosmopolitans such as Pollan construe as antidemocratic, iniquitous, and exclusionary are in fact intended to rectify injustice and benefit embattled minorities. Jordan inverted the relationship between the heterogeneous and the homogeneous, portraying native species proponents as promoters of biological (and cultural) diversity, the respecters of difference defying the onslaught of deathly uniformity. In short, he claimed the mantle of true multihorticulturalism. If anything in the garden and the wider landscape is ruthless and authoritarian, Jordan argued, it is the exotic majority that has overwhelmed local distinctiveness.[23] Like Nazi attempts to "Germanize" the landscape of occupied Poland in the early 1940s by planting trees and hedges, the behavior of invasive nonnatives was easily seen as imperialistic by native species proponents more than happy to return anthropomorphic fire.[24]

The early 1990s was also the time when the wider societal and cultural implications of the scientific debate over the consequences of alien species for native ecosystems were first fully aired among biological scientists.

Stanley Temple triggered the exchange in the journal *Conservation Biology* with a 1990 editorial seeking to communicate the urgency of a largely neglected problem. He argued that conservation biologists "should be as proficient at eradicating exotic species as they are at saving endangered species." In fact, the latter might well require the former.[25]

Ariel Lugo protested that most exotics become naturalized without causing any trouble worth mentioning.[26] Bruce Coblentz, responding to both Temple's original editorial and Lugo's riposte, echoed the latter's call for recognition of the harmlessness (and beneficence) of many exotics. Yet, like the proponents of eucalyptus removal on Angel Island, he was also critical of the excesses of the attack on indigenous species proponents. Not even the most fervent advocate of native forms, he emphasized, was recommending the repatriation of well-established agricultural staples such as wheat and cattle, which had displaced native grasses and grazers centuries ago but whose contributions to the nation were unquestionable. More recently arrived species, however, were a horse of a different color: "Responsible ecological stewardship should demand that an exotic be proven benign before being judged acceptable."[27] Unmoved by Coblentz's case-by-case approach and distinction between the past and the present, Lugo argued provocatively that judging species according to their place of origin was tantamount to judging people by their religion, nationality, or skin color.[28]

How strong is the evidence for these allegations of recent common cause between anti-immigration sentiment and environmentalists exercised by invasive alien species? As the tale of the English sparrow illustrates, immigration as an area of conservationist concern first arose among those of William T. Hornaday's generation who singled out "new" immigrants as a threat to America's native wildlife. In 1948, in his international best seller, *Road to Survival*, William Vogt went further, positing a relationship between immigrants and rising population, dwindling natural resources, and vanishing open spaces. He reacted angrily to an Indian economist's suggestion that the United States and Canada, with their vast empty lands, "should open their doors to Moslems, Sikhs, Hindus (and their sacred cows) to reduce the pressure caused by untrammeled copulation." Animals removed from their usual surroundings often proliferated wildly, he noted, selecting the starling's American exploits as a particularly grotesque example of the dispossession of native species.[29] Alluding to books with "hair-raising titles" like Vogt's, in his pioneering 1958 study of bioinvasion British ecologist Charles Elton concurred that the population problem was central to the rapid deterioration of the global environment. Expanding "like giant snails," people were the ultimate invasive species, and, he warned, "we have been introducing too many of ourselves into the wrong places."[30] During the early Cold War, however, there was more concern with ideological contamination and infiltration from communism and communist countries than with immigration per se.

Notions of racial inequality legitimated by science were thoroughly discredited by the early 1950s. During the 1920s, Franz Boas's protests against white supremacist ideology ran very much against the grain of scientific, sociological, and popular thinking. In the 1930s, though, Boas was at the forefront of what Thomas Gossett terms the "scientific revolt against racism."[31] In a revised edition of *The Mind of Primitive Man* ("the bible of antiracists everywhere," according to Marshall Hyatt), Boas ridiculed Madison Grant's "dithyrambic praise of the blond, blue-eyed long-headed White and his achievements" in *The Passing of the Great Race* (1916) and denounced eugenics and sterilization for the "mentally feeble" and "socially unfit."[32] And, after Hitler seized power, Boas had inveighed against Nazi racial beliefs and policies with the same vigor and passion he had marshalled to denounce racial discrimination and religious intolerance in his adopted country, sustaining this assault until his death in 1942.[33] Meanwhile, the cultural relativism and commitment to racial equality Boas epitomized were increasingly embraced by the American academic community and general public.[34]

While Boas's intellectual stock rose sharply (he was featured on the cover of *Time* magazine in 1936), Charles Goethe's fell precipitously. Though he had always been positioned firmly to the right of center on the conservationist spectrum, the outlook of the Californian xenophobe who had railed against the English sparrow in the 1920s had once been shared by others, forming a distinct mentality. After 1945, though, Goethe's was a lone voice in the conservationist community. The involvement in the eugenics movement of Sacramento's most famous son had deepened during the 1930s. He funded and founded the Eugenics Society of Northern California in 1933 and subsequently directed this outfit. In addition, he was president of the Eugenics Research Association of the United States. Prior to 1938, he also frequently expressed his admiration for Nazi racial ideology and sterilization policy, taking particular pride in California's pioneering eugenics work.[35]

In the 1950s, in his usual fashion, Goethe tacked back and forth between human threats and those lurking in the wider world of animate nature. Having recounted the story of the Argentine ant's displacement of Alabama's native ants, and its swift spread to California, he switched to its human counterparts. Reviving the "book of nature" approach of which the English sparrow's critics were enamored, he posed the following question: "Since low wage areas immigrants replace old-time Americans, can we not today profitably ponder Solomon's advice as to ants?" ("Go to the ant, thou sluggard"). "Do they [Argentine ants] not," he continued, "illustrate need of adequate immigration control?"[36]

The full exposure of the scale and horrors of Nazi racial hygiene policies do not appear to have moved Goethe to rethink or even modify his own belief in biological destiny. Combining a long-standing passion for horticulture with the fervent pursuit of an exclusionary immigration policy, he linked the gardener's and farmer's weeding and pest control activities with the American citizen's duty to snuff out the "human weed."[37] The lurid recent example he seized on was the arrival in Hawaii, with U.S. troop movements during World War II, of one of the world's most destructive fruit flies, the oriental fruit fly *(Dacus dorsalis)*. Only the Mediterranean fruit fly (medfly, *Ceratitis capitata*) was more feared than this prolific fly, whose maggots attack most fruits, reducing their flesh to rotten pulp, and which had been detected and eradicated on various occasions in southern California since 1949. Between 1949 and 1952, California's state legislature allocated $800,000 for research on monitoring techniques and means of extermination. Goethe contrasted political and public alertness to these "6-footed aliens" with a lackadaisical approach to the influx of "alien bipeds."[38]

During the Baby Boom years of the 1950s and 1960s, the contribution of alien bipeds to demographic growth in the United States was a minor one. The overriding source was the offspring of native-born Americans.[39] By the late 1960s, however, as the "replacement ratio" of births to deaths began a steady fall, immigration had become the major component of population expansion. In the mid-1970s, immigration—legal and illegal—reemerged as a subject of large-scale public controversy for the first time since the 1920s. This time, though, attention was pinned not on the Northeast but on California, where Los Angeles had become the focal point of the nation's largest concentration of what a *Time* reporter called "international hordes" and "exotic multitudes."[40] "Undocumented" aliens (a government euphemism adopted in the late 1970s) stirred particularly strong feelings in the context of a sluggish economy.[41] California's Republican governor, Pete Wilson, waged a populist campaign against them in the early 1990s. Proposition 187, passed by 59 percent of votes cast in November 1994, aimed to rescue California from the "Mexicanization" feared by the wealthy whites in Boyle's *Tortilla Curtain* by denying educational, social, and health benefits.

Immigration also appeared on the environmentalist agenda in the late 1970s.[42] "Not so very long ago," remarked Gerda Bikalis, "an article about United States immigration would have seemed out of place in a publication on environmental concerns: too social, surely, and outside the realm of interests of a readership dedicated to the preservation of the natural habitat." Attitudes were shifting, she explained, with increasing awareness of how a "swelling stream of immigrants landing on our shores and crossing our borders, and an immigration policy incapable of coping with this invasion" were aggravating environmental degradation and natural resource depletion.[43] Boyle's novelistic character Delaney Mossbacher embodied these concerns.

Because the average American left a far bigger ecological "footprint" than citizens of other nations, these environmentalists regarded admitting more people who aspired to this profligate American lifestyle as suicidal. Hard-won legislative protections for clean air and water would be jeopardized, whatever progress had been made toward simpler and more sustainable lifestyles would be negated, and the stabilization of population growth achieved by birthrate regulation would be endangered.[44] A prominent campaigner for immigration controls in the name of environmental protection was Garrett Hardin, a University of California–Santa Barbara biologist who belonged to a dissident element within Zero Population Growth (ZPG) that included its founders, Stanford biologists Anne and Paul Ehrlich.[45] Dissatisfied with ZPG's (lack of a) stance on immigration, they founded the Federation for American Immigration Reform (FAIR), which touted immigration as the nation's number one environmental problem.

Because racism and nativism have undoubtedly diminished in force since the 1920s, exclusionary arguments based on racial or ethnic inferiority or unsuitability are now rarely articulated in public. Racism and nativism have not necessarily disappeared, though, and defenders of current immigration levels and sources of immigrant frequently dismiss the new emphasis on environmental impacts as racism and nativism disguised under a thin green veneer. Reference to ecological consequences had certainly become mandatory in anti-immigration treatises by the mid-1990s, just as it was routine for them to reprimand "professional" environmentalists for ignoring immigration.[46]

In the U.S. Southwest, environmentalist involvement in campaigns to enshrine English as the official language at state level prompted denunciations of "green" arguments for restriction as a smokescreen for bigotry. The organization U.S. English was founded in California in 1983 by John Tanton, who had chaired the Sierra Club's National Population Committee (1971–75) and then served as ZPG's president (1975–77). Leakage to the media in 1988 of Tanton's secret internal memos to colleagues in FAIR and U.S. English in connection with Arizona's official English initiative revealed a barely concealed "Hispanophobia."[47] The case for the "greening of hate" was strengthened by the spurious allegations of Tanton and his fellow Sierra Club member, Wayne Lutton (with whom he cofounded the American Immigration Control Foundation), that the "massive [immigrant] tide" was one of the growing pressures on national parks and wilderness areas.[48]

Yet these are maverick groups and unrepresentative individual voices. Most American environmental organizations, large and small, have not debated the issues and have no formal policies on population growth or immigration. The exception is the Sierra Club, which in 1998 was deeply divided over whether to ditch its 1996 decision to "take no position on immigration levels or . . . policies" in favor of a "reduction in net immigration."[49] "Race hate" outfits quickly endorsed the proposed change.[50] The *Los Angeles Times* suggested that members of fringe groups such as American Patrol (a vigilante outfit that makes citizen's arrests at the Mexican border), as well as the 26,000-member California Coalition for Immigration Reform, were rushing to join the club for the specific purpose of voting in the forthcoming referendum. The Sierra Club's board of directors, twenty-seven local chapters, and the club's National Population Committee opposed this grassroots initiative.[51] Executive director Carl Pope felt the club was unwittingly providing distasteful elements with an opportunity to acquire legitimacy.[52]

Latino journalists endorsed Pope's warnings. Scapegoating immigrants, they insisted, was "a pain-free way to go green" that avoided hard decisions about excessive natural resource consumption.[53] One of the club's Latino members, Al Martinez, described a nightmare that featured Sierra Club "envirocops" rounding up immigrants for deportation. Loudspeakers mounted on helicopters explained that the club had "nothing personal against immigrants, but if Yellowstone and Yosemite were to survive, they had to leave." Martinez featured in his nightmare as an underground resistor against the "ultraenvironmentalism" of the Sierra Club's "immigrant-bashing Malthusians."[54]

A Scottish immigrant, Martinez stressed, had founded the Sierra Club. And members wishing to reaffirm its neutral stance on immigration also pointedly referred to their founder as "Scottish immigrant John Muir." Foreign media coverage dwelled on this alleged irony as well. But the American correspondent for the left-of-center British daily *The Guardian* took a different line, seeking to place the club's current debate within a tradition of intolerance by characterizing Muir as a man "who described Indians as filthy savages."[55] Some Americans also queried the assumption that the Sierra Club had wandered into unfamiliar territory.[56]

During the run-up to the referendum (in which 60 percent backed the club's existing stance), the renowned deep ecologist George Sessions had warned that, if it stood still, the club would be "catering to political correctness at the expense of long-term survivability of America's ecosystems."[57] Immigration restrictionists in the environmentalist community view allegations of eco-nativism and eco-racism as crude attempts to kill off the possibility of a rational debate on immigration that went beyond discredited racial theory and debatable economic and social rationales to engage with measurable environmental impacts. Otis Graham, the only historian of the United States who writes on both immigration and the environment, feels that restrictionists (like himself) have been "stigmatized, stereotyped and stifled" by "liberal McCarthyites."[58]

Whatever the reason, immigration has effectively evaporated as a major environmental issue.[59] Recent links between immigration restrictionists and environmentalists are hard to find. Pat Buchanan's populist "take back America" rhetoric during his campaigns for the Republican Party's presidential nomination in 1992 and 1996 expressed the frustrations and anxieties of blue-collar Anglo-American males. But these grievances lacked an ecological component. Champions of an ecological *campanilismo* that seeks to defend native species as the bedrock of biological diversity often speak the language of protectionism. But Buchanan's own form of *campanilismo*, made up of hostility to immigrants, opposition to the influx of foreign goods under free trade agreements, and a parochial view of America's overseas commitments, was not reinforced by a biological isolationism.

Common cause with "hate" groups is even more difficult to detect. According to Jonathan Olsen and Janet Biehl, Tom Metzger's White Aryan Resistance grafted a green cutting onto the main stem of their beliefs in the early 1990s. To make her case, Biehl quoted a statement by Metzger from an article in *The Nation* about the growth of American neo-Nazism. "I've noticed," remarked Metzger, "that there's an increased number of young people in the white racialist movement who are also quite interested in the ecology, protecting the animals from cruelty and things like that, and it seems to me that we are becoming more aware of our precarious state [the white person's] in the world, being about only 10 percent of the population, we begin to sympathize, empathize more, with the wolves and other animals." Monique Wolfing, who led the Aryan Women's League at the time, agreed: "We should save nature along with trying to save our race." Olsen also pointed out that the most notorious recent American racist, former Louisiana Klansman David Duke, wanted to limit immigration to preserve (among other things) environmental quality.[60] All the same, the purported environmentalism of the extreme right boils down to a few internet slogans such as the "white race cannot be strong if our environment is polluted" (White Aryan Resistance) and sporadic references, reminiscent of Owen Wister and Madison Grant, to "unclean," rootless metropolises and "unnatural" habitats that "suck out" natural wealth.[61] Most of these groups do not have an environmental policy of any kind, let alone a position on invasive exotics and native species. Those who belong to Aryan Nations present themselves as members of an endangered species when demanding territorial sanctuary in the mountain fastnesses of Idaho. Yet they do not patrol their compounds uprooting nonnative plants.

One of the extremist "patriot" groups that Pope worried about the Sierra Club becoming bracketed with is American Patrol, which warns of "La Reconquista." Like Delaney Mossbacher in *Tortilla Curtain,* this group accuses undocumented, invasive aliens of desecrating American soil. The desert, a representative of American Patrol testified in congressional hearings of 1999, "looks like a garbage dump where they come through."[62] More recently, in language harking back to Madison Grant and Lothrop Stoddard, the editor-publisher of a southern Arizona newspaper, the *Tombstone Tumbleweed* (apparently unaware or untroubled that his newspaper is named after an invasive nonnative), warned that a "swarm of uncontrolled refugees" is invading the United States.[63] Yet this does not make these elements natural allies of those who spend their weekends in nature reserves uprooting harmful exotics to provide breathing space for bedeviled natives.

Slim, too, is evidence that immigration restrictionists are aware of the influx of hazardous exotic species. A conspicuous exception was Tanton's short piece about a comb jellyfish *(Mnemiopsis leidyi)* in the restrictionists' house journal, *The Social Contract.* This ctenophore, native to western Atlantic waters, was probably carried to the Black Sea and nearby Azov Sea in the ballast water of a Cuban ship trading with the Soviet Union. Reproducing rapidly there in the late 1980s, these creatures ate zooplankton and crustaceans as well as fish eggs and larvae. Tanton's interest in this invasive jellyfish, which experienced a population density peak in 1993/94, stemmed partly from his views on free trade blocks, which (unlike Buchanan) he criticized for encouraging the unregulated and ecologically reckless exchange of goods. His views on immigration also shaped his concern. The ctenophore was appropriating local food supplies from humans as well as other species, destroying fisheries and aggravating regional poverty, thereby intensifying out-migration pressures.[64]

Paul Ehrlich and David Pimentel are members of the scientific community who advocate immigration controls in addition to publicizing the negative impacts of invasive nonnative species.[65] The only other immigration restrictionist who appears to have connected with the debate over nonhuman immigrants is environmental historian Otis Graham. In 2000, Graham identified invasive aliens as a "very serious new environmental threat." Citing the imported fire ant, water hyacinth, and Formosan termite (also earlier arrivals, like the boll weevil, which "came across the Mexican border"), he reflected that many natives "could not compete with the outsiders"—something Native Americans "could have warned modern environmentalists about."[66] Yet for most advocates of cuts in entry levels, the gravest dangers of immigration are racial and cultural rather than environmental (or economic).

WILTED METAPHORS AND CALLING STRANGERS NAMES

In 1999, sociologist Barry Glassner examined what he considered the pervasive culture of overblown fear in the United States. Sources of fear he cited included airplane accidents, single mothers, road rage, child abduction, teenage crime, breast implants, rap lyrics, and child pornography on the Internet. But the reader will search the index of *The Culture of Fear* in vain for entries to nonhuman aliens—even those conventionally defined (despite the conclusion's suggestive title, "The Martians *Aren't* Coming").[67]

"The Martians *Are* Coming" is nonetheless a routine example of the science fiction imagery that brightly colors the invasive species debate. "The aliens have landed in Wisconsin!" explains the web-based environmental education service for children maintained by Wisconsin's Department of Natural Resources, which includes various alien profiles—among them purple loosestrife, gypsy moth, zebra mussel, and sea lamprey. "You may see them and not even know they are aliens," the website explains, adding that "they can cause all kinds of problems for plants and animals that have always lived in our state." "Read these stories and find out how to pick aliens out of a crowd, learn how to identify imposters," it exhorts, "and how to help exterminate these alien invaders before they take over!"[68] "The Aliens Have Landed" is also a typical title or subtitle for articles about dangerous exotics. The cover of a magazine containing one of these pieces featured a startling, greatly magnified picture of the head of a wood-boring sawyer beetle (looking like a demented donkey) that customs inspectors at Charleston, South Carolina, found in a packing crate from Italy.[69] Similarly, an allusion to the Martian red weeds that engulfed England in H. G. Wells's *War of the Worlds* spiced up a report from California on German ivy that was "creeping over the Santa Cruz Mountains and advancing toward Silicon Valley."[70]

Analogies with terrestrial beings also abound. Like their human counterparts, journalists observe, "stowaway" and "hitchhiking" fauna and flora slip into the United States. Many Americans, Robert Devine reports, think of the Department of Agriculture's Animal and Plant Health Inspection Service (APHIS, founded in 1972) as the "border patrol for invasive species."[71] Yet "so far, like human immigration control," another journalist comments, "the battle against alien species has been spotty, expensive and largely ineffective."[72]

Human invaders and outlaws supply other handy reference points for purposes of rhetorical demonization. "All too many exotic plants behave as botanical barbarians," laments Devine, "laying waste to the countryside."[73] "This is a rogue's gallery unlike all others," Stephanie Flack and Elaine Forlow remark of the Nature Conservancy's alien species "hit list" ("America's Least Wanted: The Dirty Dozen"). "No human villains stare menacingly from these pages." Still, these "transplanted miscreants are ruthless in their quest for light, water, space, nutrients or the very flesh of their victims."[74]

In a 1994 article in *Sierra*, Devine described the retributive "carnage" of California "weed bashers" ripping out a "territory-gobbling imperialist" like French broom. Catching the mood of one weed warrior, he reported that "something approaching anger powers his wiry frame when he hurls himself at a hated invader." Devine also identified an almost sadistic enjoyment. One volunteer "broom basher" told him that "feeling the roots tear and finally give way produces an almost sensual pleasure." Fascinated by these reactions, Devine could not resist having a go. "I grabbed hold of a wrench, waded in, and was soon thrilling to the rhythmic ripping of roots." Toward the end of his article, he sobered up and urged the need for dispassionate assessments of potential invasiveness, lest over-zealous citizens "lynch" innocent exotics.[75]

This incendiary language tends to be the norm. "Most of us who deal with the topic of bioinvasions," reflects Yvonne Baskin, "are tempted to create linguistic maelstroms of war and pestilence, pollution and upheaval when we try to describe particularly threatening and frustrating invaders."[76] What, though, is the function and meaning of these ubiquitous images beyond their role as literary devices and consciousness-raising techniques?

Stephen Budiansky—without reference to the alien species debate—has seen the dissection of humanizing metaphors as a distorting and brazenly political exercise. Selecting a passage from an essay by environmental historian Donald Worster, this popular science writer has asserted that Worster interpreted the ecological science that emerged in the late 1970s and early 1980s—with its stress on individualism and competition among species—as a "Reagan-era apologia." Worster, he contended, regarded economic metaphors concerning how plants go about "earning their livings as best they may, each in its own individual manner" (a quotation from a 1978 book by Paul Colinvaux), as "sinister hints" of Reaganomics and a resurgent social Darwinism. "People who spend their lives combing literary texts for hidden meanings," scorned Budiansky, "think they're on to something big when they find an ecologist writing a popular essay that describes plants 'earning their livings.'" "People who understand science," he declared, "are less impressed by this game of deconstructing metaphors."[77]

Worster's analysis of the "new" ecology was more tentative than Budiansky allowed.[78] Still, Budiansky's general point enjoys some validity in connection with the nonnative species debate over the past thirty years. "Not one or two, but dozens of diseases seem poised to pack their bags for America and a perpetual feast on U.S. agriculture," warn two American plant disease specialists. "Faced with such an armada, should we capitulate?"[79] This is little more than a rhetorical flourish designed to leaven leaden textbook prose. Despite the penchant of weed warriors and conservation biologists for military metaphors (a habit that began with Charles Elton), figures of speech that once effectively served the twin causes of humanizing nonnative species and naturalizing human immigrants have lost much of their potency since the 1920s.

How the meaning and application of the term *horde* has shifted over time illustrates that metaphors fade through overuse and the emergence of fresh contexts. In the United States between the 1840s and the 1920s, the description of a human group as a "horde" was highly suggestive because those described were usually immigrants of whom the describer disapproved and because troublesome insects—often but not invariably foreign in origin—were also routinely characterized as hordes. Given the extent of hostility toward "new" immigrants among old-stock Americans after World War I, the environmental historian as well as the student of rhetoric should note that the native plant preservationist and the advocate of immigration restriction both referred to the danger of alien hordes "over-running the neighborhood."[80] At this time, in this context, for such people, these forms of speech were not simply embroidery. Rhetoric reliant on these humanizing metaphors has also been a distinctive feature of more recent American reactions to "invasive" nonnatives such as the zebra mussel, Formosan termite, Tiger mosquito, and Asian long-horned beetle. Yet the vital link that once associated humans with floral and faunal pests in meaningful fashion (sometimes regardless of nationality) has now largely been severed. Metaphor has triumphed over meaning.

When, in 1959, historian Carl Degler alluded to the "horde of unemployed" during the Great Depression, this was a prime example of the faded metaphor.[81] *Horde* had lost much of the quality that made it—in the context of the immigrant "menace" of the late nineteenth and early twentieth centuries—an effective metaphorical weapon. The sense of people marauding in a large mass remains integral—as does the notion of potential threat (to capitalism in this particular instance). But Degler did not intend to dehumanize the jobless by evoking images of insects. A more recent reference to "mongoose hordes" in a Sierra Club feature on invasive species on the U.S. Virgin Islands provides a similar example.[82] The element of threat remains central, yet the author's purpose is not to draw attention to illegal immigrants or asylum seekers or to imbue them with menacing qualities. American scientists studying bioinvasion were also using *horde* in this less functional sense during the 1980s.[83] Loss of function is the essence of what Nelson Goodman calls the wilted metaphor. A wilted metaphor is one that no longer triggers a comparison.[84]

Still, for better or worse, naturalizing and humanizing metaphors are wrapped up in the way we think and talk and write about people and the rest of the natural world. These patterns of thought and ways of communicating are so deep-seated and pervasive they seem almost second nature. Baskin explains that she has tried to "curb" the "lurid excesses" of the "sloppy and value-laden" language characteristic of "invasive species discourse," relying on the more dispassionate words frequently used in "news accounts and policy statements." Yet her prose bristles with references to "hordes," "rising tide" and "menace," to creatures that "skulk," not to mention allusions to an alien species being granted its "passport" and to "known troublemakers" seldom "stopped at most borders."[85] Even a tempered remark by a group of specialists in bioinvasion that recognizes the relative paucity of malignant newcomers is couched in this standard imagery. "The challenge" for them is to "identify the few potentially harmful immigrants among an increasing throng of innocuous entrants."[86] We simply cannot help using this language and making these allusions; they indicate our membership—often denied or insufficiently acknowledged—in a community of life that extends beyond our own kind.

Environmental historians also personify and nationalize invasive species. John McNeill refers to the boll weevil as a "well-documented alien from Mexico," dubs the imported fire ant a "fierce Brazilian," and characterizes the gypsy moth as an "unruly guest from France."[87] Australian palaeontologist Tim Flannery, discussing a now extinct South American creature that migrated northward on various occasions, comments that "wetbacks have been coming to North America ever since the first great ground sloth hauled itself ashore on the continent over 8 million years ago."[88] Again, no slur against their human counterparts is intended in these picturesque images (which remind us that faded metaphors are not necessarily colorless). A striking example of how it is entirely possible to be supportive and celebratory of human immigration despite powerful and florid criticism of invasive nonhuman immigrants is furnished by the views and prose of Dan Flores, an environmental historian of the American West. An explicit champion of native species, Flores insists that "diversity in human culture may be just as important to adaptation and evolution on earth as we have long believed ecological diversity to be."[89] He is also a dedicated weed whacker. His vivid strictures against exotics like spotted knapweed, whose "march of relentless takeover" is producing "wastelands at a dizzying rate" across the American West, are complemented by valiant, if (admittedly) vainglorious efforts to restore native species to his twenty-five-acre patch of native bunchgrass prairie in the Montana Rockies from which the wildlife and "ancient, evolved biodiversity" have fled "in panic or succumb[ed] to strangulation."[90]

The point remains, though, that such metaphors are readily misconstrued by multihorticulturalists—especially in view of the preoccupation with language that has characterized the debate over the national origin of species since the emergence of "political correctness" in the early 1990s. The same applies to terminology. Though various terms for biota that come from somewhere else are employed more or less synonymously in the United States and other parts of the English-speaking world, some commentators seek greater terminological precision because of the "casual use" of significant ecological concepts and human resonance that frequently render these terms controversial.[91]

For many in the debate over nomenclature, *nonnative, nonindigenous,* and *introduced* have the advantage of being purely technical terms. *Nonindigenous,* with its spatial rather than political or national meaning, received the official blessing of Congress's Office of Technology Assessment in 1993 as the "most neutral, inclusive, and unambiguous term."[92] Many scientists insist that *invader* is also strictly descriptive. According to British biologist Mark Williamson, "an invader can be any sort of species going into any sort of habitat." This is clearly the sense in which American ornithologist Roger Tory Peterson applied the term "world invader" to the cattle egret in the early 1950s and the spirit in which he described the areas of the United States into which it spread as "invaded territory."[93] David Richardson, a South African scientist who is equally keen to promote a standardized set of nonemotive terms, agrees that *invasive* should be a value-free term that describes a biological act and a species' biogeographic and demographic status without reference to national origins or to economic or ecological impacts.[94]

Some naturalists and ecologists, among them Peterson, use *colonist* and *colonizer* interchangeably with *invader;* Peterson's cattle egret, after all, did not impact negatively on the existing occupants of the territory it invaded "explosively."[95] Others distinguish between them according to their impact on other species (benign, innocuous, or deleterious). They confine the term *colonizer* to species that enter territories that are unoccupied or underoccupied as a result of disturbance (e.g., the site of a volcanic eruption) and initiate the process of vegetational succession. By contrast, an *invader* enters a relatively undisturbed site and assumes dominance, even displacing existing species completely. As for those species that neither "displace [n]or markedly depress the resident populations and become integrated into the communities they enter," Fakhri A. Bazzaz recommends *immigrant*.[96]

These semantic debates will sound familiar to historians of colonization and imperialism. Euro-Americans traditionally applied *colonist* to their forebears who settled in the New World. *Colonist* implies vacant niches inviting occupation, suggesting a relatively peaceful process without undue displacement. (It also implies the prior existence of unoccupied territory—a problematic notion given that the so-called unoccupied territory/vacant niche has no existence until before it is occupied; the act of occupation, in other words, creates its previous condition.) As conventional frontier history has given way to the "new" western history since the 1960s, it is increasingly recognized that the lands into which Europeans poured were far from "virgin" or "empty." Since these lands sustained long-established and complex human communities, the white colonist has been reconceived as an *invader* (invaders, according to Bazzaz's ecological terminology, enter occupied places and act to the detriment of existing species).

In view of the association of *alien* with extraterrestrial invaders and unwanted immigrants, Bazzaz recommended that its use be "minimized or altogether avoided in ecological literature."[97] But many scientists still merrily employ it. *Aliens* is the newsletter (since 1995) of the Invasive Species

Specialist Group, a New Zealand–based research unit affiliated with the Species Survival Commission of the International Union for the Conservation of Nature. The Global Invasive Species Programme (GISP), a 1997 initiative of the Scientific Committee on Problems of the Environment (SCOPE), an international nongovernmental scientific body, prefers a modified version. GISP's phrase "*invasive* alien species" (my emphasis) seeks to deflect charges of nativism by distinguishing between the benevolent or harmless majority and the troublesome handful that receive so much bad publicity.[98]

Nonetheless, Bazzaz's objections reflect a spreading unease about *alien,* modified or unmodified. As John Randall, president of the California Exotic Pest Plant Council, explained in 1994, "Unfortunately, for some, the term *[alien]* may also be used to stigmatize real people who have recently arrived in an area, especially those not granted citizenship, and for this reason it can be regarded as offensive." Casting around for more suitable terminology, he rejected *non-aboriginal* and *nonindigenous* as too formal and complex, if considerably more dispassionate. *Introduced* and *nonnative* were too bland. His choice was *exotic.*[99]

"Exotic species—sounds rather threatening, doesn't it?" declared a Minnesota horticulturist in 1996.[100] Not in my book. Instead, "exotic" arouses my curiosity. To satisfy a taste for human "exotica," native peoples from newly "discovered" lands were exhibited in sixteenth-century Britain. And old-stock Americans described "new" immigrants as exotic in appearance and origin. "Exotic" also evokes the thrill and glamor of the unusual— as in an exotic vacation destination, an exotic fruit, or an "exotic dancer."

Randall conceded that *exotic* might strike some campaigners for native biodiversity as too soft a word for the tough job of raising public awareness of the threat invasive nonnatives posed to natural areas (the danger to agricultural environments having been recognized long ago, as chapter 3 illustrates). This is why state and regional citizens' groups that confront the problem of invasive plants are called Exotic Pest Plant Councils. The inclusion of *pest,* Randall believed, would neutralize any potentially favorable construction placed on *exotic.*[101]

Yet *pest* is just as culturally and historically loaded as *alien* (and *weed*). Like *weed, pest* is a pejorative term that has no biological meaning. In an article on the dastardly activities of the Japanese beetle as a turf pest in the Northeast during World War II, *Life* magazine drew attention to the attributes it shared with the Japanese themselves (quite apart from being sneaky invaders who gave no warning): "Both are small but very numerous and prolific, as well as voracious, greedy, and devouring."[102] This and various other examples of how people have been associated with other pests, not to mention *vermin* (by no means all of them *nonnative*), illustrates how powerful charges of eco-nativism and green hatred can be—however insubstantial the current basis for these allegations.[103] The power derives from our acute sensitivity to language, the high level of public concern over immigration across the Western world (especially in northwest Europe), and, not least, the enduring value of the Nazi connection to those who wish to undermine a range of findings and viewpoints—from the links between smoking and cancer to gardening with native plants.

In her manifesto for native plants, Californian landscape designer Lorraine Johnson recapitulates the standard case for eco-nativism that is essentially grounded in language:

> The use of terms such as "exotic" and "alien" is unsettling. We're a continent of immigrants; only the native peoples are in fact native to this land, and even they arrived thousands of years ago from another place. So why call plants . . . which have been here for hundreds of years, exotic or alien? Isn't this a form of botanical racism?

No, it is not, is Johnson's answer. Why? Because plants and people are qualitatively different.[104]

Allegations of "plant racism" make little sense linguistically or biologically. Multihorticulturalists who use the same diction to describe the defamation and mistreatment of foreign people and the defamation and mistreatment of foreign plants commit the very crime they attribute to native species proponents: the deployment of humanizing and dehumanizing terminologies for plants and people, respectively. According to the racialized pseudoscience propounded by early twentieth-century nativists like Grant and Stoddard, races of people were as different from one another and as fixed in their separate racial and cultural characteristics as animal breeds. "You cannot make bad stock into good by changing its meridian," Stoddard warned, "any more than you can turn a cart-horse into a hunter by putting it into a fine stable, or make a mongrel into a fine dog by teaching it tricks." Nature, in short, invariably trumped nurture. It may well be impossible to train a bulldog to herd sheep, or—to cite Franz Boas's example—to convert the offspring of a dray horse into a race horse.[105] But the analogy between humans and animals breaks down in this context because all people belong to the same species. They are members of the human race—the only species of the genus *Homo*.[106]

In Grant's heyday, it was common to refer to races of animals. An English sparrow critic, for example, complained that, "although neither natives nor discoverers of America," the birds had become the "dominant race" among the nation's avian population.[107] Plants and animals, however, belong to countless genetically distinct species. Inasmuch as there is no such thing as a "race" of plants or animals—just species—the proper way to denote discrimination for or against a particular species of plant or animal is to adopt the rather ugly term coined in 1975 by animal rights philosopher Peter

Singer: *speciesism*.[108] Diana Rathbone wants to know why, "in this nation of immigrants, everyone is so concerned about keeping nature exactly as it was before we arrived."[109] When the elementary biological distinctions between people and plants and between people and other animals are grasped, perhaps the promotion of the interests of native flora and fauna will no longer seem quite so strange to multihorticulturalists and ecological cosmopolitans.

But this is a tall order. Casting around for other means that may offer native plant proponents a stronger defense against the assorted charges of nativism, racism, fascism, and Nazism, we inevitably confront the nature of language. It might well help all parties concerned if public and scientific discussions about nonindigenous species were conducted in a purely technical vocabulary, insofar as one exists or can be devised and is able to command a broad scientific and public consensus. Within reason, though, the conservation of linguistic variety and the tasty complexity of meaning that comes with usage in multiple contexts that span the chasm between humans and the rest of the natural world is a worthy cause to set alongside the preservation of biodiversity. For the sake of linguistic diversity (not to mention readability), the pages of this book teem with strangers, aliens, foreigners, transplants, exotics, invaders, colonists, immigrants, nonnatives, and natives.

A term that has not appeared often in this book, and one that rarely features in the scientific or popular literature, is *newcomer*. Nonetheless, *newcomer* commends itself to me as having the virtues of neutrality without the defect of blandness. My inspiration is Peterson. And here is the sentence that caught my eye in the passage on the cattle egret in his early 1950s account of an ornithological odyssey around North America: "What effect will the newcomer have on the native American herons?"[110]

Metaphorically driven language heavily freighted with historical and cultural baggage demonstrates Western thought's incorrigible and deepseated anthropomorphic tendency. Yet in the particular context of the nonnative species debate, the liberal use of loaded language by critics of invasive flora and fauna can be explained at least in part by their perception of the peculiar difficulties they face in their efforts to alert the public to the problem. Banu Subramaniam claims that some journalists and conservation biologists now highlight exotic species as the "main and even sole problem" in native species extinction, thereby obscuring the underlying problems of habitat destruction through human activity.[111] But many scientists, environmentalists, and journalists believe that the problem of invasive species has not yet secured the place it warrants on the agenda of environmental protection.

Is this because the invasive species problem is fundamentally different from other environmental problems? People are often responsible for introducing nonnatives, whether deliberately or inadvertently. Nevertheless, the idea of nature warring against nature, central to the new notion of "biological pollution" that has emerged in connection with invasive species, is hard to grasp. It is difficult to assimilate because it does not readily conform to the dualism of nature and culture—often reinforced by the dichotomy between purity and impurity—that is so ingrained in Western thought. These binary opposites are particularly entrenched in environmentalist thinking. So the idea of biological pollution brings a novel twist to conventional understandings of environmental pollution, which, since the 1950s, have pivoted on radioactive fallout, crude oil, pesticides, detergents, acid rain, smog, and other by-products of chemical-industrial processes.[112]

The effects of biological pollution are also harder to recognize. "[Native species] extinction by habitat destruction," observes Edward O. Wilson, "is like death in an auto accident: easy to see and assess." By contrast, the extinction of native species at the hands of invasive exotics is similar to "death by disease: gradual, insidious."[113] Complicating matters further, the results in many instances do not resemble a conventional wasteland. "It all looks so lush and green," remarked Diane Ragone in 1996 of the view from her office at the National Tropical Botanical Garden on the Hawaiian island of Kauai. "But practically everything you're looking at," she added, "landed from abroad."[114] For Carla Bossard of the California Exotic Pest Plant Council, public indifference is summed up in the attitude "It is still green . . . so what are you worried about?"[115]

FLORA AND FAUNA THAT ARE HERE TO STAY

Even if we fail to recognize their "foreign" origins—and no matter what we call flora and fauna from somewhere else when we do—these biota form part of our daily surroundings. When the "balance of nature" theory held sway, ecologists believed that environments least upset by human intervention—and therefore richest in native species diversity—were more resistant to nonnative incursion and that the most disturbed environments were the most susceptible.[116] Recent advances in invasion biology, however, are challenging the received wisdom by improving our understanding of the ecology and adaptation of native species. Building on the "new" ecology's emphasis on constant dynamism, these findings question the orthodoxy (which Elton reemphasized in *Ecology of Invasions*) that "ecological resistance" correlates with native species diversity. Research by Thomas Stohlgren, covering a variety of grassland and montane habitats from Minnesota to Colorado, indicates that exotics flourish in places previously thought unsuitable for new residents. "Just as human immigrants may find more opportunities in an already-overcrowded city than a small town," he noted, "invasive plants take advantage of the constant turnover and jockeying for position that characterizes species-rich ecological communities."[117] Immigrant species, in short, are everywhere, part and parcel of ecological communities that are fundamentally "recombinant" (composed of species from multiple origins).

Biotic hypermobility, which explains this recombinant character, is a fundamental characteristic of today's world. The introduction of state and federal plant quarantine laws in the United States in the 1910s and 1920s temporarily reduced but failed to curb the influx of harmful nonnative biota. International intercourse, of which cosmopolitans like Fairchild so greatly approved, accelerated rapidly as commercial aviation took off. When the *Graf Zeppelin* landed in New York City after its first transatlantic crossing, in October 1928, inspectors found that the flower bouquets in the passenger quarters were sheltering seven insect species and two plant diseases. On the German airship's second visit, in August 1929, Bureau of Plant Quarantine officials confiscated twenty insect species, six of them "uninvited, alien guests" hitherto unknown in the United States.[118] Confronted with a swelling volume of arriving vehicles, ships, and airplanes after 1945, plant inspectors at the nation's borders increasingly intercepted "hitch-hiking pests" like the citrus black fly, citrus canker, medfly, and giant African land snail. These "public enemies" sought to exploit "the land of good food and great opportunity" while contributing nothing in return.[119] The "homeland" must impose stricter entry requirements, urged the Bureau of Entomology and Plant Quarantine, for "foreign pests" were "continually and insistently knocking at our doors."[120]

Charles Goethe's own efforts to eliminate nonnative plants—water hyacinth from his irrigation canals, yellow star thistle from his range lands, and bindweed from his wheat fields—had proved expensive and largely futile. Aldo Leopold had also been more or less resigned to a rolling program of thunderous bioinvasion. As soon as one problem is solved or resolves itself, he sighed, another appears; his example was the replacement of the horse-dependent English sparrow by the starling, which capitalized on the agrarian landscape created by the tractor. "In the end," he reflected, "every region and every resource get their quota of uninvited ecological guests."[121]

If Leopold saw little point in intervening half a century ago, there is even less reason to be sanguine today. "The state, immobile and fixed to a territory," Christian Joppke explains, "is incapacitated to control hypermobile, deterritorialized economic and cultural flows."[122] This also applies to population flows. Stephen Castles and Mark Miller argue that the nation-state's efforts to restrict and regulate immigration have been largely unsuccessful, for these attempted measures "contradict the powerful forces which are leading towards greater economic and cultural interchange. In an increasingly international economy, it is difficult to open borders for movements of information, commodities and capital and yet close them to people."[123] Fairchild would have agreed.

Joppke, Castles, and Miller do not mention the hypermobile and deterritorialized ecological flows represented by the complementary movement of nonnative species. Mobile nature challenges what Jean and John Comaroff (writing in a South African context) refer to as the "nature of sovereignty and the sovereignty of nature." The outcome of nature's global mobility for the United States is that "Asian tiger mosquitoes are biting Americans, and termites from Taiwan are eating American houses" (to quote the journalist David Briscoe).[124] The Asian tiger mosquito, in particular, highlights the intimate connection between global economic and ecological systems Christopher Bright identified when he described bioinvasion as a "globalization disease."[125]

The first American breeding population of this temperate zone mosquito (named for its black-and-white markings and sharp bite) was recorded in 1984 in Houston, Texas, from where it spread as far north as New Jersey by 1997. Typical breeding sites in Asia are coconut shells and bamboo stumps, but anything that holds water (even a candy bar wrapper) will do nicely. The original American hearth was a tire dump, an American landscape staple that has ensured the spread of this considerable public health risk (it acts as a vector for malaria and dengue fever). Japanese used tires feed a massive American retreading business, and sealed shipping containers provide the ideal intercontinental "mobile pram"; rainwater that accumulates within the tire casing's rim remains there almost indefinitely.[126]

The Asian tiger mosquito's movements illustrate that few invasive species, whether yesterday or a century ago, travel entirely under their own steam. Even the English sparrow's archenemy, Elliott Coues, in one of his more reflective moments, conceded that nonnative success owes as much to us as to them. "It is always one and the same story," he lamented, "whether of plants or of animals, when exotic species, fitted by nature to thrive best under conditions which man himself affords, are imported and naturalized in any country."[127]

That one and the same story was the impoverishment of native species. In a technical sense, the result of all this intermixing during the first few centuries of biotic importation from Europe was actually enhanced biodiversity. In terms of the range of species it houses, a United States with English sparrow *and* bluebird, Japanese beetle *and* Colorado beetle, eucalyptus *and* redwood, is a biologically richer United States. Allan Fitzsimmons, an arch-conservative thinker and policy analyst, has seized on this fact, pointing out that, though the area that became the United States has lost 109 species of flora and fauna since 1600, the nation has gained over 4,500 "free-living" nonindigenous species.[128] A more relevant point, however, is that this increase in species has been accompanied by considerable reduction in the size of the populations of pre-European species. Biotic takeover rather than coexistence has been the overall long-term outcome of species migration to North America (and the other neo-Europes) over the past five hundred years.

Whether this biotic takeover is to be deplored—and measures taken to reverse its effects—is another matter. Those who actively back beleaguered native species are in no doubt about the rectitude of their stance. Responding to the multihorticulturalists who accuse them of nativism, they insist that their position is grounded in unimpeachable ecological "fact"— whereas nativism is founded on prejudice, fear, rumor, and the discredited pseudoscience of white supremacism. "We enjoy ripping out invasive plants," a California weed warrior explained, "because we know this is what mother earth needs and we are dedicated to helping heal her."[129]

But does "mother earth" really know what she needs? Do weed warriors rip up invasive plants to satisfy their own needs rather than mother earth's? Fairfax and Huntsinger are not so sure that mother earth has such a clear understanding of her own needs. They see the emphasis on natives and the need for redress against invasive exotics as a way of coping with the demise of cherished notions of how natural systems work, arguing that

> with loss of confidence in the Clementsian progression toward climax, re-source managers have lost their successional or directional compass. For the manager, this is a serious problem: what is now the goal of management? . . . we have hit upon protecting native species, a good fallback for providing clear standards for setting goals and evaluating management. . . . It is easy to rally around the cause of removing "alien species" and protecting and enhancing native ones. It is a measurable goal, one where we can create firm targets and arrive at clear results.[130]

Stephen Jay Gould observes that a preference for natives makes little evo-lutionary sense. As the success that certain nonnatives enjoy suggests, natives are sometimes less fit than the newcomers.[131] Late nineteenth-century American botanists who studied the "behavior of foreigners on our soil" admitted as much when they complained about the extermination of natives frequently "too feeble to resist the hardy invaders." So did those who—with specific reference to the English sparrow, starling, ailanthus, Japanese beetle, and San Jose scale—noted that "strange visitors seem at first to have a stamina unknown among our natives."[132] As Gould empha-sizes, a native species is not automatically the form of life best suited to a par-ticular place in perpetuity. Rather, it is the one that happens to be best suited at a given moment in time.[133] Gould's point about nature never stand-ing still was anticipated by Asa Gray in the 1870s:

> When we consider that most weeds . . . are not "to the manner born," but are self-invited intruders,—we must needs abandon the notion of any primordial and absolute adaptation of plants and animals to their habitats. . . . The har-mony of Nature and its admirable perfection need not be regarded as inflex-ible and changeless. Nor need nature be likened to a statue, or a cast in rigid bronze, but rather as an organism, with play and adaptability of parts.

To illustrate his observation, Gray noted how well the eucalyptus flourished in the heart of redwood country, how nicely the redwood was doing on many other continents, and, by no means least, how thoroughly those of his own kind—Anglo-Saxon stock—had taken "such recent but dominating possession of this New World."[134]

There is an even more persuasive argument for coming to terms with at least some nonnatives—namely, that many of them are here to stay whether we like it or not. Their presence has become permanent not only through their own invincibility conferred by millions of years of natural selection but because of the ever-expanding scale and depth of our interventions in the natural world. To concede this point is not to issue a moral blank check to introduce, willy-nilly, whatever species we like; not even the most libertarian of eco-cosmopolitans wishes to disband APHIS or throw open the doors to all comers again. Nonetheless, we should recognize the role of human subsidy in the success of certain nonnative biota. And we ought to realize that the presence of naturalized nonnatives is a sign as well as a cause of habitat degradation and biodiversity loss.[135] Even Leland Howard, one of the most fervent crusaders against the alien "insect menace" during the 1890s, conceded that the "influence of civilization" on native faunas was most direct and sweeping in terms of habitat destruction.[136]

Learning to accept creatures like the gypsy moth, balsam woolly adelgid, brown tree snake, Formosan termite, Asian long-horned beetle, and Asian tiger mosquito may seem like an insuperable challenge.[137] But we might be a bit more appreciative of the part that certain other invasive exotics play in healing a world that we are more responsible for damaging than our fellow floral and faunal immigrants.[138] John Randall, the Nature Conservancy's nonnative weed specialist, based in Sacramento, tolerates the tree that grows in California as well as Brooklyn because it "usually pops up in 'trash' areas where nothing else can survive. I've seen it growing in blighted areas . . . where any type of greenery is more than welcome." Uprooting it, in his view, would be pointless; the new spaces thereby created would simply be taken by black locust or Norway maple.[139]

James Brown, the American biologist who likened antipathy to the English sparrow to anti-foreigner feeling, goes much further than Randall in his advice. Forget trying to recover a pristine native world. Concentrate on managing and coexisting with invasive exotics.[140] An additional plank in this argument (the "you can't squeeze toothpaste back into a tube" approach) echoes Stein and Moxley's stance on the eucalyptus in California: consciousness of strangeness fades over time—especially among peoples who are often migrants themselves and whose own roots are shallow. What appears alien today will eventually become the norm (or may not seem alien at all).[141]

Timescale is a vital consideration when assessing the impact of invasive species. If the temporal baseline adopted is the advent of Europeans and their fellow organisms in the Western Hemisphere, then biotic transformations appear revolutionary. And when the timescale adopted is even shorter, the impact can appear nothing short of cataclysmic. Yet the reshuffling, displacement, and expansion of species triggered by European lifeforms was not an unprecedented convulsion; the last glacial era brought far more sweeping biotic disruption. Thinking in terms of geological time may encourage a more Olympian perspective.

The argument that massive upheaval in biotic arrangements has occurred before and is bound to happen again (so why worry?) will not impress everyone. Not all of us are ready to make our peace with invasive exotics on these grounds. What many people care about first and foremost is what their natural world looked like yesterday, what it consists of today, and what it is going to be made up of tomorrow.

For Marc Miller and Gregory Aplet, invasive species present a fundamental problem because they believe that "a concept of what is natural must include a notion of species in their proper place."[142] European beach grass was brought to San Francisco's Golden Gate Park in the late nineteenth century to stabilize dunes but quickly spread up and down the coast. In 2000, young members of the California Conservation Corps were pulling out clumps on the Mendocino coast. This is how a reporter evoked the scene: "The Pacific Ocean crashes onto the sand, creating a salty, almost imperceptible mist. Grass sways in the steady spring wind. It's a perfect day except for one thing: the grass shouldn't be there."[143]

Just as Henry Van Dyke believed that a silent spring was preferable to the English sparrow's infernal jabbering, eco-philosopher Holmes Rolston III prefers no wildlife at all if exotics are the only alternative. Agreeing that they strip the notion of "real nature" of any meaning, he cites the example of the "Asian ring-tailed [*sic*]" pheasant. Though he concedes that this bird is "rather well naturalized" in states such as Iowa, he refuses to accept it because it was introduced and owes its continued existence to grain raising, which means that the birds "are not really on their own."[144] Grappling with the strange new concept of biological pollution, Jerry E. Asher and David W. Harmon feel that invasive exotics challenge the assumed "naturalness" of wilderness areas, despite the absence of conventional evidence of intrusion. "There is little that is natural," they conclude, "about an unroaded landscape dominated by knapweed."[145] These notions of "real" nature, of nature "on its own," of nature "out of place" and "misplaced," are predicated on a predestined and autonomous natural order. The environmental historian must handle these noncontingent and noncontextualized notions—essentially ahistorical concepts—with caution.

Leaving aside the question of the naturalness of nonnatives, another prime area of misunderstanding is their degree of success. Discussing the struggle between native and nonnative flora in Hawaii, an ecologist reported that one of his students believed that an exotic species "apparently possessed a certain group spirit and cooperative action which permitted it to carry on a mass "warfare" against the indigenous flora. . . . Indigenous plants are helpless before the onslaught; the native forest, doomed, disintegrates and retreats sometimes even before the invaders have arrived. An ultimate and complete ascendancy of alien vegetation is but a matter of time alone."[146]

We can hardly accuse nonnative species of malice aforethought. But the tenacity of such views makes it easy to forget that most introductions fail to take root, let alone inflict pain and misery. Success is not the foregone conclusion the Hawaiian ecologist's students assumed. Acclimatizers in St. Louis, Missouri, released various European birds in Lafayette Park during the nineteenth-century heyday of transplantation. Yet only the tree sparrow gained anything approximating a foothold in the park (and even that bird was subsequently pushed aside by the English sparrow). Mark Williamson has calculated that only 10 percent of floral and faunal introductions become established in a continental setting (the "tens rule").[147] Trying to establish which 10 percent are likely to become naturalized increasingly occupies the attention of invasion biologists. Williamson believes that the best—perhaps the only—way to predict an introduction's fortunes is to examine its previous record elsewhere.[148] This approach takes its cue from Darwin's evolutionary ruminations. "A dominant species," he had reflected, "which has already beaten many competitors in its own home, will tend to spread and supplant many others," adding that "those species which spread widely, tend generally to spread *very* widely."[149]

Though the English sparrow's American success certainly endorses this view, the predictive power of the past is more limited than Darwin allowed and Williamson assumes. Many invasive species have no invasive history and nothing biologically to distinguish them from stay-at-homes and explain their invasive prowess. Asa Gray realized this in the 1870s, pointing out that "any herb whatever when successfully aggressive becomes a weed; and the reasons of predominance may be almost as diverse as the weeds themselves."[150] His observation rings just as true today, confounding long-standing efforts to character-profile the "ideal weed."[151] Moreover, species widely distributed at home that closely resemble those that become invasive can fail to gain a grip abroad. The aforementioned tree sparrow, a near relative of the English sparrow, and whose Eurasian range is nearly as extensive, had by 1960 barely moved beyond Lafayette Park—to which it was introduced in 1870. It has not spread much farther since (and, if its historical origins could be kept quiet, would be a candidate for endangered species listing). Nonetheless, an exotic that seems innocuous or well mannered today—as in the past—might eventually become a problem. Nor can we predict how long a problem species will remain a problem.[152] Nor can we anticipate what may alleviate the problem—witness the unforeseen relationship between the automobile's spread and the decline of the English sparrow and the more recent mystery of the ailing ailanthus in New York City.

Mary Shelley's early nineteenth-century gothic horror tale has provided a compelling metaphor for conservation biologists whose solution to the dilemma of prediction is to implement a policy of strict exclusion based on the principle of "better safe than sorry." "Until our predictive ability improves in a more general arena," advise Peter Moyle and Theo Light, "it is best to assume that the Frankenstein Effect is the one firm rule: new invasions are likely to have unexpected consequences."[153] In the United States, though, the number of exotic failures was high enough fifty years ago for a biologist discussing wildlife transplantation to introduce himself as "an importation into this country from Germany [who] appears, however, to have flourished somewhat better than some of the counterparts of which he writes."[154]

Despite an alarming initial explosion in numbers that captures scientific and public attention, a nonnative population can crash almost as quickly and graphically—doomed to rarity as native species retain the competitive advantage (witness the fortunes of North American waterweed in British rivers and lakes). And should an exotic species indeed take off, this does not inevitably spell disaster for existing species. Williamson's "tens rule" further instructs that, of the acclimatized 10 percent, only 10 percent are likely to become pests. Defenders of exotics often muddy the waters by equating criticism of invasive nonnatives with wholesale opposition to nonnative species.[155] But accusations of purism—and attempts to expose inconsistencies in that purism—are usually off-target. Many environmentalists who promote native forms are perfectly able to distinguish between naturalized exotics that invade wildlands and the benign majority of introduced crop species that are largely incompetent beyond cultivated agricultural spaces, readily acknowledging the latter's inestimable contribution to the nation's food supply.[156] Despite his vigorous sympathy for natives whose "ancient homes" had been "usurped," Alfred Crosby acknowledged that problem species like the English sparrow are far better known than the "helpful migrants" that lived up to their promise.[157]

The sheer fact of foreignness, it bears repeating, is insufficient to incur disapproval. This is borne out once again by the reception American birders and conservationists who remain hostile to the house sparrow have given to a bird that showed up nearly a century later. In terms of its distribution, the cattle egret has become like the house sparrow and starling, a "world invader" (to quote Roger Tory Peterson). Over the past century, it has expanded beyond its African homeland to wherever there are cattle pastures. Invariably found in association with livestock, the bird is attracted by the insects that grazers stir up; in Africa, it also lives among wild herbivores such as hippopotamuses and elephants. By the early 1950s, it was not only living in the adjacent continents of Asia and Europe but also in Australia and the Americas. Just as the house sparrow and starling had taken advantage of the expansion of croplands, the cattle egret also capitalized on the spread of farming. In this instance, the bird took advantage of the conversion of wild or semiwild environments into pasture that increased the number of their bovine hosts.

Here, though, the similarity with the international history of these earlier arrivals from the "Old World" ends. There is no evidence of deliberate transplantation. Cattle egrets ostensibly flew from West Africa across the Atlantic at its narrowest point circa 1930, initially alighting in British Guiana. From northeast South America, this small white heron spread northward, being spotted the length of the East Coast by the early 1950s.[158] Visiting southern Florida's cattle country in 1953, Peterson was thrilled at the prospect of seeing the first nesting cattle egrets in North America. His were not isolated sentiments. The bird received a warm, even unconditional welcome from the American ornithological community. And this welcome has endured. Conservationists also remain unperturbed.

The answers Peterson gave when he asked himself whether the bird was a "good or bad acquisition" still hold water. Acknowledging that negative experiences with the house sparrow and starling had given Americans a "jaundiced" view of exotic birds, he spelled out the exceptional features of the cattle egret's colonizing activities. Unlike native herons and egrets, it is not an aquatic bird and has different food habits as well as habitat requirements. Also, though it often nests among natives, it has done so without causing friction; in fact, the more nesting birds there are in a colony, the greater the degree of protection afforded against predators. Describing it as "beautiful and beneficial," Peterson concluded that the cattle egret was a "fine addition to the American avifauna."[159] By 1955, the bird had reached Texas. Ten years later, it had settled in California. While it continues to expand its American range as grazing acreage grows, the cattle egret still does so at no apparent cost to resident natives. Nor has it exacted an economic price—indeed, some ranchers see the bird as a more effective agent of pest control than pesticides.

If, at some unspecified and nonspecifiable future point, the cattle egret begins to adversely affect native birds, it may well be too late to do anything about it. Nonetheless, in the event of such a scenario—in the plant world as well—it is worth thinking about the arguments those who back the original occupants of land (and sky) will advance to support the case for remedial action. Green cosmopolitans often dismiss support for native species as a romantic and nationalistic fetish. Yet native plants supply vital genetic material for crops. Centuries of plant breeding has drastically reduced genetic variety, so that an entire crop can be vulnerable to a single disease or insect.

In 1970 a leaf fungus eliminated 15 percent of the U.S. corn crop; the industry was rescued with genes from wild plants in Mexico that offered resistance to blight.[160] The case for the native is now more firmly grounded in ecological and economic considerations than in sentiment. For Gould, however, the strongest argument that can be made for natives is neither scientific nor grounded in unabashed cultural preference (we like native species because they are native). Reliance on natives, he believes, teaches humility by counteracting the hubris that we can introduce anything we want anywhere we want.[161] This argument is rarely articulated as part of the current case for native species and may not win many hearts and minds. Not everyone sees transplanted species as prime evidence of the arrogance of humanism. On the contrary, many people like exotics precisely because of their spontaneous, unpredictable, self-willed natures—qualities increasingly banished from the carefully cultivated wild nature officially contained within carefully managed parks, wilderness areas, and wildlife refuges.

THE GLOBALIZATION OF NATURE
AND THE UNIVERSAL SPARROW

Rachel Carson had a more conventional view of the attractions of the natural world, whose self-willed, unpredictable, and spontaneous features were implicitly and unambiguously those of native nature. She believed that the earth was so full of beauty, mystery, and awe that natural scientists—and children—could never become bored. "There is always something new to be investigated," she marveled in the early 1950s.[162] She was not referring to recently introduced species that had enlivened and enriched existing natural communities. The earth she had in mind was the one whose marvels and mysteries predated human interventions. And many scientists and environmentalists would protest that this sense of wonder has become progressively more difficult to nurture in a natural world increasingly devoid of beauty, novelty, and the unexpected. Pondering changes in the biogeographical distribution of species, Charles Darwin pointed out that, though no mammal is common to the Americas, Europe, and Australia, cosmopolitan species were enjoying a growing ascendancy over endemic species. This process of biotic interchange has continued apace on a global scale. A century later, Australian writer Eric Rolls lamented that "we have gained animals and birds that the whole world has, and have lost and are still losing many species of our own strange, beautiful and distinct creatures."[163] According to this way of thinking, beauty, novelty, and the unexpected—qualities that green cosmopolitans associate with exotic species— are precisely those qualities that species coming from somewhere else banish in their new homes.

Australia and New Zealand have long-standing reputations as particularly

stark examples of the dramatic, deleterious consequences of species introduction. In 1998, though, American evolutionary biologist David Quammen
publicized an antipodean scenario writ large. He warned that globetrotting
invasives, distinguished by their uncannily humanlike characteristics
("scrappers, generalists, opportunists . . . aggressive, versatile, prolific, and
ready to travel"), are unifying ecosystems. The looming outcome is a "planet
of weeds." Zoologist Gordon Orians refers to a new era called the
Homogocene.[164] Alongside other cosmopolitan species like the black rat,
cockroach, and housefly, the English sparrow was a central player in
Quammen's vision of tedious and ugly sameness in which the world is
deprived of diversity and "enriched" in weedy species.[165]

The Universal Australian did not have a place in Quammen's grim scenario. But it features as the supreme survivor in T. Coraghessan Boyle's
futuristic, eco-horror novel, set in southern California circa 2025. In *A
Friend of the Earth*, Boyle evokes the view from the freeway of a land fried by
climate change, traumatized by mass extinction, and on the brink of ecological disintegration:

> The smog was like mustard gas. . . . There was trash everywhere, scattered up
> and down the off-ramp like the leavings of a bombed out civilization, cans,
> bottles, fast-food wrappers, yellowing diapers and rusting shopping carts. . . .
> The grass was dead, the oleanders buried in dust. A lone eucalyptus, twelve
> thousand miles from the continent where it had evolved, presided over the
> scene like an advertisement for blight.[166]

If not with quite such apocalyptic flair, every new book on bioinvasion
carries much the same message. "Homogeneity. Sameness. Loss of local
character." This is the opening line of a recent protest against the "globalization of nature," whose essential feature is the shift from the endemic to
the generic that Darwin identified.[167] Neltje Blanchan had mulled over the
dilemma posed by "weedy" species a century earlier in *Bird Neighbors*.
Though "self-respecting" ornithologists were loathe to concede a place on
their lists to the English sparrow, she believed that because there were so
many of them it could not be ignored. "The day is evidently not far off," she
reminded those who were still in denial, "when these birds, by no means
meek, 'shall inherit the earth.' "[168] Eugene Rolfe had also anticipated
Quammen's woeful scenario, reflecting a few years after Blanchan that "a
high state of civilization and an opulence of wild life are plainly antagonis-
tic: and only those species that possess or acquire something of the spirit of
the English sparrow can hope to survive the crush of man's advance."[169]

Though a comparably deep sense of despair and anger over the descent
into a hopelessly fallen world remained absent, Quammen's vision was
more fully rehearsed in 1948 by the president and superintendent of conservation of the Forest Preserve District of Cook County, Illinois. American

ecosystems were still untrammeled by recent headline grabbers such as the brown tree snake and zebra mussel. But these local officials could already see the emergence of a single planetary ecosystem. "The first bird a child sees, most places in the civilized world," they announced, "is likely to be an English sparrow"—for the bird was as adaptable and widespread as the cockroach, rat, and house mouse. Internationalism and global integration were very much on their minds in view of the recent establishment of the United Nations. From this perspective, the English sparrow, though "common as dirt, unloved and neglected," was undeniably "more of a world citizen than most birds." Given this borderless identity, they wondered whether the misnamed English sparrow "should be in the emblem of the United Nations."[170]

Notwithstanding this flattering proposal—and the fact that in 1960 the American Ornithologists' Union adopted "house sparrow" as the bird's official common name—its bad reputation remains nearly as widespread as its distribution. In 1971, George Laycock dismissed them as "drab little bullies of the bird world."[171] The Ivy Removal Project based in Forest Park, Oregon, refers to "the little non-indigenous bully which kicks native cavity nesters out of their homes."[172] And the bird's "pugnacious" presence in cherished national parks arouses particular indignation.[173]

A spirited defense is occasionally mounted. Creatured Connection, an organization devoted to making the world "more compassionate and environmentally friendly" by encouraging appreciation of and love for all parts of "God's creation," has taken up the bird's cause.[174] Sue Holloway, an "ecospiritualist poet" and volunteer wildlife rescuer, believes that "nativists" continue to shoulder much of the blame for the bird's defamation, which prompts her to reflect on the wider contemporary phenomenon of hostility to foreign species. She is particularly alarmed by conservationist efforts to alert young people to the presence of nonnatives, targeting an article about mute swans that "don't belong" in *Ranger Rick*, the National Wildlife Federation's magazine for younger members, rated the nation's premier nature magazine for seven- to twelve-year-olds. Echoing Blanchan's concerns a century earlier, she worries that these calls to arms might lead children to explore their familiar worlds of nature "not with awe, but suspicion."[175]

Holloway wants American children and adults to recapture the "sense of wonder" of which Carson spoke by acknowledging the value of "our ingenuous sparrow." In "The Sense of Wonder," a 1956 account of explorations with her young grandnephew in coastal Maine, Carson wrote about the importance of introducing children to nature's delights and mysteries, particularly those found in or just beyond their own backyards (not least in the city). For Carson, it was essential to learn to feel about nature before knowing about it, and she sought to arouse "a sense of the beautiful, the excitement of the new and the unknown, a feeling of sympathy, pity, admiration or love." She singled out native birds such as the song sparrow as examples of the dawn chorus's sweet voices of which "no child should grow up unaware." She did not mention that backyard fixture, the English sparrow.[176] Indigenousness was more important to her than ingenuousness.

The English sparrow is less of a fixture in the United States today than it was when Carson wrote about the natural world and a sense of wonder. Since 1966 its North American population has declined by 2.5 percent annually.[177] But there are still about 150 million of them. Pooh-poohing all the fuss over the bird during the American sparrow war, an Englishman living in New York City in the 1870s pointed out that numbers back in Britain were ten times larger.[178] This ratio has now been reversed.

In Britain, only 13 million remain. In 2000 the British press was awash with stories about the dramatic sudden decline of a bird that Peter Matthiessen had hailed as one of the New World's "hard-bitten Old World sophisticates."[179] Responding to the strong sense that an essential part of the nation's natural (and urban) heritage was disappearing, the *Independent* newspaper (May 15, 2000) offered a £5,000 prize to whoever could explain the mysterious demise of this "cultural emblem," and the matter was raised in Parliament in February 2002.[180]

The house sparrow is still classified as a pest in Britain. Yet some British conservationists are campaigning for endangered species status. If its British decline continues, the bird will take its place among the nonnatives of the world (such as Monterey pine) that are far more numerous abroad than in their original areas. There are further ironies. The chances of seeing an English sparrow may now be greater in the United States than in England, but American representatives of *Passer domesticus* are not necessarily identical to their beleaguered British cousins. Already by 1900—within thirty generations—English sparrows in the United States had begun to develop the regionally distinctive traits associated with subspecies. They have not formed hybrids through interbreeding with native sparrows. However, in line with Bergmann's rules for nonmigratory fauna, those in the northern states are bigger and darker than their counterparts in the Southwest; larger bodies retain heat more effectively while smaller, lighter ones eliminate it more rapidly.[181] These evolutionary developments that are producing a British American sparrow bolster the faint glimmer of hope that Quammen held out at the end of his Jeremiad in 1998. Posing the question, "how long will it take for evolution to fill the planet back up?" he noted that "even" rats and cockroaches can evolve into new forms and eventually boost biodiversity's floundering cause.[182]

Evolutionary potential of this sort had been far from the mind of another American biologist five years earlier. In 1993, Bill McKnight expressed amazement that a half-millennium of relentless biotic invasion in the

Americas had not produced an even larger number of extinctions and even more species impoverishment. He explained that the various case studies in the collection he had edited—which bore the title *Biological Pollution*— composed a "litany of horror stories."[183] Recent writing on the subject, popular and scientific, remains shaped by the notion of biological pollution. Much recent media coverage also implies that alien species, if not inherently bad and hell-bent on destruction, are fundamentally problematic, and that the history of the strangers on the land that make up an "Alien Nation" is essentially a tragic one.[184]

THE HISTORIAN'S CONTRIBUTION

I have not set out here to evaluate the extent of damage nonnative species have visited on native ecosystems. And I have tried to avoid the apocalyptic and castigatory "serpent in Eden" approach that informs a good deal of contemporary discussion.[185] In the late 1990s, when I first became interested in the controversial deeds of nonnative species, there were few books on the subject. Nowadays, new monographs appear on a regular basis. Yet these studies are either pitches to a scientific audience, journalistic in tone, contributions to policy formulation, or essentially contemporary in focus. None are avowedly historical and none of their authors are historians. Insofar as they do address the past, recent studies tend to use historical examples as ammunition to support positions in contemporary debates. Those involved in discussions of the impact of nonnative species essentially fall into one of two camps, The first position, which has tended to rule the roost until quite recently, seeks to pin public attention on an escalating environmental problem. Many of the accounts in this category tend to be hand-wringing cautionary tales that admonish human myopia and bemoan the repeated failure to learn from past mistakes. The problem with this approach to the past is that it is essentially reductive, driven in large part by the desire to enhance public awareness of today's problem species and to supply ammunition for today's efforts to tackle bioinvaders.

Multihorticulturalists and other champions of exotics hold a view markedly different from this influential censorious position. Ecological cosmopolitanism does not dwell on a world of nature we have lost, nor fret over what we have done *to* the world of native nature. Instead, it focuses on the interesting and valuable world we have gained through the introduction of new species and celebrates what we have done, creatively, *with* the natural world. This approach informs Pollan's work, the writings of philosopher and policy studies specialist Mark Sagoff, and one of the most recent popular studies: *Aliens in the Backyard: Plant and Animal Imports into America,* a chatty and anecdotal book by a professor of literature, John Leland.[186] For Leland (who recognizes that "weedy" aliens "can be a stand-in for unwanted immigrants" but falls into the trap of equating criticism of invasive nonnatives with nativism), growing concern over the impact of invasive nonnative species is "the green equivalent of putting a flag decal on an SUV."[187] This revisionist camp urges us to stop worrying, to relax, and to learn to appreciate—perhaps even to love—these much maligned alien species. Why? Because they aren't half as bad as they have been made out to be and, more important, are part and parcel not only of the natural world of the United States but of what it means to be American. This essentially sanguine approach, however, is no more satisfactory than a viewpoint that sees mainly doom and gloom.

American Perceptions of Immigrant and Invasive Species, the first comprehensive discussion of the cultural consequences of species transfer, falls into neither of these camps. Historians seek to understand rather than to attack or defend. Our primary allegiance is not to the present but to the past in all its infuriating complexity, ambiguity, awkwardness, and untidiness. We all crave clear messages to guide our thinking and reading and to inform our actions. My obligation as an historian, though, has been to communicate the mixed messages the past transmits. As such, my findings both bolster and undermine the two contemporary positions I have identified; they also indicate that today's debates have plenty of antecedents.

A cool historical perspective serves as an antidote to the emotionalism in which discussion of nonnative flora and fauna is often mired. My central case is for material discontinuity, despite the appearance of continuity due to rhetorical similarities, between attitudes to nonnative species of flora and fauna in the late nineteenth and early twentieth centuries on the one hand and the past three decades on the other. My main finding is that for all the racy and attention-grabbing accusations of botanical xenophobia and eco-racism, ties between conservation and prejudice, between the desire to preserve an "American" nature and to defend "old stock' America, once substantial, have largely dissolved. This is because racism and so-called eco-racism have both largely dissolved. Though by no means entirely banished to the past, prejudice against non-whites nowadays is a shadow of its ugly former self. And as racism directed against immigrants and non-whites has weakened, the vital connection that often sustained eco-racism has been severed.

So eco-racism has largely gone. But that is far from saying that suspicion and hostility toward invasive nonnatives have also disappeared. Concerns about their impacts are in fact stronger today than they were a century ago. Just as there is more tolerance of immigrants and non-whites today as ideas of cultural pluralism have taken firm root, there is less tolerance of nonhuman immigrants because of a greater awareness of their consequences for natural pluralism (a more familiar term is native biodiversity). Concern over nonnative biota is likely to intensify. Yet there is a big difference from the past. The rationale for concern is now predominantly material and rational rather than cultural and irrational. Ecological and economic considerations have replaced racism and nativism as the basis of risk assessment. To paraphrase John Higham's 1958 reappraisal of his original diagnosis of late nineteenth-century nativism in the United States, to dismiss as eco-nativism any kind of unfriendliness toward immigrant species is a bad habit to be resisted.

Immigrant fauna and flora have always been—and doubtless will continue to be—a mix of promise and menace, the good and the bad, and the beautiful and the ugly. My priority as an environmental historian is to communicate the equivocal, messy, and unpredictable character of strangers on the American land. Nature's self-willed and ungovernable qualities are exemplified by the more intrusive of nonnative species. Their natures, not our desires, will continue to determine outcomes.

This study has been more about American attitudes to these strangers, however, than about their exploits in America. Responses have been just as equivocal, messy, and enigmatic. Deciding what to do with today's troublesome nonhuman immigrants has not been part of my brief; I am no policy advisor. My task has been to demonstrate how complicated some previous debates over floral and faunal arrivals have been and, in particular, the ways in which they have connected with debates about human newcomers. The stories of human and nonhuman immigrants are rarely told together, but linking them has heightened our appreciation of how notions of nationality and debates about race and immigration have shaped American understandings of the nonhuman world of nature. For all our aesthetic appreciation of flora and fauna, for all our awareness of their ecological and economic value, for all our scientific and recreational interest in them, these considerations do not adequately capture their full meaning. I have sought to demonstrate our basic yet underappreciated need to position plants and animals in relation to ourselves and the groups to which we as individuals belong. Situating nonhuman organisms within the eminently human entities of society, community, race, and nation involves exclusion as well as inclusion, particularly from the nation-state. For many Americans, for an animal or plant to be *in* the United States is not the same as being *of* the United States. Of the various cultural polities within which we have sought to incorporate floral and faunal entities, it is the national unit that stands out. And this study has concentrated on those so-called problem species whose national citizenship has been most heavily contested.

This approach has wider implications for the history of ideas. From start to finish, my musings on immigrants both human and nonhuman have had a direct bearing on a pair of conceptual opposites that have arguably organized Western thought in more fundamental ways and for longer than any others. I am speaking, of course (naturally?), of nature and culture. We continue to pay lip service to "nature" as something apart from us and our culture, something autonomous and different. And, increasingly, as disenchantment with our role in shaping the world around us spreads, we are desperate to see in nature something better than us and our culture. Yet at the same time—as I hope this book has demonstrated—we are constantly undercutting this hallowed dualism of nature and culture with ideas and language that humanize the nonhuman world of nature and naturalize our human world. Deliberation over the nationality of plants and animals is a prime example of the type of thought and expression that cuts across the hallowed divide between nature and culture that has structured Western thinking for so long. What the examination of notions of nationality with regard to foreign bodies like English sparrows and eucalyptus trees reveals is that the mental gap between "us" and "them" is often quite narrow and sometimes virtually nonexistent.

Though sociology and biology are frequently inseparable, I do not wish to claim too much. What Americans (and other peoples) have thought about English sparrows and eucalypts does not always tell us more about people than about birds and trees.[188] Attitudes to immigrant people and actions against them may parallel and resemble attitudes to immigrant flora and fauna and policy toward them. But that does not mean that they are invariably identical or directly comparable or that there is a clear causal relationship between them. The notion of nationality is intriguing and powerful but cannot tell us everything we need to know about how we feel about, talk about, and respond to nonnative species of flora and fauna—especially as we come closer to the present. This book has been about biological entities as well as sociocultural phenomena. Metaphors can be just metaphors. And sometimes it is possible to regard a bird or a tree "merely" (to quote Frank Chapman on the starling) as a bird or a tree.

NOTES

1. STRANGERS AND NATIVES

1. "Aliens," EnvironMinute Wildlife Scripts, Environmental Health Center, National Safety Council, Washington, D.C., April 14, 1999, at www.nsc.org/EHC/minute/em990414.htm, accessed April 16, 2006; Dick Tracy, "Charming Invaders: Alien Species May Look Nice, but Native Plants Wilt under Their Attacks," *Sacramento Bee*, January 17, 1998.
2. At www.invasivespecies.gov/laws/execorder.shtml, accessed April 16, 2006.
3. The deleterious ecological impact of nonnatives (bioinvasion) is a rapidly expanding specialty within conservation ecology. For recent surveys, see Harold A. Mooney and Richard J. Hobbs, eds., *Invasive Species in a Changing World* (Washington, D.C.: Island Press, 2000); David Pimentel et al., "Economic and Environmental Threats of Alien Plant, Animal, and Microbe Invasions," *Agriculture, Ecosystems and Environment* 84 (2001): 1–20; Gregory M. Ruiz and James T. Carlton, *Invasive Species: Vectors and Management Strategies* (Washington, D.C.: Island Press, 2003); George W. Cox, *Alien Species and Evolution: The Evolutionary Ecology of Exotic Plants, Animals, Microbes, and Interacting Native Species* (Washington, D.C.: Island Press, 2004); Harold A. Mooney et al., eds., *Invasive Alien Species: A New Synthesis* (Washington, D.C.: Island Press, 2005), especially Mooney, "Invasive Alien Species: The Nature of the Problem," 1–15. For an account of the historical development of invasion biology, see Mark A. Davis, "Invasion Biology, 1958–2004: The Pursuit of Science and Conservation," in *Conceptual Ecology and Invasions Biology: Reciprocal Approaches to Nature*, ed. Marc William Cadotte et al. (New York: Springer, 2005), 1–25 (at www.cedarcreek.umn.edu/biblio/fulltext/t1972.pdf, accessed April 16, 2006). For a revisionist approach (by a nonscientist) that questions whether a sound scientific case can be made for nonnative organisms as genuinely "harmful" (based on an "operational and non-question-begging definition of 'harm'") to "biodiversity" and ecosystem "health"/"integrity," see Mark Sagoff,

"Do Non-Native Species Threaten the Natural Environment?" *Journal of Agricultural and Environmental Ethics* 18 (2005): 215–36.

4. The term *meltdown* has been coined to describe this ripple effect, while nonnative species that inaugurate these sweeping changes have been dubbed *transformer* species; see Daniel Simberloff and B. Von Holle, "Positive Interactions of Nonindigenous Species: Invasion Meltdown?" *Biological Invasions* 1, 1 (1999): 21–32; David M. Richardson et al., "Naturalization and Invasion of Alien Plants: Concepts and Definitions," *Diversity and Distributions* 6, 2 (March 2000): 93, 98, 102 (93–107).

5. Rick Gore and David Doubilet, "Florida, Noah's Ark for Exotic Newcomers," *National Geographic* 150, 4 (October 1976): 539–40 (538–58).

6. U.S. Department of the Interior, Office of the Secretary, press release, "Invasive Weeds Pose Major Threat to American Landscape," April 28, 1998, at www.doi.gov/news/archives/weedrel.html, accessed April 16, 2006.

7. Elizabeth Culotta, "Biological Immigrants under Fire," *Science* 254, 5037 (1991): 1444–47; Sally Deneen, "Going, Going . . . Exotic Species Are Decimating America's Native Wildlife," *E Magazine* 13, 3 (May–June 2000): 1–8, at www.emagazine.com/view/?729&src=QHA154, accessed 16 April, 2006.

8. *Biodiversity,* a term coined in 1986 by Walter Rosen, became a familiar buzzword in the discourse of species conservation by 1993.

9. F. Eugene Hester, "The U.S. National Park Service Experience with Exotic Species," *Natural Areas Journal* 11, 3 (1991): 127–28; Michael D. Lemonick, "Invasion of the Habitat Snatchers," *Time* 136, 11 (September 10, 1990): 68; Randy G. Westbrooks, *Invasive Plants: Changing the Landscape of America: Fact Book* (Washington, D.C.: Federal Interagency Committee for the Management of Noxious and Exotic Weeds, 1998), 6; Don Schmitz and Daniel Simberloff, "Biological Invasions," *Issues in Science and Technology* 13, 4 (Summer 1997): 33, 40 (33–40).

10. Daniel Simberloff, Don C. Schmitz, and Tom C. Brown, eds., *Strangers in Paradise: Impact and Management of Nonindigenous Species in Florida* (Washington, D.C.: Island Press, 1997); Robert Devine, *Alien Invasion: America's Battle with Non-Native Animals and Plants* (Washington, D.C.: National Geographic Society, 1998); Chris Bright, *Life out of Bounds: Bio-invasions in a Borderless World* (Washington, D.C.: Worldwatch Institute/Earthscan, 1999); Jason Van Driesche and Roy Van Driesche, *Nature out of Place: Biological Invasions in the Global Age* (Washington, D.C.: Island Press, 2000); Kim Todd, *Tinkering with Eden: A Natural History of Exotics in America* (New York: Norton, 2001); Yvonne Baskin, *A Plague of Rats and Rubbervines: The Growing Threat of Species Invasions* (Washington, D.C.: Island Press, 2002); Alan Burdick, *Out of Eden: An Odyssey of Ecological Invasion* (New York: Farrar, Straus and Giroux, 2005).

11. Edward Tenner, *Why Things Bite Back: Technology and the Revenge of Unintended Consequences* (New York: Knopf, 1996). See Banu Subramaniam, "The Aliens Have Landed! Reflections on the Rhetoric of Biological Invasions," *Meridians: Feminism, Race, Transnationalism* 2, 1 (2001): 27–28 (26–40); Jonah H. Peretti, "Nativism and Nature: Rethinking Biological Invasion," *Environmental Values* 7 (1998): 183–84 (183–92); Jean Comaroff and John L. Comaroff,

"Naturing the Nation: Aliens, Apocalypse and the Postcolonial State," *Journal of Southern African Studies* 27, 3 (September 2001): 632 (627–51).

12. For "knowing nature through labor" and "knowing nature through leisure," see chapter titles in, respectively, Richard White, *The Organic Machine: The Remaking of the Columbia River* (New York: Hill & Wang, 1995), and Paul Sutter, *Driven Wild: How the Fight against Automobiles Launched the Modern Wilderness Movement* (Seattle: University of Washington Press, 2002).

13. U.S. Congress, Office of Technology Assessment (OTA), *Harmful Non-Indigenous Species in the United States* (Washington, D.C.: Government Printing Office, 1993), 94. In view of these low numbers, I have not examined the cultural dimensions of responses to undesirable nonnative species related to notions of nationality prior to the 1850s as a prelude to this study. Regardless of numbers, responses of this kind would obviously be hard to find before American nationhood (1783). Efforts to determine conclusively the origins of that supreme scourge of American wheat farmers, the so-called Hessian fly, and the cultural-political overtones of these investigations are the most conspicuous example during the late eighteenth and first half of the nineteenth centuries.

14. Thomas R. Dunlap, *Nature and the English Diaspora: Environment and History in the United States, Canada, Australia, and New Zealand* (New York: Cambridge University Press, 1999), 97, 190. On acclimatization societies in the United States (where there were fewer and they were less influential than in Australia and New Zealand), see Christopher Lever, *They Dined on Eland: The Story of the Acclimatisation Societies* (London: Quiller, 1992), 183–90.

15. OTA, *Harmful Non-Indigenous Species in the United States*, 6, 94, 96–97. The 1920s and 1930s were hardly a quiet time insofar as several earlier arrivals, hitherto largely unnoticed, spread vigorously. The reengineered Welland Canal allowed the sea lamprey to enter Lake Erie from Lake Ontario in the early 1920s. This parasitic fish reached Lake Superior by 1946. The Argentine ant, Japanese beetle, and spruce sawfly also advanced uninterrupted.

16. OTA, *Harmful Non-Indigenous Species in the United States*, 96. Jeffrey A. McNeely, "An Introduction to Human Dimensions of Invasive Alien Species," in *The Great Reshuffling: Human Dimensions of Invasive Alien Species* (Gland, Switzerland: IUCN, 2001), 7; Francesco Di Castri, "History of Biological Invasions with Special Emphasis on the Old World," in *Biological Invasions: A Global Perspective* (Chichester, U.K.: Wiley/Scientific Committee on Problems of the Environment of the International Council of Scientific Unions, 1989), 19.

17. For "culture of fear," see Barry Glassner, *The Culture of Fear: Why Americans Are Afraid of the Wrong Things* (New York: Basic, 1999).

18. Alfred W. Crosby, *The Columbian Exchange: Biological and Cultural Consequences of 1492* (Westport, Conn.: Greenwood Press, 1972); *Ecological Imperialism: The Biological Expansion of Europe, 900–1900* (New York: Cambridge University Press, 1986).

19. Though native to most parts of Europe and a member of the finch family, the house sparrow, or European sparrow, was popularly designated the "English sparrow" in the United States—not least because most of the first generation were English imports. Adding the name of a nation as an adjectival prefix to a bird name does not have the sole function of indicating the country (or one

of the countries) from which it has been introduced. Sometimes "English" designated an entirely American bird that reminded observers of a familiar English bird; hence, "English duck" for the black duck and mottled duck, which reminded them of the mallard, and "English woodpecker" for the yellow-shafted flicker, which apparently resembled the European green woodpecker; see W. L McAtee, "Nationality Names for American Birds," *American Speech* 32, 3 (October 1957): 180.

20. Charles S. Elton, *The Ecology of Invasions by Animals and Plants* (London: Methuen, 1958), 75; Crosby, *Columbian Exchange,* 210–11; *Ecological Imperialism,* 292–93; Jerry C. Towle, "Authored Ecosystems: Livingston Stone and the Transformation of California Fisheries," *Environmental History* 5, 1 (January 2000): 60, 71, 63 (54–74).

21. Fletcher Osgood, "The English Sparrow in New England," *New England Magazine* 29, 3 (1903): 319 (317–24).

22. For definitions of *naturalized,* see David M. Richardson et al., "Naturalization and Invasion of Alien Plants," *Diversity and Distributions* (2000): 95–97, 107 (93–107).

23. OTA, *Harmful Non-Indigenous Species in the United States,* 97, 99, 69.

24. Mark Fiege, "The Weedy West: Mobile Nature, Boundaries, and Common Space in the Montana Landscape," *Western Historical Quarterly* 36, 1 (Spring 2005): 23–47.

25. For this phrase, see Edgar Anderson, *Plants, Man and Life* (Berkeley: University of California Press, 1967 [1952]), 9.

26. Judith Larner Lowry, "The Gardener and the Quail: A Bolinas Love Story," *Bay Nature* (April–June 2002), at www.baynature.com/2002apriljune/quail_2002 apriljune.html, accessed April 16, 2006.

27. Claudia Roth Pierpont, "The Measure of America: How a Rebel Anthropologist Waged War on Racism," *New Yorker,* March 8, 2004, 56–62.

28. At www.archives.gov/federal-register/codification/executive-order/11987 .html, accessed April 16, 2006.

29. Michael G. Barbour, "California Landscapes before the Invaders," in *Proceedings, California Exotic Pest Plant Council Symposium, Volume 2: 1996,* ed. Jeff Lovich, John Randall, and Mike Kelly (San Diego, October 4–6, 1996), 5–9.

30. Some early nineteenth-century botanists reckoned that the catalpa *(Catalpa bignonioides),* relatively abundant in parts of the Mississippi Valley, was native to Japan and had been introduced by the "aborigines" (and named after the Catawba tribe). Also known as the bean tree, Indian bean, and Indian cigar tree, the catalpa is now generally considered native.

31. Frances L. Jewett, *Plant Hunters* (Boston: Houghton Mifflin, 1958), viii.

32. Thirty years ago, it was believed that corn had been raised in New England for no more than two centuries before the pilgrim fathers arrived; see Mary-Alice F. Rea, "Early Introduction of Economic Plants into New England," *Economic Botany* 29, 4 (October–December 1975): 333–34 (333–56).

33. John Terborgh, "The Age of Giants," *New York Review of Books* 48, 14 (September 20, 2001): 46.

34. Russian thistle, better known as tumbleweed, has become integral to perceptions of the landscape of the American West. Canada thistle is from Eurasia

and widespread there, but it excelled to such an extent in Canada after its seventeenth-century arrival that, when it showed up in northern New York state in the early 1800s (possibly in horse feed), *Cirsium arvense* was linked with its country of immediate origin rather than its more distant homeland; see Clinton L. Evans, *The War on Weeds in the Prairie West: An Environmental History* (Calgary: University of Calgary Press, 2002), 53, 65–66, 182.

35. The Argentine ant *(Linepithema humilis)* arrived at the port of New Orleans around 1891. Two additional exotic ants from South America are the black ant *(Solenopsis richteri)* and the imported red fire ant *(S. invicta)*. They arrived in dry ship's ballast at Mobile, Alabama, circa 1918 and in the late 1930s, respectively.

36. Pam Fuller, Leo G. Nico, and James D. Williams, *Nonindigenous Fishes Introduced into Inland Waters of the United States* (Bethesda, Md.: American Fisheries Society, 1999), cited in "Book Documents Invasion of U.S. Waters," Environmental News Network (ENN), May 21, 1999, at http://edition.cnn.com/NATURE/9905/21/invasive.fish.enn/, accessed April 16, 2006.

37. Carla M. Bossard et al., eds., *Invasive Plants of California's Wildlands* (Berkeley: University of California Press, 2000), 274.

38. Robert Grese, *Jens Jensen* (Baltimore: Johns Hopkins University Press, 1992), 113–14, 117, 154.

39. Barbara L. Sleeper and Michael Hutchins, "The Horns of a Dilemma," *Pacific Discovery* 42, 1 (Winter 1989): 18. Critics of removal claim a historic presence prior to the 1920s.

40. Odd Terje Sandlund, Peter Johan Schei, and Aslaug Viken, eds., *Proceedings, Norway/UN Conference on Alien Species: The Trondheim Conferences on Biodiversity* (Trondheim, Norway: Directorate for Nature Management/Norwegian Institute for Nature Research, 1996), 7.

41. At www.presidency.ucsb.edu/ws/index.php?pid=56579&st=&st1=, accessed April 16, 2006.

42. On terminology, see Peter Coates, "Editorial Postscript: The Naming of Strangers in the Landscape," in "Theme Issue: The Native, Naturalized and Exotic—Plants and Animals in Human History," *Landscape Research* 23, 1 (January 2003): 131–37.

43. H. G. Wells, *The Future in America: A Search after Realities* (London: Chapman Hall, 1906), 2.

44. On the imported red fire ant, see Joshua Blu Buhs, *The Fire Ant Wars: Nature, Science, and Public Policy in Twentieth-Century America* (Chicago: University of Chicago Press, 2004).

45. For these terms, see Mark Sagoff, "What's Wrong with Exotic Species?" at www.puaf.umd.edu/IPPP/fall1999/exotic_species.htm, page 8 of 12, accessed April 16, 2006; and Peretti, "Nativism and Nature," 184. See also Sagoff, "Why Exotic Species Are Not as Bad as We Fear," *Chronicle of Higher Education*, June 23, 2000, B7, at http://chronicle.com/weekly/v46/i42/42b00701.htm, 4 pages, accessed April 16, 2006.

46. See Brian Nelson Fry, "Alien Notions: Varieties of Nativism and Perceptions of Threat," PhD thesis, Michigan State University, 1998, 20–56.

47. Peretti, "Nativism and Nature," 188; Michael Pollan, "Against Nativism," *New*

York Times, May 15, 1994, 54–55; Subramaniam, "The Aliens Have Landed!" 27; Nancy Tomes, "The Making of a Germ Panic, Then and Now," *American Journal of Public Health* 90, 2 (February 2000): 191–99.

48. The "greening of hate" is a phrase borrowed from an article about the debate within the Sierra Club over immigration, population growth, and environmental degradation; see Ron Russell, "The Greening of Hate," *Los Angeles Times*, March 12, 1998.

49. An American botanical scientist recently cited Napoleon's ill-fated invasion of Russia in 1812/13 to underline "the commonality of questions" facing those who assess the dynamics and consequences of invasions; see Richard N. Mack, "Assessing Biotic Invasions in Time and Space: The Second Imperative," in Mooney et al., *Invasive Alien Species*, 180–82.

50. Joseph Hooker, "The Distribution of the North American Flora," *Gardeners' Chronicle* 10 (August 3, 1878): 140.

51. Crosby, *Ecological Imperialism*, 89, 162, 287, 293. Robert Froman, *Our Fellow Immigrants* (New York: D. McKay, 1965); see also Froman, "Our Fellow Immigrants," *American Heritage Magazine* 14, 2 (February 1963), at www.americanheritage .com/articles/magazine/ah/1963/2/1963_2_60.shtm, accessed April 17, 2006.

52. J. Hector St. John de Crèvecoeur, "What Is an American?" in *Letters from an American Farmer and Sketches of Eighteenth-Century America* (Harmondsworth, U.K.: Penguin, 1981 [1782]), 69, 71.

53. Crosby, *Ecological Imperialism*, 270, 293, 288, 149–50, 154–55, 165; Lewis D. De Schweinitz, "Remarks on the Plants of Europe Which Have Become Naturalized in a More or Less Degree, in the United States," *Annals of the Lyceum of Natural History of New York* 3 (1832): 149.

54. Frederic E. Clements, *Plant Succession and Indictors: A Definitive Edition of Plant Succession, and Plant Indicators* (New York: H. W. Wilson, 1928 [1916]), 3, 75.

55. Eugene Warming, *Oecology of Plants: An Introduction to the Study of Plant-Communities* (Oxford: Clarendon Press, 1909 [1896]), 349–56.

56. Warming, *Oecology of Plants*, 349, 366. The leading British plant ecologist of the 1920s and 1930s drew explicit comparisons between "plant communities" and the "nations, tribes, and societies of mankind" (such as the British colonies in New England and Virginia); Arthur Tansley, "The Classification of Vegetation and the Concept of Development," *Journal of Ecology* 8, 2 (June 1920): 123–25 (118–49).

57. Roderick D. McKenzie, "The Ecological Approach to the Study of the Human Community," in Robert E. Park, Ernest W. Burgess, and Roderick D. McKenzie, *The City* (Chicago: University of Chicago Press, 1925), 74, 76, 77.

58. Louis Wirth, *The Ghetto* (Chicago: University of Chicago Press, 1928), vi–vii, 5–6; Ernest Burgess, "Can Neighborhood Work Have a Scientific Basis?" in Park et al., *The City*, 145–46. On the Chicago school's "invasive outgrowths of biological metaphor," see Andrew Ross, *The Chicago Gangster Theory of Life: Nature's Debt to Society* (London: Verso, 1994), 118.

59. Herbert Guthrie-Smith placed the distinction between native and nonnative at the heart of the study of ecological and human communities. A Scotsman who emigrated to New Zealand's North Island in the 1880s, he interpreted the

replacement of natives with nonnatives as part of a process of democratization that mirrored changes in the distribution of human power; *Tutira: The Story of a New Zealand Sheep Station* (Seattle: University of Washington Press, 1999 [1921]), 165, 308, 297, 298, 236, 357, 165, 172, 174.

60. Donald Davidson, "What Metaphors Mean," in *On Metaphor,* ed. Sheldon Sacks (Chicago: University of Chicago Press, 1979), 38.

61. Davidson, "What Metaphors Mean," 43; Wayne C. Booth, "Metaphor as Rhetoric: The Problem of Evaluation," in Sacks, *On Metaphor,* 55, 50–51.

62. Max Black, *Models and Metaphors: Studies in Language and Philosophy* (Ithaca: Cornell University Press, 1962), 39–41, 44, 29.

63. Lothrop Stoddard, *The Rising Tide of Color against White World-Supremacy* (New York: Scribner's, 1920), 3, 148.

64. Rodger Streitmatter, "The Nativist Press: Demonizing the American Immigrant," *Journalism and Mass Communication Quarterly* 76, 4 (Winter 1999): 678 (673–83); Madison Grant, *The Passing of the Great Race: or, The Racial Basis of European History* (New York: Scribner's, 1916), 91.

65. Leonard Dinnerstein, Roger L. Nichols, and David M. Reimers, *Natives and Strangers: A Multicultural History of America* (New York: Oxford University Press, 1996), 234.

66. Quoted in John Higham, *Strangers in the Land: Patterns of Nativism in American History, 1860s to 1920s* (New Brunswick, N.J.: Rutgers University Press, 1955), 171. The study of responses to nonnative diseases that incontrovertibly threaten human health, such as influenza, HIV/AIDS, Ebola virus, and West Nile virus, lies beyond this study's scope. Nor is there space for discussion of the Ebola and West Nile viruses as unambiguous threats to animal well-being. West Nile virus, first identified in Uganda in 1937, is a mosquito-borne pathogen that made its American debut in 1999. This neuroinvasive disease leads to inflammation of the brain in humans, birds, and mammalian animals, domestic and wild.

67. Cornelia James Cannon, "Selecting Citizens," *North American Review* 218 (September 1923): 330 (325–33); also S. J. Holmes, "Perils of the Mexican Invasion," *North American Review* 227 (March 1929): 617, 620, 616; William Deverell, "Plague in Los Angeles, 1924: Ethnicity and Typicality," in *Over the Edge: Remapping the American West,* ed. Valerie Matsumoto and Blake Allmendinger (Berkeley: University of California Press, 1999), 191 (172–200). For a "medicalized nativism" that tarred entire groups, see Alan M. Kraut, *Silent Travelers: Germs, Genes, and the "Immigrant Menace"* (New York: Basic Books, 1994), 2, 4, 31–49, 78–96.

68. Madison Grant and Charles Stewart Davison, eds., *The Founders of the Republic on Immigration, Naturalization, and Aliens* (New York: Scribner's, 1928), vi.

69. Sagoff, "What's Wrong with Exotic Species?" page 5 of 12.

70. Subramaniam, "The Aliens Have Landed!" 29, 38, 27, 34. On parallels between scientific discourse on nonnative species and the rhetoric of nativism and racism, see also Kenneth R. Olwig, "Natives and Aliens in the National Landscape," *Landscape Research* 28, 1 (January 2003): 61–63 (61–74).

71. Daniels, "Two Cheers for Immigration," in Roger Daniels and Otis L. Graham, *Debating American Immigration, 1882–Present* (Lanham, Md.: Rowman & Lit-

tlefield, 2001), 7. The hydraulic metaphors that saturated the immigration debate in the late nineteenth and early twentieth centuries illustrate the importance of immediate context. When Lothrop Stoddard, a prominent Anglo-Saxon supremacist, alluded to the "white flood" engulfing the world's empty lands, this approving usage lent a triumphal air of natural destiny to the colonizing activities of northwestern Europeans. But the idea of an uncontrollable natural force suggested calamity when twinned with human undesirables. Articulating a nature of terror, immigration restrictionist Henry Pratt Fairchild evoked "swollen streams" of eastern and southern Europeans engulfing American republicanism and religious liberty. See Stoddard, *Rising Tide of Color,* 153; Fairchild, *The Melting Pot Mistake* (New York: Arno, 1977 [1926]), 107.

72. Susanne K. Langer, *Philosophy in a New Key: A Study in the Symbolism of Reason, Rite, and Art* (Cambridge: Harvard University Press, 1957 [1942]), 140–41. Booth refers to a metaphor with no edge or twist as a non-metaphor or dead metaphor; "Metaphor as Rhetoric," 49. Davidson also refers to the dead metaphor, one of his examples being "mouth of a bottle." When we talk of the mouth of a bottle, the aim is not to drawn the listener's or reader's attention to the similarity between the apertures of a bottle and an animal: "Once one has the present use of the word, with literal application to bottles, there is nothing left to notice"; "On Metaphor," 35–36. The prominence of metaphor within ecological thinking in the late nineteenth century reflects the absence of formalization in the ecological sciences. I am grateful to Richard Minnich for this insight.

73. Thomas G. Gentry, *The House Sparrow at Home and Abroad* (Philadelphia: Claxton, Remsen, and Haffelfinger, 1878), 100; Ora Willis Knight, *The Birds of Maine* (Bangor, Maine: Charles H. Glass, 1908), 391; Roberta Friedman, "Strangers in Our Midst," *Pacific Discovery* 41, 3 (Summer 1988): 22–31.

74. John Higham, *Strangers in the Land: Patterns of Nativism in American History, 1860s to 1920s,* 2d ed. (New Brunswick, N.J.: Rutgers University Press, 1963), Preface (n.p.). In fact, this book's subtitle is rather thirdhand. Higham got his title from a celebrated scriptural plea for tolerance on the part of "native-born" Israelites toward the "strangers" in their midst (*Leviticus* 19: 33 and 34), which he quotes in his frontispiece: "And if a stranger sojourn with thee in your land, ye shall not vex him. But the stranger that dwelleth with you shall be unto you as one born among you, and thou shalt love him as thyself; for ye were strangers in the land of Egypt."

   I have slightly adjusted Higham's title, replacing *in* with *on.* This may seem pedantic. But given the shift in focus from relations between human natives and strangers to attitudes to floral and faunal strangers, this minor variation conveys a sense of plants and creatures dwelling on the land as a biological and physical entity as well as people living in the land as a cultural and social body politic.

75. Anthony F. C. Wallace, "Revitalization Movements," *American Anthropologist* 58, 2 (1956): 267, 278 (264–81).

76. Richard Hofstadter, *The Paranoid Style in American Politics and Other Essays* (London: Jonathan Cape, 1966), 3, 7, 59.

77. Lawrence Auster, "Not an Open-and-Shut-Case," *Social Contract* 2, 3 Summer 1992: 234–35.

78. John Higham, "The Politics of Immigration Restriction," in *Send These to Me: Jews and Other Immigrants in Urban America* (New York: Atheneum, 1975), 59; this essay originally appeared as "American Immigration Policy in Historical Perspective," *Law and Contemporary Problems* 21 (Spring 1956): 213–35.

79. Higham, "Another Look at Nativism," in *Send These to Me*, 105, 103, 106; this essay originally appeared as "Another Look at Nativism," *Catholic Historical Review* 44 (1958): 147–58. Higham, *Strangers in the Land*, Preface to the Second Edition, iii.

80. Juan F. Perea, "Introduction," in *Immigrants Out! The New Nativism and the Anti-Immigrant Impulse in the United States*, ed. Juan F. Perea (New York: New York University Press, 1997), 5; Joe R. Feagin, "Old Poison in New Bottles: The Deep Roots of Modern Nativism," in Perea, *Immigrants Out!* 19–25; Thomas Muller, "Nativism in the Mid-1990s: Why Now?" in Perea, *Immigrants Out!* 109.

81. Phyllis Windle, "The OTA Report and U.S. Policy on Non-indigenous Species," page 1 of 3, at www.agci.org/publications/eoc94/EOC3/EOC3-26.html, accessed April 16, 2006.

82. Subramaniam, "Aliens Have Landed!" 28.

83. John M. MacKenzie, "Editorial," *Environment and History* 7, 3 (August 2001): 253. Crosby's response is quoted in MacKenzie, "Editorial," *Environment and History* 7, 4 (November 2001): 380.

84. Hofstadter, *The Paranoid Style in American Politics*, 3, 7, 59.

85. Sagoff, "What's Wrong with Exotic Species?" pages 9 and 10 of 12.

86. *Impatiens glandulifera*, introduced as a garden ornamental in the late 1830s, is a tall cane with pretty flowers. Substantial stands started to appear along rivers in the 1960s.

87. Julian Rollins, "Red in Tooth and Claw," *Environment Action*, Summer 2002.12–13. *Environment Action* is the Environment Agency's newsletter.

88. John Muir Trust, *Annual Report 2003* (Edinburgh, Scotland: 2003), 2. For samples of current British debates, see Ian D. Rotherham, ed., "Loving the Aliens??!!? Ecology, History, Culture and the Management of Exotic Plants and Animals: Issues for Nature Conservation," *Journal of Practical Ecology and Conservation Special Series*, No. 4 (June 2005).

89. Hilda Kean, "Save 'Our' Red Squirrel: Kill the American Grey Tree Rat," in *Seeing History: Public History in Britain Now*, ed. Hilda Kean, Paul Martin, and Sally J. Morgan (London: Francis Boutle, 2000), 51–64.

90. In no sense, though, is this a full-fledged comparative study akin to Dunlap's *Nature and the English Diaspora* or William Beinart and Peter Coates, *Environment and History: The Taming of Nature in the U.S.A. and South Africa* (London: Routledge, 1995).

91. James H. Brown, "Patterns, Modes and Extents of Invasions by Vertebrates," in *Biological Invasions: A Global Perspective*, ed. James A. Drake et al. (Chichester, U.K.: SCOPE/John Wiley, 1989), 105–6 (85–109). This conference, held under the auspices of the Scientific Committee on Problems of the Environment (SCOPE), a committee of the International Council of Scientific Unions, wrapped up a SCOPE program initiated in 1982.

2. THE AVIAN CONQUEST OF A CONTINENT

1. C. G. Abbott, "European Birds in America," *Bird-Lore* 5, 5 (September–October 1903): 163.
2. Walter B. Barrows, *The English Sparrow (Passer domesticus) in North America, Especially in Its Relations to Agriculture* (Washington, D.C.: Government Printing Office, 1889), 21–22.
3. Leonard Wing, "Spread of the Starling and English Sparrow," *Auk* 60, 1 (January 1943): 80–81 (74–87).
4. The starling is thus a prime example of an introduced species that has thrived despite low genetic diversity (so-called genetic bottlenecking).
5. Jake Page, "Pushy and Brassy, the Starling Was an Ill-Advised Import," *Smithsonian* 21, 6 (September 1990): 79 (77–83).
6. Jennifer Price, *Flight Maps: Adventures with Nature in Modern America* (New York: Basic, 1999), 1–55.
7. The exception is Robin Doughty, *The English Sparrow in the American Landscape: A Paradox in Nineteenth-Century Wildlife Conservation* (Oxford, U.K.: School of Geography, University of Oxford, 1978), 6, 14, 16, 21, 24, 27–29. For brief coverage, see Mark V. Barrow, *A Passion for Birds: American Ornithology after Audubon* (Princeton, N.J.: Princeton University Press, 1998), 49–50, and David B. Williams, "The Sparrow War," *American History Magazine*, June 2002, 39–42.
8. U.S. Congress, Office of Technology Assessment (OTA), *Harmful Non-Indigenous Species in the United States* (Washington, D.C.: Government Printing Office, 1993), 63, 71.
9. Price, *Flight Maps*, 35–41, xxi.
10. William Leon Dawson, *Birds of Ohio* (Columbus, Ohio: Wheaton, 1903), 40.
11. William Brewster, *The Birds of the Cambridge Region of Massachusetts* (Cambridge: Nuttall Ornithological Club, 1906), 66.
12. *New York World* 48 (May 2, 1883), clipping, Scrapbook 56, Charles Valentine Riley Papers, Record Unit 7076, Archives, Smithsonian Arts and Industry, Washington, D.C. (hereafter Riley Papers).
13. Michael J. Brodhead, "Elliott Coues and the Sparrow War," *New England Quarterly* 44 (September 1971): 432 (420–32).
14. Elliott Coues, "The Sparrow War," *American Sportsman* 5 (November 21, 1874): 113; "The Ineligibility of the European House Sparrow in America," *American Naturalist* 12, 8 (August 1878): 499–505. Coues was a founding member of the AOU, its first secretary, and its president in the early 1890s. In the 1870s, he was assigned as surgeon and naturalist to various federal expeditions into the western territories. A member of Columbia University's medical school between 1877 and 1887, he later edited a version of the Lewis and Clark journals (published 1893).
15. Neltje Blanchan, *Bird Neighbors: An Introductory Acquaintance with One Hundred and Fifty Birds Commonly Found in the Gardens, Meadows and Woods about Our Homes* (London: Sampson, Low, Marston, 1898), Preface, 145–46, 150, 144, 163, 159.

16. William Rhodes, "Imported Birds for Our Woods and Parks," *Forest and Stream* 8, 11 (April 19, 1877): 165.

17. Henry James, *The American Scene* (London: Chapman and Hall, 1946 [1907]), 86; Owen Wister, "The Evolution of the Cow-Puncher," *Harper's New Monthly Magazine* 91, 544 (September 1895): 603–4 (602–17).

18. Bradford Torrey, "A November Chronicle," *Atlantic Monthly* 62, 373 (November 1888): 592.

19. Barrows, *English Sparrow,* 22.

20. George Laycock, *The Alien Animals: The Story of Imported Wildlife* (New York: Ballantine, 1966), 63–65.

21. Quoted in Jerry C. Towle, "Authored Ecosystems: Livingston Stone and the Transformation of California Fisheries," *Environmental History* 5, 1 (January 2000): 60, 71, 63 (54–74).

22. William A Dill, *History and Status of Introduced Fishes in California, 1871–1996* (Sacramento: Resources Agency, California Department of Fish and Game, 1997), 50.

23. The canker worm *(Paleacrita vernata),* also known as the measuring worm, inchworm, and dropworm, was later identified as the larva of the snow-white linden moth. Another tree pest of this time was the elm spanworm *(Ennomos subsignarrius).*

24. William Cullen Bryant, "The Old-World Sparrow," *Poetical Works* (New York: AMS, 1972 [1903]), 373–74.

25. Quoted in the (London) *Times,* August 17, 1869.

26. Susan Fenimore Cooper, "Later Hours" (1868), in *Essays on Nature and Landscape,* ed. Rochelle Johnson and Daniel Patterson (Athens: University of Georgia Press, 2002), 53.

27. "Some Faithful Servants," *New York Times,* December 28, 1872.

28. Thomas G. Gentry, *The House Sparrow at Home and Abroad* (Philadelphia: Claxton, Remsen, and Haffelfinger, 1878), 39, 182–3.

29. Thomas M. Brewer, "The European House-Sparrow," *Atlantic Monthly* 21, 127 (May 1868): 588 (583–88).

30. "C" (Elliott Coues), "A Nuisance in Feathers," *New York Times,* January 27, 1886.

31. Anon., "About Sparrows," *Scientific American* 37 (August 11, 1877): 80.

32. Bolles's maternal uncle was governor of New York, secretary of the treasury, and ambassador to France. His brother-in-law was a governor of Massachusetts.

33. *Boston Evening Transcript,* March 19, 1878, quoted in Barrow, *Passion for Birds,* 49.

34. Frank Bolles, "Bird Traits," *New England Magazine* 13, 1 (September 1892): 96.

35. James, *American Scene,* 85–86.

36. Wister, "Evolution of the Cow-Puncher," 603–4.

37. Henry W. Elliott, "The Sparrow War," *Harper's* 59, 354 (November 1879): 852; "The Chattering Sparrow: Shall It Be Protected or Exterminated?" *New York Times,* September 2, 1878.

38. Walter Bradford Barrows, *Michigan Bird Life* (Lansing: Michigan Agricultural College, 1912), 481.

39. The ratio of horses to people in New York City and Brooklyn in 1880 was one

to ten, and each horse produced between fifteen and thirty pounds of daily droppings. Because horses do not chew the cud, seeds pass mostly intact though the digestive tract.

40. Mabel Osgood Wright and Elliott Coues, *Citizen Bird: Scenes from Bird-Life in Plain English for Beginners* (New York: Macmillan, 1897), 182, 203–4.

41. Coues, "Nuisance in Feathers."

42. Coues, *Key to North American Birds,* vol. 1, 5th ed. (Boston: Dana Estes, 1903), 379–80.

43. Coues, *Key to North American Birds,* vol. 1, 2d ed. (Boston: Estes and Lauriat, 1884), 344; Elliott Coues and D. W. Prentiss, *Avifauna Columbiana: Being a List of Birds Ascertained to Inhabit the District of Columbia* (1883), reprinted in John Henry Gurney, *The House Sparrow* (London: W. Wesley, 1885), 61.

44. Lord Lilford, "The Destruction of British Birds," quoted in W. B. Tegetmeier and E. A. Ormerod, *The House Sparrow (The Avian Rat)* (London: Vinton, 1899), 36; Charlotte M. Yonge, *Countess Kate; and The Stokesley Secret* (London: Macmillan, 1902 [1861]), 216; William Yarrell, *A History of British Birds,* vol. 1 (London: John van Voorst, 1871–1885), 521.

45. Gentry, *House Sparrow,* 100. The city of Hamilton, Canada, provided a daily sheaf of oats in winter for a couple of years following introduction there; C. C. M., "The English Sparrow," *Birds* 3, 5 (May 1898), n.p., at www.birdnature.com/may1898/stilt.html, accessed April 16, 2006.

46. Gentry, *House Sparrow,* 100–1.

47. William Rhodes, "Imported Birds for Our Woods and Parks," *Forest and Stream* 8, 11 (April 19, 1877): 165.

48. Fletcher Osgood, "The English Sparrow in New England," *New England Magazine* 29, 3 (March 1903): 323 (317–24). In 1899, Osgood chaired a committee charged with ridding Boston Common and Public Garden of the bird.

49. Barrows, *English Sparrow,* 29.

50. Henry Van Dyke, *Fisherman's Luck and Some Other Uncertain Things* (London: Sampson, Low, Marston, 1899), 57, 97. Between 1883 and 1900, Van Dyke was minister of New York City's Brick Presbyterian Church, where his sermons won him a national reputation. He was also a major figure in the U.S. literary establishment, appointed to a chair in English literature at Princeton in 1900.

51. Claude T. Barnes, quoted in Arthur Cleveland Bent, *Life Histories of North American Blackbirds, Orioles, Tanagers, and Allies* (Washington, D.C.: Smithsonian Institution, 1958), 7.

52. Coues, "The English Sparrow," *Chicago Field* 7, 23 (July 21, 1877): 373.

53. Gentry, *House Sparrow,* 107, 64–65.

54. Olive Thorne Miller, "A Ruffian in Feathers," *Atlantic Monthly* 55, 330 (April 1885): 490, 492, 493 (490–95). Olive Thorne Miller was the pen name of Harriet Mann Miller, a well-known author of children's books. She submitted testimony (dated 1884) about the sparrow's tendency to "mob" native birds to Barrows's report (page 273).

55. "The English Sparrow," *Birds* 2, 6 (December 1897), at www.birdnature.com/dec1897/sparrow.html, accessed April 16, 2006.

56. Osgood, "English Sparrow in New England," 317–20; S. S. Rathvon, "The

English Sparrow—Passer Domesticus," *Gardener's Monthly* 29 (May 1887): 157.

57. In Australia and New Zealand, incidentally, the bird was simply called the sparrow, though this also reflected ornithological reality: there were no native birds called sparrows from which it was necessary to distinguish the newcomers.

58. Asa Gray, *Letters of Asa Gray*, vol. 2, ed. Jane Gray (London: Macmillan, 1893), 476, 490, 496, 536.

59. David Dimbleby and David Reynolds, *An Ocean Apart: The Relationship between Britain and America in the Twentieth Century* (London: Hodder and Stoughton, 1988), 27.

60. "The Sparrows' Quarters," *Washington Post*, August 7, 1893.

61. John Watson, "The English Sparrow: 1. A Sketch," in Watson et al., "The English Sparrow," *Littel's Living Age* 77, 2481 (January 16, 1892): 158.

62. John Higham, *Strangers in the Land: Patterns of American Nativism, 1860–1925* (New Brunswick, N.J.: Rutgers University Press, 1963), 25; John Reiger, *American Sportsmen and the Origins of Conservation* (Corvallis: Oregon State University Press, 2001 [1975]), 36–37, 46, 48, 110, 50.

63. Letter dated July 9, in "Further Evidence on the Sparrow Question," *Forest and Stream* 8, 25 (July 26, 1877): 420.

64. "N. D.," letter to the editor, *New York Times*, September 8, 1878.

65. Robson comments here and below drawn from the speech reprinted in *Prairie Farmer*, September 13, 1884, n.p., Scrapbook 59, Riley Papers.

66. The Know-Nothing Party, founded in 1849, effectively expired in 1856.

67. Coues, "Ineligibility," 503; "The Sparrow Nuisance," *New York Times,* July 18, 1883; "English Sparrow," *Chicago Field,* 373. "White weed" probably referred to white clover.

68. W. F. Segrave to the Marquis of Salisbury, August 23, 1889, Reports, Consuls General at New York, Baltimore, Boston, Charleston, Diplomatic, Consular, Commercial and Treaty, 1889, FO 5/2060, National Archives, London, U.K.

69. As reported in "The Sparrow in the United States," (London) *Times,* October 29, 1889.

70. "From the Editor's Scrap-Book," *Fishing Gazette,* January 4, 1913, 7–8.

71. "Argyll," "First Impressions of the New World," *Fraser's Magazine* 21 (January 1881): 48, 56.

72. Ernest Thompson Seton, *Lives of the Hunted* (London: Hodder and Stoughton, 1914 [1901]), 113, 109, 124–25.

73. Neltje Blanchan, *How to Attract the Birds; and Other Talks about Bird Neighbors* (New York: Doubleday, Page, 1902), 208–9. The exclusion act of 1882 was renewed for ten years in 1892 and more or less indefinitely in 1902; it was repealed in 1943.

74. Theodore S. Palmer, "The Danger of Introducing Noxious Animals and Birds," *Yearbook of Agriculture, 1898* (Washington, D.C.; Government Printing Office, 1899), 110, 107–8.

75. W. L. McAtee, "Economic Ornithology," in American Ornithologists' Union, ed., *Fifty Years' Progress of American Ornithology, 1883–1933* (Lancaster, Penn.: American Ornithologists' Union, 1933), 114–15, 117–18.

76. "The American Ornithologists' Union," *Science* 4, 89 (October 17, 1884): 375.

77. Quoted in Barrows, *English Sparrow*, 265, 39, 260.

78. Webster, letter to the editor (January 26, 1885), *Prairie Farmer*, otherwise unidentified clipping, Scrapbook 68, Riley Papers.

79. Barrows, *English Sparrow*, 79. The following individuals who feature in this chapter contributed evidence to the Barrows report: William T. Hornaday, L. O. Howard, Olive Thorne Miller, (Col.) William Rhodes, and (Prof.) John W. Robson.

80. A procession of European visitors echoed Buffon's belief that American birds could not sing; see Antonello Gerbi, *The Dispute of the New World: The History of a Polemic, 1750–1900* (Pittsburgh, Pa.: University of Pittsburgh Press, 1973 [1955]), 62, 161, 163, 276, 331, 344, 376, 494, 502, 594.

81. Alexander Wilson, *Wilson's American Ornithology*, ed. T. M. Brewer (Boston: Otis, Broaders, 1840 [1808–14]), 39.

82. Benjamin T. Spencer, *The Quest for Nationality: An American Literary Campaign* (Syracuse, N.Y.: Syracuse University Press, 1957), 86.

83. Spencer, *Quest for Nationality*, 51, 86.

84. Susan Fenimore Cooper, *Rural Hours* (New York: G. P. Putnam, 1850), 219; Cooper, "Later Hours" (1868) in Johnson and Patterson, *Essays on Nature and Landscape*, 53.

85. John Burroughs, "With the Birds," *Atlantic Monthly* 15, 91 (May 1865): 516 (513–28); Blanchan, *Bird Neighbors*, 159.

86. Osgood, "English Sparrow in New England," 323.

87. Thomas G. Gentry, "English Sparrows," *Natural History* 8 (November 1874): 669.

88. William T. Hornaday, *Our Vanishing Wild Life: Its Extermination and Preservation* (New York: New York Zoological Society, 1913), 334.

89. Miller, "Ruffian in Feathers," 494.

90. Gentry, *House Sparrow*, 86; "More about the Sparrows," *Lancaster Farmer*, July 1883, otherwise unidentified clipping, Scrapbook 56, Riley Papers.

91. "Tanager," "Further Evidence on the Sparrow Question," *Forest and Stream* 8 (July 26, 1877): 420.

92. Elliott Coues and D. W. Prentiss, "Remarks on the Birds of the District of Columbia," *Field and Forest 11* (May 1877): 192–93; Gentry, *House Sparrow*, 39–40, 47.

93. Osgood, "English Sparrow in New England," 317, 321.

94. Brewster, *Birds of the Cambridge Region of Massachusetts*, 66.

95. Thomas F. Gossett, *Race: The History of an Idea in America* (Dallas, Tex: Southern Methodist University Press, 1963), 306; Higham, *Strangers in the Land*, 152.

96. Prescott Hall, "Immigration Restriction and World Eugenics," *Journal of Heredity* 10, 3 (March 1919): 125–26.

97. Hiram Evans, "The Klan's Fight for Americanism," *North American Review* 223 (1926): 39 (33–63).

98. Evans, "Klan's Fight for Americanism," 41, 34, 61; see also Madison Grant, *The Passing of the Great Race: or, The Racial Basis of European History* (New York: Scribner's, 1916), 223–34, 268–80.

99. Frank Julian Warne, *The Immigrant Invasion* (New York: Dodd, Mead, 1913), 24, 4, 6–7, 9, 10–11.

100. Coues and Prentiss, "Remarks on the Birds of the District of Columbia," 192–93.

101. "X," "The English Sparrow and Our Native Birds," *Science* 20, 500 (September 2, 1892): 134.

102. Bolles, "Bird Traits," 96.

103. Grant, *Passing of the Great Race*, 91–92, 209. This book went through four editions in eight years.

104. *New York Herald Tribune*, June 2, 1937.

105. Gossett, *Race*, 353–64; Higham, *Strangers in the Land*, 265, 271–72, 274.

106. Francis Walker, "Restriction of Immigration," *Atlantic Monthly* 77, 464 (June 1896): 823 (822–29).

107. Robert De C. Ward, "Fallacies of the Melting-Pot Idea and America's Traditional Immigration Policy," in *The Alien in Our Midst*, ed. Madison Grant and Charles Stewart Davison (New York: Galton, 1930), 233.

108. Osborn, Preface, in Grant, *Passing of the Great Race;* Osborn, Introduction, in Grant, *The Conquest of a Continent; Or the Expansion of Races in America* (New York: Scribner's, 1933), ix.

109. Hall, "Immigration Restriction and World Eugenics," 125–26.

110. Susan R. Schrepfer, *The Fight to Save the Redwoods: A History of Environmental Reform, 1917–1978* (Madison: University of Wisconsin Press, 1983), 43–44.

111. C. M. Goethe, "Immigration from Mexico," in Grant and Davison, *Alien in Our Midst*, 128. Goethe refused to sell land to Mexicans or Asians; see Tony Platt, "Racist Money-Bags behind Sacramento State University," *History News Network*, March 1, 2004, at http://hnn.us/articles/3770.html, accessed April 16, 2006.

112. Osgood, "English Sparrow in New England," 321.

113. *New York Times*, January 27, 1886; "Birds or Bread?" *Rural New Yorker* 44 (July 25, 1885): 502.

114. Hornaday, *Our Vanishing Wild Life*, vii.

115. R. W. Shufeldt, "Observations on the Habits of the American Chameleon (Anolis Principalis)," *American Naturalist* 17, 9 (September 1883): 925.

116. R. W. Shufeldt, *America's Greatest Problem: The Negro* (Philadelphia: F. A. Davis, 1915), 264, 282, 2.

117. Charles Askins, "The South's Problem in Game Protection," *Recreation Magazine* (May 1909), quoted in Hornaday, *Our Vanishing Wild Life*, 110.

118. Hornaday, *Our Vanishing Wild Life*, 213, 109–10, 106, 216.

119. This is a prime example of the hydraulic metaphors historian Roger Daniels implicates in the formation of negative attitudes to immigrants; see Daniels, "Two Cheers for Immigration," in Roger Daniels and Otis L. Graham, *Debating American Immigration, 1882–Present* (Lanham, Md.: Rowman & Littlefield, 2001), 7.

120. Hornaday, *Our Vanishing Wild Life*, 94–95, 98, 96, 101; Hubert D. Astley, "A Roccolo in Italy," *Avicultural Magazine* 3, 3 (January 1912): 81, 83 (81–85).

121. Hornaday, *Our Vanishing Wild Life*, 95–98, 100, 105, 101, 102.

122. Hornaday, *Our Vanishing Wild Life*, 101, 103. See Louis S. Warren, *The Hunter's Game: Poachers and Conservationists in Twentieth-Century America* (New Haven,

Conn.: Yale University Press, 1997), 21–26. Pennsylvania's Non-Resident Licence Law (1903), which required non-residents to purchase a $10 hunting licence, defined nonnaturalized immigrants as non-residents. The state's Alien Gun Law (1909) outlawed hunting and gun possession by nonnaturalized immigrants.

123. Hornaday, *Our Vanishing Wildlife,* 101.

124. Howard, "Spread of Land Species," 398. Some western ranchers hoped the mongoose would curb the pocket gophers whose burrowing endangered their cattle.

125. H. D. Craig (secretary of the American Defense Society) to Hornaday, March 22, 1918, Box 65, Correspondence 1918, William T. Hornaday Papers, Manuscript Division, Library of Congress, Washington, D.C. (hereafter Hornaday Papers).

126. Nomer Gray (Secretary of the NECS) to Hornaday, May 3, 1917, Box 63, Correspondence 1917, Hornaday Papers.

127. William T. Hornaday, *The Lying Lure of Bolshevism* (New York: American Defense Society, June 1919), 43.

128. Sidney L. Gulick to Hornaday, October 11, 1918, Box 66, Correspondence 1918, Hornaday Papers.

129. "The Sparrow Must Go," *New England Farmer* 39 (October 11, 1884), n.p., Scrapbook 66, Riley Papers; R. W. Shufeldt, "The English Sparrow and Fruit Buds," *Pacific Rural Press* 31 (January 16, 1886): 50.

130. Gentry, *House Sparrow,* 48, 108.

131. *Indiana Farmer,* December 27, 1884, clipping, Scrapbook 58, Riley Papers.

132. When the Barrows report appeared in 1889, only Massachusetts, Rhode Island, New Jersey, Pennsylvania, and Ohio specifically exempted the English sparrow from the protection many other small birds received.

133. Mabel Osgood Wright, *Birdcraft* (New York: Macmillan, 1895), 31.

134. "The Pestiferous Sparrow," *Forest and Stream* 34, 26 (July 17, 1890): 1; C. V. Riley, "How to Get Rid of English Sparrows," *Scientific American* 65 (October 3, 1891): 213.

135. A. H. Estabrook, "The Present Status of the English Sparrow Problem in America," *Auk* 24, 2 (April–June 1907): 131, 134 (129–34). Estabrook was reporting back on the roughly eighty responses he received to a circular of inquiry regarding the status of the sparrow problem, which he had published in the leading ornithological journals in April 1906. His view that the bird was unfit to be in the United States was congruent with his eugenicist beliefs. In 1910 he was appointed a researcher at the newly established Eugenics Record Office at Cold Spring Harbor. One of his initial assignments was to examine "degenerates" in remote upper Hudson valleys; see Edwin Black, *War against the Weak: Eugenics and America's Campaign to Create a Master Race* (New York: Four Walls Eight Windows, 2003), 53.

136. Thomas M. Brewer, "The European House Sparrow," *American Naturalist* 8 (September 1874): 556–57.

137. *Prairie Farmer,* September 13, 1884.

138. Quoted in Barrows, *English Sparrow,* 274.

139. J. C. Atkinson, "A Good Word for the Sparrow," *Littell's Living Age* (Boston) 78

(June 18, 1892): 759, reprinted from a British article. Franz Boas also stressed the inadequacy of stereotypes: "We are accustomed to speak of a Scandinavian as tall, blond and blue-eyed, of a South Italian as short, swarthy and dark-eyed. . . . We are apt to construct ideal local types . . . and we forget that there are numerous individuals for whom this description does not hold true;" see "Race and Progress," *Science* 74 (1931), as reproduced in Boas, *Race, Language and Culture* (New York: Free Press, 1966 [1940]), 4.

140. Atkinson, "Good Word for the Sparrow," 757.

141. George Horton, "To an English Sparrow," *Century: A Popular Quarterly* 42 (August 1891): 640.

142. Henry Ward Beecher, "Star Paper," *Christian Union* 16 (August 8, 1877): 103.

143. The newly established Eugenics Record Office (est. 1910) showed enormous interest in this clan of pauper families, already the subject of a famous 1888 study—"The Tribe of Ishmael: A Study in Social Degradation"—which portrayed its heavily interbred members as archetypes of genetically inherited criminality and likened them to one of the most notorious of parasites, *Sacculina carcini*. Oscar C. McCulloch, "The Tribe of Ishmael: A Study in Social Degradation," *Proceedings of the National Conference of Charities and Correction,* Indianapolis, 1888, 154–59. On the group's involvement in prostitution, vagrancy, thievery, and murder—and a tracing of its origins back to a community of poor whites, escaped slaves, and American Indians in Kentucky—see Irving Fisher, *National Vitality: Its Wastes and Conservation* (Washington, D.C.: Government Printing Office, 1910), 675. Sacculina is literally a body snatcher. A barnacle that converts into a sluglike creature once it latches onto a crab's underside, it eventually covers the crab's entire body with fleshy, root-like tendrils. It is capable of castrating a male crab and forcing it to care for its own eggs.

144. Harvey Whipple, "The English Sparrow—an Ishmael," *Country Life in America* 30 (May 1916). 122.

145. Quoted in Neltje Blanchan, "Prussianizing the Campaign against Sparrows," *New Country Life* 32 (September 1917): 82.

146. Blanchan, "Prussianizing the Campaign against Sparrows."

147. Wright and Coues, *Citizen Bird*, 182, 203–4.

148. Hornaday, *Our Vanishing Wild Life*, 101–2.

149. "Plan to Wipe out English Sparrow," *New York Times*, September 15, 1916. The New Jersey Audubon Society doubted that many young boys could distinguish between an English sparrow and innocent native songsters; see "War on English Sparrows," *New York Times*, December 13, 1916.

150. Blanchan, "Prussianizing the Campaign," 82.

151. Eugene Strong Rolfe, "The Passing of the Birds," *New England Magazine* 22 (June 1900): 416, 419 (413–19).

152. W. H. Hudson, *Birds in London* (London: Longmans, Green, 1898), 7, 106, 15.

153. Elliott Coues, "On the Present Status of *Passer Domesticus* in America, with Special Reference to the Western States and Territories," *Bulletin, U.S. Geological and Geographical Survey of the Territories,* vol. 5, article 11 (Washington, D.C.: Government Printing Office, 1879), 175–93.

154. For Coues's report and Miller's article, see Gurney, *House Sparrow*, 175–193, 50–62.

155. Tegetmeier and Ormerod, *House Sparrow (The Avian Rat)*, preface, 48, 3–5, 40, iv, 90, 46, 43, 21, 9.

156. W. Warde Fowler, *A Year with the Birds* (London: Macmillan, 1891), 63–64.

157. Charlotte M. Yonge, *An Old Woman's Outlook in a Hampshire Village* (London, 1892), 16; Rev. C. A. Johns, *British Birds in Their Haunts* (London: Society for Promoting Christian Knowledge, 1899), 204; see also John F. M. Clark, "The Irishmen of Birds," *History Today* 50, 10 (October 2000): 16–18. British references had their American counterparts in the common names for the Arkansas kingbird (wild Irishman in North Dakota) and the great crested flycatcher (wild Irishman of the flycatchers); see W. L. McAtee, "Nationality Names for American Birds," *American Speech* 32, 3 (October 1957): 185.

158. Barrows's 1889 report included extracts from evidence presented to a select parliamentary committee on the protection of wild birds in 1873 (Barrows, *English Sparrow*, 98, 123–25, 330–40) and passages from Gurney's *The House Sparrow* (Barrows, *English Sparrow*, 341–47).

159. (London) *Times*, December 20, 1855; December 12 and 13, 1862; March 14, 1863; April 11, 1865.

160. *Proceedings, Boston Society of Natural History* 11 (1867): 157. On European antagonism to the house sparrow and control efforts predating the American sparrow "war," see Gentry, *House Sparrow*, 14–32, and Barrows, *English Sparrow*, 301–2.

161. Gentry, *House Sparrow*, 17–18.

162. Hinton Rowan Helper, *The Land of Gold: Reality versus Fiction* (Baltimore: H. Taylor, 1855), 87, 94.

163. *Prairie Farmer*, September 13, 1884.

164. "Dr Coues' Column," *Osprey* 1 (May 1897): 124; Osgood, "English Sparrow," 324.

165. "The English Sparrow," *New York Times*, December 26, 1892; Bent, *Life Histories*, 4–5; E. R. Kalmbach, *Economic Status of the English Sparrow in the United States* (Washington, D.C.: Government Printing Office, 1940), 4, 60–61.

166. Bent, *Life Histories*, 5; Edward Howe Forbush, *Birds of Massachusetts*, pt. 3 (Norwood: Massachusetts Department of Agriculture, 1929), 42–43.

167. Ira N. Gabrielson and Stanley G. Jewett, *Birds of Oregon* (Corvallis: Oregon State College, 1940), 518.

168. "Sparrows Are Friendless," *New York Times*, March 20, 1927.

169. Office of Information, U.S. Department of Agriculture, "American Sparrow Better Behaved than Its English Cousin," February 19, 1915; Press Service Release, Division of Publications, Biological Survey, USDA, "Most Birds Are Beneficial: Only a Few Are Injurious," October 6, 1921, both at www.fws.gov/news/archive.html, accessed April 16, 2005.

170. Kalmbach, *Economic Status of the English Sparrow in the United States*, 2, 1, 63–64.

171. *Forest and Stream* 9, 16 (November 22, 1877): 305.

172. William Walsh, "The Starlings in Central Park," *Forest and Stream* 8, 19 (June 14, 1877): 307.

173. Walsh, "Starlings in Central Park."

174. Edwin Way Teale, *Days without Time: Adventures of a Naturalist* (New York: Dodd, Mead, 1948), 17.

175. Playing on the bird's reputation for mimickry, *Henry IV* (Part One) includes the line "Nay, I'll have a starling shall be taught to speak nothing but 'Mortimer.'" Thus spoke an indignant Hotspur to his uncle, King Henry, who has instructed him never to mention his brother-in-law, Edmund Mortimer, an alleged traitor. The popular literature is riddled with unsubstantiated references to Schieffelin's impulse. Suffice to say that earlier attempted introductions had nothing to do with Shakespeare, and there would undoubtedly have been further efforts independent of Schieffelin's whims had his releases also failed.

176. John W. Miller, "Much Ado about Starlings," *Natural History* 84, 7 (August–September 1975), 38.

177. Page, "Pushy and Brassy," 79.

178. P. B. Cole, letter to the *New York Times,* May 14, 1914.

179. William T. Hornaday, *Thirty Years War for Wild Life: Gains and Losses in the Thank Less Task* (New York: Scribner's/Permanent Wild Life Protection Fund, 1931), 62–63; "European Starling Rapidly Spreading Westward—Has Beneficial Food Habits," Office of Information, U.S. Department of Agriculture, Press Release, January 5, 1929, at www.fws.gov/news/archive.html, accessed 16 April 2005.

180. Kalmbach, *Economic Status of the English Sparrow,* 62.

181. Frank M. Chapman, "The European Starling as an American Citizen," *Natural History* 25, 5 (September–October 1925): 482, 480 (480–85).

182. Chapman, "European Starling as an American Citizen," 484.

183. Chapman, "European Starling as an American Citizen," 484–85.

184. May Thacher Cooke, "The Spread of the European Starling in North America (to 1928)," Circular Number 40, U.S. Department of Agriculture (Washington, D.C.: Government Printing Office, 1928), 8, "European Starling Spreading Westward," press release, U.S. Department of Agriculture, March 13, 1925, at www.fws.gov/news/historic/1925/19250313b.pdf, accessed April 18, 2006. For the report itself, see May Thacher Cooke, "Spread of the European Starling in North America," Departmental Circular 336, U.S. Department of Agriculture, Washington, D.C., 1925.

185. Rachel L. Carson, "How about Citizenship Papers for the Starling?" *Nature Magazine* 32, 6 (June–July 1939): 317.

186. Darwin, *The Voyage of the Beagle* (New York: Doubleday, 1962 [1845]), 378–401.

187. Joseph Grinnell, "The English Sparrow Has Arrived in Death Valley: An Experiment in Nature," *American Naturalist* 53, 628 (September–October 1919): 468, 471 (468–72); Stephen J. Gould, "An Evolutionary Perspective on Strengths, Fallacies, and Confusions in the Concept of Native Plants," in *Nature and Ideology: Natural Garden Design in the Twentieth Century,* ed. Joachim Wolschke-Bulmahn (Washington, D.C.: Dumbarton Oaks/Harvard University Press, 1997), 15, 17. Grinnell was a member of the AOU's Committee on the Protection of North American Birds.

188. Joseph Grinnell, "Risks Incurred in the Introduction of Alien Game Birds," *Science* 61, 1590 (June 19, 1925): 622 (621–23).

189. H. G. Baker, "Characteristics and Modes of Origins of Weeds," in *The Genetics of Colonizing Species: Proceedings of the First International Union of Biological Sciences Symposia on General Biology,* ed. H. G. Baker and G. Ledyard Stebbins (New York: Academic Press, 1965), 141–72. This volume represents the published proceedings of the first international symposium (International Union of Biological Sciences, Asilomar, California) on the wider implications of species introductions; in this instance the focus was on the characteristics of colonizing species and colonized ecosystems.

190. Ernest Mayr, "Summary," in Baker and Stebbins, *Genetics of Colonizing Species,* 555; R. F. Johnston and R. K. Selander, "Evolution in the House Sparrow. II. Adaptive Differentiation in North American Populations," *Evolution* 25 (1971): 1–28.

191. Paul R. Ehrlich, "Which Animal Will Invade?" in *Ecology of Biological Invasions of North America and Hawaii,* ed. Harold A. Mooney and James A. Drake (New York: Springer Verlag, 1986), 79, 83.

192. Peter Vitousek, Lloyd Loope, and Carla D'Antonio, "Biological Invasion as a Global Change," 244, at www.agci.org/publications/eoc94/EOC3/EOC3-summary.html, accessed April 16, 2006. See, though, Robert I. Colautti et al., "Is Invasion Success Explained by the Enemy Release Hypothesis?" *Ecology Letters* 7, 8 (2004): 721–33.

193. James P. Porter, "A Preliminary Study of the Psychology of the English Sparrow," *American Journal of Psychology* 15 (1904): 317, 345–46 (313–46); "Further Study of the English Sparrow and Other Birds," *American Journal of Psychology* 17 (1906): 248–71.

194. Jared Diamond, "Overview of Recent Extinctions," in *Conservation for the Twenty-First Century,* ed. David Western and Mary C. Pearl (New York: Oxford University Press, 1989), 40.

195. For these terms, see OTA, *Harmful Non-Indigenous,* 1; Walter R. Courtenay and Vernon E. Ogilvie, "Species Pollution: Introduced Animals and the Balance of Nature," *Animal Kingdom* 74, 2 (April 1971): 22–28.

196. "X of Fort Edward" (author otherwise unidentified), "The English Sparrow and Our Native Birds," *Science* 20, 500 (September 2, 1892): 135; James Bryce, "The Migrations of the Races of Men Considered Historically," *Littel's Living Age* 194, 2513 (August 27, 1892): 526; William Winter, "The Broken Harp" *Harper's* 78, 468 (May 1889): 862.

197. L. O. Howard, "The Spread of Land Species by the Agency of Man; With Especial Reference to Insects," *Science* [new series] 6, 141 (September 10, 1897): 384, 398 (382–98).

198. Frank M. Chapman, *Bird-Life: A Guide to the Study of Our Common Birds* (New York: D. Appleton, 1898), 142; Wright and Coues, *Citizen Bird,* 182, 203–4.

199. James Ritchie, *The Influence of Man on Animal Life in Scotland: A Study in Faunal Evolution* (Cambridge: Cambridge University Press, 1920), 244–45.

200. "European Starling Spreading Westward," Office of the Secretary, Press Service, U.S. Department of Agriculture, March 13, 1925, at http://www.fws.gov/news/historic/1925/19250313b.pdf, accessed April 15, 2006; D. T.

Arcieri, "Undesirable Alien—The House Sparrow," *Conservationist* 46 (1992): 24–25.

201. Marc Miller and Gregory Aplet, "Biological Control: A Little Knowledge Is a Dangerous Thing," *Rutgers Law Review* 45 (1993): 297 (285–334).

202. C. V. Riley, "Insectivorous Habits of the English Sparrow" and "Our Shade Trees and Their Insect Defoliators," in Barrows, *English Sparrow*, 111–46, 324–25.

203. Barrows, *English Sparrow*, 22.

204. Jens Jensen, *Siftings* (Baltimore: Johns Hopkins University Press, 1990 [1939]), 40.

3. PLANTS, INSECTS, AND OTHER STRANGERS TO THE SOIL

The African baobab can live for thousands of years, assumes extraordinary shapes (hollow specimens have served as a prison and bus shelter), and is virtually indestructible.

1. Charles Darwin, *The Life and Letters of Charles Darwin*, vol. 2, ed. Francis Darwin (London: John Murray, 1888), 381–82, 386, 391; Asa Gray, *Letters of Asa Gray*, vol. 2, ed. Jane Gray (London: Macmillan, 1893), 472–77, 490, 496, 536.

2. Darwin, *Life and Letters*, vol. 2, 391.

3. Susan Fenimore Cooper, *Rural Hours* (New York: G. P. Putnam, 1850), 105–10. In the 1868 edition of *Rural Hours*, which included a supplement covering that year, her indignation was even more overt. In entries for May 19 and 25, she observed how "many strangers . . . steal gradually onward from the tilled fields and gardens, until at last they stand side by side upon the same bank [on the edge of woods], the European weed and the wild native flower." Moreover, displacement rather than coexistence was the usual outcome over the longer term, for "foreign intruders are a bold and hardy race, driving away the pretty natives" (just as the Indian presence had melted away); "Later Hours (1868)," in *Essays on Nature and Landscape*, ed. Rochelle Johnson and Daniel Patterson (Athens: University of Georgia Press, 2002), 81, 190.

4. Cooper, *Rural Hours,* 106; Gray, *Letters*, 492.

5. One of the first botanists to note this imbalance was Constantine Samuel Schmaltz Rafinesque in his systematic list (probably the first) of floral introductions to the United States, including weeds; "An Essay on the Exotic Plants, Mostly European, Which Have Been Naturalized, and Now Grow Spontaneously in the Middle States of North America," *Medical Repository* 2 (1811): 331.

6. Alfred W. Crosby, *Ecological Imperialism: The Biological Expansion of Europe, 900–1900* (New York: Cambridge University Press, 1986), 166.

7. William Marshall, "Excessive and Noxious Increase of Udora Canadensis (Anacharis Alsinastrum)" [letters 2 and 3 of 4], *Phytologist: A Popular Botanical Miscellany* 4 (1852): 710, 714.

8. Hewett Cottrell Watson, *Compendium of the Cybele Britannica; or, British Plants in Their Geographical Relations* (London: Longmans, Green, Reader and Dyer, 1870), 582.

9. Charles C. Babington, "On Anacharis Alsinastrum, a Supposed New British Plant," *Annals and Magazine of Natural History* Series 2, 2 (February 1848): 85.

10. Marshall, letter 1, 705–6; letter 3, 710, 708, 710; letter 4, 710–11.

11. Marshall, letter 4, 713. The plant arrived with timber imported for railroad ties; bits became attached to logs, and seeds lodged in their crannies as lumber was rafted downstream to mill sites; letter 4, 711.

12. William Marshall, "The American Water-weed: *Anacharis Alsinastrum,*" *Phytologist: A Botanical Journal* (New Series) 2 (1857): 194.

13. Marshall, letter 4, 714.

14. Kingsley, "Chalk-Stream Studies," in *Miscellanies,* vol. 1 (London: Parker and Son, 1859), 172, 176, 181–82, 210.

15. Quoted in A. O. Walker, "The Distribution of Elodea canadensis, Michaux, in the British Isles in 1909," *Proceedings of the Linnean Society of London* 124 (1912): 72.

16. The most abundant species, interestingly, was not Eurasian but from a white settler colony—New Zealand's "brass-buttons." Named for the yellow, chamomile-like flowers that have no petals, brass buttons *(Cotula squalida)* is a ground-hugging evergreen plant whose leaves resemble miniature ferns.

17. Alice Eastwood, "The Plant Inhabitants of Nob Hill," *Erythea: A Journal of Botany, West American and General* 6, 6 (June 27, 1898): 61–67.

18. Eastwood, "Plant Inhabitants of Nob Hill," 61–67.

19. Aldo Leopold, "Cheat Takes Over," in *A Sand County Almanac* (New York: Oxford University Press, 1949), 155–56.

20. Devil weed is one of the names for jimsonweed (a.k.a. Jamestown weed, which provides a heavy clue to the time and place of this poisonous plant's arrival). Wind witch is Russian thistle. Cheat grass (a.k.a. downy brome, *Bromus tectorum*) is one of the most common invasives on western rangelands. Unpalatable to livestock, this annual plant has already developed an extensive root system by the time native perennial grasses start to grow in the spring, thus appropriating most of the moisture from the topsoil before native seedlings have the opportunity to tap this supply.

21. Donald Culross Peattie, "Plant Hunters," *Yale Review* 34, 1 (September 1944): 63. In his book *Cargoes and Harvests* (1926), Peattie discussed the contributions of various introduced plants, among them quinine, rubber, breadfruit, poppy, tobacco, and cotton.

22. Claire Shaver Haughton, *Green Immigrants: The Plants That Transformed America* (New York: Harcourt, Brace Jovanovich, 1978).

23. Handlin, *Uprooted,* 3. It sometimes makes sense to address ornamentals in this chapter as well as crop plants because this fits more naturally with discussion of wider themes and specific individuals.

24. Peattie, "Plant Hunters," 59.

25. Beverly T. Galloway, "Protecting American Crop Plants against Alien Enemies," typescript, dated circa 1912, 3, 4, Box 1, Folder 16, Series III, Reports and Articles, 1897–1935, Beverly Thomas Galloway Papers, Special Collections, National Agricultural Library, United States Department of Agriculture, Beltsville Agricultural Research Center, Beltsville, Maryland (hereafter Galloway Papers).

26. Philip J. Pauly, "The Beauty and Menace of the Japanese Cherry Trees: Conflicting Visions of American Ecological Independence," *Isis* 87, 1 (March 1996): 53, 61, 68; *Biologists and the Promise of American Life: From Meriwether Lewis to Alfred Kinsey* (Princeton, N.J.: Princeton University Press, 2000), 71–92.

27. Henry N. Ridley, *The Dispersal of Plants throughout the World* (Ashford, Kent: L. Reeve, 1930), 628; Ronald Good, *The Geography of the Flowering Plants* (London: Longman, 1947), 218.

28. Robert Darnton, "A Euro State of Mind," *New York Review of Books* 49, 3 (February 28, 2002): 30.

29. Mayne Reid, *Plant Hunters, or, Adventures among the Himalaya Mountains* (London: J. & C. Brown, 1858), 1–2.

30. Reid, *Plant Hunters,* 4.

31. Frank Kingdon-Ward, *Plant Hunting in the Wilds* (London: Figurehead, 1931), 10; *Plant Hunting on the Edge of the World* (London: Victor Gollancz, 1930), 40, 38; *Plant Hunter's Paradise* (London: Jonathan Cape, 1937), 27.

32. Howard L. Hyland, "History of U.S. Plant Introduction," *Environmental Review* 4 (1977): 26 (26–33).

33. John Quincy Adams, "To a Portion of the Consuls of the United States," Circular, Treasury Department, October 4, 1827, in W. H. Hodge and C. O. Erlanson, "Federal Plant Introduction—A Review," *Economic Botany* 10, 4 (October–December 1956): Fig. 2, 303 (299–334).

34. "Note G: Thomas Jefferson's Summary of His Own Achievements," in *The Writings of Thomas Jefferson,* vol. 1 (Washington, D.C.: Thomas Jefferson Memorial Association, 1905), 258–59.

35. U.S. Civil Service Commission, "Searching the World for New Crops," typescript of radio broadcast, December 15, 1927, Historical File, 1903–39, Box 1, Bureau of Plant Industry Records, RG54, National Archives, College Park, Maryland (hereafter BPI Records).

36. Staff correspondence, "Immigrant Crops Recalled on Exploration's Centennial," June 26, 1939, Box 33, General Correspondence, 1900–40, BPI Records.

37. Victor R. Boswell, "Our Vegetable Travelers," *National Geographic Magazine* 96, 2 (August 1949): 218.

38. "25th Anniversary File" (Office of Foreign Plant Introduction), David Fairchild, Personal Correspondence, 1922, Box 38, BPI Records; Henry H. Donaldson, remarks at award ceremony, April 20, 1934, "Public Welfare Medal" file, Box 38, General Correspondence, BPI Records. Fairchild ordered more than a hundred flowering cherries from a nursery in Yokohama in 1906 to plant in the grounds of his new home at Chevy Chase, Maryland.

39. "Public Welfare Medal" file, General Correspondence, April 24, 1933, Box 38, BPI Records.

40. Fairchild, "Systematic Plant Introduction, Its Purposes and Methods," Bulletin 21, Division of Forestry, USDA (Washington, D.C., Government Printing Office, 1898), 7–8.

41. Frank N. Meyer, "China, a Fruitful Field for Plant Exploration," *Yearbook of Agriculture, 1915* (1916): 205; Fairchild, "Naturalized Plant Aliens Bringing

Wealth to U.S.," typescript, June 11, 1923, 1–5, Department of Agriculture, Office of Foreign Seed and Plant Introduction, Historical File, 1903–39, Box 1 of 1, Records of the Division of Plant Exploration and Introduction, Records of the Bureau of Plant Industry, Soils, and Agricultural Engineering, BPI Records.

42. It was renamed the Office of Seed and Plant Introduction in 1904. This, in turn, became the Office of Foreign Seed and Plant Introduction (1908–25).

43. Beverly Galloway, "The Value of the Work of the Bureau of Plant Industry to the Farmer," typescript, April 13, 1911, page 1, Box 1, Folder 14, Series III, Reports and Articles, 1897–1935, Galloway Papers.

44. Beverly Galloway, "Explorer for Alien Plants Runs Many Risks in Far Lands," *Yearbook of Agriculture, 1927* (1928): 293.

45. Meyer, "China a Fruitful Field," 205.

46. Fairchild to Meyer, Correspondence 1916–17, Box 12, File 16, Henry Meyer Records (1902–18), National Archives, College Park (hereafter Meyer Records). Meyer came to the United States in 1901 when in his mid-twenties. He was granted citizenship in 1908.

47. Fairchild, "Naturalized Plant Aliens Bringing Wealth to U.S."; "Our Plant Immigrants," *National Geographic Magazine* 17, 4 (April 1906): 182.

48. "Botany of desire" is from Michael Pollan, *The Botany of Desire: A Plant's-Eye View of the World* (New York: Random House, 2001).

49. W. J. Voss, "Millions Added to Nation's Wealth by Food Plants Sent by Agricultural Agents from World's Far Corners," *Washington Post*, August 20, 1922; George H. Dacy, "Hunters Search the World for New Crops and Fruits," *National Farm News*, March 19, 1927, in Bureau of Plant Industry, Department of Plant Exploration and Introduction, General Correspondence, 1900–40 (Fairchild, D.G.), Box 33, BPI Records.

50. J. F. Rock, *Plant Immigrants* 178 (February 1921): 1640, Bureau of Plant Industry, Division of Plant Exploration and Introduction, Bulletin of New Plant Immigrants, 1908–24, Box 1, BPI Records. The Bureau of Plant Industry's Office of Foreign Seed and Plant Exploration and Introduction published *Plant Immigrants* between 1908 and 1924.

51. A. J. Pieters, "The Business of Seed and Plant Introduction and Distribution," *Yearbook of Agriculture, 1905* (1906): 292, 297.

52. Horace Kallen, *Culture and Democracy in the United States: Studies in the Group Psychology of the American Peoples* (New York: Boni and Liveright, 1924), 11, 42–43.

53. Franz Boas, *The Mind of Primitive Man* (New York: Macmillan, rev. ed., 1938 [1913]), 20, 37, 75, 234–36.

54. Vernon L. Kellogg, *Military Selection and Race Deterioration: A Preliminary Report and Discussion* (Oxford: Clarendon Press, 1916), 168–69; *American Insects* (New York: Henry Holt, 1905), 406, 186, 181, 278, 323, 136–37, 395, 211, 404, 278.

55. Vernon L. Kellogg, "Can We Sort Them at the Gate?" *Nation's Business* 11, 6 (June 1923): 19–21; *Mind and Heredity* (Princeton, N.J.: Princeton University Press, 1923), 100. This is not to say that Boas eschewed analogies with nonhuman biota. He often drew parallels between people and domesticated animals, citing, for example, the similarity between the hair of the poodle and the

Negro. He also provided floral and faunal analogies for the absence of racial purity and the preponderance of intermixture; see Boas, *Race, Language and Culture* (New York: Macmillan, 1940), 7–8, 10 ("Race and Progress," 1931), 36–37 ("Report on an Anthropometric Investigation of the Population of the United States," 1922); 163 ("Review of Roland B. Dixon, The Racial History of Man," *Science* 57 [May, 18 1923]).

56. David G. Fairchild, "The Dramatic Careers of Two Plantsmen," *Journal of Heredity* 10, 6 (June 1919): 276 (276–80). Among his most notable introductions were the dry-land (Siberian) elm, Chinese pistachio, seedless persimmon, and a drought-resistant rootstock for apricots, plums, and peaches.

57. Meyer to Fairchild, June 5, 1917, Meyer Records, General Correspondence, Box 12, File 17, BPI Records.

58. Meyer to Fairchild, December 21, 1905, Records of Frank N. Meyer, Plant Explorer, 1902–18, Letters, Box 1, Division of Plant Exploration and Introduction, BPI Records.

59. *Plant Immigrants* 132 (April 1917): 1157. Meyer's reference to racial suicide was in the context of western European nations slaughtering each other on the battlefield, not racial intermixture and failure to reproduce. His estimate of the Chinese contribution to world population by century's end was fairly wide of the mark; in 2000, China housed a fifth of the global population. (But he did not evisage the stringent reproductive controls that have been installed.)

60. Meyer to Fairchild, September 8, 1917; Fairchild to Meyer, September 20, 1917; Meyer to R. A. Young (Botanical Assistant), September 27, 1917, Box 12, Folder 19; Meyer to Fairchild, August 1, 1917, Box 13, Folder 22, Records of Frank N. Meyer, Plant Explorer, 1902–18, Letters, BPI Records. Isabel Shipley Cunningham's biography, based largely on Meyer's correspondence, makes no reference to these views; *Frank N. Meyer: Plant Hunter in Asia* (Ames: Iowa State University Press, 1984).

61. *Plant Immigrants* 104 (December 1914): Plate 135.

62. W. E. Whitehouse, "Plant Introduction in the Last Quarter Century," *Florists Exchange*, June 15, 1935, clipping, Historical File, 1903–39, Box 1, BPI Records.

63. David G. Fairchild, *Exploring for Plants* (New York: Macmillan Company, 1930), 272.

64. S. R. Winters, "With Uncle Sam's Plant Hunters," *Popular Mechanics* 48 (February 1926): 259; Handlin, *Uprooted*, 5, 6.

65. Some immigrants inadvertently imported weeds. Russian Mennonites brought Russian thistle to South Dakota in the late 1870s in hand-threshed flax seed. By the mid-1890s, this rolling emblem of the American West had forced some homesteaders to abandon their lands, sparking resentment against the immigrant farmers with which it was associated. Mennonites were rumored to have brought the thistle as a deliberate act of revenge after a hostile reception from American farmers; see James A. Young, "The Public Response to the Catastrophic Spread of Russian Thistle (1880) and Halogeton (1945)," *Agricultural History* 62, 2 (1988): 124.

66. Prescott F. Hall, "Immigration Restriction and World Eugenics," *Journal of Heredity* 10, 3 (March 1919): 126.

67. Newton Fuessle, "Plagues That Imperil Our Trees and Plants," *Outlook* 134 (July 4, 1923): 329.

68. Cornelia James Cannon, "American Misgivings," *Atlantic Monthly* 129 (February 1922): 145–57; "Selecting Citizens," *North American Review* 218 (September 1923): 333 (325–33). Cannon and her husband (prominent experimental psychologist Walter Bradford Cannon) were keen mountaineers; an unclimbed peak whose 8,716-foot southwest summit they scaled on their honeymoon in Glacier National Park was named Mount Cannon.

69. Cornelia James Cannon, *Red Rust* (London: Hodder and Stoughton, 1928), 116, 266.

70. Isaac F. Marcosson, "Checking the Alien Tide," *Saturday Evening Post* 195, 45 (May 5, 1923): 163, 165, 160. The books referred to are *The Black Golconda: The Romance of Petroleum* (1924) and *Anaconda* (1957).

71. Voss, "Millions Added to Nation's Wealth." The number of immigrants of any given nationality was now restricted to 3 percent of the foreign-born of that nationality residing in the United States in 1910.

72. The renamed (in 1924) Office of Foreign Plant Introduction became part of the newly created Division of Plant Exploration and Introduction in 1934.

73. *Plant Immigrants* 211 (November 1923): Plate 344.

74. Theodore Roosevelt to William Williams, January 23, 1903, in *Letters of Theodore Roosevelt,* vol. 3, ed. Elting E. Morison (Cambridge, Mass.: Harvard University Press, 1951), 411. Williams was the Port of New York's immigration commissioner.

75. Henry James, *The American Scene* (London: Chapman and Hall, 1946 [1907]), 84.

76. Alfred C. Reed, "Immigration and Public Health," *Popular Science Monthly* 83 (October 1913): 329, 321 (313–38).

77. Alfred C. Reed, "Going through Ellis Island," *Popular Science Monthly* 82 (January 1913): 7, 9 (5–18).

78. "Some Present Aspects of Immigration: Report of the Committee on Immigration of the American Genetic Association," *Journal of Heredity* 10, 2 (February 1919): 68–70.

79. Anon., "Fighting the Plant Pirates," *Literary Digest* 77, 10 (June 16, 1923): 21.

80. John A. Thompson, "The Exaggeration of American Vulnerability: The Anatomy of a Tradition," *Diplomatic History* 16, 1 (Winter 1992): 25 (23–43).

81. J. G. Sanders, "Save Us from Invading Pests," *American Forestry* 23, 279 (March 1917): 148.

82. M. B. Waite et al., "Diseases and Pests of Fruits and Vegetables," *Yearbook of Agriculture, 1925* (1926): 492.

83. Nelson Klose, *America's Crop Heritage: The History of Foreign Plant Introduction by the Federal Government* (Ames: Iowa State College Press, 1950), 19; Philip J. Pauly, "Fighting the Hessian Fly: American and British Responses to Insect Invasion, 1776–1789," *Environmental History* 7, 3 (July 2002): 485, 490 (485–507).

84. Stephen A. Forbes, "Fifty Billion German Allies Already in the American

Field," *Chicago Herald,* June 3, 1917. Forbes published research in *American Naturalist* in 1881 that corroborated Riley's findings that English sparrows ate far more grain than insects; Walter B. Barrows, *The English Sparrow (Passer domesticus) in North America, Especially in Its Relations to Agriculture* (Washington, D.C.: Government Printing Office, 1889), 126.

85. Leland Ossian Howard, "The Spread of Land Species by the Agency of Man; With Especial Reference to Insects," *Science* 6, 141 (New Series) (September 10, 1897): 385.

86. Edward Howe Forbush, *Useful Birds and Their Protection* (Boston: Massachusetts State Board of Agriculture, 1905), 38–39.

87. Fletcher Osgood, "The Gypsy Moth in Massachusetts," *New England Magazine* 21, 6 (February 1900): 677.

88. Edward H. Forbush and Charles H. Fernald, *The Gypsy Moth* (Boston: Wright & Potter, 1896), 16, 14.

89. Donald Dale Jackson, "Gypsy Invaders Seize New Ground in Their War against Our Trees," *Smithsonian* 15, 2 (May 1984): 47. See also Robert J. Spear, *The Great Gypsy Moth War: The History of the First Campaign in Massachusetts to Eradicate the Gypsy Moth, 1890–1901* (Amherst: University of Massachusetts Press, 2005). This book appeared after I had completed my manuscript.

90. William Hornaday, *Our Vanishing Wild Life: Its Extermination and Preservation* (New York: New York Zoological Society, 1913), 330.

91. Galloway, "Protecting American Crop Plants," 3.

92. Charles Valentine Riley, *The Locust Plague in the United States; Being More Particularly a Treatise on the Rocky Mountain Locust or so-called Grasshopper, as It Occurs East of the Rocky Mountains, with Practical Recommendations for Its Destruction* (Chicago: Rand McNally, 1877), 28, 85, 73–74; "Insectivorous Habits of the English Sparrow," in Barrows, *English Sparrow,* 121.

93. J. M. Aldrich, "Western Spread of the Colorado Potato Beetle," *Journal of Economic Entomology* 2 (June 1909): 235.

94. "J. H. B" of Brooklyn, letter to the editor, *New York Times,* September 8, 1878.

95. "Directions for Arresting the Chinch-bug Invasion of Northern New York," New York State Museum of Natural History, Circular No. 1, October 1883, 12, Scrapbook 51, Charles Valentine Riley Papers, Record Unit 7076, Archives, Smithsonian Arts and Industry, Washington, D.C. (hereafter Riley Papers).

96. J. A. Lintner, "The Chinch-bug Must Go," *Argus* (Albany, NY), 69 (October 10, 1883), Scrapbook 51, Riley Papers.

97. Cannon, *Red Rust,* 320.

98. Kellogg, *American Insects,* 136–37; "New Habits of Old Acquaintances," *American Cultivator* 46 (September 20, 1884), n.p., Box 14, Scrapbook 59, Riley Papers.

99. Howard, "Spread of Land Species," 388, 392.

100. Kellogg, *American Insects,* 181; C. L. Marlatt, "The San Jose Scale: Its Native Home and Natural Enemy," *Yearbook of Agriculture, 1902* (1903): 169.

101. Stephen A. Forbes, *The Insect, the Farmer, the Teacher, the Citizen, and the State* (Urbana, Ill.: Illinois State Laboratory of Natural History, 1915), 12–13.

102. Oliver Peck Newman, "Foreign Plant Pests: A Narcissus Embargo Follows

Success with Our Quarantine Policy," *American Review of Reviews* 72 (October 1925): 413.

103. Fuessle, "Plagues That Imperil," 329. Meyer introduced blight-resistant specimens from China and Japan.

104. Howard, testimony, Hearings, Agricultural Appropriations Bill, 1920, 65th Congress, 3rd Session, January 8, 1919 (1919), 414, 416.

105. W. A. Orton and R. Kent Beattie, "The Biological Basis of Foreign Plant Quarantines," *Phytopathology* 13, 7 (July 1923): 305.

106. W. R. Walton, "Corn Borer Has Invaded Corn States," *Yearbook of Agriculture, 1926* (1927): 247.

107. Ralph B. Swain, "How Insects Gain Entry," *Yearbook of Agriculture, 1952* (1953): 353.

108. Will C. Barnes, "Bugs and Bureaucracy: I," *Outlook* 142 (3 February 1926): 170.

109. Howard, testimony, Hearings, Agricultural Appropriations Bill, 1920, 65th Congress, 3rd Session, January 8, 1919 (1919), 413.

110. Fuessle, "Plagues That Imperil," 332.

111. Loren B. Smith, "Asiatic Beetles of Three Kinds, Recent Invaders, Are Studied," *Yearbook of Agriculture, 1930* (1931): 120–24.

112. *Nursery stock* refers to trees, shrubs, flowers, vines, cuttings, grafts, buds, and seeds.

113. Laura D. Merrill, "Citrus Canker," in *Eradication of Exotic Pests: Analysis with Case Studies,* ed. Donald L. Dahlsten and Richard Garcia (New Haven: Yale University Press, 1989), 185.

114. F. M. Russell, "The War to Save Our Crops," *Nation's Business* 11 (May 1923): 51.

115. Howard, "Spread of Land Species," 387–88; Lyster H. Dewey, "Migration of Weeds," *Yearbook of Agriculture, 1896* (1897): 283–84.

116. F. E. Kempton and L. D. Hutton, "Barberry Eradication in Wheat Areas," *Yearbook of Agriculture, 1926* (1927): 158–62.

117. Leland Ossian Howard, *The Insect Menace* (New York: Century, 1931), ix–x, 153.

118. Anon., "Fighting the Plant Pirates," 21–22.

119. Quoted in Anon., "Fighting the Plant Pirates," 22. Dacy is best known for his research in the early 1920s on production of hemp fiber as an alternative source of pulp for paper manufacture.

120. Crosby, *Ecological Imperialism,* 165–66.

121. Kellogg, *American Insects,* 176–77.

122. This was the initial step toward a blanket ban on U.S. nursery stock eventually imposed by Austria-Hungary, Holland, Switzerland, and Turkey as well; see Gustavus Adolphus Weber, *The Plant Quarantine and Control Administration: Its History, Activities and Organization* (Washington, D.C.: Brookings Institution, 1930), 4–6.

123. Sarah Jansen, "An American Insect in Imperial Germany: Visibility and Control in Making the Phylloxera in Germany, 1870–1914," *Science in Context* 13, 1 (2000): 40 (31–70).

124. Charles Valentine Riley, "On the Cause of Deterioration in Some of Our

Native Grape-Vines, and One of the Probable Reasons Why European Vines Have So Generally Failed with Us, Part 2," *American Naturalist* 6, 10 (October 1872): 624, 630 (622–32).

125. Charles Valentine Riley, "On the Cause of Deterioration . . . , Part 1," *American Naturalist* 6, 9 (September 1872): 532–44.

126. George Ordish, *The Great Wine Blight* (London: J. M. Dent, 1972), 126–27.

127. Jansen, "American Insect," 37, 35, 34.

128. Meyer had direct experience of the rigors of the inspectorate in San Francisco; many varieties of his imported bamboo died following grueling fumigation in 1908; see Cunningham, *Frank N. Meyer,* 81.

129. C. W. Woodworth, "California Horticultural Quarantine," *Journal of Economic Entomology* 2 (October 1909): 359–60.

130. Forbes, *The Insect, the Farmer,* 12–13.

131. Pauly, "Beauty and Menace of the Japanese Cherry Trees," 51.

132. Flora W. Patterson to David Fairchild, January 19, 1910, Records, Bureau of Plant Industry, reproduced in Amy Y. Rossman, "Flora W. Patterson: The First Woman Mycologist at the USDA," April 2002, at www.apsnet.org/online/view.asp?ID = 154, accessed July 7, 2005.

133. Quoted in Jefferson and Fusonie, *The Japanese Flowering Cherry Trees of Washington, D.C.: A Living Symbol of Friendship* (Washington, D.C.: Agricultural Research Service, USDA, 1977), 15.

134. Charles L. Marlatt, "Need of National Control of Imported Nursery Stock," *Journal of Economic Entomology* 4, 1 (1911): 107–24.

135. Pauly infers that Marlatt's fears were deepened by his honeymoon travels in Japan and eastern China during 1901–2, when he witnessed the damage inflicted on Western interests during the Boxer Rebellion as well as his bride's gradual death from a disease contracted in Asia. He also notes that California's quarantine law of 1881 was imposed a year before the Chinese Exclusion Act; "Beauty and Menace of the Japanese Cherry Trees," 54, 66–67, 71, *Biologists and the Promise of American Life,* 90.

136. Marlatt to Wilson, January 19, 1910, in Jefferson and Fusonie, *Japanese Flowering Cherry Trees,* 53–54.

137. Among Simberloff's contributions are his introduction to a paperback reissue of Charles Elton's *Ecology of Invasions by Animals and Plants* (Chicago: University of Chicago Press, 2000 [1958]).

138. Letter to the editor, *Isis* 87, 4 (1996): 676–77.

139. Letter to the editor, *Isis* 87, 4 (1996): 677–78.

140. In *Biologists and the Promise of American Life,* Pauly is somewhat more circumspect than in his 1996 article on the cherry trees. "Commonplace symbolic connections between geographically identified organisms and humans were omnipresent and powerful," he observes, but he adds that "the density and pervasiveness of these thickets of meaning, however, make their overall import difficult to assess" (89). He concludes that federal scientists seeking to control floral and faunal immigration provided a "framework" and "some of the impetus" for human immigration policy (92).

141. Testimony of Marlatt, Hearings, Agricultural Appropriations Bill for 1925,

House Committee on Appropriations, Subcommittee on Agriculture, February 4, 1924, 68th Congress, 1st Session (1924), 789.

142. "'King of Scouts' Honored at Gravesite," *Kaweah Commonwealth*, August 27, 2004, at www.kaweahcommonwealth.com/8–27–04features, accessed July 6, 2005.

143. Frederick Russell Burnham, "The Howl for Cheap Mexican Labor," in *The Alien in Our Midst*, ed. Madison Grant and Charles Stewart Davison (New York: Galton Publishing, 1930), 45–46. Burnham recalled his multifarious activities in his memoirs, *Scouting on Two Continents* (Garden City, N.Y.: Doubleday, Page, 1926). For his conservationist activities, see Peter van Wyk, *Burnham: King of Scouts* (Victoria, B.C.: Trafford Publishing, 2003), 523–24, 545, and an e-mail to the author from Peter van Wyk (the pen name of Peter Craigmore), July 9, 2005. Van Wyk's study, which he refers to as a "biographical novel," lacks footnotes and references but is based on a recently opened cache of private correspondence at Yale University.

144. With Asian sources of "stoop" labor effectively prohibited, and European supplies emphatically curtailed during World War I, industrial employers and agribusiness in the Southwest relied heavily on Mexicans.

145. Between 1925 and 1932, the Imperial Valley Irrigation District paid out $33,000 in bounties on 139,000 muskrat tails; see Tracy I. Storer, "The Muskrat as Native and Alien," *Journal of Mammalogy* 18, 4 (1937): 455 (443–60).

146. Joseph Dixon, "Rodents and Reclamation in the Imperial Valley," *Journal of Mammalogy* 3, 3 (1922): 140 (136–46).

147. Dewey, "Migration of Weeds," 283.

148. Charles Lester Marlatt, "Protecting the United States from Plant Pests," *National Geographic Magazine* 40 (August 1921): 205 (205–18).

149. Marlatt, "Protecting the United States from Plant Pests," 218.

150. J. Horace McFarland, "Plant Quarantine: A Footnote to the Discussion," *Atlantic Monthly* 136, 2 (August 1925): 241 (241–45). The Plant Quarantine and Control Administration (also under Marlatt's chairmanship) assumed the Federal Horticultural Board's functions in 1928.

151. Anon., "Policing Ports against Foreign Plant Pests," *Illustrated World* 33, 3 (May 1920): 499. As a result, a shipment of Feicheng peach trees from Meyer were subject to debilitating fumigation by the Japanese authorities in April 1914; see Cunningham, *Frank N. Meyer*, 176.

152. Anon., "Policing Ports," 499.

153. U.S. Department of Agriculture, "Restricted Entry of Plants to Protect American Crops," *Journal of Heredity* 10, 2 (February 1919): 87.

154. Charles Lester Marlatt, "Plants and Plant Pests," *Atlantic Monthly* 135, 6 (June 1925): 785 (775–85); Galloway, "Plant Introduction Garden," 1–2.

155. Galloway, "Observations, Suggestions, and Recommendations Relative to Nursery Stock and Some Related Subjects. Notes. Based Mainly upon a Field Trip Made August 5 to 14, 1918," bound typescript, page 100, Box 2, Folder 27, Series III, Galloway Papers. A balled plant has earth packed around its roots.

156. Cunningham, *Frank N. Meyer*, 65.

157. Meyer to P. H. Dorsett, July 6, 1917, Box 12, File 17, Correspondence 1916–17, Meyer Records.

158. Meyer to Galloway, July 23, 1917, Box 12, Folder 18, Correspondence 1916–17, Meyer Records.

159. Meyer to Fairchild, June 14, 1917, Box 12, Folder 18, Correspondence 1916–17, Meyer Records.

160. Roderick Nash, *The Nervous Generation: American Thought, 1917–30* (Chicago: Ivan Dee, 1990).

161. Marlatt, "Plants and Plant Pests," 775–85.

162. Marlatt, "Plants and Plant Pests," 781.

163. Newman, "Foreign Plant Pests," 411.

164. "Alien Narcissus Taboo," *Outlook* 142 (January 13, 1926): 44.

165. For objections from horticultural interests, see "Bureaucracy or Democracy," *American Florist* 65 (August 13, 1925): 20.

166. Hearings, House Committee on Agriculture, Committee on Expenditures in the Department of Agriculture, "On Miscellaneous Bills, Vol. 3—Inspection of Nursery Stock, HR 23252," 61st Congress, 2nd Session, April 27, 1910 (1910), 547; testimony of William Pitkin, in "The Present Status of Imported Nursery Stock," a report on the Federal Horticultural Board hearing, May 28, 1918, in Galloway, "Observations, Suggestions, and Recommendations."

167. J. Horace McFarland, quoted in The editors, "Bugs and Bureaucracy: II," *Outlook* 142 (February 3, 1926): 171; McFarland, "Plant Quarantine," 245; McFarland, quoted in Stephen F. Hamblin, "Plants and Policies," *Atlantic Monthly* 135, 3 (March 1925): 354 (353–62).

168. Hamblin, "Plants and Policies," 360, 355.

169. McFarland, "Plant Quarantine," 241. McFarland wrote in response to Marlatt, "Plants and Plant Pests."

170. Hamblin, "Plants and Policies," 362.

171. Galloway, "A Plant Introduction Garden. What It Is and What It Does," typescript, 1924, 4, Box 2, Folder 34, Series III, Galloway Papers.

172. Marlatt, "Protecting the United States from Plant Pests," 209, 208.

173. Galloway, "Florida. A Home for New Plant Immigrants," typescript, October 19, 1925, 4, Box 2, Folder 39, Series III, Galloway Papers. See also George H. Dacy, "Our Agricultural Ellis Island," *Scientific American* 83 (July 1927): 48–51. Stations were located in Florida (Miami, Coral Gables, Brooksville, and, finally, Coconut Grove), California (Chico, the destination for many of Meyer's plants), and Washington (Bellingham). The Yarrow station (Rockville, Maryland, 1910), which monitored plants certified disease-free but recommended for further observation, was superseded, with implementation of PQN37, by a plant detention station at nearby Glenn Dale.

174. P. H. Dorsett, "The Plant-Introduction Gardens of the Department of Agriculture," *Yearbook of Agriculture, 1916* (1917): 135–44.

175. Galloway, "Foreign Plant Introduction and Its Contribution to the Agriculture of the U.S.," 3, Box 6, Folder 187, Subseries X. 3.1, U.S. Department of Agriculture Papers (1914–1937), Special Collections, National Agricultural Library, U.S. Department of Agriculture, Beltsville Agricultural Research Center, Beltsville, Maryland (hereafter NAL). See also Fred Wilbur Powell, *The*

Bureau of Plant Industry: Its History, Activities, and Organization (Baltimore: Johns Hopkins University Press, 1927), 17, 38.

176. Russell, "War to Save Our Crops," 51.
177. Galloway, "Plant Introduction Garden."
178. Galloway, "Plant Introduction Garden."
179. Knowles A. Ryerson, "Plant Immigrants Pass Numerous Tests before Becoming Established," *Yearbook of Agriculture, 1928* (1929): 491.
180. Galloway to Fairchild, June 8, 1918, Box 4, Folder 15 (Correspondence, 1914–1926), Series IV, Correspondence, 1914–37, NAL.
181. Ryerson, "Plant Immigrants Pass Numerous Tests, 493; B. T. Galloway, "Immigrant Plants Hold Large Place among U.S. Crops," *Yearbook of Agriculture, 1928* (1929): 381, 379.
182. Galloway, "Plant Introduction Garden."
183. Galloway, "Foreign Plant Introduction and Its Contribution," 6. Galloway cited the yam, mango, papaya, and avocado as examples of plants whose full potential in the United States remained to be realized.
184. David G. Fairchild, *The World Grows around My Door: The Story of Kampong, a Home on the Edge of the Tropics* (New York: Scribner's, 1947), 425, 471.
185. Fairchild, *Exploring for Plants*, 52.
186. David G. Fairchild, "The Independence of American Nurseries," *American Forestry*, 23, 280 (April 1917): 216.
187. David G. Fairchild, *Garden Islands of the Great East* (New York: Scribner's, 1944), 27–28; *Exploring for Plants*, 307.
188. Fairchild, *World Grows around My Door*, 89–90.
189. David G. Fairchild, *The World Was My Garden: Travels of a Plant Explorer* (New York: Scribner's, 1938), 328.
190. Frederick Lewis Allen, *Only Yesterday: An Informal History of the 1920s* (New York: Harper, 1931), 225, 230.
191. The cabbage palmetto has a wider, bushier crown and a thicker trunk than the palmyra palm and is often squatter, but it can attain a comparable height.
192. Fairchild, "Notes on Seeds from Kandy, Ceylon," January 1926, file "Allison V. Armour Expedition, 1925–26," in General Correspondence 1900–40 (Fairchild), Box 37, BPI Records; *Exploring for Plants*, 296–300.
193. Quoted in William H. Bischoff, "Dr Fairchild Leaves Growing Monument," *Miami Daily News*, August 6, 1954.
194. *Plant Immigrants* 111, 2 (July–August 1915): Plate 161. The native range of Cuban pine (*Pinus caribaea*, a.k.a. pitch pine and yellow slash pine) stretches from the lowlands of the southeast United States to Central America.
195. Fairchild, "The Everglades National Park as an Introduction to the Tropics," February 23, 1930, Presidential Papers, Everglades National Park, 1926–1934, Richter Library, University of Miami, Coral Gables, Florida (Reclaiming the Everglades: South Florida's Natural History, 1884–1934, State University System of Florida, Textual Collections. See also, Tropic Everglades National Park Association, script, radio address on Everglades National Park, W.I.O.D., University of Miami, Coral Gables, April 13, 1931, 3–4 (4 pp.), Presidential Papers, Everglades National Park, 1926–1934.
196. David G. Fairchild, "Are the Everglades Worth Saving?" *National Parks Magazine*

80, 1 (January–March 1945): 3–8, 28–29; *The Proposed National Park in Southern Everglades of Florida* (Tallahassee: Florida Department of Agriculture, 1929), 7, 11, 20, 12. The American Forestry Association (est. 1875) subsequently shortened its name to American Forests.

197. David G. Fairchild, "My Favorite Tree," *American Forests* 52, 10 (October 1946): 451, 511.

198. For "Universal Australian," see Stephen Pyne, *Burning Bush: A Fire History of Australia* (New York: Holt, 1991), 15.

4. ARBOREAL IMMIGRANTS

1. At www.arborday.org/nationaltree/ntResults.cfm, accessed April 17, 2006. The oak, redwood, and palmetto received 101,146, 80,841, and 15,519 votes, respectively. The redwood category encompassed both members of the redwood family: the coastal redwood and the giant sequoia. The giant sequoia's champions wanted its individual identity acknowledged and urged a write-in vote. In November 2004, Congress officially designated the oak, symbol of American strength, the National Tree.

2. Thomas Pakenham, *Meetings with Remarkable Trees of the World* (London: Cassell, 2002), 7. The American Forestry Association (now known as American Forests) has maintained a National Register of Big Trees/Register of American Champion Trees since 1940.

3. Charles Eliot, "Anglomania in Park Making," *Garden and Forest* 1, 6 (April 4, 1888): 64.

4. To distinguish trees and shrubs in the garden from their woodland counterparts makes little sense, not least because Americans of this period usually treated flowers, fruits, trees, shrubs, gardens, and forests as aspects of a single subject; witness the name of the first American journal on these matters— *Garden and Forest: A Journal of Horticulture, Landscape Art, and Forestry.* The brief of this journal encompassed horticulture, botany, landscape design and preservation, national and urban park development, scientific forestry, and the conservation of forest resources.

5. Edgar Anderson, *Plants, Man and Life* (Berkeley: University of California Press, 1967), 9.

6. In his preface to the second edition of *Ecological Imperialism*, Crosby recognized that the eucalyptus constituted an exception to the basic thrust of his thesis; Alfred W. Crosby, *Ecological Imperialism: The Biological Expansion of Europe, 900–1900*, 2d ed. (New York: Cambridge University Press, 1993), xiv.

7. Abbot Kinney, *Eucalyptus* (Los Angeles: B. R. Baumgardt, 1895), 24.

8. J. C. Loudon, *Arboretum et Fruticetum Britannicum; or, The Trees and Shrubs of Britain, Native and Foreign, Hardy and Half-Hardy*, vol. 1 (London: Henry Bohn, 1854 [1838]), v, vi–vii, 201, 12.

9. From *Edinburgh Review* (January 1820), in *The Faber Book of America*, ed. Christopher Ricks and William L. Vance (London: Faber and Faber, 1992), 289.

10. The opposite phenomenon can often be seen in the grounds of the wealthy in

the United States. The Huntington estate in San Marino, California, is distinguished by exotic plantings.

11. Loudon, *Arboretum et Fruticetum Britannicum*, 191.

12. George Vasey, "Exotic Trees in Washington," *Field and Forest* 1, 3–4 (August–September 1875): 17. Vasey was editor of the botanical department of the journal *American Entomologist and Botanist*.

13. Alistair H. A. Scott and Harold R. Walt, "A Californian Abroad," *Fremontia* 16, 1 (April 1988): 22.

14. Katherine Parsons, letter to the editor, *Garden and Forest* 1, 10 (May 2, 1888): 18. Chief Sequoyah, for whom the tree was originally named, was the early nineteenth-century Cherokee tribal leader.

15. William Robinson, *The Wild Garden, or the Naturalization and Natural Grouping of Hardy Exotic Plants with a Chapter on the Garden of British Wild Flowers* (London: Scolar Press, 1977 [1870]), 40, 211–12.

16. Robinson, *Wild Garden*, 9, 113.

17. For a balanced view, see "Shall We Plant Native or Foreign Trees?" *Century* 34, 5 (September 1887): 792–94.

18. The Sterculiaceae family of tropical plants is large, including cacao and cola, and it is not clear which one is indicated. It might have been *Sterculia brevissima*, the smallest member of the family, which is distinguished by its star-shaped red fruit.

19. E. N. Plank, "Botanical Notes from Texas, XXIV," *Garden and Forest* 8, 365 (February 20, 1895): 72.

20. Mary Treat, "Wayside Plants in the Pines," *Garden and Forest* 7, 336 (August 1, 1894): 302.

21. T. H. Douglas, "Vaccinium ovatum as a Hedge-plant," letter to the editor, *Garden and Forest* 6, 263 (March 8, 1893): 116.

22. C. S. Sargent, "The Planting of Home Grounds," *Garden and Forest* 4, 177 (July 15, 1891): 325–26. Sargent was the founder and first director of Harvard University's Arnold Arboretum.

23. Sargent, "Correspondence: Foreign Plants and American Scenery," *Garden and Forest* 1, 35 (October 24, 1888): 419. Sargent's comments followed a letter from Frederick Law Olmsted (dated September 1888), published on pages 418–19 of the same issue.

24. C. S. Sargent, "Note," *Garden and Forest* 1, 23 (August 1, 1888): 266.

25. Olmsted, "Correspondence: Foreign Plants and American Scenery," 418.

26. Sargent editorial response to Olmsted, "Correspondence: Foreign Plants and American Scenery," 419.

27. Sargent, "Shrubs, Native and Foreign," *Garden and Forest* 9, 430 (May 20, 1896): 202.

28. Watrous, as quoted in Sargent, "Hardy Trees for a Trying Climate," *Garden and Forest* 1, 23 (August 1, 1888): 265–66. In fact, the Department of Agriculture had been importing varieties of crab apple from Russia, Germany, and Scandinavia for many years.

29. Quoted in Sargent, "Hardy Trees for a Trying Climate," 255–66.

30. Olmsted, "Correspondence: Foreign Plants and American Scenery," 419, 418.

31. Thomas M. Brewer, "The European House-Sparrow," *Atlantic Monthly* 21, 127 (May 1868): 586.

32. W. L. Jepson, "Alien Plants in California," *Erythea* 1 (1893): 141–42.

33. Sargent, "The Ailanthus," *Garden and Forest* 1, 1 (October 10, 1888): 385.

34. Walter T. Swingle, "The Early European History and the Botanical Name of the Tree of Heaven, *Ailanthus Altissima,*" *Journal of the Washington Academy of Sciences* 6 (August 19, 1916): 497–98.

35. On these grounds, official plantings were banned in Washington, D.C., in 1875; see Elbert L. Little, "Fifty Trees from Foreign Lands," *Yearbook of Agriculture, 1949* (1949): 826.

36. Andrew Jackson Downing, *Rural Essays,* ed. George William Curtis (New York: Leavitt & Allen, 1858), 311–13.

37. "The Awful Ailanthus," *New York Times,* July 4, 1859.

38. *New York Times,* July 25, 1855; July 7, 1859; July 18, 1855.

39. *New York Times,* August 12, 1925.

40. Letters to the editor, *New York Times,* July 26 and 30, 1934.

41. Letter to the editor, *New York Times,* October 28, 1944.

42. Betty Smith, *A Tree Grows in Brooklyn* (New York: Harper and Brothers, 1943), epithet.

43. H. W. Longfellow, "Evangeline, A Tale of Arcadie," *Poetical Works* (Oxford: Henry Frowde, 1893), 142.

44. Smith, *Tree Grows in Brooklyn,* 3–4. Unlike Nantucket's majestic but ineligible pagoda tree, the ailanthus qualifies for the Big Tree register.

45. Smith, *Tree Grows in Brooklyn,* 89, 442–43. The ailanthus even excels in competition with other exotics, whether from overseas (Norway maple and London plane) or other parts of the United States (black locust).

46. Jason Van Driesche and Roy Van Driesche, *Nature Out of Place: Biological Invasions in the Global Age* (Washington, D.C.: Island Press, 2000), 252.

47. Ted Williams, "America's Largest Weed," *Audubon* 104, 1 (January–February 2002): 26 (24–41).

48. Joseph Hooker, *The Botany of the Antarctic Voyage of H.M. Discovery Ships Erebus and Terror in the Years 1839–184, Part IV, Flora Tasmaniae* (London: Lovell Reeve, 1860), 253, cv.

49. Louis Margolis, *Yield from Eucalyptus Plantations in California* (Sacramento: W. W. Shannon/California State Board of Forestry, 1910), 6.

50. William Robinson, *The English Flower Garden and Home Grounds* (London: John Murray, 1921 [1883]), 467.

51. Before the advent of germ theory (ca. 1900), medical authorities and lay wisdom alike maintained that malaria (Italian for "bad air") resided in the miasmatic exhalations of decaying organic matter.

52. Jules Emile Planchon, *The Eucalyptus Globulus from a Botanic, Economic, and Medical Point of View, Embracing Its Introduction, Culture, and Uses* (Washington, D.C.: Government Printing Office, 1875), 15.

53. A few come from Papua New Guinea, Timor, and the southern Philippines.

54. Planchon, *Eucalyptus Globulus,* 13–14, 20.

55. Quoted in Alfred James McClatchie, *Eucalypts Cultivated in the United States,* Bureau of Forestry, Bulletin No. 35 (Washington, D.C.: USDA, 1902), 16.

56. Quoted in Stan Kelly, *Forty Australian Eucalypts in Colour* (Sydney: Dymocks, 1949), 3.

57. Review of Ian Tyrrell, *True Gardens of the Gods: California-Australian Environmental Reform, 1860–1930* (Berkeley: University of California Press, 1999), in *Western Historical Quarterly* 31, 1 (Spring 2000): 87.

58. Tim Bonyhady, *The Colonial Earth* (Melbourne: Melbourne University Press, 2000), 170–71.

59. Quoted in Gayle M. Groenendaal, "Eucalyptus Helped Solve a Timber Problem: 1853–1880," from "Part 1. History of Eucalypts in California," in *Proceedings of a Workshop on Eucalyptus in California,* ed. Richard B. Standiford and F. Thomas Ledig (Berkeley, Calif.: Pacific Southwest Forest and Range Experiment Station, 1983), 2–3 (1–8). In North America, "new countries" meant fresh territory.

60. Gifford Pinchot, "Letter of transmittal" to James Wilson, Secretary of Agriculture, at the front of McClatchie, *Eucalypts.*

61. U.S. Department of Agriculture, Introduction, Planchon, *Eucalyptus Globulus,* 1; Carl Purdy (of Ukiah), "The Redwood Forest," *Garden and Forest* 3, 116 (May 14, 1890): 235.

62. Asa Gray, "Address of Professor Asa Gray, Ex-President of the Association [On the Origin of the Flora of North America]," *Proceedings of the American Association for the Advancement of Science* 21 (1873): 3, in *Essays on North American Plant Geography,* ed. Ronald L. Stuckey (New York: Arno Press, 1978); Kinney, *Eucalyptus,* 12.

63. Kenneth Thompson, "The Australian Fever Tree in California: Eucalyptus and Malaria Prophylaxis," *Annals of the Association of American Geographers* 60 (June 1970): 230.

64. A. R. Heath, *The Eucalyptus Hardwood Trees of California* (Chicago: The Author, 1913), 8. For "apostle," see Kinney, *Eucalyptus,* 11.

65. F. D. Cornell, "Hickory's Younger Brother—The Eucalyptus," *Sunset: The Magazine of Western Living* 22, 3 (March 1909): 278; Russell Grimwade, *An Anthology of the Eucalypts* (Sydney: Angus and Robertson, 1920), 12.

66. Cornell, "Hickory's Younger Brother," 274.

67. Alfred James McClatchie, "The Eucalypts of the Southwest," *Out West* 31, 4 (November 1909): 858.

68. Cornell, "Hickory's Younger Brother," 282.

69. Charles Sargent, "Trees for Planting in America," *Garden and Forest* 1, 6 (April 4, 1888): 61.

70. "Tree Planting in California," *Garden and Forest* 1, 10 (April 11, 1888): 82–83.

71. Heinrich Mayr, "The General Condition of the North American Forests: I," *Garden and Forest* 3, 133 (September 10, 1890): 445–46.

72. Viola Lockhart Warren, "The Eucalyptus Crusade," *Historical Society of Southern California Quarterly* 44 (1962): 41 (31–42).

73. McClatchie, *Eucalypts,* 31.

74. Propagated from seed in California, the tree's customary diseases were left at home. So were the distinctive marsupials that browsed its leaves, bark, and seedlings. California's soils were also exceedingly fertile by Australian standards.

75. In addition, the switch to gas and electricity; the advent of reinforced concrete and steel beams and girders after 1914; and the replacement of wooden carriages and wagons by automobiles all served to lift the pressure on timber supplies.

76. This development gave the blue gum a limited new lease of life as a windbreak.

77. Tyrrell, *True Gardens of the Gods,* 57–58, 61, 65, 68.

78. Cornell, "Hickory's Younger Brother," 274.

79. McClatchie, "Eucalypts of the Southwest," 852, 858.

80. C. R. Orcutt, "The Blue Gum Tree," *Garden and Forest* 3, 123 (July 2, 1890): 319; George Nicholson, "Holiday Notes in Southern France and Northern Italy: XI," *Garden and Forest* 3, 105 (February 26, 1890): 99; William Garden Blaikie, "The French Riviera," *North American Review* 168, 509 (April 1899): 446.

81. Charles H. Shinn, "Notes from Santa Barbara (Correspondence to the Editor)," *Garden and Forest* 9, 434 (June 17, 1896): 248. Monterey cypress *(Cupressus macrocarpa)* is not to be confused with Monterey pine *(Pinus radiata).*

82. Warren, "Eucalyptus Crusade," 37.

83. Abbot Kinney, "Forestry in California, II," *Garden and Forest* 1, 32 (October 3, 1881): 380–81.

84. John H. Barber, "Notes from Santa Monica Forestry Station," *Garden and Forest* 10, 497 (September 1, 1897): 342.

85. Mary Cone, *Two Years in California* (Chicago: S. C. Griggs,1876), 82; Ludwig Salvator (Archduke of Austria), *Los Angeles in the Sunny Seventies: A Flower from the Golden Land,* trans. Marguerite Eyer Wilbur (Los Angeles: B. McCallister/Jake Zeitlin, 1929), 75; Charles Frederick Holder, *All about Pasadena and Its Vicinity* (Boston: Lee and Shepard, 1889), 103.

86. *Papers of Frederick Law Olmsted,* vol. 5: *The California Frontier, 1863–1865,* ed. Victoria Post Ranney (Baltimore: Johns Hopkins University Press, 1990), 480; Olmsted, "Correspondence: Foreign Plants and American Scenery," 419.

87. Lawrence Clark Powell, "Eucalyptus Trees & Lost Manuscripts," *California Librarian* 17 (January 1956): 32; Norman Douglas, *Old Calabria* (London: Secker and Warburg, 1956 [1915]), 99–100.

88. *Argonaut* 1 (April 22, 1877): 4.

89. Charles H. Shinn, "The California University Gardens," *Garden and Forest* 3, 107 (March 12, 1890): 122–23.

90. Merritt Berry Pratt, *Shade and Ornamental Trees of California* (Sacramento: California State Board of Forestry, 1922), 69–70.

91. Charles Sargent, "The Madronia," *Garden and Forest* 3, 139 (October 22, 1890): 510.

92. Robin W. Doughty, *The Eucalyptus: A Natural and Commercial History of the Gum Tree* (Baltimore: Johns Hopkins University Press, 2000), 102, 131, 109, 127.

93. Robert Fyfe Zacharin, *Emigrant Eucalypts: Gum Trees as Exotics* (Carlton, Victoria: Melbourne University Press, 1978), vii. Willis was a retired director of the National Herbarium at Melbourne's Royal Botanic Gardens.

94. Zacharin, *Emigrant Eucalypts,* xvii.

95. Stan Kelly (with G. M. Chippendale and R. D. Johnston, *Eucalypts* (Melbourne: Nelson, 1969), vii, 1. On the eucalypt's emergence as archsymbol of "Aus-

tralianness," see Ashley Hay, *Gum: The Story of Eucalypts and Their Champions* (Sydney: Duffy and Snellgrove, 2002), 3–4, 115–17.

96. Zacharin, *Emigrant Eucalypts*, 113, 32, 124.

97. So did deer; nor will birds eat the hard seeds; see Harriet Lamb and Steve Percy, "Indians Fight Eucalyptus Plantations on Commons," *New Scientist* 115, 1569 (July 16, 1987): 31; Vandana Shiva and J. Bandyopadhyay, "Eucalyptus—A Disastrous Tree for India," *Ecologist* 13 (1983): 184–87.

98. William D. Montalbano, "Environment: on Iberian Peninsula," *Los Angeles Times,* December 4, 1990; Lars Kordell et al., "Eucalyptus in Portugal," *Ambio: A Journal of the Human Environment, Research and Management* 15 (1986): 6–13.

99. Powell, "Eucalyptus Trees & Lost Manuscripts," 32.

100. J. Smeaton Chase, *California Coast Trails: A Horseback Adventure from Mexico to Oregon in 1911* (1913), at www.ventanawild.org/news/fall05/chase/chapter 2.html, accessed April 17, 2006.

101. Eric Walther, "A Key to the Species of Eucalyptus Grown in California," *Proceedings of the Californian Academy of Sciences,* 4th series, 27 (June 1928): 67.

102. Raymond F. Dasmann, *The Destruction of California* (New York: Macmillan, 1965), 79.

103. See Nancy Dustin Wall Moure, "Impressionism, Post-Impressionism, and the Eucalyptus School in Southern California," in *Plein Air Painters of California: The Southland* (1982), ed. Ruth Lilly Westphal, at www.tfaoi.com/aa/2aa/ 2aa638.htm, accessed April 17, 2006.

104. Planchon, *Eucalyptus Globulus,* 11.

105. Testimony, Senator Alan Cranston, Hearings, "Predisaster Assistance for Eucalyptus Trees in California (S241–33)," U.S. Congress, House of Repesentatives, Committee on Banking, Housing and Urban Affairs, Subcommittee on Small Business, 93rd Congress, 1st Session, May 9, 1973 (1973), 2.

106. Hearings, "Federal Predisaster Assistance for Eucalyptus Tree Fire Hazard," U.S. Congress, House of Representatives, Subcommittee on Forests, Committee on Agriculture, May 29, 1973, 54.

107. Testimony, Cranston, Hearings, "Predisaster Assistance for Eucalyptus Trees in California," May 9, 1973, 20.

108. Lance Williams, "Eucalyptus Trees Getting Blamed for East Bay Fire," *San Francisco Chronicle,* December 22, 1991.

109. Joseph Williamson, "Oakland Fire, One Year Later: 'Don't Blame the Eucalyptus,'" *California Eucalyptus Grower* 7 (October 1992): 1. Others agreed that it was easier to scapegoat the eucalyptus than face the blunt facts of wooden houses and poorly maintained yards.

110. Cecily Miller, as quoted in Harriet Chiang, "Hearing on Angel Island Trees," *San Francisco Chronicle,* July 13, 1988.

111. H. M. Lai, "Island of Immortals: Chinese Immigrants and the Angel Island Immigration Station," *California History* 57 (Spring 1978): 100 (88–103).

112. Him Mark Lai, Genny Lim, and Judy Yung, *Island: Poetry and History of Chinese Immigrants on Angel Island, 1910–1940* (Seattle: University of Washington Press, 1980), 23, 136, 56. Detainees copied some 130 poems in the early 1930s and eventually published them.

113. Lai, Lim, and Yung, *Island,* 38, 84, 102, 73, 141, 159, 94, 160–61.

114. Lai, Lim, and Yung, *Island,* 105.

115. *San Francisco Chronicle,* January 12, 1910, quoted in Elliot A. P. Evans and David W. Heron, "Isla de Los Angeles," *California History* 66, 1 (March 1987): 36 (24–39, 71–72).

116. *Chinese World* (March 16, 1910), as quoted in Lai, Lim, and Yung, *Island,* 140.

117. Mark Davison, *Cultural Landscape Report: Angel Island Immigration Station, Angel Island State Park, Tiburon, California,* vol. 2: *Existing Conditions, Analysis and Treatment* (75% draft, May 2002), 4.

118. Richard Henry Dana, *Two Years before the Mast* (New York: Viking Penguin, 1981 [1840]), 301.

119. David Boyd, "Eucalyptus," *Fremontia* 12, 4 (January 1985): 19–20.

120. Joe R. McBride, Neil Sugihara, and David Amme, "The History of Eucalyptus on Angel Island" (Berkeley, May 18, 1988), in California Department of Parks and Recreation (CDPR), "Focused Environmental Study: Restoration of Angel Island Natural Areas Affected by Eucalyptus" (July 1988), 23–24; David Boyd, "Eucalyptus Removal on Angel Island," *CalEPPC Symposium* 3 (1997): 73.

121. Jones and Stokes Associates, Inc., "Draft Environmental Impact Report, Restoration of Angel Island Natural Areas Affected by Eucalyptus" (May 1989), 1–4.

122. J. B. Kirkpatrick, "Eucalyptus Invasion in Southern California," *Australian Geography* 13 (1977): 387, 392, 391 (387–93).

123. David Boyd, "Eucalyptus Globulus," in *Invasive Plants of California's Wildlands,* ed. Carla C. Bossard et al. (Berkeley: University of California Press, 2000), 185–86.

124. CDPR, "Focused Environmental Study," 43; Jones and Stokes, "Draft Environmental Impact Report," S-1, S-2, 5–1.

125. Boyd, "Eucalyptus," *Fremontia,* 19–20.

126. Marla S. Hastings, "Resource Management Plan: Eucalyptus Removal, Angel Island State Park," CDPR, Northern Region, Santa Rosa, Fall 1988, 1, 7, 8, 10.

127. Brian O'Neill (General Superintendent, National Park Service, Golden Gate National Recreation Area) to Carl Chavez (Regional Director, CDPR), July 28, 1988, David Boyd, Office Files, Northern Region, CDPR, Novato, California (hereafter DBOF).

128. Williams, "America's Largest Weed," 26.

129. Anon., "The Trees That Captured California," *Sunset: The Magazine of Western Living* 117, 2 (August 1956): 48; Robert Sward, "The Tree That Destroyed California," at www.ventana.org/archive/poetry.htm, accessed April 17, 2006.

130. Nancy E. Lubamersky to CDPR, Northern Region (Santa Rosa), October 22, 1987, DBOF.

131. Margaret Azevedo to CDPR, Northern Region, July 13, 1988, DBOF.

132. Frank G. Goodall (San Rafael) to David K. Boyd, October 14, 1987, DBOF.

133. John G. Trezevant to David Boyd, October 9, 1987, DBOF.

134. Dale Champion, "Public Hearing on Eucalyptus Removal," *San Francisco Chronicle,* October 14, 1986.

135. Betty Dietz, "Group Plans to Stop Eucalyptus Clearcut," *Marin Independent Journal,* November 17, 1986; Jeanne Price, "A Group Unites in Support of Trees," *The Ark* (Tiburon), April 29, 1987. Estimates of POET's active membership

varied between twenty and seventy. On POET, see Judd A. Howell, "Citizen Mobilization in the Fight to Save the Golden Gate Eucalyptus," *George Wright Forum* 7, 1 (1990): 18–27.

136. I have taken this phrase from the heading to a letter to the editor from Jack Moreschi, objecting to Angel Island removal plans; *Pacific Sun* (Marin County), September 30, 1988.

137. David C. Haase to David Boyd, September 23, 1987, DBOF.

138. Flora Davis to James Doyle, June 16, 1989, in Jones and Stokes Associates, Inc., "Final Environmental Impact Report: Restoration of Angel Island Natural Areas Affected by Eucalyptus" (July 1989), III-37.

139. CDPR, "Focused Environmental Study: Restoration of Angel Island Natural Areas Affected by Eucalyptus" (July 1988).

140. CDPR, "Focused Environmental Study," 1.

141. R. Burton Litton, "F. Aesthetics of Eucalyptus on Angel Island: A Report for the California Department of Parks and Recreation Pursuant to Contract 84–04–295," May 24, 1988, in CDPR, "Focused Environmental Study," 202–3, 205–6.

142. Jean Severinghaus to Carl Chavez (Director, CDPR, Northern Region), July 20, 1988, DBOF.

143. David Haase and Flora Davis to David Boyd, April 6, 1989, DBOF.

144. Walter M. Scott (Mill Valley), Letter to the editor, *Marin Independent Journal,* October 1, 1987.

145. Silvia Lange to James Doyle, June 15, 1989, CDPR, Final Environmental Impact Report, III-62.

146. Thomas F. Jones, "Day of the Locust for Trees in the Parks," *San Francisco Chronicle,* July 6, 1996.

147. "POET (Preserve our Eucalyptus Trees) Chris Womack, David Haase, Flora Davis, Petitioners v. State of California Department of Parks and Recreation, Henry Agonia, Director, and Does 1–50, inclusive, Respondents, Petition for Writ of Mandate and Complaint for Injunctive and Declaratory Relief ("CCO 1085, Pub. Resources Code 21668.5"), Superior Court of the State of California in and for the County of Marin, October 6, 1988, copy, DBOF. The Resources Agency of California had granted CDPR an EIR exemption for its Angel Island plans in April 1984.

148. Jones and Stokes, "Draft Environmental Impact Report," S-3, 6–1, 6–5.

149. Jones and Stokes, "Final Environmental Impact Report," S-7. The final EIR took the form of an addendum to the draft report.

150. The majority of California's exotic flora—17.4 percent of the state's plant species—are European grasses.

151. Quoted in Jim Doyle, "Loggers Busy on Angel Island: Hikers Angered over Efforts to Get Rid of Nonnative Trees," *San Francisco Chronicle,* June 28, 1996. See also Walter E. Westman, "Managing for Biodiversity: Unresolved Science and Policy Questions," *BioScience* 40, 1 (January 1990): 29; "Park Management of Exotic Plant Species: Problems and Issues," *Conservation Biology* 4, 3 (September 1990): 254–56.

152. Walt Westman to James M. Doyle (Environmental Review Section, CDPR), June 4, 1989, in Jones and Stokes, "Final Environmental Impact Report," III-

9; Ray Siemers (Historian, City Hall, San Francisco) to James Doyle, June 21, 1989, in Jones and Stokes, "Final Environmental Impact Report," III-27.

153. For an account from a previously treeless region of California (Buena Park) that stresses the tree's value for native birds as food, shelter, and nesting site, see John McB. Robertson, "Birds and Eucalyptus Trees," *Condor* 33, 1 (July–August 1931): 137–39.

154. C. Nagano and J. Lane, *A Survey of the Location of Monarch Butterfly (Danaus plex-ippus L.) Overwintering Roosts in the State of California, U.S.A.: First Year, 1984/85* (Washington, D.C.: World Wildlife Fund, 1985).

155. Dan Dickmeyer, "Wildlands Restoration Team and Eucalyptus Trees," *Ventana*, November 1997, at www.ventana.org/archive/letters.htm, accessed April 17, 2006.

156. Quoted in Doyle, "Loggers Busy."

157. Walter Westman (for POET), "FACT SHEET: Eucalyptus Groves in the Golden Gate National Recreation Area (GGNRA)," December 17, 1986, 5 (5-page typescript), DBOF.

158. At www.arborday.org/nationaltree/ntResults.html, accessed April 17, 2006.

159. "Historical Trees May Be Spared," *San Francisco Chronicle*, May 23, 1969. The trees were dedicated in the early 1990s. Set in the sidewalk under the trees at the corner of Bush and Octavia streets is a marker placed by the San Francisco African American Historical and Cultural Society engraved with the words "Mary Ellen Pleasant Memorial Park"; see Mike Sullivan, *The Trees of San Francisco* (Petaluma, Calif.: Pomegranate Publications, 2004), 40.

160. Donald R. Hodel, *Exceptional Trees of Los Angeles* (Los Angeles: Los Angeles Arboretum Foundation, 1988), 30; "Exceptional Trees of Los Angeles: Ten Years After," *Arboretum News*, Fall/Winter 1997, page 2 of 3, at www.arboretum.org/arboretum/arti . . . /fallwinter1997, accessed April 16, 2005.

161. *San Francisco Chronicle*, July 6, 1996.

162. Memorandum, Frank Lortie (State Historian II, CDPR) to John W. Foster (Supervisor, Cultural Resource Management Unit), March 27, 1984, DBOF.

163. Anon., "The Trees That Captured California," 48.

164. Roberta Friedman, "Strangers in Our Midst," *Pacific Discovery* 41, 3 (Summer 1988), 27

165. Marshall Wilson, "Burlingame Seeks Strategy to Save El Camino Trees: Residents Pack Council Meeting to Share Ideas," *San Francisco Chronicle*, December 17, 1996.

166. Marshall Wilson, "A Tree Battle Grows in Burlingame: City Buzzing over Plan to Raze Landmark Eucalyptuses," *San Francisco Chronicle*, December 14, 1996.

167. Friedman, "Strangers in Our Midst," 27.

168. Marshall Wilson, "Battle over Burlingame Trees Rages On: Opposition Began in Early 1900s," *San Francisco Chronicle*, January 24, 1997.

169. Wilson, "Battle over Burlingame Trees Rages On."

170. Marshall Wilson, "Burlingame Trees Cut down for Tests: Rot Findings May Doom Over 100 Others," *San Francisco Chronicle*, August 22, 1997.

171. Dan Dickmeyer, "Eucalyptus Part of California History," *Ventana*, March/April 1998, at www.ventana.org/archive/letters.html, accessed April 16, 2005.

172. Achva Benzinberg Stein and Jacqueline Claire Moxley, "In Defense of the

Nonnative: The Case of the Eucalyptus," *Landscape Journal* 11, 1 (1992): 42, 45, 46 (35–50). Stein was a Los Angeles–based landscape architect specializing in urban public spaces and Moxley a Canada-based agrologist and plant physiologist who promoted sustainable agroforestry.

173. Edward L. Greene, "Native Shrubs of California: IV," *Garden and Forest* 3, 128 (August 6, 1890): 378.

174. Mary Curtius, "Au Naturel," *Los Angeles Times,* July 21, 1996.

175. See Kevin DeLuca, "In the Shadow of Whiteness: The Consequences of Constructions of Nature in Environmental Politics," in *Whiteness: The Communication of Social Identity,* ed. Thomas K. Nakayama and Judith N. Martin (London: Sage, 1998), 217–46.

176. Stein and Moxley, "In Defense of the Nonnative," 47.

177. Stein and Moxley, "In Defense of the Nonnative," 37, 38–39, 43.

178. Friedman, "Strangers in Our Midst," 25.

179. M. R. Jacobs, *Eucalypts for Planting* (Rome: Food and Agriculture Organization of the United Nations, 1979), 216.

180. Kinney, *Eucalyptus,* 37; Philip Taubman, "Editorial Observer: Days of Protest and Remembrance at Stanford," *New York Times,* May 12, 1999.

181. Stein and Moxley, "In Defense of the Nonnative," 43.

182. Taubman, "Editorial Observer."

183. Mills College, *Newsletter,* October 1996, 10–11; at www.mills.edu/PROV/CSCH/NEWS/oct96.news.p.10–11.html, accessed April 6, 2005. Another Australian pest, the red gum lerp psyllid, was detected in southern California in 1993. A third Australian insect, the eucalyptus tortoise beetle, a bark-dwelling insect the size of a ladybug, has defoliated trees in San Diego, Riverside, Orange, and Los Angeles counties since 1998.

184. Quoted in Dana Nichols, "Con-tree-versy: Eucalyptus Lovers Take on State over Cutting Plan," *Los Angeles Times,* October 31, 1987.

185. Quoted in *San Francisco Chronicle,* July 6, 1996.

186. Doyle, "Loggers Busy."

187. Quoted in Azevedo, "Of Eucalyptus and Ecology," 16–17.

188. Guy Wright, "State Hatchet Job: Angel Island's Eucalyptus Trees," *San Francisco Examiner,* September 9, 1988.

189. S. B. Parish, "The Immigrant Plants of Southern California," *Bulletin of the Southern California Academy of Sciences* 19, 4 (October 1920): 3 (3–30); Elizabeth McClintock, "The Displacement of Native Plants by Exotics," in *Conservation and Management of Rare and Endangered Plants: Proceedings of a California Conference on the Conservation and Management of Rare and Endangered Plants,* ed. Thomas S. Elias (Sacramento: California Native Plant Society, 1987), 185.

190. Boyd, quoted in Azevedo, "Of Eucalyptus and Ecology," 16–17, and Mitchel Benson, "State Parks Get Back to Nature," *San Jose Mercury News,* August 20, 1987.

191. David G. Fairchild, *Exploring for Plants* (New York: Macmillan, 1930), 134.

192. J. J. Burdon and G. A. Chilvers, "Preliminary Studies on a Native Australian Eucalypt Forest Invaded by Exotic Pines," *Oecologia* 31 (1977): 1–12.

193. Quoted in Doyle, "Loggers Busy."

194. Andrea Pickart and Julie Goodnight, "Aliens, Invaders and Exotics," *California Waterfront Age* 6, 1 (Winter/Spring 1990): 11 (11–14).

195. Guy Wright, "Spare Those Trees," *San Francisco Examiner*, July 28, 1987.

196. Curtius, "Au Naturel"; Jones, "Day of the Locust."

197. "Euk lovers" is a term that Dave Kavanaugh, director of research at the California Academy of Sciences, used in a memorandum to departmental heads in the academy's research division, August 13, 1987, DBOF.

198. James K. Sayre to James Doyle, May 12, 1989, in Jones and Stokes, "Final Environmental Impact Report," III-52–53. The Fourteenth Amendment guarantees citizenship to everyone born in the United States (so-called "birthright citizenship"—*jus soli*). In 1994, immigration restrictionists in California campaigned to narrow citizenship to exclude the American-born children of undocumented aliens.

199. Cited in Friedman, "Strangers," 25.

200. See David Boyd, "Synopsis of Speakers' Comments: Public Hearings on Removal of Eucalyptus at Angel Island, Tuesday, July 12, 1988," 2 (5 page typescript), DBOF.

201. Anne and John West to State Senator Milton Marks and Assemblyman William Filante, August 15, 1988, DBOF.

202. Severinghaus to Carl Chavez, July 20, 1988, DBOF. In the latest controversy over removal—focusing on San Francisco's Presidio National Park—eucalyptus supporters continue to label advocates of removal nativists: "plants and trees without the proper papers to show their pre-Mayflower lineage are called 'invasive exotics,'" insists city supervisor Leland Yee; see Patricia Leigh Brown, "Ancient Dunes vs. Exotic Trees," *New York Times*, March 6, 2003.

203. Sally Fairfax and Lynn Huntsinger, "An Essay from the Woods (and Rangelands)," in *The New Western History: The Territory Ahead*, ed. Forrest G. Robinson (Tucson: University of Arizona Press, 1998), 205.

204. Sharon Callahan, as quoted in James K. Sayre, "Blue Gum Trees Are Back," *San Francisco Chronicle*, May 10, 1996.

205. Stein and Moxley, "In Defense of the Nonnative," 36, 47.

206. Maura Thurman, "Angel Island Trees Spark New Dispute," *Marin Independent Journal*, July 8, 1988.

207. Williams, "America's Largest Weed," 31.

208. Michael G. Barbour, "California Landscapes before the Invaders," *Proceedings, California Exotic Pest Plant Council Symposium* 2 (1996): 5, 6–7.

209. For these terms, see, respectively, Mike Davis, *Ecology of Fear: Los Angeles and the Imagination of Disaster* (New York: Henry Holt, 1998), and Barry Glassner, *The Culture of Fear: Why Americans are Afraid of the Wrong Things* (New York: Basic, 1999).

5. THE NATURE OF ALIEN NATION

1. Michael Pollan, "Against Nativism," *New York Times*, May 15, 1994, 54–55.

2. Gary Koller, "Native Dictates," *Arnoldia* 52, 4 (1992): 23.

3. Pollan, "Against Nativism," 52, 54.

4. Ken Druse, *The Natural Habitat Garden* (New York: Clarkson Potter, 1994), acknowledgments, 6, 9, 82.

5. Pollan, "Against Nativism," 54–55. Talk of "crimes" against natives by troublesome exotics reminded a British journalist of allegations that non-whites/immigrants committed most of the nation's street crime; Paul Evans, "Invaders from the Lost World," *Guardian*, August 9, 1999.

6. Gert Gröning and Joachim Wolschke-Bulmahn, "Some Notes on the Mania for Native Plants in Germany," *Landscape Journal* 11 (1992): 117–18, 116, 124.

7. Joachim Wolschke-Bulmahn, "The Mania for Native Plants in Nazi Germany," in *Concrete Jungle*, ed. Dion, Mark and Alexis Rockman (New York: Juno Books, 1996), 65, 67; "The Ideology of the Nature Garden: Nationalistic Trends in Garden Design in Germany in the Early Twentieth Century," *Journal of Garden History* 12, 1 (1992): 79–80 (73–80). The bulk of the translated quotation from Borchardt appears in its original form in the postscript to Rudolf Borchardt, *Der leidenschaftliche Gärtner* [The Passionate Gardener] (Stuttgart, Germany: Ernest Klett, 1968 [1938]), 268–69. Borchardt's comments were in fact directed at the advocate of hardy plants ("this Eskimo of his only nominally temperate land" [author's translation]), whose ultimate test of eligibility was whether or not a species could survive a German winter without assistance.

8. T. Coraghessan Boyle, *Tortilla Curtain* (London: Penguin, 1995), 220, 242, 41, 11.

9. A nonfictional counterpart to *Tortilla Curtain* soon appeared. In *Ecology of Fear: Los Angeles and the Imagination of Disaster* (New York: Henry Holt, 1998), Mike Davis, an urban geographer, is equally intrigued by the humanization of natural threats and the naturalization of human threats. "Too often," he asserts, "wildness is equated with urban disorder, and wild animals end up as the symbolic equivalents of street criminals." Coyotes and cougars are "discursively assimilated to 'serial killers' or 'gangbangers,'" he explains, referring to the white suburbanite response to a rising number of unwelcome encounters with the animal denizens of Los Angeles's "wild edge." "Reciprocally," he continues, "the urban underclass is incessantly bestialized as 'predators,' 'wilding youth,' and 'wolf packs' in an urban 'wilderness'" (267, 207–8, 238).

10. On the connection between Shakespeare, starlings, and the Shakespeare "buff" (Eugene Schieffelin), see chapter 2, note 175. Boyle had previously published a short story (1981) about the introduction of the starling and its American exploits that emphasizes the bird's invincibility: "A Bird in the Hand," in *T. C. Boyle Stories* (New York: Viking, 1998), 602–11. The starling also serves Mike Davis as an example of the cosmopolitan creatures that often thrive in built-up environments. He also refers to that other highly adaptable bird that flourishes in human proximity—the house sparrow; *Ecology of Fear*, 206. Davis seems unaware, though, that starlings were originally imported from Britain, specifying the East Coast as their source. And he errs in attributing the sparrow's arrival to Spanish colonists.

11. Boyle, *Tortilla Curtain*, 220, 242, 41, 11, 242, 39, 215, 108–10, 318, 319, 332.

12. Wolschke-Bulmahn, "Mania for Native Plants," 69.

13. George Miller, *Landscaping with Native Plants of Texas and the Southwest* (Stillwater, Minn.: Voyageur Press, 1991), 11–12.

14. Miller, *Landscaping with Native Plants of Texas*, 11–12. Banu Subramaniam, "The Aliens Have Landed! Reflections on the Rhetoric of Biological Invasions," *Meridians: Feminism, Race, Transnationalism* 2, 1 (2001): 26–40, and Jonah H. Peretti, "Nativism and Nature: Rethinking Biological Invasion," *Environmental Values* 7 (1998): 183–92, also tend to use nationalism, native species advocacy, and nativism as synonyms.

15. David Lowenthal, "British National Identity and the English Landscape," *Rural History* 2, 2 (1991): 206.

16. "Heritage, not hate," a phrase popularized in the early 1990s, is a bumper sticker slogan popular among southern whites defending the display of the Confederate flag.

17. Sara Stein, *Noah's Garden: Restoring the Ecology of Our Own Back Yards* (Boston: Houghton Mifflin, 1993), 202–3.

18. For "eco-jingoism," see David Matless, *Landscape and Englishness* (London: Reaktion Books, 1998), 225.

19. Subramaniam, "Aliens Have Landed!" 36.

20. Ivy is invasive at home too—so are a clutch of notorious fellow natives: bracken, bramble, nettle, and gorse.

21. Similarly, in Britain, there is no correspondence between the main recent sources of human immigrants and those of the most problematic floral and faunal immigrants. According to Judy Ling Wong, director of the U.K.'s Black Environment Network, terms like "Rhodo-bashing" (a reference to efforts to eliminate rhododendron from woodlands) "resonate too closely to Paki-bashing"; "Cultural Aspects: The 'Native' and 'Alien' Issues in Relation to Ethnic Minorities," in Ian D. Rotherham, ed., *Loving the Aliens??!!? Ecology, History, Culture and the Management of Exotic Plants and Animals: Issues for Nature Conservation* (*Journal of Practical Ecology and Conservation Special Series*, No. 4; Sheffield, U.K.: Wildtrack Publishing, June 2005), 94. Yet the geese that dominate many British public parks are from Canada, not Nigeria. The flatworm, which gobbles up native earthworms, arrived in 1965 from New Zealand, not Jamaica. The 8-inch bullfrog (*Rana catesbeiana*), which can swallow native frogs whole, comes from eastern North America, not Pakistan (breeding populations were detected in 1999). Floating pennywort—first found in 1990, and forming such thick mats on rivers, ponds, and lakes that livestock mistake them for solid ground and drown—is also North American.

22. Edmund P. Russell III, "'Speaking of Annihilation': Mobilizing for War against Human and Insect Enemies, 1914–1945," *Journal of American History* 82, 4 (March 1996): 1506, 1508, 1522, 1524 (1505–29); *War and Nature: Fighting Humans and Insects with Chemicals from World War I to Silent Spring* (New York: Cambridge University Press, 2001), 132–33, 232.

23. William R. Jordan III, "The Nazi Connection," *Restoration & Management Notes* 12, 2 (Winter 1994): 113–14. See also Janet Marinelli, "The Nazi Connection, Continued," *Restoration & Management Notes* 13, 2 (Winter 1995): 180. Jordan founded this journal (now known as *Ecological Restoration*) in 1981.

24. Kim Sorvig, "Natives and Nazis: An Imaginary Conspiracy in Ecological Design: Commentary on G. Gröning and J. Wolschke-Bulmahn's 'Some Notes

on the Mania for Native Plants in Germany,'" *Landscape Journal* 13, 1 (Spring 1994): 61.

25. Stanley Temple, "The Nasty Necessity: Eradicating Exotics," *Conservation Biology* 4, 2 (June 1990): 113.

26. Ariel Lugo, letter to the editor, *Conservation Biology* 4, 4 (December 1990): 345.

27. Bruce Coblentz, "A Response to Temple and Lugo," *Conservation Biology* 5, 1 (March 1991): 6.

28. Lugo, "More on Exotic Species," *Conservation Biology* 6, 1 (March 1992): 6.

29. William Vogt, *Road to Survival* (London: Victor Gollancz, 1948), 228, 89.

30. Charles Elton, *The Ecology of Invasions by Animals and Plants* (London: Methuen, 1958), 144. The giant African land snail spread from East Africa around half the world between circa 1800 and 1940. It showed up in Hawaii in 1936 and in Guam and California during World War II.

31. Thomas Gossett, *Race* (Dallas, Tex.: Southern Methodist University Press, 1963), 409–30.

32. Marshall Hyatt, *Franz Boas, Social Activist: The Dynamics of Ethnicity* (New York: Greenwood Press, 1990), 113; Boas, *Mind of Primitive Man* (New York: Macmillan, rev. ed., 1938), 37, 237.

33. The Nazis responded by burning the German version of *The Mind of Primitive Man;* Melville J. Herskovits, *Franz Boas: The Science of Man in the Making* (New York: Scribner's, 1953), 4–5, 117–18.

34. Some credit Boas with a major role in shaping the thinking of the Supreme Court justices who struck down segregated schools in the *Brown v. Board of Education* ruling of 1954; Hyatt, *Franz Boas, Social Activist,* 99.

35. Edwin Black, *War against the Weak: Eugenics and America's Campaign to Create a Master Race* (New York: Four Walls Eight Windows, 2003), 277, 315, 343–44. On links between California conservationists (especially Goethe) and eugenicist beliefs, see also Alexandra Minna Stern, *Eugenic Nation: Faults and Frontiers of Better Breeding in Modern America* (Berkeley: University of California Press, 2005), 115–49. This book appeared after I had completed my manuscript. A quick reading, however, indicates that Stern does not cover attitudes to native and nonnative species of flora and fauna.

36. Charles Goethe, *Garden Philosopher* (Sacramento, 1955), 152. The Argentine ant's success in California can be partly attributed to the genetic similarity of its populations there, which results in far less aggression within the species (and formation of "supercolonies"). In Argentina, where the species displays far greater genetic diversity, different colonies constantly war against one another.

37. Goethe, *Garden Philosopher,* 241, 218, 190, 239, 187. Goethe's close links with California State University–Sacramento, one of the major beneficiaries of his wealth during the 1950s and recipient of the largest portion of his substantial estate when he died in 1966, have become increasingly controversial. The university's arboretum, established in 1959, was named for Goethe in 1961, and campaigners seek to remove the association from what is now a three-acre botanical garden. In 1965 student protest defeated a proposal to attach his

name to a new science building; see www.changethesign.org, accessed May 2005.

38. Goethe, *Garden Philosopher*, 131–32, 103, 238, 187, 267.

39. Paul R. Ehrlich, *The Population Bomb* (New York: Ballantine, 1968), 84–85.

40. Kurt Andersen, "The New Ellis Island," *Time,* June 13, 1983, 10–11.

41. Otis L. Graham, "Illegal Immigration," *Center Magazine* 10, 4 (July–August 1977): 56–57 (56–65); John D. Huss and Melanie Wirken, "Illegal Immigration: The Hidden Population Bomb," *Futurist* 2 (April 1977): 114–20.

42. Robert M. Hardaway, "Environmental Malthusianism: Integrating Population and Environmental Policy," *Environmental Law* 27, 4 (Winter 1997): 1239. On environmentalism and population, see Roy Beck and Leon Kolankiewicz, "The Environmental Movement's Retreat from Advocating U.S. Population Stabilization (1970–1998): A First Draft of History," *Journal of Policy History* 12, 1 (2000): 123–56.

43. Gerda Bikalis, "Immigration Policy: The New Environmental Battlefield," *National Parks and Conservation Magazine* 51 (December 1977): 13.

44. Bikalis, "Immigration Policy," 16, 13; Robert Rienow, "Can We Still Close the Gates?" *Humanist* 41, 6 (1981): 14, 15, 17.

45. Elizabeth Midgley, "Immigrants: Whose Huddled Masses?" *Atlantic Monthly* 241, 4 (April 1978): 20; Garrett Hardin, "Living on a Lifeboat," *BioScience* 24 (October 1974): 561–68.

46. Peter Brimelow, *Alien Nation: Common Sense about America's Immigration Disaster* (New York: Harper Perennial, 1996), 187–90. A green-tinged critique of immigration emerged simultaneously in western Europe; see Mark Shapiro, "Browns and Greens: Europe's New Eco-Fascists," *Amicus Journal* 14, 1 (Winter 1992): 6–7. With reference to the "new," officially "post-racist" South Africa, Jean and John Comaroff suggest that "alien-nature" supplies a medium for "voicing new forms of discrimination" in societies where public expressions of racism are taboo; see their "Naturing the Nation: Aliens, Apocalypse and the Postcolonial State," *Journal of Southern African Studies* 27, 3 (September 2001): 627 (627–51).

47. Raymond Tatalovich, "Official English as Nativist Backlash," in *Immigrants Out! The New Nativism and the Anti-Immigrant Impulse in the United States*, ed. Juan F. Perea (New York: New York University Press, 1997), 244–53.

48. Wayne Lutton and John Tanton, *The Immigrant Invasion* (Petoskey, Mich.: Social Contract Press, 1994), 39, 85–93. Recent immigrants are probably the population sector least likely to be visiting national parks.

49. In 1989 the club had announced that immigration "should be no greater than that which will permit achievement of population stabilization in the U.S."; Dick Schneider and Alan Kuper, "Why We Need a Comprehensive U.S. Population Policy," *Sierra* 83, 1 (January–February 1998): 105–7.

50. Environmentalists troubled by immigration rates try to distance themselves from the far right by emphasizing numbers, not composition. Californians for Population Stabilization (CAPS—the former California branch of ZPG, which seceded in 1986) supports "replacement-level" immigration without regard to race, ethnicity, or national origin; see James Ricci, "Tuning in to the Cacoph-

ony of California's Population Crunch," *Los Angeles Times Magazine,* September 10, 2000.

51. Ron Russell, "The Greening of Hate," *Los Angeles Times,* March 12, 1998; Alexander Cockburn, "Column Left," *Los Angeles Times,* October 2, 1997.

52. William Branigin, "Immigration Policy Dispute Rocks Sierra Club," *Washington Post,* March 7, 1998.

53. Emil Guillermo, "The Sierra Club's Nativist Faction," *San Francisco Examiner,* December 7, 1997, A-27.

54. Al Martinez, "Listen to the Wind," *Los Angeles Times,* October 7, 1997.

55. Peter H. Kostmayer and Karen Kalla, "Let's Focus on Underlying Causes, Not Symptoms," *Sierra* 83, 1 (January–February 1998): 105, 107; Christopher Reed, "Immigration Splits Greens," *Guardian,* March 18, 1998.

56. A letter to the *Los Angeles Times* (April 23, 1998) referred to the eugenicism of founder member David Starr Jordan, who promoted sterilization for the "genetically defective"; see Edward McNall Burns, *David Starr Jordan: Prophet of Freedom* (Stanford, Calif.: Stanford University Press, 1953), 66–77.

57. CAPS press release, February 28, 1998, at www.cap-s.org/pressreleases.html, accessed May 2005; William Branigin, "Sierra Club Votes for Neutrality on Immigration: Population Issue 'Intensely Debated,'" *Washington Post,* April 26, 1998; Otis Graham, "The Unfinished Reform: Regulating Immigration in the National Interest," in *Debating American Immigration, 1882–Present,* by Roger Daniels and Otis Graham (Lanham, Md.: Rowman & Littlefield, 2001), 174–75.

58. Otis L. Graham, "The Wind Has Shifted: A New Agenda for Immigration Reformers," *Social Contract* 2, 2 (Winter 1991–92): 93. Graham's survey of recent U.S. history foregrounds the relationships among population/immigration increase, natural resource depletion, and environmental degradation; *A Limited Bounty: The United States since World War Two* (New York: McGraw-Hill, 1996), xviii, 11–15, 47–49, 94–96, 156–59, 172–74, 241–45, 300–02. Graham, who is a director of the Federation for American Immigration Reform, has recently published *Unguarded Gates: A History of America's Immigration Crisis* (Lanham, Md.: Rowman & Littlefield, 2004).

59. But it flared up again within the Sierra Club in 2004, when several restrictionists with alleged connections to far right groups stood unsuccessfully for election to the club's board; see "Hostile Takeover," *Intelligence Report* 113 (Spring 2004): 55–63.

60. Jonathan Olsen, *Nature and Nationalism: Right-Wing Ecology and the Politics of Identity in Contemporary Germany* (Houndmills, U.K.: Macmillan, 1999), 137; Janet Biehl, "'Ecology' and the Modernization of Fascism in the German Ultra-Right," in Biehl and Peter Staudenmaier, *Ecofascism: Lessons from the German Experience* (Edinburgh, U.K.: AK Press, 1995), 64–65; Elinor Langer, "The American Neo-Nazi Movement Today," *Nation,* July 16–23, 1990, 86.

61. At www.resist.com/positions/Environment.html, accessed July 20, 2005.

62. At www.americanpatrol.com/IRAW/barnett-testimony990615.html, accessed July 20, 2005.

63. Chris Simcox (October 24, 2002), in Bob Moser, "Open Season," *Intelligence Report* 109 (Spring 2003): 8.

64. John Tanton, "Alien Invasion!" *Social Contract* (Winter 1993/4): 119.

65. A conservation biologist at Cornell University and editor of *Biological Invasions: Economic and Environmental Costs of Alien Plant, Animal, and Microbe Species* (Boca Raton, Fla.: CRC Press, 2002), Pimentel is active in organizations such as Sierrans for U.S. Population Stabilization and Carrying Capacity Network.

66. Otis Graham, "Introduction: A Long Way from Earth Day," in "Special Issue: Environmental Politics and Policy, 1960s–1990s," *Journal of Policy History* 12, 1 (2000): 9.

67. Barry Glassner, *Culture of Fear* (New York: Basic, 1999), 88, 135, 203.

68. See www.dnr.state.wi.us/org/caer/ce/eek/earth/aliens.htm, accessed July 20, 2005.

69. John Tibbetts, "Exotic Species: The Aliens Have Landed," *Coastal Heritage* 11, 4 (Spring 1997): 3–9; David Malakoff, "Biological Invaders Sweep In," *Science* 285 (September 17, 1999): 1834–43; Henry Tepper, "Attack of the Aliens," *New York Times*, October 16, 2005.

70. Christopher Weir, "Biological Warfare: Alien Species Have Escaped from Their Native Habitats and Hit California's Shores," *Metro*, May 1–7, 1997, page 1 of 8, at www.metroactive.com/papers/metro/05.01.97/plants-9718.html, accessed April 17, 2006. Imported as a house plant, German ivy—also called Cape ivy—is actually from South Africa.

71. Robert Devine, *Alien Invasion: America's Battle with Non-Native Animals and Plants* (Washington, D.C.: National Geographic Society, 1998), 52, 189. APHIS began life in 1971 as the Animal and Plant Health Service, assuming its current name the following year. At www.cbp.gov/xp/cgov/toolbox/about/history/aqi_history.xml, accessed April 17, 2006.

72. Joseph B. Verrengia, "Exotic Species Turning Ecologists into Killers," *Associated Press*, September 28, 1999.

73. Devine, *Alien Invasion*, 52.

74. Stephanie Flack and Elaine Forlow, "America's Least Wanted: Alien Species Invasions of US Ecosystems," at www.tnc.org/news/magazine/nov-dec/index.html, accessed May 15, 2004; see also Bruce A. Stein and Stephanie R. Flack, ed., *America's Least Wanted: Alien Species Invasions of U.S. Ecosystems* (Arlington, Va.: The Nature Conservancy, 1996).

75. Robert Devine, "Botanical Barbarians," *Sierra* 79, 1 (January–February 1994): 51, 53, 56, 71.

76. Yvonne Baskin, *A Plague of Rats and Rubbervines: The Growing Threat of Species Invasions* (Washington, D.C.: Island Press, 2002), 13. Inflammatory language is not a peculiarly American trait; see Tim Lowe, *Feral Future: The Untold Story of Australia's Exotic Invaders* (Ringwood, Victoria: Harmondsworth, 1999), xvii, xv.

77. Stephen Budiansky, *Nature's Keepers: The New Science of Nature Management* (London: Weidenfeld and Nicolson, 1995), 64–65. For the passage in question, see "The Shaky Ground of Sustainable Development," in Donald Worster, *The Wealth of Nature: Environmental History and the Ecological Imagination* (New York: Oxford University Press, 1993), 149–52. The quotation from Colinvaux's *Why*

Big Fierce Animals Are Rare is from a different essay in Worster's *Wealth of Nature: "The Ecology of Order and Chaos,"* 165–67.

78. Worster does not refer to Reaganomics in *Wealth of Nature,* but he alludes to the revisionist view of nature "populated by rugged individualists, eager opportunists, and self-seekers" and the "desire to be less disapproving of economic development" than 1960s and 1970 environmentalists; "Shaky Ground," 150, 152).

79. R. D. Schrum and R. D. Schein, "Prediction Capabilities for Potential Epidemics," in *Exotic Plant Pests and North American Agriculture,* ed. Charles L. Wilson and Charles L. Graham (New York: Academic Press, 1983), 420.

80. James Brown, "Help to Preserve the Native Flora," *Gardener's Chronicle* 29, 5 (May 1925): 134.

81. Carl Degler, *Out of Our Past: The Forces That Shaped Modern America* (New York: Harper & Row, 1984), 422.

82. Andrew Hultkrans, "Invasion of the Parks," *Sierra* 73 (November–December 1988): 24.

83. L. E. Ehler and L. A. Andres, "Biological Control: Exotic Natural Enemies to Control Exotic Pests," in Wilson and Graham, *Exotic Plant Pests and North American Agriculture,* 396.

84. Nelson Goodman, "Metaphor as Moonlighting," in *On Metaphor,* ed. Sheldon Sacks (Chicago: University of Chicago Press, 1979), 175.

85. Baskin, *Plague of Rats,* 12–13, 143, 124, 2, 163, 15, 145.

86. Richard N. Mack et al., "Biotic Invasions: Causes, Epidemiology, Global Consequences, and Control," *Ecological Applications* 10, 3 (2000): 701.

87. John McNeill, *Something New under the Sun: An Environmental History of the Twentieth Century* (New York: W. W. Norton, 2000), 253.

88. Tim Flannery, *Eternal Frontier: An Ecological History of North America and Its Peoples* (New York: Atlantic Monthly Press, 2001), 145.

89. Dan Flores, "Environmentalism and Multiculturalism," in *Reopening the American West,* ed. Hal K. Rothman (Tucson: University of Arizona Press, 1998), 36 (24–37).

90. Dan Flores, *The Natural West: Environmental History in the Great Plains and Rocky Mountains* (Norman: University of Oklahoma Press, 2001), 196, 198.

91. R. I. Colautti and H. J. MacIsaac, "A Neutral Terminology to Define 'Invasive' Species," *Diversity and Distributions* 10 (2004): 136 (135–41).

92. U.S. Congress, Office of Technology Assessment (OTA), *Harmful Non-Indigenous Species in the United States* (Washington, D.C.: Government Printing Office, 1993), 52.

93. Roger Tory Peterson and James Fisher, *Wild America: The Record of a 30,000 Mile Journey around the Continent by a Distinguished Naturalist and His British Colleague* (London: Collins, 1955), 103–13.

94. Mark Williamson, *Biological Invasions* (London: Chapman and Hall, 1996), 77; David M. Richardson et al., "Naturalization and Invasion of Alien Plants: Concepts and Definitions," *Diversity and Distributions: A Journal of Biological Invasions and Biodiversity* 6, 2 (March 2000): 93, 98, 102 (93–107). On the other hand, Mark A. Davis contrasts what he sees as the more strictly scientific and value-free terminology of *colonizer, introduction,* and *new arrival,* which prevailed in

the 1960s and 1970s, with the more metaphorically suggestive, applied ecological and explicitly environmentalist language of *alien, exotic, invader,* and *invasion* (traceable to Elton's book) that has dominated more recent and current debates; "Invasion Biology, 1958–2004: The Pursuit of Science and Conservation," in *Conceptual Ecology and Invasions Biology: Reciprocal Approaches to Nature,* ed. M. W. Cadotte, S. M. McMahon, and T. Fukami (New York: Springer, 2005), at www.macalester.edu/~davis/kluwer, 3, 15–16, accessed July 20, 2005.

95. Roger Tory Peterson, *A Field Guide to the Birds East of the Rockies* (Boston: Houghton Mifflin, 1980), Map 94.

96. F. A. Bazzaz, "Life History of Colonizing Plants: Some Demographic, Genetic, and Physiological Features," in *Ecology of Biological Invasions of North America and Hawaii,* ed. Harold A. Mooney and James A. Drake (New York: Springer-Verlag, 1986), 97. Mack et al. note that a nonnative species can progress from *immigrant* (integrated or inconspicuous) to *invader* status over an unspecified (and usually unspecifiable) period; "Biotic Invasions: Causes, Epidemiology, Global Consequences, and Control," *Ecological Applications* 10, 3 (2000): 691 (689–710).

97. Bazzaz, "Life History of Colonizing Plants," 97, 107.

98. Baskin's book, sponsored by GISP, adopts this modified term; see *Plague of Rats,* 12.

99. John Randall, "What's in a Name?" *CalEPPC News* 2, 2 (Spring 1994): 3.

100. Anne Hanchek, "The International Garden at Your Door: Examining the Role of Exotic Plants in our Landscapes," *Minnesota Horticulturalist: The Magazine of Northern Gardening* 121, 9 (December 1993): 11.

101. D. E., "Barbarians at Our Gates," *American Horticulturist* 74, 3 (March 1995): 6; Randall, "What's in a Name?" 3. Florida's Exotic Pest Plant Council (est. 1984) was the prototype.

102. Anthony Standen, "Japanese Beetle: Voracious, Libidinous, Prolific, He Is Eating His Way across the U.S., Destroying $7,000 Worth of Plant Life Every Year," *Life,* July 17, 1944, 39–46.

103. Nazi Germany's consignment of various groups of people to pest status is the most notorious example of the "racialization of vermin"; see Shireen R. K. Patell, "The Language of Pests," in *Concrete Jungle,* ed. Mark Dion and Alexis Rockman (New York: Juno, 1996), 62–64.

104. Lorraine Johnson, *Grow Wild! Low Maintenance, Sure-Success, Distinctive Gardening with Native Plants* (Golden, Colo.: Fulcrum, 1998), 9, 6.

105. Lothrop Stoddard, *Rising Tide of Color* (New York: Scribner's, 1920), 258; Franz Boas, "Report on an Anthropometric Investigation of the Population of the United States," *Journal of the American Statistical Association* 18 (June 1922), in Boas, *Race, Language and Culture* (New York: Macmillan, 1940), 45.

106. Pierre Binggeli, "Misuses of Terminology and Anthropomorphic Concepts in the Description of Introduced Species," *Bulletin, British Ecological Society* 25, 1 (February 1994): 12 (10–13). As Boas emphasized, animal breeds are produced by meticulous selection, "by means of which physical and mental characteristics are fixed in each separate strain," for which there was no human parallel; "Report on an Anthropometric Investigation," 45.

107. "The Sparrows' Quarters," *Washington Post,* August 7, 1893.

108. Peter Singer, *Animal Liberation: A New Ethics for Our Treatment of Animals* (New York: Avon, 1975), 7.

109. Diana Rathbone, "In Defense of the Politically Incorrect Garden," *San Francisco Examiner,* May 26, 1999.

110. Peterson and Fisher, *Wild America,* 113.

111. Subramaniam, "Aliens Have Landed!" 35–36.

112. Genetically modified species also require us to adjust our customary ways of thinking about pollution and the relationship between nature and culture.

113. Quoted in Don Schmitz and Daniel Simberloff, "Biological Invasions," *Issues in Science and Technology* 13, 4 (Summer 1997): 33–34 (33–40).

114. Quoted in Carey Goldberg, "In Hawaii, Flora Fights for Its Turf," *New York Times,* August 4, 1996.

115. Carla Bossard, "President's Message," *CalEPPC News* 4, 3 (Summer–Fall 1996): 3.

116. Frederic E. Clements, *Plant Succession and Indictors: A Definitive Edition of Plant Succession, and Plant Indicators* (New York: H. W. Wilson, 1928 [1916]), 75–76.

117. Elton, *Ecology of Invasions,* 116–17; U.S. Geological Survey, news release, "USGS Research Upsets Conventional Wisdom on Invasive Species Invasions," May 13, 1999, Midcontinent Ecological Science Center, Fort Collins, Colorado, at http://biology.usgs.gov/pr/newsrelease/1999/5-18.htm, accessed April 17, 2006.

118. F. A. Johnston, "Aviation Brings Foreign Plant Pests and Makes Quarantines Necessary," *Yearbook of Agriculture, 1934* (1935): 143.

119. "Hitch-Hiking Pests," *USDA Bulletin,* October 24, 1951, Box 8, "Clippings," Bureau of Entomology and Plant Quarantine, Plant Quarantines 1912–49, Records, Record Group 7, National Archives, College Park, Maryland.

120. W. A. McCubbin, "Preventing Plant Disease Introduction," *Botanical Review,* 12, 1 (January 1946): 124, 101, 103, 107.

121. Aldo Leopold, "Cheat Takes Over," in *A Sand County Almanac* (Oxford, U.K.: Oxford University Press, 1949), 154.

122. Christian Joppke, ed. *Challenge to the Nation-State: Immigration in Western Europe and the United States* (Oxford, U.K.: Oxford University Press, 1989), 189.

123. Stephen Castles and Mark Miller, *The Age of Migration: International Population Movements in the Modern World* (London: Macmillan, 1993), 266.

124. Comaroff and Comaroff, "Naturing the Nation," 627, 633; David Briscoe (AP), "'Smart Pollution,'" *Palm Beach Post,* October 11, 1998.

125. Christopher Bright, "Invasive Species: Pathogens of Globalization," *Foreign Policy* 114 (Fall 1999): 51 (50–64). Further research is required to see if efforts to combat nonnative species can be treated as part of a "tribalist" critique of "McWorld"; for these terms, see Benjamin Barber, "Jihad versus McWorld," *Atlantic Monthly* 269, 3 (March 1992): 53–56 (53–65).

126. Donald Kennedy and Marjorie Lucks, "Rubber, Blight, and Mosquitoes: Biogeography Meets the Global Economy," *Environmental History* 4, 3 (July 1999): 370, 376–79 (369–83); William A. Hawley, "Adaptable Immigrant," *Natural History* 110, 7 (July 1991): 56 (55–59).

127. Elliot Coues, "The Sparrow Nuisance," *New York Times,* July 18, 1883.

128. Allan Fitzsimmons, "Ecological Confusion among the Clergy," *Markets and Morality* 3, 2 (Fall 2000), page 3 of 18, at www.acton.org/publicat/m_and_m/2000_fall/fitzsimmons.html, accessed April 17, 2006.

129. Ken Moore, "Volunteers and Long-Term Community Support for Effective Pest Plant Control," in *Proceedings, California Exotic Pest Plant Council Symposium 1995*, ed. Jeff Lovich, John Randall, and Mike Kelly (Sacramento, Calif.: The Council, 1996), 59.

130. Sally Fairfax and Lynn Huntsinger, "An Essay from the Woods (and Rangelands)," in *The New Western History: The Territory Ahead*, ed. Forrest G. Robinson (Tucson: University of Arizona Press, 1998), 205.

131. Stephen Jay Gould, "An Evolutionary Perspective on Strengths, Fallacies, and Confusions in the Concept of Native Plants," in *Nature and Ideology: Natural Garden Design in the Twentieth Century*, ed. Joachim Wolschke-Bulmahn (Washington, D.C.: Dumbarton Oaks/Harvard University Press, 1997), 17 (11–19).

132. W. L. Jepson, "Alien Plants in California," *Erythea: A Journal of Botany, West American and General* 1, 6 (June 1893): 141 (141–43); "The Sparrow's History," *Washington Post*, May 22, 1928.

133. Gould, "Evolutionary Perspective," 17. Extending this critique, Peter Del Tredici of Harvard's Arnold Arboretum has described the pro-native stance as a "form of creationism"; see Anne Raver, "What's Eating America? Weeds," *New York Times*, September 16, 1999. Whether nonnative success illustrates the free play of evolutionary forces is unclear. How big is the difference between a seed attaching itself to a migratory bird's foot and a snake traveling halfway across the world in an airplane's cargo hold?

134. Asa Gray, "Address of Professor Asa Gray, Ex-President of the Association [On the Origin of the Flora of North America]," *Proceedings of the American Association for the Advancement of Science* 21 (1873): 4.

135. We might also think about whether our distaste for invasive exotics may, therefore, in part, be an unconscious form of self-criticism.

136. Leland Howard, "The Spread of Land Species by the Agency of Man; With Especial Reference to Insects," *Science* 6, 141 (September 10, 1897): 397 (382–98).

137. Alan Burdick, the popular science writer, has certainly tried to rise to this challenge. In a publicity statement for his *Out of Eden: An Odyssey of Ecological Invasion* (New York: Farrar, Straus, Giroux, 2005), he explains that "I wanted to give myself, and by extension the reader, permission to be impressed by [globe-trotting organisms], to admire their victories—to sympathize with them, even." See www.aburdick.com, accessed November 15, 2005.

138. We could also give them some credit for providing an opportunity for natural scientists to learn more about the fundamental operation of ecological communities and the characteristics of native species.

139. Quoted in Dick Tracy, "Charming Invaders: Alien Species May Look Nice, but Native Plants Wilt under Their Attacks," *Sacramento Bee*, January 17, 1998.

140. James Brown, "Patterns, Modes and Extents of Invasions by Invertebrates," in *Biological Invasions: A Global Perspective*, ed. J. A. Drake et al. (Chichester, U.K.: John Wiley, 1989), 105–6 (85–109).

141. Mark Sagoff suggests that Americans could neutralize problematic nonnatives by eating them: "The problem may be that [the green crab, from the Sea of Japan] is alien to our cuisine. . . . executive orders may be less effective than recipes"; see "Native to a Place, or What's Wrong with Exotic Species?" in *Values at Sea: Ethics for the Marine Environment,* ed. Dorinda G. Dallmeyer (Athens: University of Georgia Press, 2003), 96 (93–110). This "if you can't beat them, eat them" approach has been tried before. Eat them instead of calling them names, recommended those who promoted English sparrow pie in the 1880s and 1890s. Elevating exotics to culinary delight may create a vested interest in maintaining (even expanding) populations.

142. Marc Miller and Gregory Aplet, "Biological Control: A Little Knowledge Is a Dangerous Thing," *Rutgers Law Review* 45 (1993): 288 (285–334).

143. Heather Millar, "Generation Green," *Sierra* 85, 6 (November–December 2000): 42.

144. Holmes Rolston III, "The Wilderness Idea Reaffirmed," in *Unmanaged Landscapes, Voices for Untamed Nature,* ed. Bill Willers (Washington, D.C.: Island Press, 1999), 183 (179–83).

145. Jerry E. Asher and David W. Harmon, "Invasive Exotic Plants Are Destroying the Naturalness of U.S. Wilderness Areas," *International Journal of Wilderness* 1, 2 (December 1995): 36 (35–37). The belief in authentic nature in its rightful place can foster a highly interventionist management policy. Witness Angel Island.

146. Frank Egler, "Indigene versus Alien in the Development of Arid Hawaiian Vegetation," *Ecologist* 23, 1 (January 1942): 14, 15–16 (14–23).

147. James C. Merrill, "The European Tree Sparrow in the United States," *American Naturalist* 10 (January 1876): 50–51; Williamson, *Biological Invasions,* 28–54, 115.

148. Mark Williamson, "Measuring the Impact of Plant Invaders in Britain," in *Plant Invasions: Ecological Mechanisms and Human Responses,* ed. U. Starfinger et al. (Leiden, Netherlands: Backhuys, 1998), 67 (57–68).

149. Charles Darwin, *The Origin of Species* (New York: New American Library, 1958 [1859]), 127.

150. H. G. Baker, "Characteristics and Modes of Origin of Weeds," in *The Genetics of Colonizing Species: Proceedings of the First International Union of Biological Sciences Symposia on General Biology,* ed. H. G. Baker and G. Ledyard Stebbins (New York: Academic Press, 1965), 147–72; Asa Gray, "The Pertinacity and Predominance of Weeds," *American Journal of Science and Arts,* 3d Series, 18, 105 (September 1879): 162.

151. Baker, "Characteristics and Modes of Origin of Weeds," 147–72.

152. The Brazilian pepper tree arrived in Florida in the 1890s but did not expand vigorously until the 1950s. On the other hand, the Asian tiger mosquito may already have reached the limits of its expansion in North America; in a decade, it could be just a curiosity—and extinct within twenty years.

153. Peter Moyle and Theo Light, "Biological Invasions of Fresh Water: Empirical Rules and Assembly Theory," *Biological Conservation* 78 (1996): 149 (149–61).

154. Herbert W. Levi, "Evaluating Wildlife Importations," *Scientific Monthly,* 74, 6

(June 1952): 315–16. Levi chaired the Nature Conservancy's Committee on Exotics.

155. Mark Sagoff, "Why Exotic Species Are Not as Bad as We Fear," *Chronicle of Higher Education,* June 23, 2000. For a rejoinder, see Daniel Simberloff and Donald R. Strong, "Exotic Species Seriously Threaten Our Environment," *Chronicle of Higher Education,* September 8, 2000. Sagoff implies that those who criticize the ecological impact of nonnative species tend not to discriminate between the harmful minority and beneficial majority. He also queries whether there is a truly scientific case for nonnative species being "harmful"; see Sagoff, "Do Non-Native Species Threaten the Natural Environment?" *Journal of Agricultural and Environmental Ethics* 18 (2005): 215–36.

156. David Pimentel et al., "Environmental and Economic Costs of Nonindigenous Species in the United States," *BioScience* 50, 1 (January 2000): 61 (53–65).

157. Alfred Crosby, *Columbian Exchange: Biological and Cultural Consequences of 1492* (Westport, Conn.: Greenwood Press, 1972), 210–11. Sagoff believes that the study of nonnative impacts is overreliant on selective historical evidence and insufficiently based on properly conducted scientific studies of a "sample of species or sites selected randomly or on neutral grounds"; "Do Non-Native Species Threaten?" 229.

158. Peterson and Fisher, *Wild America,* 103–13.

159. Peterson and Fisher, *Wild America,* 113.

160. See www.nps.gov/plants/wildwealth.html, accessed May 15, 2004.

161. Gould, "Evolutionary Perspective," 15.

162. Rachel Carson, "A Statement of Belief" (unpublished speech, April 21, 1954), in Paul Brooks, *The House of Life: Rachel Carson at Work* (Boston: Houghton Mifflin, 1973), 324.

163. Eric Rolls, *They All Ran Wild: The Story of Pests on the Land in Australia* (Sydney: Angus and Robertson, 1969), 209.

164. Quoted in Harold Mooney, "Invasion of Exotic Species," page 1, at California Academy of Sciences, "Bioforum for High School Science Teachers," www.accessexcellence.org/BF/bf04/mooney/bfo4c4.html, accessed April 17, 2006. The identification of a looming "Homogocene" could be premature. The next geological era is likely to be another glacial epoch, which, given that intervals between glacial ages have invariably been less than 12,000 years long over the past half-million years or so, could be here sooner rather than later. My thanks to Richard Minnich for this insight.

165. David Quammen, "Planet of Weeds: Tallying the Losses of the Earth's Animals and Plants," *Harper's Magazine* 297, 1781 (October 1998): 67 (57–69).

166. T. Coraghessan Boyle, *A Friend of the Earth* (New York: Penguin, 2001), 305.

167. Jason Van Driesche and Roy Van Driesche, *Nature out of Place: Biological Invasions in the Global Age* (Washington, D.C.: Island Press, 2000), 1, 2, 5, 7.

168. Neltje Blanchan, *Bird Neighbors* (London: Sampson, Low, Marston, 1897), 151.

169. Eugene Rolfe, "The Passing of the Birds," *New England Magazine* 22, 4 (June 1900): 413 (413–19).

170. William N. Erickson and Roberts Mann, "The English Sparrow," Nature Bulletin 139, Forest Preserve District of Cook County, Illinois, January 24, 1948,

at www.newton.dep.anl.gov/natbltn/100–199/nb139.htm, accessed April 17, 2006.

171. George Laycock, *Animal Movers: A Collection of Ecological Surprises* (Garden City, N.Y.: Natural History Press, 1971), 15.

172. At "No Friend of Trees," www.noivyleague.com/Pages/pers_no_friend.html, accessed April 17, 2006.

173. "National Parks Find Balancing Nature a Tough Act to Perform," *San Diego Union-Tribune*, December 27, 1985. There is some evidence, though, of declining hostility. In the New York Public Library's exhibition "Urban Neighbors: Images of New York City Wildlife" (October 11, 2000 to February 1, 2003), the house sparrow featured in the "Street and Backyard Neighbors" section rather than alongside the likes of the Norway rat, gypsy moth, and Asian longhorned beetle in "Unwelcome Neighbors" ("animals for whom almost no one has a good word"); at http://urban neighbors.nypl.org/checklist/checklist2.html, accessed April 17, 2006. Moreover, a sign on an ivy-covered wall at Central Park Zoo explains that "This ivy wall provides nesting habitat for house sparrows, a species native to Europe and Asia that now also makes its home in New York City" (viewed April 2, 2006).

174. See also Chris Chester, *Providence of a Sparrow: Lessons from a Life Gone to the Birds* (Salt Lake City: University of Utah Press, 2002), 5–13.

175. Sue Holloway, "Alien Birds? When Nativism Is Applied to Sparrows," 1–3 pages, at www.all-creatures.org/cc/op-alienbirds.html. This originally appeared in *The Day* (New London, Conn.), August 29, 1999. The article referred to is "Adventures of Ranger Rick: Troubles with Mute Swans," *Ranger Rick* 33, 5 (May 1999): 29–32. Mute swans, introduced from Eurasia in the late nineteenth century, flourish from Maine to Florida, where they uproot vegetation and displace native waterfowl and fish.

176. Rachel Carson, *The Sense of Wonder* (New York: HarperCollins, 1998 [1965]), 55, 56, 85. This essay first appeared in *Woman's Home Companion*, July 1956.

177. Moreover, at least one native bird has come to terms with city life and house sparrows over the past few decades: the black phoebe.

178. "N. D.," Letter to the editor, *New York Times*, September 8, 1878.

179. Peter Matthiessen, *Wildlife in America* (New York: Viking Press, 1959), 64.

180. Robyn Dixon, "Silent Warning? Sparrows Are Vanishing throughout Great Britain," *Los Angeles Times*, July 12, 2002; Stephen Moss, "The Fall of a Sparrow," *BBC Wildlife*, November 2001, 45. Some investigators implicate traffic noise, which makes it difficult for sparrows to hear their own songs and mating calls. Others point to loss of nesting sites as eaves disappear from building design, cat predation, viral infection, the intensification of agricultural practices that has reduced fallow winter food, and the decline of weed seeds and insects due to growing pesticide and herbicide use. Cleaner streets have also been suggested as a factor in shrinking urban food supply. Others blame automobile emissions, arguing that a substance added to unleaded gasoline as an antiknock agent is killing the aphids sparrows feed to their newborn fledglings.

181. J. B. Calhoun, "The Role of Temperature and Natural Selection in Relation to the Variations in the Size of the English Sparrow in the United States," *Ameri-

can Naturalist 81 (1947): 203–28; R. F. Johnston and R. K. Selander, "Evolution in the House Sparrow. II. Adaptive Differentiation in North American Populations," *Evolution* 25 (1971): 1–28. For the potential of an evolutionary history that looks at change within species over historical time, see Edmund Russell, "Evolutionary History: Prospectus for a New Field," *Environmental History* 8, 2 (April 2003): 204–28.

182. Quammen, "Planet of Weeds," 69.

183. Bill McKnight, ed., *Biological Pollution: The Control and Impact of Invasive Exotic Species* (Indianapolis: Indiana Academy of Science, 1993), x.

184. "Alien Nation," *Harper's Magazine* 301, 1804 (September 2000): 88.

185. See, for example, Brenda Z. Guiberson, *Exotic Species: Invaders in Paradise* (Brookfield, Conn.: Twenty-First Century Books, 1999). The most literal example of the serpent in Eden is the brown tree snake and its impact on the avifauna of Guam since World War II, when it arrived from New Guinea as a stowaway on a military cargo plane; see Mark Jaffe, *And No Birds Sing: The Story of an Ecological Disaster in a Tropical Paradise* (New York: Simon and Schuster, 1994).

186. I read *Aliens in the Backyard* in the fall of 2005, having completed my own manuscript, and was amazed at the minimal overlap in terms of content and approach. Checking Leland's references, I found that only ten or so are shared.

187. Leland, *Aliens in the Backyard: Plant and Animal Imports into America* (Columbia: University of South Carolina Press, 2005) 5, 22, 130, 199.

188. Nor do we invariably learn something about animals or plants from discussions of people. The year after he wrote an article comparing Mexican immigrants to English sparrows in California, Charles Goethe published a comparable diatribe against Filipino agricultural laborers. He contended that the fast-breeding "coolies" "flock" to California's cities in winter and that their willingness to work for low wages was a "menace" to the living standards of American workers. On this occasion, though, he did not deploy the English sparrow analogy; C. M. Goethe, "Filipino Immigration Viewed as a Peril," *Current History* 34, 3 (June 1931): 353–54.

INDEX

Text: 10/12 Baskerville
Display: Baskerville
Compositor: Bookmatters, Berkeley
Printer and binder: Maple-Vail Manufacturing Group